The American Kings

The American Kings

Growth in Presidential Power from George Washington to Barack Obama

ROBERT KIMBALL SHINKOSKEY

RESOURCE *Publications* · Eugene, Oregon

THE AMERICAN KINGS
Growth in Presidential Power from George Washington to Barack Obama

Resource Publications
An Imprint of Wipf and Stock Publishers
199 W. 8th Ave., Suite 3
Eugene, OR 97401

www.wipfandstock.com

ISBN 13: 978-1-62564-194-6

Manufactured in the U.S.A.

For My Children and Yours

Contents

Introduction

This is a book about presidents who cared more about power for themselves than they did about power for the people. They made promises they knew they could not keep, subverted the law, raided the public treasury, and went abroad looking for dragons to slay. By and large each successive president made the government more autocratic than the one before.

The student of high school social studies or college political science will remember that in a democracy, citizens either make laws themselves directly or indirectly through elected representatives. Ideally, they guarantee human rights, make sure that bad officials get quickly removed from office, and that even good ones have a limited length of stay. Their citizens make sure to get a good education in both the law and the history of their country so politicians can't trick them into giving up their rights and their paychecks.

On the other hand, in any kind of government, whether a monarchy or a democracy, kings or elected rulers inevitably try to take the law-making power away from the people and their legislatures. They get their lawyers to find high-sounding reasons why the law allows them to rule on their own. They try to stay longer in office than law or tradition allows, often declaring emergencies to justify expanding their terms or changing the law.

Both hereditary kings and elected tyrants tend to make war and alliances without the consent of the people, and conduct many domestic and international activities in secret. Often spurred on by business or political party interests, they take power away from local governments and concentrate it in the executive department of the central government. They do all this by taking advantage of the people's ignorance, and by adding to that ignorance through deliberate misinformation and lies.

Such a situation of lawless behavior is called tyranny. There are several types of tyrants, and there are an abundance of these among the

American presidents. There are those who promise to be "president of all the people," and not just represent one political party. They talk about "bi-partisanship" or about occupying the moderate "center," but often end up pushing the political programs of only one party, favoring the interests of the wealthy part of society, or spending the country into debt by passing out benefits to as many groups of voters as they can. These are the "practical" or "flexible" or "re-election" tyrants, who want a "great" name for themselves in history.

Another type of tyrant tries to make the national government more powerful by taking power away from states, counties, and cities. These are the "nationalist" or "progressive" tyrants. They do not believe the people can solve problems on their own in localities or that local programs meet a high enough standard.

Another type of tyrant is very clear about having a favorite party and goes about repressing not only other political parties but all manner of citizens who oppose them. Such tyrants may even turn the army inward on their own people to "unify" different parts of the country. These are the "oppressor" tyrants.

Yet other tyrants start wars or make treaties to try to increase their popularity when things aren't going so well at home. They often want also to expand the boundaries of the nation or bring "democracy" to other nations, while actually taking resources away from their own people who need them and leaving other countries with something other than democracy. These are the "imperialist" tyrants. An ambitious tyrant usually mixes together several of these tyrannical purposes and methods.

Bad kings and tyrants in European and Asian history are well known. Kings like George III (whom the American revolutionaries rebelled against), Charles I, Louis IX, and Kaiser Wilhelm made life miserable for the people of their countries. Bismarck, Napoleon, Disraeli and other popular leaders took power away from the people and soaked it up for themselves. In earlier times, tyrants like Peter the Great, Catherine the Great, Alexander the Great (you get the picture) made a name for themselves while hurting people at home and abroad. In ancient times the kings of Egypt, called pharaohs, were notorious tyrants and predators, as were the "great" kings of Assyria, Babylon, Persia, India, China, and the emperors of Rome and Byzantium.

By the time of the American revolution in 1776, the American colonies had had 170 years of democratic history on the North American continent. The long distance from England meant that even though they owed allegiance to the parent country, in practice the colonies experienced self-government. The mother nation spawning the colonies, England, had a fairly good democratic tradition for periods of times. The ancient Anglo-Saxon witenagemot, or national council, was based on principles of representative government. Then Magna Charta in 1215, the English "Glorious Revolution" in 1688 and the English Bill of Rights in 1689 helped to enshrine certain basic rights.

The distance between individual settlements in the colonies meant that local towns had a good deal of independence from higher colonial authorities. Also, the colonies were filled with religious groups, like Quakers, Puritans/Congregationalists, and Baptists, which had very democratic church government traditions. The first representative government in the colonies began at Jamestown in 1619 with the election of the House of Burgesses, the forerunner of the Virginia General Assembly. In fact, the whole purpose of the various migrations to America from the earliest days, and even down to modern times, was to get away from European and Asian governments where power was centralized and unbalanced rather than decentralized and separated into somewhat balanced branches of government. The French author Montesquieu summarized the need for balanced government on a national level not long before the American revolution, and the American revolutionaries were very aware of his writings.

The colonies and the first national government under the Articles of Confederation acted like a loose league of self-governing mini-nations. When the Constitution was hammered out in 1787 in order to bring the league of states a bit closer together, the founders did all they could to keep any one of the three branches of government from becoming too powerful. They gave the president power to administer (carry out) the laws, but made sure the Congress had the sole power of making laws, entering wars, and raising and spending money. Most believed that the executive branch was the most dangerous. If a single individual could exercise any of the powers given to Congress, he would quickly make decisions to make himself popular, keep himself in power and glorify his place in history at the expense of the people. The founders even considered having two or more presiding officers, or "presidents," to administer the law like ancient Rome's two "consuls," so there would be balance of opinions even within the executive branch.

The purpose of this book is to give a brief portrait of each one of the American presidents so the reader can make a judgment about the real contribution, good or bad, that each president made to the nation. Another purpose of this book is to teach a little bit of constitutional law and to show how presidential disrespect for law came to be. The presidents, even more than the Congress and the judiciary, are the ones who got the nation into a hot mess with high taxes, a massive national debt, an immense standing army, and cowed state and local governments. The people, of course, did their part by trusting what the tyrants told them.

Handsomely paid "court" historians put a glossy shine on the periods of rule of ancient kings by publishing supposedly glorious accomplishments on stone monuments and in "king lists." They were telling history from a very biased point of view. That is why the biblical historians (writers of the books of Kings and Chronicles), and independent political commentators in other democratic traditions around the Mediterranean Sea, like Plato and Aristotle, gave a sort of people's view about rulers in their own lands. The Bible finds many of those political rulers "evil" rather than "good" because they neglected the laws, called "commandments," or took over the powers lawfully given to other bodies of the government. The founders of the United States believed that an elected ruler became a king when he exercised the war-making power on his own, that is, without the consent of the legislature.[1] If that is the case, then elected American kingship started with Harry Truman in 1950 and has continued in an unbroken line ever since.

This book also seeks to demonstrate the growth in the federal bureaucracy, the exploitation of religion to help the president increase his power, the movement toward "idolatry" in the presidency, and the record of propaganda, dishonesty and corruption of each of the presidents. It tells a story you likely did not hear about in high school, and possibly not even in college. It surely is nowhere to be found in the offices or speeches of the Republican and Democratic parties today, parties whose activities are far different from what their names suggest.

1. Adler and Genovese, *Presidency and the Law*, 29.

1

Makers of the Republican Nation

The first five presidents can rightly be regarded not only as revolutionary founders of the American republic, but also guardians of the rule of law on the national level for the first forty years of the nation. The Constitutional Convention had decided to create a single presidency—only one leader for the executive branch—in spite of their desire to curb the executive appetite for power. Some Convention delegates had advocated for a three-person committee, others for a single person sharing power with a council of judges. Most delegates wanted a person of great character like Washington who was strong but not oppressive and who was "acceptable to the people."[1]

The new United States of America was to be a "government of laws and not of men."[2] The presidency was to be an office that confined its occupants to the legal limitations placed on the office no matter how exciting the personality or how oceanic the ambition of the individual. To assure that these rules are adhered to, the president takes an oath of office to support the foundational constitutional law. The presidential oath is a vow to be faithful to the hundreds of founding lawmakers and the tens of thousands of amazing ancestors who sacrificed to make the new nation. It is an oath to be faithful to the farmers and merchants and soldiers, who, at the end of their lives, left their lands and their fortunes to their children and grandchildren, not to the king of England, and not even to their own government. The president was not to become "great" while in office. His

1. Nelson, *Presidency*, 9.
2. Ibid., 15.

responsibility was only to become good as a private citizen, which usually took place in the years before he took office, and often only well after he left the presidency.

Jefferson, for example, made a name for himself in state education policy after his presidency. John Quincy Adams spent a long and productive career in the Congress, where the real national power lay, *after* his two terms in the presidency. During their time in the presidency, the first five leaders limited themselves to seeing that the laws were faithfully executed. Focus on outward personality and political innovation while serving in the executive branch was seen as political idolatry, meaning the worship of a fallible human being. Presidential idolatry did not appear on the American national political scene in full force until the seventh president, Andrew Jackson. The fifth president, James Monroe, however, got the nation worried about idolatry when he made an extensive tour of the country during his time in office. The reputations of the candidates and presidents were supposed to be debated, but their faces were not to be seen except on special occasions. Monroe traveled to show himself to the people partly because there was so little to do in his position. But he also wanted to increase his popularity in order to get reelected.

The early presidents did little to actively seek the office, but responded when called to serve. They all worked with only a handful of cabinet members. They carried pistols to defend themselves, having no paid palace guard like European leaders. Prior to the Buchanan administration in 1857, Congress gave the president no money to hire staff of any kind. They had to pay any clerical help out of their own salaries. Washington, for example, paid his nephew to help with correspondence. The position, according to Roger Sherman of Connecticut, was "nothing more than an institution for carrying out the will of the legislature." The Constitution provided the president with four limited legislative-related powers: convene Congress for special sessions to deal with urgent issues; report on the state of the union; veto certain bills if they offended the Constitution; and "recommend measures."[3] On the other hand, the Constitution specified that Congress, not the president, "make all laws," create and fund cabinet departments, and "declare war."

The presidents were expected to demonstrate loyalty to wives, children, friends, employees, local government, political parties, and, most of all, the great law for preventing autocracy that had been written for the

3. Nelson, *Presidency*, 53.

benefit of all Americans. In other words, they were to ensure that all the other agencies and individuals in society were deeply empowered. But they were not supposed to devote themselves to accumulating political power for themselves.

The makers also were determined to prevent an extended term of office for the president and to take popular excitement out of the national political equation. Madison's Virginia Plan at the constitutional convention proposed a single term of office for the president, and presidential election by Congress. They finally left the matter of term-limits open, and felt satisfied that it was settled in tradition when Washington and Jefferson, representing the two opposing parties, each voluntarily retired after two terms of four years each. The makers settled upon a presidential election process half-way between direct popular election and Congressional election. They called it the electoral college. It was to be a process of voting by elected local representatives who had education, passion for the Constitution, and political experience. They would vote for who they thought would be best regardless of the person some in their districts might want. An age requirement was set for the president to ensure some real life experience, and a residence requirement thrown in so skilled tyrants from other countries could not move to America and make a play for the office.[4]

The early presidents were heavily set against a "standing army," a national military force that would obey only the president. They wanted the states to loan their own militias to the president in times of need, as Article II, Section 2 of the Constitution specified. The regular national army would have only a few small outposts on the frontier to protect against the British to the north in Canada, the Spanish to the south in Florida, the French to the west in Louisiana, and unhappy Indian tribes.

George Washington

Early in his adult professional career, George Washington was focused on acquiring land and pursuing military achievements. He was very likely the wealthiest man in America, having inherited wealth, married into further wealth, and made smart investments. He was part of a very

---

4. Nelson, *Presidency*, 10.

wealthy class then, just as politicians are today. Some two percent of the nation's families sold twenty percent of the nation's exports.[5]

In military matters, Washington's record was not always good. During the French and Indian War he was "more courageous than wise." Nevertheless, he hated the English for exploiting Americans and won the decisive battle of the Revolutionary War at Yorktown, the only decisive military battle he ever won.[6] After this he retired like Cincinnatus, the law-abiding ancient Roman military hero, until the people called on him to be president. He served as president from 1789 to 1797.

The new president was galled to learn there were some in the Congress who wanted to give him a title like "His Elective Majesty," or "His Highness the President of the United States and Protector of the Rights of the Same." He did not want to see monarchy in America. On the other hand, he did lend an air of aristocracy to the office, since he rode around the capitol in a luxurious carriage. He also demonstrated "monarchical aloofness" by cutting down the number of visitors he would receive, limiting public gatherings at the president's house to a couple per week. His policy was also not to return any visits and not to accept invitations.[7]

The nation did not want to get involved in political idolatry, yet they adored George Washington. Even while he was still president, the nation celebrated his birthday in what one newspaper called "a monarchical farce." Another newspaper said "the President has been pictured as spotless and infallible."[8]

Washington understood that his actions as president would serve to mold the behavior of future presidents. He reminded, "There is scarcely any part of my conduct which may not hereafter be drawn into precedent."[9] In a move extraordinarily important for the future of the nation, he refused to run for a third term, and thus set the pattern for treating the national executive as a short-term rather than a life-time occupation.

The Constitution was not clear as to the extent to which cabinet heads were responsible to the president, as opposed to the Congress. It was clear, however, that the executive departments were to be fairly

5. McDonald, *Washington*, 21.

6. Ibid., x.

7. McDonald, *Presidency*, 213; Nelson, *Presidency*, 65; McDonald, *Washington*, 26.

8. McDonald, *Washington*, 132.

9. Crenson and Ginsberg, *Presidential Power*, 51.

independent of the president. Washington used the department heads as a sort of advisory counsel. This beefed up the power of his office and diminished their responsibility toward Congress. His taking of personal responsibility for their actions and placing them under his leadership was a precedent he set for future generations that helped to erode Congress' relationship with the executive departments.[10]

Washington said "no" to a group asking him to act like a military tyrant. Soldiers of the revolutionary army seeking back pay wanted him to lead them in a march on Congress. But that would have made him like Caesar and his army crossing the Rubicon River headed for Rome to become an emperor. Instead, he persuaded the soldiers to disperse.[11] Early American tyrants did not follow his example. Jackson and Lincoln moved armies toward Washington, DC in order to intimidate Congress or protect personal political interests.

Washington was anti-faction (anti-political party). He didn't want one section of the electorate to fight against another to support the interests of popular tyrants. He was a "unifier" in the good sense, in that he sought to encourage the people to close ranks voluntarily around a set of political principles rather than have them forcefully united around an opportunistic politician's wishes. He wanted to stay away from partisan politics and to serve as a moderator among competing interests and points of view during his presidency. He did this by seeking opinions from a variety of individuals from various parties before making decisions. He tried for balance in his appointments to his three cabinet departments— treasury, state, and war. He wanted to set a precedent for making job appointments on the basis of ability and loyalty to the Constitution (civil service), rather than loyalty to only part of the Constitution or to one political party (patronage). His heads of treasury and state, Hamilton and Jefferson, eventually headed up competing political parties. Washington made approximately 1,000 appointments on a non-partisan basis. Once the basic character of job applicants was established, the only vetting (researching) he did was to determine whether the applicant was an avowed enemy of the new Constitution. This was because the statutes (laws) establishing the State and War departments indicated that their "duties . . . (must be) agreeable to the constitution."[12]

---

10. McDonald, *Washington*, 8, 95, 184.
11. Nelson, *Presidency*, 65.
12. McDonald, *Washington*, 38; McDonald, *Presidency*, 224.

Washington attempted to set a good constitutional example by submitting his first foreign policy proposals to the Senate for them to "advise and consent," as the Constitution required. When the Senate did not rubber-stamp them, but subjected them to considerable debate, he withdrew from his visit to the Senate in a huff and decided that after this both advice and consent should come only after he took action. Unfortunately, many senators believed that the law required prior consent, rather than after-the-fact consent. Washington himself had apparently interpreted the Constitution this way as well, as evidenced by his trip to the Senate to seek their consent in the first place. Subsequent presidential interpretation of this provision of the law was thus held captive to the first president's personal thin-skin with regard to the matter.[13]

The Constitution was silent as to the details of public finance, and in particular, how to manage public debts. A large amount of the Revolutionary War debt was held in the north by citizens and banks who loaned money to the revolutionary army. They not only wanted to be paid back by the successful new government, but also to be beneficiaries of continuing government use of their financial services.[14] While Washington understood how to manage land and personal finances, he left the more complex public financing matters to his treasury secretary, Alexander Hamilton. Hamilton had studied the British system and wanted to install it in America. The British favored nationalization of the monetary and credit systems, which meant that money would be coined on the national level and banking would be controlled in the nation's capitol. Those who supported this system were called Federalists. Those who supported local operation and control of money affairs were called Republicans, or Democratic-Republicans, or Democrats, or Jeffersonians.

Washington centralized power in the new government by assuming (promising to pay) state debts owed to private parties who financed the revolutionary war. The states were seduced into giving up the power to decide how to pay off these debts when they figured out that a federal repayment plan removed the need for state taxation. Privately, Hamilton promised favorable policies for states wavering over the debt proposal, such as additional federal money for state activities like geographic explorations. Washington also followed Hamilton's push to "fund" those debts, that is, just pay interest on them and keep the national government

13. McDonald, *Presidency*, 221–22.
14. McDonald, *Washington*, 8, 17, 91.

in constant debt like a long-term mortgage. Washington ultimately supported Hamilton's call for a national banking system even though his attorney general and secretary of state said it was unconstitutional. The program of Washington and Hamilton "bound the interests of the wealthy . . . to the national government."[15]

Washington's administration paid off the revolutionary war debt incurred by the new government by imposing tariffs, essentially taxes on imported goods, and by a tax on liquor. The tax on whiskey boiled over into a rebellion in Pennsylvania. Washington acted hastily and militarily to deal with the problem when federal marshals and the courts might have handled the situation.

The Constitution specified that federal troops could be used to intervene in a state only when requested by the governor, and the governor of Pennsylvania insisted he would handle the situation by himself. Washington raised a militia army of 12,950 and made a big show of marching to western Pennsylvania. He could only find and arrest twenty suspected rebels, only two of which could even be convicted. Jefferson remarked, "an insurrection was announced and proclaimed and armed against, but could never be found." Madison charged the incident was used to "establish the principle that a standing army was necessary for enforcing the laws." Washington, perhaps feeling the heat of the people, pardoned them both. This was the first presidential use of an emergency power to deal with insurrection. In using this power, Washington in some ways set a good example. He coordinated with both Congress and the courts.[16] But Washington, unfortunately, also set a bad precedent which Woodrow Wilson and Franklin Roosevelt were happy to build upon. Those two presidents each conducted huge round-ups of citizens, providing much more egregious examples of federal response way out of proportion to the actual threat.

Washington let the Congress make the laws. He stood firmly with the Constitution in stressing that the people through their representatives made policy for the nation. He wrote that the president would not introduce "any topick which relates to legislative matters, lest it should be suspected that he wished to influence the question before it." The reason for this is that the Constitution says "The Congress shall have Power

15. Ibid., 72, 76, 184.

16. McDonald, *Washington*, 145, 147; McDonald, *States' Rights*, 38; Cooper, *By Order*, 130.

. . . To make all Laws which shall be necessary and proper . . ." (Article I, Section 8) While he made several legislative suggestions in his inaugural address, he left Congress alone to deliberate on them and draft laws. In fact, he did not veto laws or interfere with their execution even when he disagreed with them, unless there was a clear constitutional concern. He vetoed his first on that basis in April of 1792, but vetoed only one more during his entire presidency. This set a precedent followed by the next five presidents. He thus refused to follow the advice of his treasury secretary Hamilton, who wanted the president and department heads to aggressively draft legislation. Washington also refused to endorse or oppose candidates for the Congress.[17]

If Hamilton, and indeed the entire country, did not gather his philosophy of governance and his strict interpretation of the Constitution from his actions during two terms of office, he determined to make it clear in his Farewell Address to the nation. On the topic of separation of powers between the legislative functions of Congress, and the implementing function of the executive branch, he had this to say: "It is important . . . in a free country . . . to confine themselves within their respective constitutional spheres; avoiding in the exercise of the powers of one department to encroach upon another. The spirit of encroachment tends to consolidate the powers of all the departments in one, and thus to create . . . a real despotism." As to whether a president could single-handedly change a policy of the Constitution he was equally clear: "The basis of our political systems is the right of the people to make and to alter their Constitutions of Government . . . let there be no change by usurpation . . . (even if it) may be the instrument of good, it is the customary weapon by which free governments are destroyed."

Washington, together with the other founders and framers, had a great disdain for the maintenance of a peacetime national army, termed a standing army. The federal Militia Acts of 1792 and 1795 allowed for the formation of state militias and for their call up to national service not more than three months in a year. There was no penalty for failing to sign up. Washington demonstrated his respect for states rights and state supremacy in military matters during his good-will tour of New England. He was invited to review the militia troops in Cambridge, Massachusetts, but declined, stating that those troops were under state jurisdiction, and

---

17. Healy, *Cult of the Presidency*, 35; McDonald, *Presidency*, 218, 223; McDonald, *Washington*, 39, 78.

not his. He indicated that "overgrown military establishments . . . under any form of government are inauspicious to liberty, and . . . are to be regarded as particularly hostile to Republican Liberty." The standing army during Washington's time was a mere 600 soldiers. In fact, seven of the first nine states to ratify the Constitution wanted a prohibition of standing armies in time of peace to be placed in the Bill of Rights. Five states wanted a guarantee of the right of states to control their own militias and four wanted bans on unconstitutional treaties to be placed in the Bill of Rights as well.[18]

Washington used executive orders to enforce neutrality in the war between Britain and France and to punish citizens who violated it.[19] Although he thus asserted the right of the president to take leadership in foreign affairs, his use of executive orders was in pursuance of constitutional law, whereas many presidents after him used executive orders to upset constitutional law in both domestic and foreign affairs.

Congress quickly confirmed the neutrality proclamation, and forbade Americans from entering in the military service of a foreign power, thus taking a stand against the monarchic practice of using mercenary armies. At the same time, Washington oversaw the creation of a navy and expenditures to build six war ships, ostensibly to deal with Algerian pirates in the Mediterranean. He pushed through these measures even though the pirate situation was being resolved through treaty.[20]

In his Farewell Address, he indicated that in "extending our commercial relations" with other nations, the nation should "have with them as little political connection as possible." It went without saying, but he said it anyway in the Farewell in 1796, that the nation's strength could and should never come from "passionate attachments" to "permanent alliances" with other nations. He spoke of the "insidious wiles of foreign influence," and elsewhere allowed that "temporary alliances" might be undertaken only in "extraordinary emergencies." He said that "'Tis our true policy to steer clear of permanent alliances with any portion of the foreign world."[21]

18. Crenson and Ginsberg, *Presidential Power*, 231–32; McDonald, Presidency, 215–16; Morley, *Freedom and Federalism*, 140; McDonald, *Washington*, 27, 35.

19. Cooper, *By Order*, 123.

20. McDonald, *Washington*, 141, 144–45.

21. Morley, *Freedom and Federalism*, 134; Healy, *Cult of the Presidency*, 43; Herring, *Colony to Superpower*, 83.

In fact, the problems that come with foreign entanglement were very clear during the Washington administration itself. Britain, France and Spain were totally unreliable governments as far as basic relations with other nations. Each of those monarchies changed political posture like chameleons. When one monarchy became weak due to internal political difficulties, others looked to take over parts of the struggling neighbor's foreign territories. This happened, for example, when France was in the throes of revolution. The idea was to plunder the other guy's empire in America while he was up to his neck in domestic politics at home.[22] Even America's 1778 treaty with France during the revolutionary war came with tremendous strings attached. France required American aid in the event France went to war, and this happened in 1793, when she went to war against England. However, the treaty only required aid in the case of a defensive war, and France had launched an offensive one in 1793, so America did not have to get involved militarily.

When Britain began seizing ships of the American merchant marine in the West Indies, American citizens got war fever. Rather than ask for war against Britain, Washington proclaimed an embargo against the British and sent John Jay to England to negotiate a treaty to end the British seizures and obtain compensation for them. He also asked Jay to deal with a couple of other issues unresolved from the revolutionary war. For example, Washington sent Jay with instructions to ask for compensation for American slaves the British army freed during the Revolutionary War. The south was not asking for return of the slaves, but just some partial compensation for them. He was also instructed to ask for the evacuation of northwest posts that Britain had not yet abandoned. On the other hand, Hamilton, working through backroom channels, told Britain they should pay no compensation to the former owners of the slaves. Since he was one of the three most powerful men in the U.S. government, this carried a lot of weight. Hamilton also pushed the British to demand that the U.S. pay debts owed by farmers to England before the revolution broke out.[23] Hamilton was subverting Washington's position, trying to move the United States back into the British imperial orbit, and positioning himself to try to be the next president.

The final treaty that was brought back to the U.S. had tabled the items concerning compensation for seizures, pre-revolution debts, and

22. McDonald, *Washington*, 114, 116, 134.
23. Ibid., 142–43.

settlement of boundaries between the northern states and Canada and referred them instead to binding arbitration commissions. The treaty amounted to a renouncing of the U.S. claim to freedom of the seas. As a result of these concessions, the south would have to pay pre-war debts of about $20 million, and lost compensation for slaves worth around $10 million. This was a tremendous loss for the south and essentially amounted to an economic alliance of the northern states with Britain, at the expense of the southern states.[24]

When Congress demanded diplomatic papers related to the negotiation of Jay's Treaty, Washington claimed executive privilege and refused to turn over the papers. This set a precedent for increasingly illegal activities by later presidents along the same lines. Washington was arguing, essentially, that the lowest form of law, foreign treaties, could trump the highest form of U.S. law, the Constitution, and the second highest form, laws passed by the Congress pursuant to the Constitution. This would be the case if the Congress was forced to be a mere rubber stamp of the president's treaties. In fact, the treaty usurped (took over) two of the most important functions of the House of Representatives, its appropriations function (to approve money for the debt commissions), and its regulation of commerce. As it turned out, there was nothing in the Jay papers related to national security. The sensitivity was all about Washington's and Hamilton's and Jay's political security instead.[25]

Washington tolerated dissent by pardoning Whiskey rebels during his term of office. He tolerated dissent in other ways too. In fact, in 1794, near the end of his administration, newspapers took pot shots at him regarding John Jay's treaty normalizing diplomatic relations with the British and betraying the southern states. Washington upheld the Constitution by refusing to shut down the newspapers, and did not even respond publically to the attacks against his character. He also upheld the Constitution by firing federal employees tainted by corruptions such as bribery. One such notable dismissal was Edmund Randolph. In this, he set a precedent for presidential dismissal of high level appointees. In the future, the president and Congress argued about having control of dismissals, since the Constitution said nothing about it.[26]

---

24. Ibid., 154, 156.
25. Ibid., 171–72.
26. Miller Center, *Washington—Foreign Affairs*.

John Adams

John Adams' wife Abigail sounded the theme of this book. She wrote to her husband warning, "Remember, all Men would be tyrants if they could." Adams came to his inaugural in a carriage-and-two (horses) rather than Washington's carriage-and-six white horses. In the inaugural address he spoke of states' rights and the need to expand education throughout the nation. The greatest threats to the fledgling country, he said, were sophistry (deceptive reasoning), faction (a contentious or self-serving political group or party within the citizenry), and foreign influence. Accordingly, he tried to be clear-eyed and practical in reason, not to follow party lines in government appointments (at least initially), and to demonstrate "inflexible determination" to maintain peace with all nations. He served from 1797 to 1801.[27]

Adams can be seen as an advocate of an expanded presidency in a number of ways, and an advocate of a restrained presidency in an equal number of ways. After having spent ten years abroad as an American envoy in the imperials courts of European kings, he tended to give more respect to "pomp and protocol" than his revolutionary companions. In his role as President of the Senate during Washington's term, he had wanted to explore European-style honorific titles for both the president and vice president, "to lend an air of dignity and majesty to government," and also because other nations might sneer at American leaders with small titles like "President" and "Vice President." Senator Maclay objected to Adams' suggestion that the president be called "Protector of Their Liberties," because it might easily have led to the war power slipping into the hands of the president rather than Congress, where the Constitution placed it. The Senator said, "The power of war is the organ of protection . . . this is placed in Congress by the Constitution. Any attempt to divest . . . and place it elsewhere, even with George Washington, is treason against the United States, or, at least, a violation of the Constitution." Maclay called such thinking "idolatrous." He pointed to Article 1, Section 9, Clause 8 of the Constitution, which read, "No Title of Nobility shall be granted by the United States."[28]

Adams promoted a strong presidency when he supported Washington's right to remove presidential appointees confirmed into office by the

---

27. Flagel, *Guide*, 268; McCullough, *Adams*, 468–69.
28. Whitney, *Biographies*, 23; Healy, *Cult of the Presidency*, 16–17.

Senate. He also appointed John Marshall to the Supreme Court, which had grave consequences for states' rights. He asserted a presidential right to executive privilege to keep a diplomatic controversy with France from boiling over. He asked the Congress and nation to expand its military capacity, specifically by building up a standing army. He used the same heavy-handed means to suppress the Fries Rebellion of 1799 that Washington had used against the Whiskey Rebellion. He also supported and enforced the Alien and Sedition acts, widely viewed by historians as snuffing out First Amendment guarantees, at least for his opponents. He was the first to be obviously ambitious for the office of president. In fact, he patiently bided his time for eight years while he was Washington's Vice President. These are all red-flags that devoted democratic republicans could legitimately point to as worrisome to the principles found in the Declaration of Independence.[29]

On the other hand, Adams respected the legislative prerogative of the Congress to such an extent that he never used the veto to stop legislation. He understood and deplored tyranny to the extent he was an ardent promoter of term limits for politicians. He admired the Roman republican practice, and the practice in the American states, of electing important public officials for a term of one year, rather than to a term of two or more years. He wrote, "Where annual elections end, there slavery begins." And though he was an ardent supporter of Washington as president, he worried during the revolution that the people of the nation were succumbing to political idolatry by means of "the superstitious veneration which is sometimes paid to General Washington." This caused even some members of the Congress, he said, to "idolize an image which their own hands have molten." On balance, then, Adams should be seen as a defender of liberty rather than a threat to it, since the executive branch promotions he made were not overwrought.[30]

Adams believed in a participatory political science. However, historians have suggested that later in his career Adams likely was upset when new states coming into the union during his presidency, like Kentucky and Tennessee, weakened property requirements for voting by extending the right to vote to all white males at the age of twenty-one. The original thirteen states still limited the vote to property owners/taxpayers. Adams wrote, "Inequalities are a part of the natural history of man . . . That all

29. Whitney, *Biographies*, 23; Nelson, *Presidency*, 68; McDonald, *Presidency*, 306.
30. McDonald, *Presidency*, 83 fn 25, 139, 223 fn 27.

men are born to equal rights is true. But to teach that all men are born with equal powers and faculties, to equal influence in society, to equal property and advantages through life, is . . . a fraud . . ." Later presidents, like the Tennessean Andrew Jackson, would take advantage of hordes of new and uneducated voters to push methods and policies not in the peoples' best interests, and even later presidents, like Franklin Roosevelt and Lyndon Johnson, did the same by passing out benefits from Washington to people who had no idea the Constitution wanted those benefits only passed out on the state level, or by private agencies.[31]

Adams was a religious man and obliquely suggested that his position was a calling that entitled him to a vision that his department heads could not ascertain as well as he. He wrote, "It always gives me pain when I find myself obliged to differ in opinion from any of the heads of departments; but, as our understandings are not always in our own power, every man must judge for himself."[32]

Many historians believe Adams' greatest achievement was avoidance of war with France. The leaders of the French revolution wanted America to join them in a war with Britain. This was a sure sign the French revolution was on a bad footing, as the French should have worked on improving their own democratic government instead of looking beyond their boundaries for glory in war. In order to punish Adams for his pro-British leanings and ancestry, they refused to recognize U.S. diplomats and threatened to hang American seamen found on British ships. Hamilton pushed an alliance with Britain and war with France, largely to further his political ambitions. Hamilton wrote that if he could get war with France, "Tempting objects will be within our grasp." He wanted "offensive operations . . . our game will be to attack where we can." Adams wrote regarding Hamilton, "This man is stark mad, or I am." He believed Hamilton had "total ignorance" of the state of affairs in Europe. Abigail wrote, "That man would . . . become a second Bonaparte." Once he discovered Hamilton's various schemes to promote war, he purged his cabinet of Washington holdovers who had secretly been supporting Hamilton.[33]

31. Miller Center, *John Adams – The American Franchise*; Adams, *Political Writings*, 199–201.

32. McCullough, *Adams*, 527.

33. Whitney, *Biographies*, 19, 25; McCullough, *Adams*, 478, 518, 522–23, 531, 535, 539; Napoleon overthrew democratic government in France in a coup in November, 1799.

Adams had in mind to do what the French should have done, kept their noses out of other nation's affairs. He believed, like Washington, that war would be disastrous for the new constitutional republic and thus he ardently pursued Washington's policy of neutralism.[34] He wrote, "Great is the guilt of an unnecessary war." His "peace with honor" policy he called "the most splendid diamond in my crown."[35] Although the reference to his "crown" was not particularly becoming, modern presidents have not been nearly as careful to promote the interests of the nation over their own. For his efforts, Adams lost a second term.

When France began attacking U.S. merchant ships off the coast of Long Island, Adams sent a peace mission to France rather than press for war. France at first refused to receive the envoys, thus pouring more fuel on the war fire back home. Next, representatives of the French Revolution quietly sought concessions from the United States in the form of a program of bribes and loans, known as the XYZ Affair. Unbeknownst to the American public, the French foreign affairs leader Talleyrand specifically demanded $250,000 for himself as a bribe, the guarantee of a $10 million loan to France, and an apology from Adams, all in compensation for Adams' supposed insults to the honor of France. Talleyrand clearly was hoping either for personal enrichment or war, either of which were attractive to him personally.[36]

When the American envoys returned home, Adams believed information about the incident should not be made public, as it would unduly enflame American sentiment against France. He thus classified the documents, and resisted calls for making them public, citing executive privilege. Unfortunately, members of Congress believed the diplomatic mission had failed because Adams had sabotaged it in favor of Britain. They therefore loudly demanded to see the documents relating to the mission. Adams finally relented and released the records. When the nation learned of the affair, they understood Adams was not at fault, and they called for war preparations. In April, 1798, legislation for arming merchant ships passed, and money was appropriated for harbor fortifications and cannon foundries.[37]

---

34. Politicians and historians later on found it useful to call this policy "isolationism," in order to cast a negative, culturally backward connotation on the policy.

35. McCullough, *Adams*, 515; Boyer, *Oxford Companion*, 7.

36. McCullough, *Adams*, 495–96; Flagel, *Guide*, 312.

37. McCullough, *Adams*, 499.

Expecting France to invade, Adams asked for a small, "provisional" standing army. The Congress then authorized the building of the standing army the Federalist party had longed for. It debated the idea of an army of from 25,000 to 50,000, but ultimately knocked the figure down to 10,000, still more than Adams wanted. It also provided for authority to call up 80,000 state militiamen. Adams' preferred buildup of the navy rather than a national army, because it was harder for a navy to be turned against its own people than an army. He wrote, "There is no more prospect of seeing a French army here than there is in heaven."[38]

Congress also took the step of trying to deal with potential enemies at home, such as French agents and sympathizers. The Alien and Sedition Acts, which Adams signed, were aimed at dealing with French aristocrat refuges from slave uprisings on Haiti, and also Irish who were anti-British and therefore could potentially ally with the French if war broke out. The Alien Act allowed the president to exile any of these foreigners who became suspect. The acts tended to crush opposition from 25,000 French émigrés to the U.S. and allowed the President to deport any foreigner who was a threat to national security. He did not deport any, although members of his cabinet and party pushed for him to do so. But hundreds, and possibly thousands, got the message and left on their own. The Alien Enemies Act is still in force today, 2014.[39]

The Naturalization Act was aimed at limiting the clout of immigrants, most of whom tended to vote for Jefferson's Democratic-Republican party, rather than Adams' Federalist party. Some new immigrants fled the country as a result of this law. The law extended the residency requirement for citizenship from five to fourteen years. The Sedition Act outlawed conspiracy against federal laws and punished subversive speech with fines and prison. Specifically, it was against the law to say "false, scandalous, and malicious" things about the U.S. president, but not about the U.S. vice president, who was of a different party. The acts essentially made it illegal for people to criticize Adams.[40]

Jefferson was worried enough by the acts that he suspected his own mail was being searched by Federalist-appointed post official officials. Twenty newspaper editors were prosecuted under the act. Jefferson and Madison drafted Kentucky and Virginia state resolutions condemning

38. Ibid., 499, 513.
39. Ibid., 505.
40. Fagel, *Guide*, 70.

the Alien and Sedition Acts and pronouncing them null and void. This positioned the party of Jefferson in the revolutionary tradition against centralist tyranny and propelled that party into power in due time. It also established the supremacy of states' rights for the next several generations of U.S. citizens.[41]

Adams' biographer reminds that the Sedition Act was "clearly a violation of the First Amendment." Cabinet member John Marshall openly opposed the legislation. Jefferson believed the legislation would be used to persecute opposition party members. The legislation did allow the truth of a libelous statement against the president as a legitimate defense. Prosecutions and convictions under the Act were obtained from all sectors of society, from a Vermont Congressman to a drunk New Jersey tavern "loafer," to republican party pamphleteer James Callender.[42]

The French invasion never came, and the army was never formed. Both Congress and Adams worked to dismantle what had begun of the new army in the summer of 1800. Adams attempted once again to re-open diplomatic relations with France, which his own Federalist party opposed. When Federalists in the Senate told him they refused to support this effort, he threatened to resign the presidency and leave the country in the hands of his Vice President Jefferson, who was much more friendly to the French than he was. This took great courage, and the Senate backed down. Adams then sent a second delegation to Talleyrand, over the objections of Congress and even his own cabinet, after receiving a variety of indications France did not want war with the U.S. The envoys signed a treaty with Napoleon that released the U.S. from its Revolutionary War dabbling with France and set the nation up into a situation of real neutrality between Britain and France. Adams might have won a second term if news of the peace treaty had arrived sooner.[43]

To pay for the nation's new Navy Department, the Federalists enacted heavy new national government fees increases, called "stamp taxes," and new property tax requirements, called "house taxes."[44] Farmers in Pennsylvania rioted and attacked the federal tax collectors because they did not believe the nation should maintain

41. Ibid., 70.

42. McCullough, *Adams*, 536–37.

43. Flagel, *Guide*, 236; Whitney, *Biographies*, 26; McCullough, *Adams*, 523, 540, 552, 556; Crenson and Ginsberg, *Presidential Power*, 216–17; Miller Center, *John Adams—Foreign Affairs*.

44. McCullough, *Adams*, 507.

an army in peace time. Leaders of the rebellion arrested for treason were pardoned by Adams in 1800 in what might be termed an election eve vote-buying maneuver to get the support of poor farmers. At the end of his lame duck term in early 1801, Adams and his party passed a revision of the Judiciary Act of 1789 which created federal circuit courts and sixteen judgeships for them and extended the jurisdiction of the federal courts. Adams then packed these new courts with anti-states rights political appointees, and also installed John Marshall as Chief Justice of the Supreme Court, a man instrumental in expanding the scope of the national government over the next several decades. Jefferson wrote, "The Federalists have retired into the Judiciary . . . (and from there) Republicanism (will be) beaten down and erased." This legislation expanded the federal judiciary at the expense of state courts.[45]

Adams legacy might be summed up thusly: he did what was right, rather than doing what would personally glorify him, and left the country better off for it, even though it cost him a second term. He lost reelection because he checked rather than accommodated a dangerous militaristic faction in his own party. In the process he very possibly prevented a devious tyrant from taking power at a very early time in American government. Not insecure, like many politicians, he wrote "Extravagant popularity is not the road to public advantage." He would rather sacrifice his popularity than unleash forces that would harm the republic. He left office having demonstrated "incorruptible integrity" throughout his term. One historian wrote, "At the risk of his career, he chose not to go to war."[46]

Thomas Jefferson

Jefferson believed that the only secure basis for liberty was in freedom of speech and learning, and in government encouragement to education. Jefferson's civic philosophy was based on the idea people can change things for the better by obtaining land and improving it, getting educated, participating in government, allowing freedom of religion and pursuing free trade.

Jefferson got his political support from the tobacco belt: North Carolina, Virginia, Central Kentucky and Tennessee. Religion had been

45. McDonald, *States' Rights*, 53.
46. McCullough, *Adams*, 470–71, 557, 566.

declining generally in the states, and in particular in Virginia. However, a revived form of religion based on individual responsibility for salvation, and individual responsibility for good local government was sweeping across the south and west in 1800. While God, for Jefferson, supported land acquisition and resale to hard working farmers with consequent profit for the seller, God did not support other kinds of unearned gain like that promoted by bankers in the form of paper money, bank notes, and public debt. God also did not support lavish spending by government. Tobacco belt dwellers were constantly at odds with creditors, and were not averse to stalling payments to them since they were believed to be a swindler profession. For Jefferson and his supporters, Europe was the scene of "exterminating havoc" due to constant warring and banker financing of those wars. European heads of states like Napoleon and Pitt were thus bandits and tyrants. Jefferson was also hostile to navies because they were expensive and could easily be used to get a nation involved in war.[47]

To get involved in entangling economic, political or military relations with such "madmen" was a death sentence for a republic. European countries were devoted to taxation and public debt to support large, standing armies and navies, territorial ambitions of their rulers, and parliamentary systems of government whereby the executive branch of government took the lead in pushing for legislation. They set up systems of economic treaties with weaker nations to entrap them, and collected import duties that favored one set of homeland interests over another. Their leaders flip-flopped constantly back and forth from one opportunistic alliance to another, while their citizenries hardly knew what was going on. Already Europeans, and especially the British, owned a large percentage of the public debt of the United States and held stock in the American national bank, and thus could manipulate U.S. economic policy to their benefit. British subjects owned $16 million of the original U.S. public debt, $8 million of bonds for the purchase of Louisiana, and $4 million in stock of the Bank of the United States. For this reason, Jefferson was determined to purge the national government workforce of monarchists, repeal taxes, slash expenses and liquidate the national debt as much as possible. He also wanted to establish greater respect for the constitutional separation of powers between the legislative and executive branches, depoliticize the judiciary, gradually extinguish slavery, and

47. McDonald, *Jefferson*, 10–11, 15, 17–19, 54–55, 101.

purchase new territories to provide land for the ever-increasing American population. Rice and cotton planters in his political base wanted to obtain Indian and Spanish lands in furtherance of the republican land policy. In the parlance of Jefferson's political party, tax collectors were called excise men, bankers were called paper shufflers, stock jobbers, and monopolists, and government employees were called placemen.[48]

Any appointments Adams made after the moment of election of the new president, Jefferson considered unethical, if not technically illegal. He refused to sign their commissions of appointment. The Judiciary Act of 1801 also transferred jurisdiction of land title problems to the federal courts, which Jefferson disagreed with. That law also instituted an intentional decrease in Jefferson's power as president, reducing the court from six to five judges by leaving the next retirement from the court vacant. Jefferson signed the Judiciary Act of 1802 after his group repealed the 1801 Act and postponed the next meeting of the Supreme Court for a year.[49]

Jefferson served from 1801 to 1809. Ultimately, Jefferson presided over a one-third turnover of federal employment in his first two years, and a 50 percent turnover by the end of his first four-year term. Jefferson inherited about 4,000 civilian federal employees. Some 316 of these could be appointed by the president, some 700 of them could be appointed by cabinet chiefs, and 3,000 could be appointed by the postmaster general. Jefferson was determined, as Washington was, to only remove political monarchists, those who were corrupt, and incompetents. He had no intent to introduce a spoils system, where the wining political party would sweep out all the appointees of the losing political party. He had to modify his thinking somewhat, of course, not only when he saw Adams appoint a slew of Federalists to the newly expanded federal judiciary, but also when he began to get pressure from his supporters for federal jobs. He cut back the number of presidential appointments open to him, the size of the standing army, the navy and the diplomatic corp. He left in place most of the clerks and postal workers, but overall reduced the nation's 316 appointed positions. He cut Adams' swollen national army down to two regiments (3,350 men), and instead founded West Point and the Army Corp of Engineers. He put the navy essentially in moth-balls, out of active service, and thus cut navy expense by two-thirds.[50]

48. McDonald, *Jefferson*, 21–22, 24, 107, 163.
49. Ibid., 48–50.
50. McDonald, *Jefferson*, 34–38, 166; Whitney, *Biographies*, 40.

Jefferson delivered his message to Congress in writing rather than in person, since he did not want to imitate the annual English royalty ritual. In his first message he was careful not to give any tone of command, and in fact said his purpose was not to make laws but to "carry that [legislative] judgment into faithful execution." He wrote that Congress had "the sovereign functions of legislation." By this time, both major political parties on the national scene had made clear their understanding of the distinct separation of powers between the Congress and the president. Jefferson established free and easy communication with Congress. It has been said that he did not use the tyrannical techniques of so-called "strong" presidents in trying to influence Congress, including "popular pressure, naked power, bribery, flattery, cajolery, blackmail, or shrewd trading." Although Congress respected and took up many of his legislative proposals, he did not openly initiate legislation. He conducted democratic discussions with his cabinet until they came to a consensus. Opinions were voiced freely. Cabinet meetings were "a democracy of equals."[51]

Jefferson believed that the individual citizen's secret to limiting despotism was to be found "in the making himself the depository of the powers respecting himself, so far as he is competent to them, and delegating only what is beyond his competence." Government at the highest level had an extremely limited purpose—to "restrain men from injuring one another." He abhorred war and announced candidly, "Peace is my passion." With so limited a function, national government must necessarily be "frugal," or inexpensive.[52]

Jefferson set about as president to cut back on the level of national debt so it could be liquidated within 15 years. He reduced the national debt by 30 percent during his time in office, from $80 million to $57 million, and left a rainy-day fund of $14 million, even after making the $15 million Louisiana Purchase. His efforts in reducing the debt resulted in part from the bonanza shipping business enjoyed by the nation's ship owners (the "carrying" trade). This happened because American shippers were allowed to be neutral carriers to Britain and France, engaged in war since about 1793. France and Spain had to martial their shipping fleets into war-use, necessitating the use of outside shippers such as the U.S. Jefferson also worked with Congress to abolish most internal taxes

51. Healy, *Cult of the Presidency*, 63; McDonald, *Presidency*, 259; McDonald, *Jefferson*, 31, 34–38, 42, 166.

52. Jefferson, *Works*, 6:543; Miller Center, *Jefferson—Domestic Affairs*; Herring, *Colony to Superpower*, 97.

such as excise, carriage, and property taxes, including the war tax of 1798, leaving only the tariff to provide revenue for the national government. He worked to repeal the Alien and Sedition Acts as well. He freed political prisoners incarcerated under the Alien and Sedition Acts, pardoning ten mostly Republican party newspaper publishers convicted under those laws. He restored with interest the fines extracted from them under those laws, as well. This was essentially a retro-nullification of that chapter of American life.[53]

Jefferson signed the Land Act of 1804, which reduced the price of public land and the minimum purchase by half from 320 to 160 acres, so more Americans could participate in land ownership and political governance. He also signed the Ohio Enabling Act, which reserved one section in each township for education. The government also agreed to buy or otherwise obtain Indian land in Georgia for white settlement. This later became the basis for Jackson's harsh policy of Indian removal from the state.[54]

Jefferson believed that not only each branch of the national government, but each state and its own branches and conventions had the right of "judicial review," that is, to decided what laws are constitutional. In other words, while the judiciary ought to be independent of undue interference, it should not be sovereign, not the only final authority. Jefferson also believed the president was the equal of the Supreme Court in interpreting the Constitution. For this reason, he felt empowered to use a presidential veto to stop measures passed by Congress that he felt were unconstitutional. In particular, Jefferson asserted that the presidential veto exists to "protect" the states from "invasions" by the national government. Thus he set a precedent that a major part of presidential duty was to protect the states. In his inaugural he spoke of the rights of the states in domestic affairs. But he was firm in his position that the chief executive should not veto bills that he merely had a preference for or policy difference with. In this, he set a pattern that was followed for a lengthy period of time.[55]

Jefferson is criticized by some historians for betraying his strict construction principles in making the Louisiana Purchase. The original

53. McDonald, *Jefferson*, 5, 41–44, 56, 86; Whitney, *Biographies*, 40.

54 McDonald, *Jefferson*, 47, 172 n. 10.

55. McDonald, *States' Rights*, 31; McDonald, *Presidency*, 251; Crenson and Ginsberg, *Presidential Power*, 66.

states did not plan for the addition of more territory by treaty. Thus, the Constitution, in fact, says nothing about purchasing new territory to add to the existing United States. An addition like the Louisiana Purchase would double the size of the nation and it would clearly diminish the overall power of the old states in the newly expanded nation.[56]While later presidents like Teddy Roosevelt and George W. Bush would argue that they can do anything the Constitution does not prohibit (a proposal that the founders would have viewed as absurd and tyrannical), Jefferson saw that the Constitution was clear in stating that the national government could only do the things explicitly spelled out ("enumerated" or "delegated") for it to do. The silence of the Constitution regarding things like new territory was not a green light, but a red light.

In fact, Jefferson was troubled also because the purchase would double the national debt. Jefferson therefore held off so he could discuss a constitutional amendment with Congress. In fact, he actually drafted up the amendment himself. But when he heard that Napoleon might be having second thoughts about selling the land, he went ahead with the purchase and presented the treaty to Congress without mentioning the constitutional issue.[57]

In spite of all the financial entanglement the deal brought (the U.S. had to borrow money from European bankers), Jefferson at least was able to reduce the chance of war with France to zero percent, since France would not be nipping at America's western flank any more. And he pulled off a huge real estate deal at the same time, so most other Americans were not swallowing as hard as he was. Jefferson also increased the tariff to help pay for Louisiana, disguising it as a measure necessary to protect against Barbary pirates in the Mediterranean by adding to the navy.[58]

Jefferson was reelected to a second term by huge margins across the country because he abolished national taxes, reduced the size of civilian government and the military, decreased the public debt, avoided war, and increased the size of the country by two times. Shortly after his election, he announced he would not seek a third term, and thus honor Washington's precedent.[59]

---

56. McDonald, *Jefferson*, 70.

57. Flagel, *Guide*, 207; McDonald, *States' Rights*, 59; Herring, *Colony to Superpower*, 106.

58. McDonald, *Jefferson*, 68.

59. Ibid., 86, 97.

In Jefferson's second term, foreseeing a treasury surplus if the nation could avoid war, he proposed a constitutional amendment to allow Congress to fund internal improvement projects and fund public education. He also advanced legislation to improve coastal defenses, either reorganize the state militias or enlarge the regular standing army, and abolish the slave trade. The Constitution allowed the slave trade for a period of twenty years, long enough to educate the next generation against it, after which the nation would hopefully abolish it. Now Jefferson proposed to do just that, and Congress agreed. This was an example of gradual abolition of slavery in practical action, a course that Lincoln might have championed sixty years later, but did not. The slave trade legislation was the only part of Jefferson's second term agenda that Congress agreed to do, as they were even more conservative constitutionally than he.[60]

In the meanwhile, Britain had continued and expanded its practice of "impressments" of American merchant sailors. Jefferson was determined to avoid war, and took extreme measures to do so. He prohibited all American ships from leaving port, not just for Britain but for France. This was a policy of "no trade at all." This embargo would give time to prepare for war, if that had to be resorted to as a last measure, but he was determined that Britain would have to declare war first. Because there was severe unemployment in New England as a result of the embargo, some shippers ignored the law, and continued to conduct trade with British Canada.

James Madison

James Madison was educated at Princeton. He had no law degree, but he knew the country's constitutional law well, because he helped to write it. He was an old-school president, a politician who, he says, "despised" campaigning. He never made a campaign speech, and didn't even acknowledge his candidacy for the presidency after it was put forward by others. This was a day when presidents were "heard not seen," that is, known through their writings and others' writings and speeches about them. His philosophy of government was simple: "You must first enable the government to control the governed; and in the next place, oblige it to control itself." He served from 1809 to 1817.[61]

60. Ibid.,130.
61. Rutland, *Madison*, xii, 1, 3, 5, 8, 14–15, 27, 118, 205.

At the Constitutional Convention in 1787, Madison had argued for a fairly strong executive branch. He succeeded in getting the delegates to give the president, instead of the Congress, power to appoint ambassadors, federal judges and cabinet members. But he didn't want to go as far as some in promoting presidential power. Near the end of Jefferson's term, Madison opposed a proposal in Congress to put Washington's facial image on all American coins. This is what kings in Europe were accustomed to do to so that their people would dote upon the image and cherish the ruler's ways. Madison got Congress to use instead "an emblematic figure of liberty." It was another century before America gave in to the practice of molten political image-making. President Teddy Roosevelt put Lincoln's face on the penny, suggesting the president was now more important than liberty.[62]

Madison kept the federal government small, after Jefferson had cut it back from Adams' term of office. In fact, there was little change in the pattern or amount of federal government employment over the 20 years from 1801 through 1821, that is, the end of the term of James Monroe, who came after Madison. Each department of government had about 6 clerks to run its business. The treasury department had 50 in Washington, DC, and 700 across the nation, including tariff collectors, inspectors, and anti-smuggler crewmen. There was no army general staff, and only a paymaster and two clerks to run the war department. Naval department agents purchased timbers and stored them for potential use in building ships in the future. There were 2,000 post offices, but only a dozen clerks to run the department in Washington. When war clouds gathered in 1808, new officers were commissioned for the military for a while. There were only eighteen people employed at the White House.[63]

Madison elaborated his overall theory of checks and balances in republican government in Federalist, No. 51. He wrote that in the new U.S. republic, the power of the people is "first divided between two distinct governments [national and state], and then the portion allotted to each [is] subdivided among distinct and separate departments [legislative, executive, judicial]. Hence a double security arises to the rights of the people." Furthermore, the states were to have power over "all the objects which, in the ordinary course of affairs, concern the lives, liberties, and properties of the people, and the internal order, improvement, and

62. Ibid., 28.
63. Ibid., 34–36, 53.

prosperity of the State." These powers together are generally referred to as the "police powers."[64]

Clearly, then, Madison envisioned that economic affairs ("prosperity," and "property"), and health, education, and welfare activities ("improvement") should fall within the power of the states, and not the national government. Madison's ideas later influenced first northern, and then southern states to threaten secession (leaving the union of states) when their local rights were manhandled.[65]

Madison's concern about presidential usurping of the legislative power under one or another guise like the General Welfare Clause was serious indeed. He wrote, "The accumulation of all powers, legislative, executive, and judiciary, in the same hands, whether of one, a few, or many, and whether hereditary, self-appointed, or elective, may justly be pronounced the very definition of tyranny."[66]

Madison supported term limits on the presidency. In Federalist No. 39, he wrote that the very definition of a republic is that kind of government where the executive holds power "for a limited period, or during good behavior." Furthermore, the people of a republic must have full access to information. A "popular government without popular information or the means of acquiring it is but a prologue to a farce or a tragedy, or both." Accordingly, he would have staunchly opposed the government-by-secrecy policies of twentieth century presidents.[67]

During the Constitutional Convention, Madison had been outspoken in favor of making it difficult to go to war. This could be achieved by placing the war power in the hands of the legislative branch. He suggested that legitimate executive powers "do not include the Rights of war and peace . . . but the powers should be confined and defined . . . (if not) we shall have the Evils of elective monarchies." The one who has the power to mold military activity in his own political interests often does so for self-promoting reasons: "In no part of the constitution is more wisdom to be found, than in the clause which confides the question of war or peace to the legislature, and not to the executive department . . . the temptation would be too great for any one man." He added, "The strongest passions and most dangerous weakness of the human breast,

64. Morley, *Freedom and Federalism*, 32, 169.

65. Boyer, *Oxford Companion*, 468.

66. Madison, *Federalist No. 47*.

67. Morley, *Freedom and Federalism*, 6, 196.

ambition, avarice, vanity, the honorable or venial love of fame, are all in a conspiracy [within the executive branch] against the desire and duty of peace. Hence it has grown into an axiom that the executive is the department of power most distinguished by its propensity to war."[68]

There must be a separation of the power to declare and the power to conduct: "Those who are to conduct a war cannot . . . be proper or safe judges whether a war ought to be commenced . . ." War challenges rights at home: "No nation could preserve its freedom in the midst of continual war." Again, "The means of defense against foreign danger have always been the instrument of tyranny at home." In the Helvidius letters, written anonymously, Madison warned about the use of propaganda in war: "War . . . (is) the parent of armies; from these proceed debts and taxes . . . the known instruments for bringing the many under the domination of the few. In war, too . . . all the means of seducing the minds, are added to those of subduing the force of the people."[69]

Madison carried over the anti-war policies Jefferson had instituted into his own term as president. He signed the Non-Intercourse Act Congress passed just before his first term in office. This forbade all American commerce with the two warring nations in Europe, Britain and France. It allowed trade with other European nations. But it gave the two nations an escape clause allowing them to trade with America if they would only allow the U.S. to function as a neutral shipper to the warring parties, instead of blocking U.S. trade with the other warring party.[70]

Napoleon used the law to manipulate Madison into war against Britain by saying France would agree to the new American neutrality law, but upon terms that would be hard for Britain to meet. The old anti-war horse John Adams wrote of Napoleon's offer, "It is a trap to catch us into war with England." In fact the U.S. was not prepared for war. Madison took Napoleon's bait and headed for war. Nevertheless, he still did not want to enact any taxes before his reelection campaign, because the people would not like that. He decided to fight the war by taking the nation into debt.[71]

68. Herring, *Colony to Superpower*, 53; Healy, *Cult of the Presidency*, 29; Crenson and Ginsberg, *Presidential Power*, 357.

69. Herring, *Colony to Superpower*, 159, 169; Healy, *Cult of the Presidency*, 43.

70. Rutland, *Madison*, 13, 37–39, 52, 90.

71. Nelson, *Presidency*, 74; McDonald, *Presidency*, 261; Boyer, *Oxford Companion*, 467; Rutland, *Madison*, 40–42, 46, 62–63, 66, 92, 94, 102.

Washington, Adams, Jefferson, and Madison believed that the best way for a nation to stay at peace was not to build up a standing army (permanent and professional). In Madison's day, the nation still utilized a largely voluntary force to handle defense of its borders. The military consisted of state militia men and a small number professionals employed on the national level. The officers that commanded these forces were mostly appointed by governors, not the president.[72]

In order to underscore the nation's commitment to non-entanglement in military treaties with foreign nations, Madison undertook the task of winning the War of 1812 without external assistance from other nations. He also did not use the War of 1812 as an excuse to suppress his political opposition within the Federalist party or to assume extreme powers.[73]

Madison was not unlike other American war presidents who came after him in at least one important sense. Polk, Lincoln, McKinley, and Wilson were idealists who thought that war would be short and easy. Madison listened to "armchair generals" like John Calhoun, who assured him that "in four weeks . . . Canada will be in our power." The war lasted 20 months, and the U.S. still had not taken an inch of Canada.[74]

Many of the citizenry were actively opposed to Madison's War. Madison wrote, "The enlistments for the regular army fall short of the most moderate calculation . . . The volunteer act is extremely unproductive. And even the Militia detachments are either obstructed by the disaffected Governors, or chilled . . ." The Massachusetts militia, for example, had 70,000 skilled and drilled men, but the Massachusetts legislature essentially nullified Madison's war by passing a resolution urging the citizenry to resist the war. They proclaimed a day of fasting and prayer to protect against "entangling and fatal alliances with foreign powers," thinking that the war would push the U.S. into an alliance with France.[75]

The New England states got together in December, 1814 in what was called the Hartford Convention. Their stated goal was to insure "security against conscription, taxes and the dangers of invasion." Madison was subjecting the citizens of those states to forced military servitude, unnecessary taxation, and British hostility toward them, when they considered

72. Crenson and Ginsberg, *Presidential Power*, 282.

73. Herring, *Colony to Superpower*, 132–33; Nelson, *Presidency*, 74.

74. Rutland, *Madison*, 105.

75. Ibid., 112, 115–16, 141.

themselves friendly toward Britain. While the northeast states were gathered together, they showed the depths of their commitment to the political ethics of the founders by proposing new and severe limits on the power of the president. They proposed constitutional amendments which would mandate a two-thirds vote in Congress for declaring war, imposing a trade embargo, and admitting new states; limit the president to one term; and mandate that a new president could not come from the same state as the previous president. These were concerns about southern power, as well as national power.[76]

The War of 1812 between the U.S. and Great Britain lasted two and a half years, cost more than 2,000 American lives, and cost $158 million in national government debt. Madison had cut the national debt from $83 million to $45 million before the start of the war, but the war increased it to $127 million by 1816. The $68–72 million cost of the war was more than Polk's later war on Mexico. Thus, even though Madison understood in general terms the historical cost of war in debt and taxes, he greatly underestimated, like later presidents would, the money and manpower necessary for new wars. Total British and Canadian casualties were around 9,000 and American casualties at nearly 8,000.[77]

After the war, in his message to Congress in December, 1815, Madison successfully asked for a protective tariff for textile and iron manufacturing, perhaps to shore up his reputation with northerners. He may have initially been opposed to the tariff measure that passed, but signed it either because he later supported it or because he did not think it unconstitutional. The latter was in accord with his philosophy that "In a republican government, the legislative authority necessarily predominates." He also asked for more military schools across the country, a stronger navy, a national university, and a tax bill. Of these, only the tax bill passed. Congress once again was more conservative than the president.[78]

Meanwhile, in 1817 Henry Clay submitted his Bonus Bill asking that $1.5 million left over from the start up of the National Bank be used for roads and canals across the country. Madison argued that the Article 1, Section 8 list of enumerated constitutional powers of the national government did not contain such a power, and furthermore such

76. Ibid., 20, 24, 147, 174, 180, 183, 186.

77. McDonald, *Presidency*, 257; Rutland, *Madison*, 196; Flagel, *Guide*, 129, 247, 251; Herring, *Colony to Superpower*, 127.

78. McDonald, *Presidency*, 257; Nelson, *Presidency*, 74; Whitney, *Biographies*, 49; Healy, *Cult of the Presidency*, 37; Rutland, *Madison*, 195, 197.

a power did not fall under the "power to make the laws necessary and proper" for carrying out the functions that *were* on the list either. He also rejected the interpretation that the General Welfare Clause could justify such expenses. Therefore, Madison broke republican tradition of signing whatever the Congress passed, and vetoed the bill. He explained his veto by stating he thought "the permanent success of the Constitution depends upon a definite partition of powers between the General and State governments."[79]

Madison did not believe the third great plank of the national centralizers—the expenditure of federal funds on "internal improvements" like roads and canals—could be done without an amendment to the Constitution. He understood infrastructure improvement to be the bailiwick of the states. For example, New York State, having this same understanding, had begun construction on the Erie Canal at its own expense. Madison did sign legislation providing $100,000 for a westward extension of the national road, called the Cumberland Road.[80]

James Monroe

James Monroe was well educated at the College of William and Mary. He then studied law with Thomas Jefferson. He served three one-year terms as governor of Virginia, the maximum span of office allowed by the state constitution. In the Senate he was opposed to the national bank. He opposed direct taxation by the federal government like the kinds imposed during the War of 1812, which included taxes on alcohol, refined sugar, stamp taxes, the carriage tax, and sales at auction. He asked for their repeal. He wanted some level of national control over state militias, but only as a way to prevent a standing army. Later, as Madison's secretary of war, he flip-flopped and called for a permanent army establishment of 20,000, two times the pre-1812 level. Monroe served as president from 1817 to 1825.[81]

In Monroe's 1822 message to Congress, he re-iterated the common understanding that the legislative branch is "by far the most important." Monroe had the power of veto, but used it only once to block an extension

79. Whitney, *Biographies*, 49.

80. McDonald, *States' Rights*, 74–76; Nelson, *Presidency*, 74; Rutland, *Madison*, 198, 205–06.

81. Cunningham, *Monroe*, 1, 3–4, 7, 13, 15, 46–47.

of the Cumberland road and set up tolls and tollgates. He believed that national internal improvements and subsidies for manufacturing could happen only with a constitutional amendment. In this case, Congress was quicker to abandon the rule of law than the president was. It did not think an amendment was needed and sent him a bill to repair the national Cumberland Road and collect tolls on it. Monroe vetoed the bill and indicated the states should collect the tolls. He said if a constitutional amendment failed, Congress could repair roads it had already built. He signed a general survey bill to make estimates for military, commercial or postal uses. Congress had raised the tariff in 1816, but Monroe signed another tariff increase in 1824.[82]

Monroe earlier had taken a position against a number of specific weak provisions of the Constitution which he now swore to uphold when he became president. He had spoken against the final form of the impeachment power because he believed there was a flaw in the treaty power involving the relationship between the president and the Senate. The Senate was given power to try impeachments of the president. But the Senate and president were mandated to consult frequently with each other in foreign affairs. This meant they could easily be cozy with one another and not inclined to maintain an arms-length relationship. When the president got involved in misbehavior, his friends in the Senate would be little inclined to hold him to account.[83] This flaw came home to roost during the impeachment trials of Andrew Johnson, Richard Nixon, and Bill Clinton.

At the start of his first term as president, Monroe traveled 3,000 miles across the nation for 16 weeks to meet the people and promote the military. He wanted a chain of forts on the American frontier and an increase in the size of the navy. He paid for the trip out of his own pocket. But he also wanted to glorify himself and the presidential office. One newspaper spoke of "all the idle pageantry, all the ridiculous and noxious pomp." One historian wrote that Monroe "missed few opportunities to bolster his political position." An editor wrote in 1824, "I am not one of those who 'fell and worshipped' Mr. Monroe . . . He was praised without decency . . ." Monroe's travels and personal promotions were not the only inclinations toward idolatry during this time. There also was a call for a

82. Healy, *Cult of the Presidency*, 37; McDonald, *States' Rights*, 91; McDonald, *Presidency*, 223, n. 27; Cunningham, *Monroe*, 24, 29–30, 165–67, 190.

83. McDonald, *Presidency*, 197–98.

national monument in George Washington's name to be housed at the nation's capitol. The eighty-four-year-old John Adams did not think this was a good idea.[84]

The national government, in spite of Monroe's early writings against it, grew greatly during his term of office. There were 75 post offices in Washington's term, 1,025 at the start of Jefferson's, and 3,459 at the start of Monroe's. Postal employees in the nation's capital continued to grow during his term, from fifteen to twenty-seven. The departments of war, navy, and state grew moderately during his two terms, but he added new auditors in treasury and doubled the number of land officers. In contrast to growth in the executive departments, Monroe had no money even for a personal secretary in the White House, or for hospitality. Members of his family had to perform clerical duties for the government. Monroe decreased the national debt from $127 million in 1816 to $84 million by the end of his term in 1825, largely due to de-mobilization after the war.[85]

When the depression of 1819–23 dimmed the luster of his presidency, bringing employment and foreclosures, Monroe believed, with most people in the country, that it was not the president's responsibility to rescue either the economy or his own popularity. Even though manufacturers called for a bailout, including a "very liberal policy as to the payment of money," and "the making of paper money in a time of peace," Monroe declined to call a special session of Congress. While Monroe tinkered with the toys of tyranny, he did not have many of them to play with. He signed the Land Act of 1820, providing several million acres west of the Appalachians for sale with a minimum down payment. In fact, land giveaways and debt relief historically have been two of the most effective tools "reformist" tyrants have used, often disingenuously, to charm an electorate dogged by poverty and misery. About the only thing he could do to help the economy was instruct the secretary of the treasury to loosen payment terms on lands purchased from the federal government. He left private land transactions alone, since they were clearly not the jurisdiction of the national government. He left to Congress whether to raise the tariff and protect American industries.[86]

The debate over the Missouri slavery question gave Monroe an opportunity to show off his conservative constitutional chops, and he came

84. Cunningham, *Monroe*, 31, 33, 35, 73, 86, 185.

85. Ibid., 24, 42, 51, 116, 121, 123.

86. McDonald, *Presidency*, 257; Cunningham, *Monroe*, 2, 46, 83–85.

down in favor of traditional constitutional law over political expediency. Missouri was petitioning for admission as a state. Abolitionists wanted to prohibit slavery not only in the territories but in new states like Missouri. Monroe vetoed a measure to put a specially tailored slavery restriction on Missouri's admission to the union. He gave out the "decided opinion" that "new states cannot be admitted into the union, on conditions other than the old." He did so not because he wanted to keep new slaves from entering the state and adding to the ones already there, but because the Constitution did not allow the enacting of discriminatory laws such as this one. This legislation was a little like the detested private legislation that kings in Europe used to harass their political opponents and uppity sections of the country. Also, it was widely believed that Congress could not interfere in state government except to ensure a liberal form of government and to help keep it that way. Article IV, Section 4 stated, "The United States shall guarantee to every State in this Union a Republican Form of Government, and shall protect each of them against Invasion . . ." This was called popular sovereignty, and both old and new states thought Missouri ought to be able to decide slavery policy on its own. For example, the Kentucky legislature passed a resolution saying that "The general assembly refrains from expressing any opinion either in favor or against the principles of slavery; but to support and maintain state rights . . to preserve the liberties of the free people of these United States." The founders believed democratic government could still have slavery, as long as progress was being made to end it. In fact, in the main Monroe stayed out of the fractious debates in Congress on policy issues like slavery because it was not his constitutional place to make or push policy. He said, "I take no part in these concerns . . ." [87]

Eventually, Monroe and John Quincy Adams, Monroe's secretary of state, supported the Missouri Compromise of 1820, as it was "all that could be effected under the present Constitution." This allowed Missouri as a slave state and Maine as a free state. It also banned slavery in the northern area of the Louisiana Purchase. Monroe privately let it be known he favored the compromise, but took no active role in the legislative debate leading to it, and thus maintained constitutional separation. Monroe also did not give an opinion whether the nation could now legislate more extensively to stop slavery in the territories, north or south. But he believed it would have been even better to have allowed the peaceful

87. Miller Center, *Monroe—Domestic Affairs;* Cunningham, *Monroe,* 87–88, 92.

separation of the north and south, and a new constitutional convention called in the north to end slavery. This would create "a new Union of thirteen or fourteen States unpolluted with slavery." This example of "the universal emancipation of their slaves" in the north he believed would then "rally [the southern states] to the standard . . ."[88]

Andrew Jackson was one of Monroe's generals in the small standing army. Monroe sent Jackson to the border of Spanish Florida to chase away Indians causing trouble for settlers near there. Jackson personally wanted to take east Florida as tribute for claims of U.S. citizens against Spain, but this would cause war with Spain. Jackson exceeded his orders and attacked Spain, taking Pensacola. Monroe's entire cabinet agreed that this was an act of war, was unauthorized by the president, and was not constitutional, since only Congress could declare war. Monroe ordered the territory returned. Monroe then negotiated Spain's sale of Florida to the U.S. by means of the Adams-Onis Treaty. He believed in expansion by purchase, not by conquest.[89]

Monroe also signaled a change in Indian policy toward more harshness and away from a neutral posture toward their communities and lands: "We have treated them as independent nations without their having any substantial pretensions to that rank." He said, "Their sovereignty over vast territories should cease." The new policy was to be assimilation: "The right of soil should be secured to each individual . . . and funds . . . for the education of their children . . ." This meant they should move away from communal ownership of land to private ownership.[90]

We mentioned above that Monroe had changed his mind once about a standing army and now he approved of a standing army during the time of peaceful relations with Spain. He wanted the permanent army reduced only about 1,000 or so from the 7,421 in service during the Florida war scare. But Congress reduced his army request even further and cut fort construction by three fourths. Monroe grew the navy to twenty-one ships in his two terms and positioned a permanent navy presence on the Pacific coast.[91]

---

88. Cunningham, *Monroe*, 96, 98, 104; Boyer, *Oxford Companion*, 513, 693–94; Nelson, *Presidency*, 80.

89. Cunningham, *Monroe*, 58–69, 75.

90. Ibid., 114.

91. Ibid., 111, 118–19.

In the arena of foreign affairs, Monroe espoused isolationism—or more properly, neutralism. In his 1823 annual message to Congress, he said, "In the wars of European powers in matters relating to themselves we have never taken any part, nor does it comport with our policy so to do." Furthermore, "Our policy in regard to Europe . . . nevertheless remains the same, which is, not to interfere in the internal concerns of any of its powers . . ." He also issued the bold statement that "The American Continents . . . are henceforth not to be considered as subjects for future Colonization by any European Power."[92]

With this doctrine, which came to be known as the Monroe Doctrine, he re-iterated the long-standing Washingtonian policy of non-entanglement in European political and military affairs. But it also established the U.S. as protector of the Americas from any further European conquest. The idea was to provide a safe haven in the Americas from European kingship for the development of democratic governments throughout the hemisphere. This sentiment contrasted mightily with the political philosophy of later presidents, who sided with kings and despots in the Americas, Europe, Africa, and Asia whenever their autocratic power was threatened by democratic movements. They turned the Monroe Doctrine on its head.

John Quincy Adams

John Quincy Adams served one term as President, from 1825–1829. He was a transitional figure in American politics. He was the last of the early "big government" nationalists, and big government would not surface again until the time of Abraham Lincoln forty years later.[93] Of course, the "big" of Adams' day would be deliriously small and libertarian today.

Adams was known to be haughty, cerebral, and distant. He could also be confrontational. He was a puritanical scholar who read the Bible through once a year. He was perhaps the most public of all presidents before or since in his expressions of faith. As a member of the Unitarian Congregational church, like his father, he questioned the virgin birth, a divine Jesus, the holy trinity, and predestination, but he strongly believed in God. After thirty years in the company of monarchs in Europe, he

---

92. Morley, *Freedom and Federalism*, 134; Cunningham, *Monroe*, xv, 42–43, 45, 52, 151–52, 157.

93. Miller Center, *John Quincy Adams—Domestic Affairs*

was also a wine aficionado. He believed in vigorous exercise, and walked several miles a day and swam the Potomac River in the summer. Madison offered Adams an appointment to the Supreme Court of the U.S., but Adams was too ambitious to settle for the court. He wanted the presidency. Like Jimmy Carter 150 years later, he refused to follow the dictates of either of the major two parties in Congress, or popular opinion.[94] Accordingly, he suffered the same fate Carter also suffered, abandonment by both party and people after only one term.

As Monroe's secretary of state, he negotiated away U.S. claims to Texas by means of the Adams-Onis treaty. But he still had a vision of the American nation extending all the way to the Pacific. He wanted the U.S. to "be like the nations." He announced that Madison's 1816, eight-year naval building program was completed and that it was the destiny of the U.S. "to become in regular process of time and by no petty advances a great naval power." Still, he hated British imperial rule and saw that its government was "full of Coronations and Adulteries, Liturgy, prayers and Italian Sopranos . . . High Treasons, and Petty Treasons, Pains, Penalties and Paupers . . ."[95]

Before Adams' election, he had switched from the Federalist party of his father, to the states' rights party of Jefferson. Like President Tyler after him, he took cover in the popular party of the day in order to disguise his minority, nationalist views. Privately, he said that southern republican congressmen fancied themselves "a guardian of the people against Executive encroachments . . . Jealousy of state rights and jealousy of the Executive were the two pillars." These types "never originated a measure of any public utility." He was discouraged by what he called the "perpetual struggle in both Houses of Congress to control the Executive—to make it dependent upon and subservient to them. He said, "They are continually attempting to encroach upon the powers and authorities of the President."[96]

Adams soon came out and openly avowed broad national policies. When he presented his first message to Congress, he shocked many with his ideas. He favored regional specialization in the American economy, where southern cotton and western food products would be marketed to northern and eastern manufacturing concerns. Such economic planning

94. Whitney, *Biographies*, 59; Rutland, *Monroe*, 57; Flagel, Guide, 23, 26, 104, 272.

95. Cunningham, *Monroe*, 119, 191; Cole, *Jackson*, 68, 105.

96. McDonald, *Jefferson*, 41; Cunningham, *Monroe*, 126.

worried Republicans because it smacked of direction of state and regional, and even small business interests by the national government. He wanted not only a system of national roads and canals, but also a national university and a national astronomical observatory. He said that internal improvements were "the most important means" of bettering the lives of the American people. He put his recommendations in almost cultic terms: "The spirit of improvement is abroad upon the earth." Congress did not think his massive program of internal improvements was constitutional, and his own Jeffersonian party, in particular, were infuriated. He spent more on internal improvements than any previous president. Yet Adams still reduced the national debt by half during his term. He was also pro-bank and heaped scorn on opponents of the U.S. Bank.[97]

While Adams wanted an assertive national government, he believed that legislative assertiveness must issue forth from the legislative branch. He underscored his view about the superiority of the legislative branch by not using the veto at all during his term of office.[98]

Adams was against corruption in international diplomatic relations. European diplomats were notorious for the use of bribery. He instructed U.S. envoys to turn down gifts. He also elaborated a doctrine of term limits for such envoys. They should serve a maximum of six years, in part to protect them and the country from the kind of corruption that often accompanied long-term service.[99]

In a July 4, 1821 speech delivered before he became president, Adams had indicated the U.S. should be "the well wisher to the freedom and independence of all . . . the champion and vindicator only of her own." As president, Adams held to his aversion for European political entanglement. When the Greeks revolted against Turkish rule, he declined to recognize the new Greek government. Rather than trying to impose an American political or economic system on other nations he spoke of projecting "the benignant sympathy of our example" only. The founding fathers had subscribed to the idea of creating a society in the homeland worthy of emulation, but not of active export. Foreigners like the Frenchman Alexis de Tocqueville might come to study or observe America, but the U.S. would not insist on his country becoming like ours.[100]

97. Miller Center, *John Quincy Adams—Domestic Affairs*; Whitney, *Biographies*, 64; Nelson, *Presidency*, 80; Cole, *Jackson*, 63, 66–67, 102.

98. Flagel, *Guide*, 145.

99. Herring, *Colony to Superpower*, 139.

100. Ibid., 4, 152, 155, 160.

In the spirit of non-entanglement even in the Americas, Adams did not recognize new Latin American revolutionary governments. He also rejected proposals by Columbia and Brazil for political and military alliance. His policy was "strict and impartial neutrality." New Latin American republican governments could easily turn in the direction of tyranny. Americans were shocked when Simon Bolivar advocated a life-time presidency for himself that brought his thinking very close to that of European monarchy. That was good reason for staying aloof from them. On the other hand, he wanted to expand U.S. trade in the hemisphere, and so won permission from Congress to send delegates to the Panama Conference in 1826. He made reciprocal economic treaties with Austria, Brazil, the Central American Federation, Denmark, Norway, and Sweden. As a result of the treaty with Brazil, there was a great surge in imported coffee.[101]

Adams was eager to be a part of policy-making by the superior authority in the national government, so when he left the presidency he served in the House of Representatives for nine terms. There he led the opposition to Polk's War with Mexico. He supported expansion westward, but not conquest of a neighboring country. Perhaps he had time to reflect upon his experience as ambassador to Russia, where he had witnessed Napoleon's invasion of Russia in 1814 and saw the devastating effect it had upon the people. He also he headed the protectionist House Committee on Manufactures. He sponsored the McLane-Adams tariff bill. Average rates were lowered to thirty-three percent from the Tariff of Abominations of 1828.[102]

101. Herring, *Colony to Superpower*, 161; Miller Center, *John Quincy Adams—Foreign Affairs;* Cole, *Jackson*, 122–23, 125, 136.

102. McDonald, *States' Rights*, 133, 257; Boyer, *Oxford Companion*, 8; Flagel, *Guide*, 27; Cole, *Jackson*, 106–07.

2

Jackson and the Party of Expansionism and Conquest

The bulk of the next chronological group of presidents follows in name only the Jeffersonian democratic tradition. While Jefferson and his associates were democratic in their love of supremacy of local government, they also respected the self-determination and independence of other territories and nations round about the American states, although not so much the Indian nations scattered here and there around the home soil. They took a decidedly neutralist stance toward international conflicts unless they threatened the U.S. Jackson and his followers, while talking a good game on states' rights and the sovereign independence of nations abroad, wanted to intimidate or conquer foreign lands, exile Indian nations, and generally serve as controllers rather than good neighbors to all.

Of the nine presidents in this group, fully six were states' rights democrats, which is good, but virtually all had the blood of Indian nations or Spanish colonies dripping from their hands, which is bad. Two of the remaining three—Harrison and Taylor, members of the anti-Jackson Whig party—were soldiers who had the blood of native Americans and Mexicans on their hands, so were not without Jacksonian impulses as well.

Three democrats of this group—Van Buren, Polk, and Buchanan—and one Whig—William Henry Harrison—earn true republican distinction not only for defending states' rights, but also for loudly championing term limits for the office of the president. In addition, like the six founding presidents, the nine presidents in the second group did not try to use tax money to hire personal staff to help them expand executive power. They had the appointment patronage power instead, which was the ability to switch out the previous president's cabinet and federal workers with their own. Jackson initiated the first real tyrannical use of the patronage power by purging the government of northerners and placing a huge number of his southern supporters in paying positions instead. He set a precedent for others after him who did not care much for professionalism or experience in government employment either. This animated northern distasted for the southern way of doing politics and amped up the sectional conflict that Lincoln later exploited for his own political interests.

Presidents in this group actively aspired to the presidency and actively used their past military experience as a substitute for republican political ethics and historical intelligence. They had agendas, but most of them in both parties kept them secret during their campaigns so as not to alienate portions of the electorate. Such secrecy also gave them the appearance of not wanting to usurp the policymaking function of Congress. These presidents also tended to subvert earlier treaties made with Native Americans, which served as a sad precursor to presidential treachery in international relations during the wars and adventures of the twentieth century.

Two of these presidents so alienated Congress due to their heavy partisanship (factionalism) that one of them motivated the start of a new party, and the other an impeachment process. Presidents in this group also rattled sabers saying they wanted to preserve the "union," which meant preserving politics and economics on terms dictated by their own section of the country. This was a political ethic hardly acceptable for a government by the entire people.

One last caution must be advanced here. The southern-oriented presidents championed states' rights not just to protect slavery and the plantation, or the right of each state to decide about slavery on its own, but truly to protect all the constitutional legislative powers of democratic local government. They knew what the rest of the world knew. The direction the European world and the South American nations were taking with regard to slavery was clear. The trend was to peacefully end the institution. Without Lincoln's civil war, many or all of the states might well have relented to local, national, and international pressure and voluntarily given up slavery, like Tennessee did. Some in both the south and north, like Jackson, Taylor, and Lincoln, and the northern armaments industry did not think a blood bath over slavery and over states' rights was bad, unless they were the ones in the tub. But most of the presidents in this group took a course of peaceful tolerance and compromise regarding slavery in order to avoid carnage.

Andrew Jackson

Andrew Jackson lived life on an elemental level. Born in a log cabin on the border between North and South Carolina, he lost his father a few days before his birth. Abandonment occasioned emotional insecurity issues. It also meant that he would have to take on too much of manliness before he was ready for it. He joined the army at age thirteen and fought in the Revolutionary War. He apprenticed in the study of law as a teenager after the War, grew to the height of six feet one inch, and moved to Nashville, Tennessee about the time the Constitution was being developed.

Jackson practiced law, speculated in land, became a farmer, got involved in politics, married, and felt like he had to defend the honor of his wife on several occasions. Quick to anger, he fought in brawls, including one with future senator Thomas Hart Benton in a Nashville hotel. He also fought in some eight different duels. As a "keenly sensitive and excessively irritable" man he took slights as a matter of the highest importance. He killed at least one man by all accounts, and perhaps as many as a dozen by other accounts. And those were just his civilian killings. His violent temperament led him to continue to pursue military work. He became a military leader in the War of 1812, where he became known for his victory over the Creeks in 1814. As a commander in the war with the Creeks, he arbitrarily executed six of his own militia men. He also became known for his toughness and his victory over the British at New Orleans in 1815, which was fought after the peace treaty was already signed. After the battle of New Orleans, he was fined $1,000 for contempt of court for refusing to recognize a writ of habeas corpus. In 1818, he exceeded his instructions, followed the Seminole Indians into Spanish Florida and fought war on foreign soil without a Congressional declaration.[1]

Jackson was drawn to politics, apparently seeing the possibilities for some respectable use of power to add to help dilute the perception of his disrespectful use of it. In part because of his name recognition after the

---

1. M. Nelson, *Presidency*, 83; Cole, *Jackson*, 5, 80.

war, and in spite of his violence, he was elected Tennessee's first representative in Congress, and soon after its first senator. In politics he worked at softening his image, but colleagues could see in his eyes and in his debate speeches the potential for havoc on a more sophisticated level. Jefferson said that Jackson's "passions are terrible." He added, "I have seen him . . . often choke with rage." In the Senate he was pro-tariff protection and pro-federal internal improvements. Jackson served as president from 1829 to 1837.[2]

Andrew Jackson was America's first certifiable tyrant. Henry Clay, candidate for president in 1824 and no slouch of a political manipulator himself, said that Jackson attempted to bring about "a total change of the pure republican character of the government . . . the concentration of all power in the hands of one man." One biographer notes that Jackson was "capable of the profoundest dissimulation (concealing one's opinions)." He intended to exercise power in a new way, using many un-republican (that is, un-democratic) means to achieve some republican (democratic) ends.[3]

Jackson convinced people that highly partisan political parties were no longer bad for America, that self-interest and sectional interest and class interest were all reasonable to use to marginalize other weaker interests. His view was that the most manly party should prevail as long as it could get enough voters on its side. He thus undermined the age-old democratic emphasis on consent of all the governed, respect for minority views and respect for the methods Americans used to hammer out union in the first place. At the time of the founding, peaceful methods like debate and compromise over time brought even reluctant colonies voluntarily into the initial union of thirteen states. Jackson didn't have time and he didn't use compromise. Jackson fell perfectly into the hands of political handlers in the Democratic party who helped him organize new voters in the South and West on the basis of his personality and war exploits rather than his stance on issues. Popularity was now the decisive factor in elections rather than principles.

Jackson's corrupt use of the political process was assisted by the fact that between 1815 and 1830 twelve states had increased the percentage of voters by lowering or eliminating property, taxpayer and religious qualifications, and moving the choice of presidential electors from the

2. Cole, *Jackson*, 18, 20; Flagel, *Guide*, 268.
3. Cole, *Jackson*, ix, 16.

legislature to the people. The people, and in particular, the mob of ignorant frontiersmen and poor farmers, chose electors in all but two of
the nation's twenty eight states in 1828. By 1824, when Jackson ran for
the presidency for the first time and lost to John Quincy Adams, almost
all white males could vote, where in Washington's day only about four
percent of white men could vote. In effect, the middle class was overtak-
ing the aristocratic class in political power, or at least in numbers and
potential political power.[4]

Jackson was essentially the nation's first "progressive," since he pitted
farmers and workers against corporate leaders. This kind of class warfare
could easily be exposed as a sort of "artful propaganda" to win voters to
his personal cause. In order to entice the poor to his camp, he advocated
that public lands be sold to them at a cheaper price. Jackson raised the
banner of "nationalistic democracy," that is, centralism in democratic
decision-making. This was a process of empowering the majority who
elected him to rule things nationally through him without checks and
balances.[5] It was precisely the kind of "mob" rule possibility that the
founding fathers understood took place when minority rights were marginalized and executive power went uncontrolled.

Jackson was the first president to actively promote what political
scientists of the period referred to as idolatry, essentially a cult of personality. In his first campaign in 1828, he made one of the first presidential
"campaign tours," traveling to New Orleans to celebrate the anniversary
of his military victory over the British in 1815. He made another campaign tour in 1833 before his second term. During his campaigning, he
hammered so hard on his military ties that he later had to re-iterate his
belief in civilian control of the military.[6]

Jackson introduced new vote-getting techniques. He made use of
extensive graphic images of himself on campaign buttons, jugs and other
memorabilia. He converted his various portrait paintings into engravings
to be sold to the masses, who could then adore his image in their own
homes.[7]

---

4. Ibid., 16–17, 20.

5. Flagel, *Guide*, 58; Boyer, *Oxford Companion*, 400; Morley, *Freedom and Federalism*, 73.

6. Whitney, *Biographies*, 76–77, 80.

7. Boyer, *Oxford Companion*, 400; Crenson and Ginsberg, *Presidential Power*, 77.

Jackson provoked reactive opposition from the first moment of his appearance in Washington. He was the first president to not make a courtesy call on an outgoing president. He had "none of the magnanimities" required for the job as chief politician of the nation. He was not interested in healing political wounds, or in uniting people around the country to support his policies. In fact, he set about appointing friends, relatives, and old soldier comrades to positions of power in the government. He appointed cronies as secretary of the navy and as attorney general and "neither was especially qualified for his position." In his cabinet selections he avoided potential future rivals for power and thus had a weak cabinet. He had no strong political figures in the cabinet except for his loyal promoter Van Buren. He appointed no one with experience in commerce. His reasoning was soon enough to be known—he did not believe the national government should be sticking its nose into economic matters.[8]

In his first annual message, delivered in December, 1829, he curried favor with voters in the northern opposition by indicating he would collect money owed to American merchants by foreign nations. He said he would support a constitutional amendment to distribute any budget surplus to the states so they could construct their own internal improvements. He also called for voluntary Indian removal from the east. Those who stayed, he said, should be subject to white law.[9]

Jackson was the first president to use numerous different levers of tyrannical power, which required him to sidestep or break a number of constitutional laws or traditions. For example, he appointed five members of Congress to his cabinet. This violated the spirit if not exactly the letter of the Constitution. Article I, Section 6 said "No Senator or Representative shall, during the Time for which he was elected, be appointed to any civil Office . . . which shall have been created . . . during such time . . ." It had long been taboo to appoint members of Congress to the president's cabinet since that was seen to erode the separation of the legislative and executive branches. For example, it put those of legislative mentality into administrative positions, where they would be tempted to continue legislating. Jackson appointed forty-one members of Congress to executive department positions in his first five years on the job, thus almost transferring the legislature to his own supervisory control. Not surprisingly,

8. Cole, *Jackson*, 26, 28–29, 31, 44.
9. Ibid., 55–56, 136.

he was the first president to publically promote a legislative agenda, and thus to usurp Congress' constitutional legislative prerogative.[10]

Jackson was the first president to go over the heads of Congress and rouse public opinion. He was like an early version of twentieth century presidents because he relied on unauthorized informal advisers, used the press as a propaganda vehicle, dramatized politics, used the veto, and appealed to "the people" above the heads of their legitimate representatives. He filled the national government up with southerners and essentially made the north a colony of the south by making southern concerns count more than northern ones.[11]

Jackson called his federal worker removal policy "rotation." Long before Franklin Roosevelt cleaned house and filled it with his toadies, Jackson made sweeping re-organizations in two of the governments largest departments, Post Office and Land Office and filled them with party appointments. He concluded partial re-organizations twice in the War department and three times in State. In doing so, he made the bureaucracy heavily dependent upon his will. He asserted, with some historical justification, that too much time spent in government caused people to become corrupt and act like a privileged class. He alleged, too, that some had used their offices to interfere with state elections. The federal workforce had grown from 3,000 in Jefferson's first year to 11,500 in 1831, just before Jackson took office. Jackson removed about 10 percent of the 11,500 in a massive purge that came to be known as "the spoils system." This was removal of top- and mid-level leadership in order to implement presidential policy rather than to faithfully and professionally enact congressional policy. Jackson removed more officers in one year than all prior presidents had in the previous forty years. He also greatly increased the percent of new appointments made directly by the president, rather than by department heads, personally appointing about forty-five percent of them. In addition, a great many of these appointments were "recess appointments," during the period of many months when Congress was out of session. This meant that many new appointees got settled into jobs for six to eight months before Congress could confirm them.[12]

10. Ibid., *Jackson*, 42–43.

11. Crenson and Ginsberg, *Presidential Power*, 74; M. Nelson, *Presidency*, 84; Miller Center, *Jackson—Domestic Affairs;* Cole, *Jackson*, 274.

12. Crenson and Ginsberg, *Presidential Power*, 80–81; Cole, *Jackson*, 40–44, 47, 75–76, 91, 93.

When the Senate did convene, they reacted strongly to Jackson's quick and excessive removals and appointments. They asked Jackson to give them reasons for the removals, but he refused. The Senate ultimately rejected forty-nine of his appointments, an average of twenty-five per term. This was four times the average of previous appointment rejections. Jackson did not educate his appointees particularly well in the high ethics the nation expected of them on the job. To his appointee to the U.S. attorney position in New York, he said, "Go do the duties of your office, and make as much money as you can; but remember you are to be always at my command." The commander of the army was now the commander of politicized justice in the nation. Jackson also built up a huge propaganda apparatus under his control by appointing pro-Jackson newspaper editors to government positions, some fifty-nine all told. A fellow Democratic party member, John Calhoun, noted that Jackson used appointments "as an instrument to perpetuate power."[13]

Jackson was the first president to not follow the traditional practice of obtaining consent of the Senate before removing a major cabinet appointee who had received Senate consent for the appointment in the first place. For this, in 1833 he was the first president to be censured by Congress. Ultimately, Jackson's political shenanigans proved to be so offensive to others that long-time enemies like Clay and Calhoun came together, along with others, and formed an anti-Jackson political party which they called the Whigs, after the anti-monarchy party in England. In fact, many citizens of the day referred to Jackson as King Andrew.[14]

Jackson increased federal employment in the land office from eighteen workers to one hundred, in the main post office from thirty-eight to ninety, and also in the patent office. Local offices of the postal service increased from 8,000 to 11,000 and doubled in number of employees during his term. Jackson also established the Office of Indian Affairs, a new federal bureaucracy. Jackson signed a law increasing the federal judiciary via new appeals circuits, which expanded the Supreme Court from seven to nine. These two new court positions were on top of two vacancies, all of which he filled with Democrats, adding five southerners altogether. In return, the court institutionalized slavery in the Dred Scott

13. Cole, *Jackson*, 40–44, 47, 75–76, 91, 93.

14. Crenson and Ginsberg, *Presidential Power*, 349; McDonald, *Presidency*, 318; Miller Center, *Jackson—Domestic Affairs*.

case. Overall, Jackson increased federal employment by 7,000.[15] He built a most un-republican (un-democratic) style national bureaucracy while railing against big government.

Jackson was the first president to treat Native American tribes as other than independent sovereign communities. He treated them rather as disenfranchised wards of the government, somewhat like blacks in the north and south after the Civil War, and Japanese-Americans during World War II. As such, he was able to justify breaking treaties that the government had previously signed with them. He believed that Indian sovereignty within enclaves of the existing states was "absurd." Jackson viewed Indians as inferior. As Governor of Florida he called himself the Indians' "father" and demanded his "children" remove from the coastal areas. Cherokees in Georgia, however, had a rather advanced civilization with their own language, a written constitution, and their own newspaper. Nevertheless, Jackson wanted them to assimilate or remove, especially after the discovery of gold on Cherokee land. Evangelical Christians, on the other hand, wished to have Indian populations stay and be assimilated.[16]

Jackson's Indian Removal Act of 1830, which many believed was unconstitutional because it violated states' rights, required federal financing for Indian exile, and broke existing treaties, like the U.S. treaty with the Cherokee nation that had previously committed the U.S. to honor their tribal government and tribal lands. The removal act forced southwest tribes into exile, ultimately forcing 46,000 to leave their ancestral lands and march to locations west of the Mississippi.[17] As in the case of large national projects before and since, Jackson vastly underestimated the cost of the Indian exile project.

To save money, Jackson promoted cheap contracts to provide food, and even pushed a policy for Indians to go into exile at their own expense. But still the expense of removing the Choctaws alone almost busted the budget for removal of all of the tribes. Jackson spent $70 million total for local Indian land allotments for those who wished to stay and assimilate, for land in the west, and for removal costs, betraying his promise for limited, economical government. In fact, federal discretionary spending in

15. Cole, *Jackson*, 238–42, 246, 252–53, 273, 275.

16. Miller Center, *Jackson—Domestic Affairs* ; Herring, *Colony to Superpower*, 173, Cole, *Jackson*, 68–69.

17. Miller Center, Jackson—Domestic Affairs; Cole, *Jackson*, 54; Herring, *Colony to Superpower*, 173.

1828, Adams' last year, had been $13.3 million, but rose to $30.7 million in Jackson's last year, an increase of 130 percent. Expenses for locating parts of the regular army in Florida continued for many years after that. Despite this increase in national expenditures, Jackson still liquidated the national debt by January 1835.[18]

While Jackson did not promote much in the way of positive legislation beyond the Indian Removal Act, he let his legislative mind be known in a negative way by using the veto more than all previous presidents combined. Thus, he essentially tried to thwart Congress from carrying out its constitutional duty to make laws. In fact, he was the first president to make use of the veto for mere policy differences rather than constitutional concerns. He shocked the nation by vetoing a re-charter of the national bank. He virtually ended all national public improvements during his term by use of such vetoes. For example, he vetoed Maysville Road legislation in 1830. He determined that the road was located entirely in Kentucky and decided that national money spent on it would not be for the "general welfare." He was also the first president to use the pocket veto. Jackson was the sole legislative decider in his administration. He never asked for cabinet approval for a veto. In fact, he never took a vote in his cabinet for anything.[19]

Part way through his first term, Andrew Jackson came out against the National Bank by opposing its re-chartering, which would be coming up in 1836. Part of his problem with it was its political nature. He believed that the bank's head, Nicholas Biddle, was a political "broker," or manipulator who favored Jackson's "national republican" opposition, rather than just a bank manager. He saw that Biddle had decreased loans to Democrats and Jackson supporters. Furthermore, the bank was too large, in Jackson's estimate. The bank's capital was two times the annual expenditure of the U.S. government and thus it challenged the economic power of the government itself. Biddle, in addition, had boasted he had the power to destroy state (i.e., private) banks, by manipulating credit.[20]

Daniel Webster defended the bank by saying that it promoted "great public interests, for great public objects." But it was these monumental projects that many in the country disagreed with. Ultimately, Jackson

---

18. Cole, *Jackson*, 110–12, 115–17, 197, 229, 232–33.

19. He used the veto twelve times, Nelson, *Presidency*, 83; Crenson and Ginsburg, *Presidential Power*, 78, 352; Boyer, *Oxford Companion*, 400; McDonald, *Presidency*, 350; Flagel, *Guide*, 58; Cole, *Jackson*, 93.

20. Cole, *Jackson*, 57–59, 203.

vetoed the bank re-charter legislation. Henry Clay accused Jackson of using the legislative veto like the King of France, who by law had the power to initiate and disapprove legislation.[21]

During his second term, Jackson wanted to remove deposits in the national bank well before it was scheduled to go out of business. Two members of the cabinet threatened to resign. Clay introduced a resolution to censure Jackson for the removals, saying Jackson was "approaching tyranny." The resolution passed. It stated that Jackson had taken on "authority and power not conferred by the constitution and laws." In fact, Jackson explained privately that God told him the bank deposit removals were "right." He called pro-bankers "worshippers of the golden calf." Jackson demonstrated an ability to manipulate God for the needs of the Democratic party on other occasions as well. During his terms of office, there was a Sunday closing, or sabbatarian, movement afoot across the land. Jackson took care personally not to travel on the Sabbath, but he didn't feel that God should want to close the post office on Sunday.[22]

Another great policy issue Jackson dealt with was that of public lands. Western lands of the original states had been ceded to the federal government, which then had to decide what to do with those lands during the time before states were organized in those outlying areas. Clay wanted to use federal land sales to finance three programs: federal internal improvements, a federally-supported program of education, and a colonization program to send free blacks out of the country. Jackson initially proposed to eliminate federal income from land sales by selling public land to the states, and distributing the proceeds to all the states. Many opposed "distribution" because some states would benefit more than others due to population imbalances. Also, citizens were put in the position of having to buy back their own land from the government. Jackson eventually sided with "preemption," a policy of allowing squatters preference in purchasing land, and signed a bill establish that policy in May, 1830. This helped him buy a lot of votes for his reelection campaign.[23]

Jackson also believed that corruption—particularly logrolling (trading of votes) and pork-barrel legislation (local interest projects)—pervaded the process of nationalized internal improvement spending.

21. Ibid., 102–6.
22. Ibid., 69, 131, 188–95, 199, 202, 206–8, 234–35, 272.
23. Ibid., 61, 107–8.

Internal improvements were clearly constitutional only in the territories and in the District of Columbia, and in rivers and harbors used for broader than state-only commerce. Jackson ended up supporting some national projects, because they were sought by his western supporters. But he drew the line at projects that constituted merely a local scope. For example, he supported extensions of the National Road, and the Survey Bill, but vetoed the Maysville (Kentucky) Road. He also vetoed or pocket vetoed other projects like the Washington Turnpike and the Louisville Canal, and a lighthouse bill. In fact, Jackson used the pocket veto more often than Madison, the leader among the first six presidents. In fact, while speaking out against national infrastructure projects, Jackson ended up spending two times what all other presidents before him had spent combined, after even adjusting for inflation. He doubled the level of spending of his nationalist-oriented predecessor John Quincy Adams, the previous leader in internal improvements. Much of the increased spending was due to the National Road, running west through Ohio, and a second national road, running southwest from Buffalo to New Orleans.[24]

Jackson bought and sold slaves and used them to work his own plantation in Tennessee and had slaves working for him in the White House. Jackson used censorship to support slavery while in the White House. When abolitionists mailed out anti-slavery tracts into the South, Jackson's postmasters intercepted the mails and refused to deliver them, with Jackson's approval. Jackson asked Congress for a law to prohibit abolitionist tracts altogether, saying they threatened the union by appealing to the passions of the slaves. This proposal for the use of federal power to interfere with freedom of speech was extraordinary and influenced other presidents after him. Jackson was the first president to send troops to suppress a riot where he was not enforcing a federal law. In Maryland, his troops sided with management in the face of labor troubles there. On the other hand, Jackson sided with labor when he limited public workers to twelve hour work days at a naval yard.[25]

Jackson saw tariff protectionism primarily as a means of obtaining income with which to reduce the national debt. Once the debt was eliminated, he would reduce the tariff, except as it was "essential to national defense." Such was the case of the domestic iron industry. Clay, on the other hand, wanted to cut duties on products not competing with

24. Ibid., 63–67, 109.
25. Miller Center, *Jackson—Domestic Affairs* ; Cole, *Jackson*, 222–27.

American goods, and protect others. Shortly after the start of Jackson's second term, South Carolina asserted its right to nullify, or ignore, a federal tariff policy that financially discriminated heavily against the south. They also indicated their readiness to secede from the union if Jackson made an effort to collect federal tariffs after a certain date. Jackson asserted great hostility toward the idea of secession in a Proclamation on Nullification, saying "Disunion by armed force is treason." In fact, Jackson began to prepare for civil war and issued a nationwide call for volunteers. At first he promised to raise an army of 50,000, then threatened to raise an army ten times the size of the existing standing army, increasing it from 20,000 to 200,00, in order to stop any secession. His letters were peppered with words like "treason," "rebellion," and "war." He also asked Congress for a new sedition law that would allow him to arrest leaders. However, even the nationalist Daniel Webster and many Democrats of his own party cried out against the use of force. Jackson finally accepted a tariff compromise when South Carolina overturned its nullification law.[26]

Jackson was determined to diminish the institutional power of the federal government with respect to the states. Accordingly, he spent so little federal money that he was able to extinguish the national debt during his term of office. He retired the federal debt in his last year of office. He wanted the federal government to then be able to give any surpluses back to the states, and approved an act in 1836 to do so. He wrote, "Our Government [was not] to be maintained or our Union preserved by invasions of the rights and powers of the several States." He continued, "[In] attempting to make our General Government strong we make it weak. Its true strength consists in leaving individuals and States as much as possible to themselves—in making itself felt, not in its power, but in its beneficence; not in its control, but in its protection; not in binding the States more closely to the center, but leaving each to move unobstructed in its proper orbit."[27] Jackson also gave an opinion on the subject of term limits. Regarding long tenure in government service, he said "I can not but believe that more is lost by the long continuance of men in office than is generally to be gained by their experience."

In his second inaugural address in 1833, Jackson declared a love for two great "objects": "the rights of the several States and the integrity

---

26. Whitney, *Biographies*, 80; Flagel, *Guide*, 58; Cole, *Jackson*, 106. 161–77.

27. Whitney, *Biographies*, 80–81; McDonald, *Presidency*, 258; McDonald, *States' Rights*, 97, 110-11.

of the Union." Unfortunately, his administration called into question the extent of his commitment to both, for he betrayed states' rights in the nullification controversy, and showed that his fixation on maintaining the "integrity of the Union" was really more like maintaining the "unity of his command" over all things. His domestic affairs program was a classical case of tyranny, since he defended the rule of democratic law in some ways, but subverted it in even more ways.[28]

Jackson left foreign conquest to one of his chosen successors, James Polk, perhaps smarting from his unauthorized invasion of Florida in 1818 during the Monroe administration. When Jackson traveled to Washington to defend his actions after that incident, Clay made references to Caesar crossing the Rubicon.[29]

Jackson, however, had real "enthusiasm for extending the frontier" of the American nation by more peaceable means. He was willing to purchase Texas from Mexico and sent money to bribe magistrates there to get around Mexican constitutional issues. He told Van Buren that $3 million should "amend the Mexican constitution." When the news of the Jackson legate's financial activities surfaced, Jackson tried to deny having given him instructions to use bribery. However, Jackson had told the emissary that he could use those millions either for "purchase of men or to pay their national debt," and that it didn't matter to him. Jackson's efforts in Mexico were so "crude" and "corrupt" that it helped sewed the seeds for war with Mexico. Jackson claimed to be neutral during Texas' subsequent revolt for independence from Mexico, but the world saw Jackson's hand in it, as he and Sam Houston had always been close. He did "little to prevent the start of the Texas revolution" or to prevent American volunteers from joining the Texas military. He also quickly recognized Texas as a new nation. Jackson viewed Texas as a buffer to secure New Orleans and American trade. Texas was also necessary, since the "God of the universe had intended [all of] the great Valley [of the Mississippi] to belong to one nation."[30]

As president, Jackson gave high priority to expanding U.S. trade. He signed commercial treaties with Russia, Turkey, Thailand, and Vietnam, and several other nations. He worked to open up the British West Indies to American exports and to open American ports to British ships from

28. Whitney, *Biographies*, 80.
29. Herring, *Colony to Superpower*, 129, 133, 177; Whitney, *Biographies*, 75–76.
30. Cole, *Jackson*, 133–35, 267.

the West Indies. In the process, he suppressed his anti-British feelings. In spite of his trade efforts, the nation still ran a trade deficit. Consequently, U.S. banks could not repay their notes to British banks, and the Panic of 1837 ensued after Jackson left office.[31]

Congress rejected a secret treaty Jackson had made with Turkey to help rebuild its navy, thus rejecting Jackson's attempt at military entanglement in the Middle East. The nation would have to wait 110 years (from 1830 to 1940) before Franklin Roosevelt would fulfill Jackson's hopes for entanglement there. In his favor, Jackson did oppose an alliance with the South American confederation of nations proposed by Simon Bolivar.[32]

Martin Van Buren

Martin Van Buren has been called America's first presidential "politician by trade." In fact, he pursued politics as a professional career, not as a volunteer civic duty. In fact, he was the first president born after the nation declared independence. As a young man he apprenticed in law, but did not pursue formal, liberal college education. He admits that he suffered from a "disinclination to mental efforts." He read for amusement or not at all and did not think critically about the world around him. He liked intrigue instead, and organizing the citizenry to vote Democrat. He thrilled in teamwork to promote his political cause. He wrote to Jackson, "I go with you against the world." While in Congress, he pushed through a higher tariff to help Jackson win votes in the Mid Atlantic and western states. He was a close friend and companion to Jackson, serving in his cabinet. He also "ministered shamelessly to Jackson's egomania," a necessary condition of such closeness. He served in presidential office from 1837 to 1841.[33]

Van Buren is venerated for the contributions he made in developing the newly revamped Democratic political party that put first Jackson, then he and others in power. The party reached out to newly enfranchised groups of voters, and mobilized white males so well on election day that even individuals who were not citizens, or residents, or property owners ended up voting. This roused concerns of unfairness. The new political

31. Herring, *Colony to Superpower*, 166; Miller Center, *Jackson—Foreign Affairs*; Cole, *Jackson*, 123–25, 234–35.

32. Herring, *Colony to Superpower*, 162, 168.

33. Wilson, *Van Buren*, xi–xii, 18, 22–24, 31, 39, 41, 117.

party enforced a degree of party loyalty that was deemed by critics to be "degrading subservience." Van Buren himself was involved in much of the party intrigue and the jockeying for bureaucratic power on the state and national levels. He was seen by some as manipulative and power-hungry. His nick name was "the Sly Fox." John Quincy Adams spoke of Van Buren's "profound dissimulation and duplicity." It was said of him that "He rowed toward every objective with muffled oars." Contemporaries called him "a giant of artifice," and a master of "non commitalism." He left most of Jackson's political appointments in office, since he had helped to put them there in the first place. All four of Van Buren's sons worked as his office assistants in the White House.[34]

As president, Van Buren was a legislative minimalist. He offended one of the modern promoters of presidential activism because he "prepared no great bills." He pledged to leave citizens alone to govern themselves so they can "reap . . . the rewards of virtue, industry and prudence." He stated, "All communities are apt to look to government for too much." He wanted to keep the federal government out of economic development. In Van Buren's term of office, there was destined to be no national spending program on roads, canals, and bridges, and no national bank. In his inaugural, he mentioned that federal infrastructure projects were "wisely arrested by . . . my predecessor." He believed the national government should be limited to delivering the mail, and collecting enough tariff to service the small public debt and meet the federal payroll. In fact, he ended his term with a $1.5 million surplus in the federal budget.[35]

Many Americans blamed Van Buren for the Panic of 1837. Not having a clue about what was coming just around the corner, in his inaugural, Van Buren had used biblical language to predict the future happiness of a "thousand generations" of Americans. Van Buren did not support national government solutions to regional or national economic difficulties, even as severe as those in 1837. He opined that it is "not (government's) legitimate object to make men rich . . . or (give) direct grants of money." As a result, he failed to win a second term of office. Therefore, like John Adams before him, he sacrificed political expedience in order to support political principle. However, he did call a special session of the Congress

34. Crenson and Ginsberg, *Presidential Power*, 84; Miller Center, *Van Buren— Domestic Affairs*; Morley, *Freedom and Federalism*, 165; Wilson, *Van Buren*, 25, 38–39; Boyer, *Oxford Companion*, 801; Whitney, *Biographies*, 85, 273.

35. Crenson and Ginsberg, *Presidential Power*, 84; McDonald, *States' Rights*, 121–22; Whitney, *Biographies*, 89.

to deal with the panic. He wanted them to pass one piece of conservative banking legislation calling for an "independent treasury." Although he worked long and hard for the legislation, it did not pass until near the end of his term in 1840. In the meanwhile, he started implementing some of its features. Supporters believed that the move was his greatest achievement. One said that the Declaration of Independence delivered America "from the power of the British throne," while the independent treasury delivered them "from the power of British banks."[36]

The basic idea of the independent treasury was to keep the nation's money in the Treasury's own vaults rather than in private bank vaults. The nation would then disburse it directly to creditors of the federal government. This would make the federal government essentially a bank of deposit, rather than place its finances into banks of issue, also called credit banks, where the funds could be loaned out to others. Van Buren's new system was halted in 1841 shortly after it officially began. But it was revived again in 1846 and remained in use until 1913, when Woodrow Wilson re-introduced the country to national credit banking in the form of the Federal Reserve system.[37]

Van Buren continued Jackson's easy, populist-oriented land policies. In 1838 he called for another preemption act to give title to those who had squatted on public lands after Jackson's 1834 legislation, and called for it again in 1840 as a reelection measure. He also reduced the price of unsold western land below $1.25 per acre to further assist homesteading.[38]

Van Buren continued Jackson's policy of exile of native Americans. He engaged in the better part of a six-year war with the Seminoles, which took place from 1836 through 1842, resulting in the death of thousands. The Van Buren administration supervised the removal of the Cherokees in 1838, the infamous "Trail of Tears" migration during which twenty-five percent of the Cherokee nation perished. Van Buren borrowed $11.5 million for ongoing Indian removal costs. In part because of his Indian exile policy, Van Buren enlarged the standing army from 8,000 to 12,000 in July, 1838.[39]

In the summer of 1839, Van Buren traveled around the country to show himself to the people and help himself get reelected. He participated

36. M. Nelson, *Presidency*, 86, 88; Wilson, *Van Buren*, 54, 58, 123.
37. Wilson, *Van Buren*, 64–65, 72, 83, 210.
38. Ibid., 102, 141, 175, 179.
39. Nelson, *Presidency*, 86; Wilson, *Van Buren*, 182, 187–89.

in party "pageants," which included parades that had a religious revival flavor. However, he did not take an active part in the presidential campaign in 1840, though he was the party's candidate. It is widely believed he lost the election in part because he advised against the annexation of Texas and sought peaceful relations with Mexico. He believed that the Constitution raised questions about the annexation of an "independent foreign state." Louisiana and Florida, previous to incorporation into the U.S., had been "colonial possessions" and thus came in as territories, not states. Also, Van Buren was sensitive to harmony between the north and south and knew that acquisition of Texas would cause concerns about the balance of power between slave and non-slave states.[40]

William Henry Harrison

William Harrison is an interesting figure because he further exemplifies the politics of a new republic in the process of rapidly losing its moorings and turning instead to anti-republican thinking and methods. Harrison's father signed the Declaration of Independence, which stressed the somber responsibility of all citizens to understand and correct abuses in the government. But Harrison and his handlers were content to encourage the people to trust in military prowess as a sufficient basis for independence, much as they had by trusting in Jackson.

Harrison is generally regarded as the "first candidate to campaign openly for the presidency." He ran against Van Buren in 1836 and lost. He indicated his support then for federal aid for internal improvements, and denounced the Democrats for Jackson's use of the veto and the efforts to expunge the censure of Jackson. His Whig backers felt he could be used to overturn Van Buren's independent treasury and renew the "credit system" of national funds management, and so they backed him again in 1840.[41]

Harrison traveled around the country giving speeches on behalf of his own candidacy, thus revealing the fact that he did not have the kind of track record that could be communicated to the people in his behalf. This tactic turned out to be offensive enough to the electorate that it was abandoned for the next fifty years until the time of William Jennings Bryan.

40. Wilson, *Van Buren*, 131–32, 149–51, 206.
41. Cole, *Jackson*, 261–63; Wilson, *Van Buren*, 132, 144.

William Harrison has the distinction of having the shortest term of office of any American president. He died after only a month in office in 1841. He was "an irresolute man with a somewhat bogus reputation as a military hero." However, his election is an extremely important one in American history. Backers of Harrison seized upon Andrew Jackson's methods of electioneering and turned it against Jackson's party with a vengeance. The Whigs hid Harrison's cultural background, economic status, and political beliefs and instead played up his military activities in the War of 1812 and as Governor of the Indiana Territory, where he fought Indians. His colorful military history was somewhat like Jackson's, in that it lent itself to dramas that were interesting to the public.[42]

The campaign pushed political idolatry to an unprecedented level in the U.S., using logos, banners, giant painted buckskin balls patched over with Whig slogans that were rolled across the countryside, songs, rallies two and three days long, marches, all focusing on the glory of the person and the fun of elections without mentioning his politics. One author writes, "His campaign consisted of slogans and gimmicks rather than issues." His literature was replete with slogans like "Battle of the Thames," referring to a battle through which Harrison's troops smashed an Indian confederacy devoted to local tribal rule. Another slogan was "Harrison and Reform," an early version of "Obama and Change." These slogans left it up to the voters to hope that the particular reform or change would be exactly the kind they wanted. The campaign set the standard for future political campaigns designed to hide the real candidate and his real policies from the view of voters. They would not vote for him so readily if they knew what he intended to do and what he was really like. He and his party virtually presented no platform at all.[43]

As is suggested by all the diversionary use of entertainment and hero worship, a deeper element of deception was involved. The Whigs used one of the primary tools of ancient tyranny to advance his campaign, that of secrecy. One prominent Whig strategist wrote, "Say not one single word about . . . principles or creed . . . say nothing, promise nothing . . . let the use of pen and ink be wholly forbidden." It is hard to imagine a more forceful or sophisticated one sentence summary of the method of tyrannical manipulation and political idolatry. The idea is to use the face, the figure, the profile, the stories about the person as the vehicle to seize

42. McDonald, *Presidency*, 319.
43. Nelson, *Presidency*, 87; Boyer, *Oxford Companion*, 329 .

power, and to use disappearing ink regarding anything of substance that can be used to hold him to legal or constitutional accountability. It is the virtual formula for overthrow of the rule of law by the rule of the imperial personality.[44]

In fact, Harrison was a Whig who was picked to re-assert national power and corporate power versus the states and the working class. He believed in traditional big federal government programs like federal expenditures on internal improvements. But just like Jackson before him, he embodied a welter of contradictory tendencies within that fundamental position. His party were in fact opposed to one aspect of tyranny, specifically that usurpation of the legislative power carried out by Jackson. Thus Harrison pledged to stay out of the debate on national fiscal policy in Congress. He stated that the president "should never be looked to for schemes of finance," apparently referring to Jackson's propensity for involvement in banking, monetary, revenue, and appropriations policy, all admittedly the constitutional bailiwick of the legislative branch. The idea was to let Congress do the legislating, since he asserted that Congress is "the first Branch." He spoke of the "impropriety of Executive interference in the legislation of Congress." He promised to only use the veto if a bill was deemed to be unconstitutional, not because it ruffled his feathers personally. In fact, he agreed that executive decisions would be made by a majority in the cabinet. During his month in office, he then allowed executive decisions to be made by democratic vote in the cabinet.[45]

In his inaugural address he also touched upon another lever of tyranny that would come prominently into play in the time of Lincoln and again in the twentieth century. He declared that the president should not get too involved in military affairs, an intrusion he no doubt felt having served as a military commander himself under the direction of politicians. It was especially important to limit the presidential term of office due to the imperial lure of foreign affairs. He sensed that presidents are tempted to initiate wars and prolong conflicts in order to gain glory: "It is the part of wisdom for a republic to limit the service of that officer [the president] at least to whom she has entrusted the management of

44. Crenson and Ginsberg, *Presidential Power*, 89; An argument can be made that the Biblical admonition against "idolatry" contained in the second commandment actually refers to the glorifying of mortal personalities to the detriment of the humane written laws of ancient Israel and the God that promoted those laws.

45. McDonald, *States' Rights*, 123; Whitney, *Biographies*, 94; McDonald, *Presidency*, 319.

her foreign relations, the execution of her laws, and the command of her armies and navies to a period so short as to prevent his forgetting that he is the accountable agent, not the principal; the servant, not the master . . ." In the address he spoke of the excess of power that comes from one individual serving multiple terms of office like Jackson. He thundered, "Under no circumstances will I consent to serve a second term." Once again, on his death bed, he referred to such things as states' rights, presidential respect of the legislative authority of Congress, and term limits as "the true principles of the government."[46]

John Tyler

As Harrison's Vice President, Tyler was expected to kow-tow to the Whig party and its national leaders like Henry Clay once he took office after Harrison's death. He served from 1841 to 1845. In fact, originally he was a Democrat who had flip-flopped to become a Whig to get into Washington and to give Harrison's ticket some Southern flavor. After Harrison's death he flip-flopped back again to being a Democrat once he assumed power. His states' rights views were nearly as sturdy as Calhoun's. For example, like Van Buren before him, he supported states' rights to soften creditors' hold on debtors. This was a measure to endear the party's base of common folk. However, he began to act like Andrew Jackson immediately, doing things never done before and alienating party, Congress, and Harrison's own cabinet.[47]

Congress soon sent Tyler a bill bringing back the Bank of the United States. He asserted a states' rights' position and indicated the bill was unconstitutional because the national bank would operate in states not wanting it. Tyler vetoed not only this bill but a revised one sent to him later. Congress did not have enough support to override the vetoes. All but one of his entire Whig cabinet resigned in protest. Whigs denounced him as a traitor to the party and demanded that he resign. He refused to resign and filled the cabinet with new appointments in order to try to build a southern Democrat power base. While Jackson had purged some forty-five percent of government appointees available for him to remove,

---

46. Miller Center, *Harrison—Domestic Affairs* ; Miller Center, *Harrison—Foreign Affairs* ; Flagel, *Guide*, 96.

47. Crenson and Ginsberg, *Presidential Power*, 89, 92; Cole, *Jackson*, 48.

Tyler removed nearly fifty percent. However, some of the new appointees did not stay long.[48]

In 1842, when he began to get assassination threats resulting from the bank veto, and a mob rioted outside the White House, Tyler asked Congress for a police force for the Capitol and for Washington, DC. A senator from Kentucky believed such a police detail would be used as "a political guard for the Executive" which could then be used to "overthrow the liberties of the people." Eventually a different bill was passed assigning several police to the White House to guard the facility but not the president. These policemen were given the title of "doormen."[49] Congress gave the Mayor of the District of Columbia the power to appoint this police force, but the president was advised he would have to hire private bodyguards from his own funds.

In his second year, when Congress sent him bills instituting higher tariffs, Tyler vetoed them, thus indicating that he would also be going down the Jackson road of vetoing bills that were clearly constitutional, just not to his policy liking. In response, Congress proposed that a constitutional amendment be sought allowing Congress to override presidential vetoes by a majority vote, rather than a two-thirds majority, but that did not pass.[50]

Whigs in the Congress began a slow impeachment process based on the idea Tyler used the veto for an unconstitutional reason. Tyler thus occasioned the first presidential impeachment effort in U.S. history. The Congress were not about to see another Jackson running loose on the national landscape. The 27th Congress accused him of "withholding his assent to laws indispensable to the just operations of the government." Also, in the meantime, Congress voted to censure him for withdrawing federal deposits from the Bank of the United States.[51]

Tyler by now had exposed himself as an actual Democrat, passionately opposed to protective tariffs, internal improvements at federal expense, and a national bank. In fact, Tyler did not even like the idea of the national government giving the proceeds of the sale of public lands to the states for internal improvements. This was too much central intrusion.

48. Whitney, *Biographies*, 99; Cole, *Jackson*, 44, 85; McDonald, *Presidency*, 319; McDonald, *States' Rights*, 137.

49. Healy, *Cult of the Presidency*, 249; Flagel, *Guide*, 171.

50. Miller Center, *Tyler—Domestic Affairs*.

51. Flagel, *Guide*, 132; Miller Center, *Tyler—Domestic Affairs*; Whitney, *Biographies*, 98.

He finally signed a law to increase the tariff, but only when the treasury was almost empty. Tyler, a slaveholder himself, felt that if a state wanted to contest a federal law, they should first try all means necessary to have a federal law overturned. If that could not be successfully done, rather than simply not enforce the law in their jurisdiction (nullification), the state should simply secede from the union.[52]

Tyler was firmly set upon winning a second term for himself by supporting the annexation of Texas. Having alienated the Whig party, he was hoping to form a new political party based on annexation, even though not all in the Democratic party favored it. To win election, he was willing to overlook the absence of constitutional support for annexation of previously independent nations. His "new" political party he named the Democratic Republican party after Jefferson's earlier party. He picked up the branding process that was so effective for Harrison by making his slogan, "Tyler and Texas." Unfortunately, Martin Van Buren, now back in the Senate, undermined the annexation treaty there. Tyler, in another display of brilliant usurpation of the Constitution, re-packaged the treaty as a simple domestic bill rather than as foreign affairs legislation. Since such a bill needed only a majority vote, he got it passed and signed it in March 1845 three days before leaving office. This maneuver set a bad precedent which would be used by twentieth century presidents to get treaties passed when they didn't have the two-thirds majority needed.[53]

This president announced what might be called the Tyler Doctrine, which added Hawaii to the Monroe Doctrine, thus extending America's sphere of influence out into the Pacific, far away from the Western Hemisphere. He warned the British to stay away from Hawaii by stating the U.S. would make "a decided remonstrance" toward any nation threatening Hawaii's independence. It was said that he was "Pacific-minded," and could see the importance of Hawaii to interests the U.S. were seeing in Asia. Tyler implemented what has been called "hitchhiking imperialism" in China by taking advantage of British imperial gains made at cannon-point there. He sent envoys to China to wrest economic and consular relations with the country. He succeeded in gaining "most favored nation"

---

52. Miller Center, *Tyler—Domestic Affairs* ; Whitney, *Biographies*, 100; McDonald, *States' Rights*, 124.

53. Miller Center, *Tyler—Domestic Affairs*

status, which meant that China would have to automatically cede to the U.S. any favorable trading concessions given to any other nation.[54]

Tyler had an interesting political career after the presidency. He supported Virginia's secession from the union and was elected to the House of Representatives in the Confederate States of America. He also served as leader of the Confederate peace commission, chartered to try to meet with Lincoln to prevent the civil war.[55] Lincoln, as we will see, had no interest in a peaceful solution.

James Polk

James Polk studied law and practiced law in Tennessee. He served in Congress for fourteen years, where he was Jackson's man on the ways and means committee, which dealt with issues like the bank, tariff, and internal improvements. He was speaker of the House for four years, then governor of Tennessee. He set his sight on the vice presidency in 1840, the year that Harrison won, and again in 1844. But in 1844 Van Buren made the political mistake of opposing Texas annexation, which Polk did not, and as a result Polk won the party nomination for president with Jackson's support. Polk served in the office from 1845 to 1849.[56]

James Polk was a little more open about his domestic agenda than Harrison and Tyler. For example, he made a campaign promise to revive the independent treasury system initiated earlier by fellow Democrat Van Buren. He also campaigned against high protective tariffs. Once elected, he worked to fulfill both promises, and he succeeded, with some compromise, in doing so in 1846. For example, in July, 1846, he signed a law decreasing tariffs on coal and steel. He opposed protectionism, and argued for tree trade. He wanted minimal tariffs only for the purpose of raising necessary revenue for the government. Protectionist tariffs benefitted manufacturing mainly, rather than the consumer or farmer broadly. Low tariffs would allow farmers to export excess products. Polk also reduced national funding for internal improvements.[57] During the campaign, his

54. Herring, *Colony to Superpower*, 208, 211.

55. Flagel, *Guide*, 21; Nelson, *Presidency*, 88; Boyer, *Oxford Companion*, 790.

56. Bergeron, *Polk*, 3, 10–12, 15–16, 243.

57. Miller, *Polk – Domestic Affairs*; Boyer, *Oxford Companion*, 607; Whitney, *Biographies*, 106; Nelson, *Presidency*, 92; Herring, *Colony to Superpower*, 148; Bergeron, *Polk*, 18–20, 185–86.

Democratic party also projected an expansionist platform with the slogan "54' 40" or Fight," meaning that the U.S. should go to war with Britain to obtain a far north boundary for the U.S., well into present day Canada.

As a party man, Polk had labored to cultivate the new sectors of the party's base: the uneducated immigrants from Ireland and Germany, factory workers and unionists, western migrants, and tenant farmers. As president, he was now in a position to exploit the naïve views of these masses that had put him into office. A calculating and methodical individual, he knew his politics well.[58]

Part of the reason Polk retained effective administrators from Tyler's administration was that he had pledged to serve only one term of office. That philosophy kept the party open to fresh, new faces, and Polk liked the idea. Thus, he needed his staff to travel a shorter learning curve in order to get what he wanted done. The opposition Whig party had pledged itself to one term as well. Later in his term when recruited by the party to run again, he reminded them of his one term promise and kept it, the first president to turn down the call of his party.[59]

Polk imitated the model of executive assertiveness established by his mentor, Andrew Jackson. It has been said that "Polk set out to dominate the nation's capitol." That assertiveness did not extend to baldly usurping the legislative power from Congress, but it did include actively pushing a legislative agenda that he believed represented the wishes of the people who elected him. He believed that he could use the veto for policy reasons, justifying it by saying Congress could overrule his veto. But he undercut that argument by going so far to promote his program as to deny patronage appointments to friends of Congressmen who did not support his legislation. Thus, he tried to control Congress as well as the executive branch.[60]

Polk controlled the executive branch by not allowing cabinet heads to dispense their own patronage, including even army and navy appointments. Those appointments were especially numerous, as the Mexican war soon brought about ten new regiments, with a need for five new generals. He asked the cabinet to submit lists to him of current employees and their political loyalties. He retained some Whigs, but ordered that

58. Crenson and Ginsberg, *Presidential Power*, 86; Miller, *Polk—The American Franchise*; Bergeron, *Polk*, 23.

59. Bergeron, *Polk*, 17, 247.

60. Ibid., xi, 183–84.

they could not be promoted. Polk removed 700 postmasters in his first year, and 13,500 by the end of his term. He only removed 1,600 outright, but his administration was so partisan that 10,000 actually resigned. Polk also kept tight control on appointments in the judicial branch and appointed eight federal district judges during his term. [61]

Polk did not want competition for the power he intended to wield among his cabinet members, so he asked each one to forswear any presidential ambition during his term, a sort of political celibacy. Unlike Jackson, he consulted cabinet members on most matters, and worked for democratic consensus. He had no executive office of the president, so he used the cabinet as advisers, including helping with the annual message. Cabinet members could comment on matters before other departments, but Polk took initiative in dealing with issues in most cases. His controlling nature masked an insecurity due to frail health. He was like Teddy Roosevelt, in that he was frail of body as a youth, although strong of mind. Hard work and aggressiveness made up for his physical insecurity growing up in a very manly environment. "Polk's personality demanded that initiative come from him in almost all instances." In addition, Polk controlled the national bureaucracy and its policies by studying the details of the six departments, and even the treasury, which had always functioned fairly independently of the president. He wrote, "I have . . . probably given more attention to details than any of my predecessors." He recommended expansion of the Attorney General office into a full-fledged Justice Department, but Congress declined to act on this early attempt at usurping the criminal justice power of the states. While Polk knew he was a hard worker, and could have taken quiet satisfaction in that, he was driven to get acclaim for his habits. He said, perhaps overstating the case, "I am the hardest working man in this country." Polk also organized and controlled a major war almost single-handedly.[62]

Polk announced that he intended "to be myself President of the United States." So he purged Blair, Jackson's man, who had served as the party communications chief as editor of the party newspaper, the Globe. He set up his own newspaper, the Union, and hired an editor who would be subservient to the president alone. He said, "I must be the head of my own administration, and will not be controlled by any newspaper."

61. Ibid., 139, 142, 144, 149–50, 155–56, 167–70.
62. Ibid., xii–xiii, 25, 35, 37, 40, 45–46, 243.

He directly controlled the paper as none before him, and even wrote a number of its editorials.[63]

Polk stated in his fourth annual message that he represented the "whole people," while Congress only represented portions of the people. The implication of this was that it gave him the power to enact his will on the country. This is the standard assertion of tyrants. If that were truly the case, the constitutional law would not bother to specify a legislature at all. In fact, the Congress is the truly representative body in the government. The Constitution requires the president to get the consent of Congress for what he does, but the Congress does not need to get the consent of the president for what they do.

Polk did several things to enhance the power of the executive at the expense of the Congress. For example, he invented the executive budget. Prior to him the departments submitted budgets directly to Congress. But Polk required the department budgets to be submitted to him first, and he then made up a consolidated budget which he forwarded to Congress. Polk asked the departments to operate "on the most economical scale," and screened out unconstitutional projects like internal improvements. The bureau heads were often "Federalist" holdovers, so he had to pare down their requests. They tried to smuggle in rivers and harbors projects in their budget requests. But Polk wanted to reduce the national debt, in the tradition of Jackson. This practice of presidential budget making fell into disuse after he left the office until some seventy years later in the 1920s.[64]

In the main, Polk remained faithful to the party program of states' rights. He was a slave owner and supported a state's right to allow slavery within its bounds. Such a philosophy dictated that the number of free states be balanced by the number of slave states, so that the agricultural economy of the south would not be politically bullied or marginalized by the manufacturing economy of the north. During Polk's term, four states came into the union, two slave states (Florida and Texas), and two free states (Iowa and Wisconsin).[65]

As we have suggested in the section on Jackson, the issue of states' rights had less to do with slavery and more to do with tariffs, and the overall philosophy of government and economics. The south had only

63. Ibid., 171–76.
64. Bergeron, *Polk*, 40, 43; McDonald, *Presidency*, 283.
65. Miller, *Polk—the American Franchise*.

a small manufacturing base, so it purchased its finished goods from the north or from Europe. Since they were so dependent upon trade, they were paying the lion's share of the tariff tax.[66] The north wanted to reap the economic benefit of the efficiencies of slavery in southern agriculture by buying low-cost southern raw materials for their manufacturing concerns, while protecting themselves against competition from inexpensive manufactured goods from abroad. Protective tariffs against foreign goods put them in a position to do this.

But the protective tariff against foreign manufactured goods also limited opportunities for the south to sell their produce abroad. Foreign countries would retaliate against high American tariffs by erecting their own barriers. In sum, the north set themselves up as effectively the only inexpensive source of manufactured goods the south could buy. When the south bought from Europe it had to pay the tariff tax, while the north supplied its own people with local manufactures.

Tariffs had been high since 1832. Polk, true to his methodical character, commissioned a scientific study of tariffs before structuring legislation. He sent out a questionnaire to importers and customs officials to get statistics. He wanted to learn the level at which duties became so high as to reduce imports and revenue. He then suggested rates be set to produce only the revenues than needed for an economical central government program. He then asked for repeal of the 1842 tariff and had his people in Congress work to set up ad-valorem, or proportional to value, rates according to seven categories of products beginning with luxury goods like distilled spirits, which got the highest rates, down through manufactured items and raw materials, which got lower rates. Polk called the resulting Walker Tariff "the most important domestic measure of my administration." It was not passed without the customary negotiations and battles over items such as tea and coffee and without manufacturing lobbyists' efforts to bribe votes.[67]

The north also wanted a stronger central government than the south could tolerate. They envisioned a certain amount of national stimulus of the economy, whereas the south wanted local political and economic priorities to prevail. Polk vetoed two internal improvement measures during his term, and had always voted against them while he was in Congress. He saw no clause in the Constitution permitting federal involvement in

---

66. DiLorenzo, *Real Lincoln*, 125–26.
67. Bergeron, *Polk*, 186–90.

transportation projects, commonly called harbors and rivers bills, unless related to the national defense. High tariffs brought in an unconstitutional level of income to the federal government and internal improvements spending used this tainted money on unconstitutional development projects.

The first internal improvement bill he vetoed designated a long list of watercourse bills, including an improvement of the James River below Richmond. In his veto message the president protested that "to call the mouth of a creek or a shallow inlet on our coast a harbor can not confer the authority to spend the public money in its improvement." He said that some twenty projects to be funded as harbors were "at places which have never been declared by law either ports of entry or delivery . . . from which there has never been a vessel cleared for a foreign country." The second bill called for hundreds of projects all across the country, and especially in Wisconsin. He asked his hearers to "Let the imagination run along our coast . . . and trace every river emptying into the Atlantic and Gulf of Mexico to its source . . . let it pass to Oregon and explore all its bays, inlets, and streams . . . and the mind will be startled at the immensity and danger of the power which the principle of this bill involves." He added, "The treasure of the world would hardly be equal to the improvement of every bay, inlet, creek, and river in our country." He said he was "convinced I am right upon the subject," and further suggested, "The usefulness and permanency of this Government and the happiness of the millions . . . will best be promoted by carefully abstaining from the exercise of all powers not clearly granted by the Constitution."[68]

Polk's domestic economic program also included his "independent," or "constitutional" treasury bill. He had denounced national banks in his inaugural address and his first message to Congress in December, 1845. He had said that the people and their government did not need national or even state banks, which just decentralized corruption and money-jobbing, but could manage their money on their own without professional money managers. He supported Van Buren's idea that money should be held for safekeeping in the Treasury itself. Whigs had repealed Van Buren's independent treasury system and returned to the state or "pet bank" program. By a strict party vote, the House and Senate approved Polk's legislation.[69]

68. Ibid., 193–200.
69. Ibid., 191–93.

Polk's wife Sarah required him to go church each Sunday, and he went not unwillingly. At the White House, Sarah banned dancing, but allowed the serving of wine. Polk's personal inclination toward Methodism and free will living, and his family history of Calvinist Presbyterianism likely affected his views of presidential power and territorial expansionism. The Manifest Destiny of his day was a political phenomenon bordering on the religious. The idea was that the nation should expand to its "natural" geographic borders, perhaps as far as the Pacific sea. This was a sort of "geographical predestination" with an element of crass territorial opportunism thrown in. But Americans coveted expansion for economic reasons as well, and the discovery of gold in California only added to that fever. The war-making needed to obtain the additional real estate temporarily had an opposite economic effect, as it diminished the recovery underway after the Panic of 1837.[70]

Polk's war with Mexico was mixed up with the problem of slavery and with the problem of Texas. Southerners desired Texas in the union to allow for the expansion of slavery. Northerners wanted free blacks from border states and further north to migrate to Texas and thus relieve their communities of what they believed was an inferior race and also relieve their workplaces of labor competition. Texas had come into the union as the fifteenth slave state during the Tyler administration, and Mexico still harbored a lingering claim to this "stolen province of Mexico." In fact, Congress' vote to annex Texas was the U.S.'s first serious provocation to war in the nation's brief history. Mexico called it "an act of aggression."[71]

Polk was looking for a way to take California from the Mexicans, since they would not sell it to him. He knew about the boundary dispute between Texas and Mexico, and allowed annexation knowing that the border problem still festered. Mexico claimed that the Texas border was the Nueces River, while Polk insisted that the Rio Grande was the border, some 200 miles further south. The U.S. had assured Texas that the Rio Grande would be a guaranteed boundary if she were annexed, even though that boundary lacked solid evidence. The new state then sent a letter requesting U.S. military assistance in the event Mexico should cross

70. Ibid., 4, 8–10, 48, 236.

71. Bergeron, *Polk*, 51, 53, 67; Miller, *Polk—Foreign Affairs*; Whitney, *Biographies*, 105.

the border, and Polk sent Zachary Taylor from Louisiana to camp fairly far north of the Rio Grande.[72]

In public, Polk spoke of defending Texas, and in private he spoke of wanting California. He disguised his imperial ambitions as a simple border dispute rather than a conspicuous and humongous land grab. Polk therefore hoped for action at the Rio Grande, which would trigger the rollout of his real agenda. The action at the river happened April 25, 1846. Polk sent Zachary Taylor to guard the "U.S." side of the Rio Grand and a skirmish broke out between a Taylor reconnaissance patrol and a contingent of Mexican troops. Polk claimed that Mexico attacked and killed Americans on American soil, and on the strength of this he got Congress to declare war. He argued, "War exists by the act of Mexico itself." Opponents among Whigs and Calhoun democrats called it "Mr. Polk's War" and voted against the war declaration. Polk's newspaper brayed, "We shall invade her territory; we shall seize her strongholds; we shall even TAKE HER CAPITAL."[73]

Polk asked for state volunteers to come mostly from the south and the Ohio valley rather than enlarge the standing army. He also appointed army officers from the civilian population. Congress authorized up to 50,000 volunteers. Polk went so far as to authorize the taking of the capitol, Mexico City, and General Scott captured it in October, 1847. The peace negotiation took place February, 1848, at Guadalupe Hidalgo.

Polk's claim that Mexico provoked the war was later determined to be false. Polk was censured by the House, which declared that the war had been "unnecessarily and unconstitutionally begun by the President of the United States." "Mr. Polk's War" of 1846–48 was American's first concerted war of imperial expansion. It was American's first military intervention in a foreign country, and the first time America occupied a foreign country.[74] Polk used the press to report on his war and the exploits of his army in order to keep up enthusiasm among those who actually supported the war.

The United States took half of Mexico's land. It was the greatest expansion of U.S. territory since the Louisiana Purchase. The war destroyed Mexico, plunging it deep into a debt level from which it has never really

72. Nelson, *Presidency*, 92; Flagel, *Guide*, 224; Bergeron, *Polk*, 62–63, 72.

73. Flagel, *Guide*, 225; Herring, *Colony to Superpower*, 199; Boyer, *Oxford Companion*, 608; Bergeron, *Polk*, 75–77, 87.

74. Healy, *Cult of the Presidency*, 5, 41; Herring, *Colony to Superpower*, 194, 201

recovered. American loss of life was about 13,000 to 15,000, and wounded about 4,000. Some in the Congress urged Polk's impeachment for the loss of these American lives. Mexico suffered the loss of 26,000 lives and overall 50,000 casualties.[75]

During the Mexican War, volunteer state militias accounted for over seventy percent of troops mustered. At the end of the war, the U.S. standing army was slashed from 30,000 to 12,000, since the Congress believed the militias could always handle national needs.[76]

In what might be called the "Polk Corollary" to the Monroe Doctrine, the president asserted, "Our Union is a confederacy of independent States, whose policy is peace with each other and all the world . . . to enlarge its limits is to extend the dominions of peace over additional territories and increasing millions."[77] This bit of sophistry married states' rights to national imperialism. It turned the corner away from the founders' neutralism policy while still holding onto the idea of state sovereignty.

James Polk took the nation to the edge of war once again with Great Britain at the same time the Mexican war was unfolding. He wanted the Oregon territory for markets for the original northwest states. There were 3,100 settlers in Oregon by the time Polk took office. There had been a boundary dispute there since the decision for joint occupation of the area in 1818. The two main solutions were the 49th parallel, bending it to allow Vancouver Island to fall to the British, and the 54/40 line wanted by the "All Oregon" movement, which extended much further north. The British, on the other hand, wanted the Columbia River as the boundary, which would have left most of present-day Washington state to them. Polk asked the Congress for notice to end the joint occupation, which he obtained in April, 1848, thus forcing negotiation over the boundary. He also invoked the Monroe Doctrine against European intervention in the hemisphere. Most took this as a step toward war and it led to a Senate resolution to investigate the state of military preparedness in the west. British warships set sail for Canada. The U.S. and British eventually settled on the 49th parallel in June, 1848.[78]

75. Crenson and Ginsberg, *Presidential Power*, 86; Herring, *Colony to Superpower*, 204–5; Flagel, *Guide*, 225.

76. Crenson and Ginsberg, *Presidential Power*, 232.

77. Flagel, *Guide*, 192.

78. Bergeron, *Polk*, 113–14, 117, 123–26, 128, 130, 133.

Polk also made eight major Indian treaties. The U.S. government acquired 18.5 million acres of land by means of treaties removing Indians westward of Arkansas, Missouri, and Iowa. The Winnebagos ceded land in Minnesota.[79]

Zachary Taylor

Before he gained the presidency, Taylor acquired plantations and many slaves in Louisiana. As a military officer, he honored Indian treaties and prevented white settlement of Indian lands. But he also served the illegitimate wishes of president Polk, who sent him deep into Mexico to intimidate that nation into releasing its northern states into permanent U.S. custody. In 1848 the Democrats bandied about a political cartoon titled "One qualification of a Whig Candidate." It showed a U.S. general atop a mound of human skulls.[80] This opposition notwithstanding, the nation was about to reward its first Caesar with political power. Taylor, like Caesar, conquered the American equivalent of neighboring Gaul— Mexico—and was now making noises, much like Caesar, that he would punish any sections of the country that did not like his personal policies or points of view, as we will see below.

As in the case of William Henry Harrison, Whig handlers suggested that Taylor write no letters during the campaign that might disclose his political views. In fact, Taylor rarely read books, and had difficulty spelling, since he had little formal education. Thus he could not be tempted to write very much anyway. His Democrat opponent tried to draw him into debate on whether slavery should be permitted in the new territories, but Taylor was non-committal. He was a party man, and did what the party said. He said nothing about the extension of slavery into the new states even in his inaugural address. In fact, he said nothing about any other issue in that address. He was the first president with no political experience. The outgoing former president Polk said of the totally inexperienced Taylor, "the country will be the loser by his election."[81]

---

79. Ibid., 220, 223.

80. Boyer, *Oxford Companion*, 764; Flagel, *Guide*, 82.

81. Crenson and Ginsberg, *Presidential Power*, 89; Flagel, *Guide*, 80; Nelson, *Presidency*, 93; Miller, *Taylor—Domestic Affairs* ; Whitney, *Biographies*, 110; Flagel, *Guide*, 80, 83.

Zachary Taylor served only sixteen months in presidential office before he died, serving from 1849 to 1850, but he did finally take a stand on slavery. He encouraged California and New Mexico to be admitted to statehood, knowing they would opt to be free states. Like Jackson, he believed the union should be preserved, even if over the objection of great sections of the country. So, although he supported states rights, he did not want secession to take place. He told southerners he would march on any state that might secede. He would hang secessionists if they left because they did not like his statehood proposal for California and New Mexico. He also threatened Texas with military intervention if it moved to seize New Mexico by force. Texas had motivation to do this to prevent that area from becoming another free state, such as Californians were wanting to do. He said "I will command the army in person" if any southern state tried to drive federal troops out of New Mexico.[82]

In retrospect, Taylor appears to have been dead set on provoking a civil war. He wanted new states to come in as free states, thus deliberately upsetting the balance of political power so the sections would tend toward conflict. But then he told them he would not tolerate compromise or conflict and would happily go to war to support the unequal state of things. This was an early version of the same provocation to war that Lincoln exploited so effectively in his day. Taylor's lack of literacy in European history and worldwide current events relative to the peaceful abolition of slavery meant that he seemed not to understand there were pathways other than war to achieve changes in public policy with respect to slavery.

Taylor's threats served to initiate a great Congressional debate leading to the Compromise of 1850. This compromise admitted California as a free state, and gave territorial status to New Mexico and Utah without prohibiting slavery there, so they could decide slavery on their own.[83]

In his December, 1849, state of the union address, Taylor announced that the Mexican War and the fire sale "purchase" of California and New Mexico at the end of the war had put the U.S. budget in debt $16 million. He therefore called on Congress to raise tariffs to increase revenues, and also to support economic development. The party had apparently whispered in his ear that it was time to announce the Whig program. He was now prepared to pass out national largesse to the northern section of

82. Boyer, *Oxford Companion*, 764; Whitney, *Biographies*, 111, 113.
83. Nelson, *Presidency*, 93.

the country. He reported, "I do not doubt the right or duty of Congress to encourage domestic industry, which is the great source of national as well as individual wealth and prosperity." This was a nice statement in favor of both economic central planning and the expansion of corporate wealth that would become the mainstay of future Republican political values.[84]

Taylor was a Congress-has-the-lead-in-legislation president, as were the great majority of presidents before him. Thus he declined to develop a relationship with Congressional leaders. It was his job to contain brush fires, not to start them. If Congress passed unconstitutional legislation, he would veto it. In his inaugural, he said he would look to Congress "to adopt such measures of conciliation as may harmonize conflicting interests . . ." One presidential historian who supports the tyrannical presidency laments that "[Taylor] never addressed the legislature with a clear policy statement, nor did he use his influence to direct legislation . . ." Coming in as he did, however, after a Democratic administration, Taylor took care to install Whig appointees in place of Democrats, removing two-thirds of presidential appointees in his first year in office, even more than Jackson and Tyler had done before him.[85]

Taylor backed off the Monroe Doctrine a bit. He lessened U.S. imperial influence in Latin America by signing the Clayton-Bulwer Treaty with Britain whereby both countries renounced control or ownership over any canal to be built across Central American in the future. This gave Britain a little more equality of influence in the Americas than they had had before.[86]Zachary Taylor thus was a picture in contrasts. He conquered Mexico upon orders of an earlier president, but saw little constitutional merit in Manifest Destiny imperialism when he himself became president. On the other hand, he wanted war within his own country to lay down the law of Whig political and economic orthodoxy. He died suddenly after only 16 months in office. Daniel Webster said that Taylor's death prevented civil war and allowed the Compromise of 1850, which his successor endorsed.

---

84. Whitney, *Biographies*, 111.

85. Whitney, *Biographies*, 110; Miller, *Taylor—Impact and Legacy*; McDonald, *Presidency*, 320; Cole, *Jackson*, 44.

86. Miller, *Taylor—Foreign Affairs*.

Millard Fillmore

Millard Fillmore worked as a teacher before studying law. In the state legislature, he worked to end imprisonment of debtors. Thus, he had a mindset that government liberality should overshadow private contractual arrangements between free and willing citizens. As a member of Congress before he attained the presidency, he supported Henry Clay's American System of strong central government, and helped write the Tariff of 1842. Once in office, he spent half of every working day processing applications for office. He removed Whigs of his own party from government patronage positions when they opposed his policies. He was known for personal vindictiveness, like Jackson before him, and Franklin Roosevelt after him.[87]

Though he and his predecessor Taylor were from the same Whig party, and though he succeeded to the presidency upon Taylor's death and served out the term from 1850 to 1853, Fillmore held a different view on how to handle the slavery issue. Where Taylor had actively flirted with secessionism and war by proposing to unbalance the number of slave and free states, Fillmore wanted to keep balance and keep the union together by compromise, rather than by military threat and bluster. Therefore, he reversed Taylor's overall policy.[88] As Taylor's vice president and president of the Senate, he had supported the Compromise of 1850. When Taylor died, Fillmore became president and strategized with Congress on how to get the legislation passed.

Congress broke up the compromise package that had stalled during Taylor's short term into smaller bills, and each one was passed separate from the others. He said, taking a bit of a stab at his former boss, "Compromise must necessarily be unwelcome to men of extreme opinions." Fillmore appointed Brigham Young as territorial governor in the Utah Territory in 1850 and allowed the territory to operate largely independent of the federal government. That independence included sidestepping decisions of federal judges.[89]

In order to stall southern secession threats, Fillmore strictly enforced the Fugitive Slave portion of the compromise. This law required runaway slaves to be returned to their owners. Fillmore supported treason charges

87. Whitney, *Biographies*, 115; McDonald, *Presidency*, 320; Boyer, *Oxford Companion*, 265–66.

88. Nelson, *Presidency*, 93.

89. Whitney, *Biographies*, 116; Miller—Fillmore, *The American Franchise*.

against forty people involved in killing a slave-master pursuing after a runaway slave. However, the Supreme Court held that rebellious actions like that which the forty people undertook to prevent return of a slave did not qualify as a crime of treason.[90]

Fillmore's reconciliation policy kept America from civil war for the next decade, and for this he is vilified by historians. His own party dumped him because of his enforcement of the Fugitive Slave law and his dumping of Taylor's Whig party appointees in favor of his own. They thus denied him the nomination in his own right in 1852 in order to take a chance on another war hero, General Winfield Scott.[91]Scott lost to the Democrat Franklin Pierce. During Pierce's time in office, Fillmore accepted the nomination of the American Party, and campaigned on the anti-immigration platform of the group, which was also known as the Know Nothings.

Fillmore was heir to the aggressive economic expansionism of a number of his predecessors, including Monroe, John Quincy Adams, Jackson, Tyler, and Polk. He followed the lead of the world's greatest imperial power, Britain, in bull-dozing an increasingly constitutionally illiterate nation into the Asia trade. Prior presidents had fought to keep the great imperial powers from interfering in American affairs and dictating economic policy. But the U.S. now felt comfortable dictating economic policy to nations on other continents and thus acting the part they once hated in others.

Fillmore used gunboat diplomacy to force commercial relations with Japan. He needed Japan as a fueling station for trade with China and Southeast Asia, so he sent representatives to request favorable trade concessions. In 1852, Fillmore sent Commodore Perry with four large ships, 61 guns, and 1,000 men. This was a relatively large scale military deployment without Congressional authorization. If Perry could not persuade the Japanese gently, his instructions were to "change his tone" and tell them "They will be severely chastised." Japan expressed disinterest, so Perry essentially threatened the same fate for Japan as America had just imposed upon Mexico in the War of 1846–48. Perry's ships maneuvered close to Tokyo, an obvious and severe provocation to war of the type that later presidents would find handy as a means to provoke a war when it was clear it was not in the interests of national security, or self-defense.

90. Miller—*Fillmore, Domestic Affairs.*
91. Whitney, *Biographies*, 118.

Japan did not bite. A year later, the U.S. navy came back with a larger force demanding an economic treaty. Fillmore sent ten ships and 2,000 officers and men, approximately ten percent of the U.S. armed forces. In 1856, Japan finally agreed to make concessions. American forces were dispatched to Japan six more times in the decade of the 1860s.[92]

It is not surprising that blowback against this aggressive stance erupted immediately in the form of extreme hostility toward U.S. diplomats sent to negotiate trade arrangements in 1856. In fact, over a period of time, seven U.S. diplomats were killed on Japanese soil.[93] That hostility was still alive and well in the twentieth century when Franklin Roosevelt inflamed it even more by interfering with traditional U.S.-Japanese trade relations before U.S. entry into World War II.

In Hawaii, a way station on the Pacific journey to Japan, the French tried to implement an annexation treaty. Fillmore warned Napoleon III that the U.S. was opposed. He engineered a secret document in 1851 transferring sovereignty of Hawaii to the U.S. in the event of war in Hawaii involving France or Britain. By means of this preventive protectionism, the U.S. would then be authorized to use force.[94]This is one of the earliest examples of the type of entangling alliance hated by the founders, but destined to be used a century later to bind the U.S. to regular war activity in Europe.

Franklin Pierce

While in the U.S. Senate, Pierce was an ardent states' righter, a position that undergirded many of his decisions as president. He was a northern Democrat who respected slave states' rights to decide the slavery question on their own. He was, however, elected because many northerners had not researched his pro-Southern views. In his inaugural address, he said, "I believe that involuntary servitude, as it exists in different States of this Confederacy, is recognized by the Constitution." Free blacks had often been denied citizenship privileges such as preemption rights to homestead, or "squat" on and obtain title to land in the west. They also

92. Historians who admire the dashing nature of Fillmore's activities used the word "open" commercial relations instead ; Herring, *Colony to Superpower*, 212–13; McDonald, *Presidency*, 393.

93. McDonald, *Presidency*, 393.

94. Miller, *Fillmore—Foreign Affairs*; Herring, *Colony to Superpower*, 208–9.

were not able to obtain minor government employment, and obtain passports to travel out of the country. Pierce adopted a national policy against free black passports.[95]

As a Democrat, Pierce disapproved of federal funds for infrastructure (internal improvements). As a result of his meager spending, he reduced the national debt from $60 million to $11 million during his four years in office from 1853 to 1857. He favored land grants to railroads and loosened up some federal money for construction of an Atlantic telegraph cable. Facing an often hostile Congress not happy with his sensitivity to southern and western local interests, Pierce had five of his nine vetoes overridden.[96]

In 1850, Millard Fillmore had appointed the Mormon leader Brigham Young as governor of the territory of Utah. When Congress denied the Mormon petition to write a constitution and become a state, the Mormons wrote a constitution and set up a government as a separate national entity anyway. Pierce simply ignored the new development at first. However, in 1855, he appointed federal judges who greatly antagonized the Mormons in the matter of land claims and national/territorial relations.[97]

Pierce was a modest and honest man. During a visit to Britain, Oxford University tried to heap on him one of the familiar glories of European political leadership, consistent with the growing importance of the U.S. in the fraternity of colonial empires. They offered him an honorary degree, which he declined. Pierce may have sensed the smug scent of monarchic entanglement in the invitation. Pierce said he did not deserve the degree, unlike Andrew Jackson who accepted an honorary degree from Harvard. In fact, Pierce had graduated from Bowdoin College and had also studied law. But he did not have as broad a liberal education as he had wanted. He said, "I have not the advantage of a classical education, and no man should, in my judgment, accept a degree he cannot read."[98] Pierce thus admitted that he did not have as much knowledge of the history of republican government as the founders clearly did.

95. Boyer, *Oxford Companion*, 598; Whitney, *Biographies*, 122; Smith, *Buchanan*, 28, 197.

96. Whitney, *Biographies*, 123–24; Flagel, *Guide*, 132; McDonald, *Presidency*, 355.

97. Smith, *Buchanan*, 66.

98. Nelson, *Presidency*, 95.

Pierce, like Fillmore, tried to prevent national civil war. But he could not keep civil war breaking out in one place—the state of Kansas. He made compromises to try to keep the peace, but war lords on both sides of the slavery issue fanned the flames of conflict. Pro-slavery and anti-slavery whites had flooded into the new territory of Kansas. Pierce appointed a territorial governor who was anti-slavery. Next, the pro-slavery folks acted the part of usurpers and installed their own government in order to try to oust the territorial governor. They asked for federal recognition of their pro-slavery government. Pierce then appointed a compromise governor who was more sympathetic to slavery. But the anti-slavery faction then tried to organize their own government. Pierce then supported the governor and legislature of the pro-slavery side, and condemned the others as rebels.

Historians who support a strong-arm presidency chide Pierce for not sending federal troops into Kansas to decide things by force of arms. They assume that local self-determination is an antiquated concept.[99] They also assume that the president has the power, if he would just seize it, to do such things without Congress' blessing. Pierce was a peacemaker and compromiser, and a believer in state control, while many historians want war and conquest, and national control of everyone's lives.

In his final state of the union message, Pierce noted that radical abolitionists "pretending to seek only to prevent the spread of the institution of slavery into (other) . . . States, are really inflamed with desire to change the domestic institutions of existing States . . ." He made the prediction that their activities would promote "burning cities, and ravaged fields, and slaughtered populations." He also predicted a military state of "a vast permanent camp of armed men like the rival monarchies of Europe and Asia." He defended his decision not to intervene in Kansas to suppress conflict and supervise elections, saying, "It needs little argument to show that the President has no such power." In fact, to exercise such power would make of the executive "a monarchy in fact." States, if let alone, "will . . . remedy in due season any such incidents . . ." With such firm sentiments in mind, it is not surprising that after his presidency, Pierce harshly criticized the political usurpations of Abraham Lincoln, whose mindset was intervention, war and central concentration of power at all costs. He also decried the Emancipation Proclamation as unconstitutional, since it did not have the blessing of Congress. A friend said that Pierce could not

---

99. Miller, *Fillmore—Domestic Affairs.*

give in to "ideas that were not entertained by the Fathers of the Constitution and of the Republic."[100]

The Whig-Republican platform in 1856 accused Pierce of "murder, confiscation of private property, false imprisonment, and tyrannical subversion of the Constitution in Kansas." He had appointed governors on both sides of the issue, and was damned for his conciliatory efforts both times. If the Republicans should win with their candidate John Fremont, they promised to jail and possibly execute Democrat leaders who disagreed with them on Kansas. This earned them the nick name of the Black Republicans.[101]

Pierce, like many other Democrats, was keen on American expansionism. He announced, "The policy of my Administration will not be controlled by any timid forebodings of evil from expansion." He spoke of "the acquisition of certain possessions not within our jurisdiction eminently important for our protection . . . (and for) the rights of commerce and the peace of the world."[102] By such means he was apparently indicating that he would continue Fillmore's intimidation of Japan and pursue further land appropriations on the continent.

Pierce continued the economic and territorial exploitation of Mexico first engineered by James Polk by sending a railroad senator to extort thirty-nine million acres of Mexican territory from Santa Anna for $15 million. The railroad interests wanted a southern route for a transcontinental railroad through what is now southern Arizona and southern New Mexico. The deal was called the Gadsden Purchase after the name of the senator.[103] Pierce sent a military mission to Japan in 1856 to complete the work of forced treaty-making that Fillmore had begun there.

James Buchanan

James Buchanan was a northern Democrat from Pennsylvania who served from 1857 to 1861. He was sympathetic to the south's right to maintain slavery, although he was personally opposed to slavery. He was the only president never to marry. He told people he was wedded to the Constitution. However, he took financial care of several orphaned nieces

---

100. Nelson, *Presidency*, 95; Whitney, *Biographies*, 124–26.
101. Smith, *Buchanan*, 5–6.
102. Flagel, *Guide*, 123.
103. Herring, *Colony to Superpower*, 215.

and nephews. In addition, he refrained from alcohol. During his first four terms in Congress, he supported the national-power Federalist party. At a later point, he became a supporter of Andrew Jackson and tilted toward states' rights. Generally speaking, he opposed homestead programs, rivers and harbors projects, and land grants for schools. He straddled the fence on the question of Indian removal. He supported the annexation of Texas as a place where freed border-state slaves would go instead of to the north. Jackson appointed him minister to Russia. Still later he served as Polk's Secretary of State and as minister to Britain under Pierce. During Polk's term, Buchanan performed a number of athletic flip-flops, as he positioned himself as a champion of the people's wishes. He first was against the 54/40 boundary in Oregon and then was for it. He was against and then for annexations in the Mexican War. He took both sides of the tariff issue, both sides of the issue regarding state regulation of banks, and both sides of the hard money issue.[104]

As a candidate, Buchanan followed traditional national political advice to hold his opinions to himself. He spoke so generally people could often not get his point. It was said he could "speak vacuums." He had worked to become president for more than 10 years. He was not about to falter at the finish line by letting people know what he would actually do as president. However, he carried on an active correspondence, which meant that he was active in building political bridges during the campaign.[105]

As president, Buchanan expressed a passionate belief in states' rights and slave state political preferences. He believed territories as well as states should have the right to decide for or against slavery. In his inaugural speech he said, "It is the imperative and indispensable duty of the government of the United States to secure to every resident inhabitant the free and independent expression of his opinion by his vote . . . nothing can be fairer than to leave the people of a territory free from all foreign interference to decide their own destiny for themselves . . ."[106] Buchanan thus held the widespread belief that each state and territory should be treated almost like an independent foreign nation in terms of

---

104. Whitney, *Biographies*, 127; Flagel, *Guide*, 281; Nelson, *Presidency*, 97; Smith, *Buchanan*, 11–14, 31; Cole, *Jackson*, 74.

105. Crenson and Ginsberg, *Presidential Power*, 90; Smith, *Buchanan*, 6.

106. Miller, Buchanan—*Domestic Affairs*.

its preferences. In the 1856 campaign, accordingly, he promised to try to conciliate between northern and southern interests.

In the inaugural address, he also stated his conviction as to term limits, and said he would retire after one term. Some presidential scholars rank Buchanan as one of the worst presidents, since he distrusted federal power and would not strong-arm the southern states. In fact, however, Buchanan used many of the levers of activist presidential power that they so admire in later presidents. For example, he purged Pierce's appointments if they did not go along with his policies.[107]

Some historians argue that Buchanan failed to prevent secession because he was excessively partisan at the time the nation needed a statesmanlike president to calm irrational fears on both sides. He uniformly ignored the Northern side of the slavery question and had a profound emotional attachment to the South, believed wrongly that all Republicans were abolitionists and were themselves so partisan that they wanted disunion, and acted the part of a demagogue in Kansas. He might have promoted peace by appointing a Republican or two, or even by promoting balance in his cabinet by appointing a few Douglas democrats, but he did neither.[108]

Buchanan vetoed bills to grant lands for support of agricultural colleges on the grounds states should not get gifts from the federal government. As a result of his tightwad spending habits he was able to announce a large surplus in the national treasury. No sooner did he make the announcement, the nation sank into recession during the panic of 1857, which converted Buchanan's surplus into a $27 million deficit.[109]

When federal territorial survey officials fled Utah, claiming that Indians had been incited by Mormons to drive them out, Buchanan appointed a new governor to replace Brigham Young, and other federal officials, including judges. He also sent 2,500 troops to accompany the new governor. Brigham Young announced his people would fight "in the mountains, in the canyons, upon the plains, on the hills, along the mighty streams, and by the rivulets." After several skirmishes, escalations, and retreats between the parties, Thomas Kane, an outsider who had lived in Utah, negotiated an agreement which gave the new governor supremacy in secular affairs, and Young supremacy and independence in church

107. Smith, *Buchanan*, 20–21; McDonald, *Presidency*, 320.
108. Smith, *Buchanan*, 1, 6–8, 15–16, 18, 20, 43, 148.
109. Whitney, *Biographies*, 131; Smith, *Buchanan*, 60.

affairs. Buchanan issued pardons to Mormons accused of violence, and federal troops agreed to stay a distance away from Salt Lake City.[110]

The Missouri Compromise of 1820 made slavery illegal in Kansas and Nebraska. The Compromise of 1850 allowed the territories of New Mexico and Utah to decide on slavery when they wanted to become states. As a part of that later compromise, California was admitted as a free state, Texas gave up its claims on New Mexico, and the Fugitive Slave law was enacted. This latter law called for returning runaway slaves to their owners. This was like an extradition treaty between two independent nations. The peaceful balancing of slave and free territory suggested that the two great sections, with their agreed upon demarcations between slave and free domains, could peacefully coexist with each other either as respectful partners in union or as separate nations demonstrating good will with one another as sovereign neighbors. As far as Buchanan was concerned, the 1850 legislation signaled that the two sections were far enough apart that, in due time, they would peacefully separate into two independent nations.[111]

Nevertheless, by the end of Pierce's administration the nation was still at one and new rules had to be established to deal with the inevitable circumstance of one or the other section wanting to enlarge its boundaries. Northern Democrats wanted voting on the slavery question to be done when a territory was open to settlement. Southern Democrats, whom Buchanan sympathized with, wanted the voting to be done later, near the time of statehood. In 1854, Stephen A. Douglas engineered a reversal of the Missouri compromise with his Kansas/Nebraska Act, which opened Kansas to the possibility of slavery by allowing citizens to decide the question on their own. By the start of Buchanan's term, there was a legal, but minority pro-slavery government at Lecompton, Kansas, and an illegal, majority anti-slavery government at Topeka, Kansas. People did not know what Buchanan would do, because he had been in England in the early days of the Kansas struggle.[112]

In the Kansas territory, Buchanan, like Pierce, illegitimately supported the pro-slavery Lecompton Constitution. Even his own appointed governor in Kansas urged him to reject this constitution. But Buchanan upheld the Lecompton Constitution in December, 1857 and in February,

110. Smith, *Buchanan*, 66–68.

111. Ibid., 15.

112. Smith, *Buchanan*, 3–5, 15, 23; Boyer, *Oxford Companion*, 150.

1858, asked Congress to accept Kansas as a slave state. Buchanan used his government appointment patronage power to influence the legislation and allowed cabinet members to fire opposing postmasters. The debate was heated, and in the House a physical fight broke out involving more than fifty congressmen, "with the damage limited only by the age and poor physical condition of the combatants." In the end, Congress declined to accept the Lecompton Constitution. Buchanan then revived the bill, spicing it up with a pledge of a land grant of several million acres to help finance the new pro-slavery state government. The Lecompton government voted this offer down because they wanted more in the land grant than the legislation had offered. Kansas could then not apply for statehood until it grew in size, at which time slavery would surely be a dead letter. Kansas ultimately was admitted as a free state. The pro-slavery group in Kansas was found to have accepted in their vote total some 1,500 names copied out of the Cincinnati, Ohio, phone book. Their constitution forbade emancipation of slaves without the consent of the owner and compensation. It also excluded freed slaves from living there. Many free-soilers (anti-slavery people) in the Lecompton area refused even to vote. Buchanan was thus tainted by what appeared to be election tampering.[113]

Buchanan did not believe the states had a right to secede unless their concerns were so broad that the activity rose to the status of a revolution, which was a right that he said existed "independently of all constitutions." He believed the federal government had no legal power to stop a state from seceding in any event. However, his administration's newspaper, the Constitution, advocated and defended secession, and published according to Buchanan's wishes "on pain of immediate dismissal." Thus, Buchanan seems to have engineered a simultaneous policy flip-flop on this, the biggest issue of his career. In truth, on numerous occasions he refused to deal with the secession issue, passing the buck to Congress, saying the executive branch had no right on one hand to use force against secession or, on the other hand, to recognize secession.[114] He did, however, try to prevent a civil war by calling for amendments to the Constitution.

In a special message to Congress, Buchanan called for something like a return to the Missouri Compromise that the Supreme Court had

---

113. Whitney, *Biographies*, 131; McDonald, *States' Rights*, 183; Smith, *Buchanan*, 41–46.

114. Smith, *Buchanan*, 124, 143, 146, 149–51, 180.

just overturned. He said he did not want to provoke civil war "by any act of this government," a hesitation that his successor Abraham Lincoln did not share. But Buchanan actually did much to provoke war. In the first place, in an effort to build a legacy as a decisive leader, he took a strong stand on the north's need to hold onto its forts in the south, including Fort Sumter. He essentially taught Abraham Lincoln how to start a civil war when he sent a naval vessel to Sumter. The events there signaled the depth of southern hostility to northern political and economic exploitation. Southern shore batteries opened fire on the vessel. One historian notes, "The results . . . could not have been lost upon president-elect Abraham Lincoln." In fact, Buchanan also helped provoke war by aligning with one faction of Democrats to the exclusion of others. This divided the Democrats and allowed the war-minded Republicans to win in 1860. He also upset political stability by means of his expansionist foreign policies, which convinced the north he was trying to obtain more slave territory. Over the southern forts issue and a variety of other issues, fully half his cabinet resigned. Once the war broke out, Buchanan supported the Union side, since he lived in the north, but he believed the war could have been averted.[115]

Buchanan was an avid hemispheric expansionist. He asked Congress for authorization to conquer and annex northern Mexico's provinces of Chihuahua and Sonora and establish a military protectorate there. The Senate nixed his plans.[116]

He also asked Congress for a resolution giving him a blank check for using military force in Latin America. Congress rejected his request. He did, however, get approval for U.S. transit rights across Nicaragua and obtained tribute from Mexico, Costa Rica, and Columbia for alleged damages to American property. He also considered buying Alaska and using it as a Mormon colony, tried to purchase Cuba for $30,000,000, sent nineteen ships to intimidate Paraguay, and tried to get commercial concessions in China. However, he declined a British and French invitation to join them in a war against China.[117]

115. Whitney, *Biographies*, 133; Smith, *Buchanan*, 15, 170, 181–84, 196–97; Cole, *Jackson*, 85.

116. Miller, Buchanan—Foreign Affairs; Smith, *Buchanan*, 75–76.

117. Smith, *Buchanan*, 60, 72, 69–75.

3

Lincoln and the Party of Discriminatory Taxation, Domestic War, and Repression of Human Rights

The next group of four presidents can be thought of as achieving a spectacular new degree of concentration of power at the national level and in the executive branch of that level. The name of the new party of the northeastern industrial and banking interests tinkled pleasantly in the ears of Americans, but the actions of its presidential figureheads betrayed almost every notion of actual republicanism.

The Whig Party, founded in opposition to executive branch tyranny, morphed into the new Republican party, which, ironically, in Lincoln's hands, extended Jackson-style Democratic party tyranny to the north. The south, due to an oppressive scheme of tariff taxation, had long been placed in the same position of taxation without representation that the thirteen original colonies had once been placed in. Lincoln showed that he could match the military violence of King George III as well. As the first Republican president, Abraham Lincoln matured from an extremely ambitious, wealthy, highly capable political manipulator and representative of railroad interests early in his career into an adept despot in the White House.

Lincoln's unnecessary Civil War took the lives of 800,000 Americans. It also set the stage for the blossoming of a corporate elite for whom money would replace respect for law, ethics, and community government as the standard of human success. The dominance of the northeastern corporate elite under Lincoln set the stage for the era of robber barons of the Gilded Age at the end of the nineteenth century. A cowed and servile post-war people, greatly dumbed-down in political intelligence, were no match for a new breed of court historian, who, over time, taught them to admire a tyrant who used illegitimate means (repression and war) to attain illegitimate ends (massive concentration of power in the hands of the central government). The one good outcome during the autocracy that was Lincoln's brief reign, was the end of slavery in peacetime, something he, in fact, had little to do with.

No president was ever more ambitious for unlawful power than Lincoln, and none before or since has reached the depths of twisted insincerity and political bestiality that he achieved. Lincoln's favorite general, the blood-thirsty, drunken Grant followed sometime later in his footsteps in the presidency, and did a great deal to raise the level of corruption the national government would come to know in its patronage appointments in the future. Lincoln's immediate successor, Andrew Johnson, to his credit, moderated the level of oppression that the left-wing radicals of Lincoln's Republican party coalition wanted to impose on the south after the war. But Johnson still used enough of the tools in Lincoln's bag of tyrannical tricks that the Congress and country seriously tried for the first time to knock an American president off of his powerful perch.

The third Republican president to come after Lincoln, Rutherford B. Hayes, in 1868 made a deal to become president similar to the deal John Quincy Adams' made to shut out Andrew Jackson from the presidency in 1824. Under default decision-making by Congress in the throes of a close election, Hayes cake-walked into office based on the winks and handshakes of a handful of men operating like European princes or Spartan oligarchs, far outside the light of day. But Hayes turned out to be a pretty good president after all, salvaging some honorable mention for the new party.

What might have become a gross abuse of the presidential term limit concept was solved in Lincoln's case by an assassin's bullet. Had he not been assassinated, he might either have been impeached or elevated to lifetime rulership. Grant, for his part, openly lusted for a third term, but the many reports of corruption during his administration denied him that possibility.

Abraham Lincoln

Abraham Lincoln was a life-long proponent of an enlarged national gov-ernment, but no one could have guessed how huge he would make it grow during his presidency. On the other hand, he was constantly equivocating about the slavery issue. During the campaign his policy on the matter was "having no policy." Once sitting in power he began to push the main Federalist/Whig/Republican party planks: higher protective tariffs, a na-tional bank system, national expenditures for internal improvements like rivers and harbors, national support for education, and a Pacific railroad. Until southern states began to show they were serious about seceding, this centralizing program had stalled in the Congress. With the seces-sionists gone, it still wasn't easy to enact the Republican centralization program, because even Republicans opposed parts of the program. Seces-sion made the national government into a one-party system. Objections to large-scale national spending were essentially gone from the Congress. Absence of the southern Democrats also made it easy to get Lincoln's patronage appointments through. The Senate rubber stamped them.[1]

Lincoln's record as a Republican office-holder exposes a consider-able hypocrisy between his earlier words and his deeds once he obtained the presidency. He had attacked Polk's authority to start a war on his own, and then did so himself. He also warned against executive policy formulation. Once in power, he orchestrated an immense legislative pro-gram from the offices of his right hand.[2] He also had spoken out against tyranny. But Lincoln, while praising republicanism, then overturned the most sacred principle of republicanism—that a true leader governs only with the consent of the people. Lincoln wanted to force the south to sub-mit to the union and to policies they had had no part in formulating.

Lincoln, while a candidate, had maintained, "No man is good enough to govern another man, without that other's consent."[3] But when Lincoln denied that southern states could secede, he essentially denied their right to give consent to the government and its policies, in much the same way the thirteen colonies asserted a right to consent or secede, and King George then denied them that right.

1. Paludan, *Lincoln*, 7, 36, 143, 169.
2. Ibid., 27.
3. Paludan, *Lincoln*, 18.

With a stunning quickness that must have spun the head of the most studied southern politicians, Lincoln ran hard in the direction of the Whig/Republican program after gaining office. He signed measures implementing a hundred percent of their program as if he had been chosen by the entire nation with a great mandate to do so. In fact, he won only thirty-nine percent of the national vote and won zero electoral votes in the eleven states that eventually seceded. That zero vote was hardly what founder presidents would have called sufficient consent to govern. In fact, Lincoln won only two out of 996 southern counties in the election of 1860. He did not even get a majority of the votes in the non-seceding states. Yet the laws Lincoln signed remained a part of the national law even after the south came reluctantly back into the union. Once the war was over, Lincoln announced that if he could only get ten percent of southerners to consent to a government rejoining the union on his terms, he would recognize that government, and shun the other ninety percent.[4]Ten percent consent was good enough.

Presumably underlying his belief in consensual government, Lincoln dishonestly told political friends after the election that he considered potential northern raids into state or territorial soil "under what pretext, as the gravest of crimes." He wrote, "The South would be in no more danger . . . than it was in the days of Washington." A Lincoln speech was delivered in Springfield promising that "Each and all of the States will be left in as complete control of their own affairs respectively and at as perfect liberty to choose, and employ, their own means of preserving and protecting property, and preserving peace and order within their respective limits, as they have every been under any administration."[5]

Lincoln's policy of consent with specific reference to slavery was just as deceitful as his overall policy on consent of the governed. Republican party bedrock policy was to work on full political equality for blacks over a long, peaceful process of fifty to a hundred years effort. William Seward, Lincoln's secretary of state, offered the majority view this way, "The laws of political economy, combining with the inevitable tendencies of population, are hastening emancipation." The most important Republican in the land after Lincoln, Seward believed the federal government could not force the southern states into obedience. He was clear, "Only an imperial or despotic government could subjugate thoroughly disaffected or

4. Boyer, *Oxford Companion*, 448; Paludan, *Lincoln*, 250–51.
5. Ibid., 31.

insurrectionary members of the state." Indeed, Seward believed the nation would get to full emancipation quicker by compromising with the south and keeping it in the union. The victory of the free soil movement in Kansas was a perfect example of the wave of the future, he believed.[6]

While Lincoln's own party was fast forgetting how to govern democratically, the southern states remembered well how to do so. When the seven states from the deep south formed a new constitution, that document prohibited their own Congress from enacting a protective tariff like that enacted by the powerful lords of the northeast states, so that the new south could not build up a class of powerful bankers and ruling oligarchs. It also prohibited the national government from financing monumental public works improvement projects. This action demonstrates that secession was about more than protecting local decision-making regarding slavery. It was about protecting local decision-making relating to distribution of economic wealth and about local power versus national power. Furthermore, the new Confederate constitution limited the confederate presidency to one six-year term. This signaled southern intention to cut short the duration of any popular tyranny that might crop up in the new southern nation. In other words, the south provided able, traditional, constitutional antidotes to the Whig/Republican legislative juggernaut currently being imposed upon them.[7]

Lincoln's political ambition was evidenced in the political deals he made the Chicago Republican convention to get himself nominated. He made deals with major opponents to give them cabinet positions in exchange for folding their supporters into his lap. To make sure the deck was thoroughly stacked against the south, he picked no southerners at all to sit in his cabinet, even from the upper south, which had not seceded at this point. Lincoln's ambition was to attain ultimate power, not merely the presidency, but the presidency without constitutional constraints. He planned to do this by means of the emergency conditions of war, which conditions he would bring upon the country himself. Secession played perfectly into his hands. He also needed to marginalize northern Democrats and individual Republicans who might remember what he was trying to make the citizenry forget. What he was left with in the Congress and in his cabinet after secession were largely members of his own party. What Lincoln did was position his specific supporters in positions of power

6. Ibid., 34, 38, 171.
7. Miller Center, *Lincoln—Domestic Affairs.*

to an extent no other president in U.S. history had done to this time. Jackson had shocked the country by purging forty-five percent of those appointed directly by the president in the federal government. The percent rose to sixty percent by Zachary Taylor's time. But Lincoln removed fully ninety percent of these federal employees, thus doubling Jackson's great purge of thirty years earlier and creating "the largest turnover in history." In order to make room for all those he owed favors to, he had to give jobs to notoriously corrupt individuals like Simon Cameron, who himself used patronage to the fullest in Pennsylvania, and bribery when patronage failed. Cameron was extremely pro-protectionist tariff. Lincoln put him in as secretary of the war department. Cameron was perfect for a department in which industrial ties were important and perfect for the subterranean activities Lincoln would be undertaking in that department: A contemporary said of Cameron, "[He is] a tricky man in whom no reliance is to be placed." Another judged him to be "an unprincipled rascal." In fact, after the war started Cameron's department then let huge contracts for military supplies to crooks. Fremont, Lincoln's agent in the west, did the same, letting "the most stupendous contracts, including an almost unprecedented waste of public money." In addition, Lincoln gave government contracts to Republican newspapers and hired newspaper editors in his government. Lincoln tended to disregard Congress' war appropriations directions, and thus gave precedent to the later practice of presidential "impoundment" of duly appropriated funds. For example, he used funds marked for other programs to fund iron plate ships when Congress denied his funding request for them. Lincoln agreed to allow cabinet members to control their own patronage appointments, with one caveat. They must honor Lincoln's wishes "in cases where . . . I have such wishes." Eventually, he purged two cabinet members Jackson-like for their insufficiently loyal behavior. All he needed to do now was fashion a propaganda initiative that would distort the views of the nation's founders and co-opt their names and reputations into the service of his own program. This program of shifting rationalizations for his actions he called "true views," as we shall see below.[8]

Even during the alleged "crisis" at Fort Sumter, Lincoln was busily about the business of his partisan removals and patronage replacements so as to assure loyalty to the program he had initiated and allegiance and alliance for his activities further down the road. He purchased complicity

8. Paludan, *Lincoln*, 43–45, 85–86, 121, 287–88.

in his war policy by passing out jobs "to every element in his party." Lincoln was all about removing federal employees for political rather than professional reasons: "Lincoln . . . removed Democrats from practically every office they held." Some eighty percent of his 1,520 removals were Democrats. Lincoln did not accept the advice and consent of the Senate regarding his new appointments. He was, in the words of one commentator, becoming "an increasingly independent presiden[t]." When it became known to the members of his own party in the Congress that Lincoln was not using even his own cabinet to help him formulate policy, a delegation of senators met with him and confronted him. They confided to him, "The President should be aided by a Cabinet council . . . all important public measures . . . should be the result of their combined wisdom and deliberation." Indeed, John Quincy Adams had allowed himself to be overruled by a majority vote of his cabinet. The Senators told him that the Senate was designated by the Constitution as an even broader and more democratic body of advisers than the cabinet. When they asked if he would be willing to entertain the advice of the Senate, he answered them, "I think not." Lincoln used his cabinet members only as lightning rods. He sent them out to float up a new policy that he desired but did not want to take the blame for. If the public did not like the policy, it was the surrogate who would take the heat, and not he.[9] His talent for political manipulation and autocratic control exceeded even Jackson's considerable talents.

Later, during the war, he relentlessly purged generals from his armies when they exercised independent judgment or enacted local policies in the field, or when they did not pursue the southern general Lee with sufficient bloodthirstiness. He fired top generals McDowell, McClellan, Pope, Buell, Butler, Burnside, Hooker and Meade and many lesser lights.[10]

Lincoln soon enough began a program of reelection vote-buying policies designed to nurture and develop as broad a political base in the north as possible. He started with the all-important military-industrial base in the northeast and the sheepish liberal and conservative wings of his own party, whom he courted with contracts and appointments. He then used virtually every major political vote-buying tool known to mankind to woo the rest of the people, including governmental welfare programs like protectionist tariffs and internal improvements for labor

9. Ibid., 106, 171–72, 175.

10. Ibid., 27, 35–36, 44, 84, 97, 100, 104, 106, 153, 159–60, 205, 217

and industry, free land giveaways for railroads and citizens, debt relief through banking and monetary policies, and an "emancipation" proclamation to free up southern black workers for re-assignment into northern wartime labor projects.

Lincoln hinted that he would adopt a soft position regarding the collection of tariffs by stating he would not send "obnoxious strangers" to enforce tariff laws in the south. Indeed, he then quickly flip-flopped on the tariff enforcement issue after breathing in the air of autocratic control of the country. In his inaugural address he promised military invasion of any state that declined to collect the specified tariff revenues: "The power confided in me will be used to hold, occupy, and possess the property . . . and to collect the duties and imposts . . ."[11]

The new tariff program was contained in the Republican-sponsored legislation awaiting him on his desk when he was elected. This was known as the Morrill tariff, which, together with subsequent Lincoln/Republican-imposed tariffs, raised tariffs from almost free-trade levels up to an average of forty-seven percent in the 1860s. Even before the Morrill tariff, southerners were paying more than half of all federal revenue while having well less than half the population of the north. Now, they were to be plundered unmercifully. The editor of the Daily Chicago Times in December, 1860, admitted that this situation amounted to the payment of a tribute bounty from the south to the north. In effect, the south had become an economically exploited colonial possession of the north. In July, 1862, Lincoln increased the Morrill Tariff levels in order to "encourage the development of the industrial [i.e., war] interests," like iron processors in Pennsylvania.[12]

The north was in fact much sturdier economically than the south, and thus could have moderated its tariff demands on the south. The value of manufacturing in the north was ninety-two percent of the value of manufacturing in the whole nation. Banking capital in the north amounted to eight-eight percent of the nation's total.

Lincoln also took advantage of his stranglehold on the Congress to enact the Homestead Act of 1862. This law gave 160 acres to farmers over the age of 21 who worked the land for five years and built a home on it. Unfortunately, much of the land fell into the hands of speculators and ultimately made tenant laborers and farm hands out of citizens who had

---

11. Paludan, *Lincoln*, 53, 129; DiLorenzo, *Real Lincoln*, 236–37.

12. DiLorenzo, *Real Lincoln*, 283–42; Paludan, *Lincoln*, 112–13.

hoped to be home and farm owners. Lincoln also wooed western farmers and the poorer classes, and at the same time found a way to finance the war, by promoting and signing the Legal Tender Act of 1862. This provide the nation with $150 million in paper money, backed by government promises, not gold or silver: "Thus began the printing of federal money." This meant that poor debtors could pay back their debts with money worth less than what they borrowed in the first place. But inflation of up to eighty percent "gobbled up wage increases." What remained was for the government to tax the people on the national level to get the means to pay its debts. Historically, the act of instituting a national currency was a key sign of a nation's tilt toward centralization and tyranny. Lincoln's "greenbacks" were used as legal money except for the payment of import duties, which went directly into government coffers and had to be paid in gold. The government, on the other hand, could pay its own debts in paper rather than gold. Congress and Lincoln put another $300 million in paper money in circulation by the end of the war. This $450 million in paper money "increased the economic influence of the national government."[13] In addition, Lincoln lobbied for a national banking system, which he obtained from his captive Congress in February, 1863. Lincoln's new national bank system favored north eastern bankers and gave them additional profits. The new bank system eliminated state bank notes by taxing them out of existence.

Lincoln also enacted massive internal improvements programs in the north, including rivers and harbors projects. He signed legislation to provide for "a railroad to the Pacific Ocean," the Pacific Railroad Act of July, 1862. The new railroad act gave "millions of acres of public lands and millions of dollars of loans" for track between Omaha and Sacramento. Railroads received $500 million from the land giveaway and gained effective control of the states in the West, serving essentially as the central government's economic development agent there. The 1862 Morrill Act also funded "agricultural and mechanical" colleges by means of land given to states that the states could in turn sell, with the money going to local, land-grant, colleges. These colleges were to including military education, to help bolster Lincoln's new militarized national government. Lincoln also created a new department of agriculture in May, 1862. The war which raged while these major pieces of legislation were

---

13. Drewry and O'Connor, *America Is*, 356; Paludan, *Lincoln*, 109.

being enacted, "eliminated from Congress effective Southern challenges to Republican economics."[14]

One historian writes, "For anyone to give Lincoln advice on politics was superfluous at best." John Hay, his personal secretary, said "It is absurd to call him a modest man." He believed in the power to manipulate, and spoke of the power of "the all-conquering mind." He was a sophisticated speechwriter and misinformation specialist whose words went in a good direction while his deeds went the opposite way. When he spoke of "emancipation," for example, most people thought of freedom for blacks. They did not realize Lincoln meant switching African-Americans from permanent plantation servitude in the south to temporary military servitude in the service of the north, and then finally to permanent exile outside of the United States, the only land most had known. Loving his newly-found flexibility as an autocrat to initiate legislation by means of decrees, Lincoln reminded that as a situation presented, "It may be my duty to make some new announcement." He prided himself upon flexibility: "I shall adopt new views so fast as they shall appear to be true views."[15] As soon as his mind told his hands what to do, he would have his presidential security apparatus execute those ideas. He hinted that God was guiding his great mind to execute those activities as well. Lincoln led his hearers at the second inaugural address to believe that his ethical decision-making during the war was based upon "the right as God gives us to see the right." But the "us" he was speaking of was his right hand and his left hand. Thus, Lincoln used God to justify and explain away the great slaughter that a great many of the day attributed to his personal doing. In fact, the religious slogan, "In God We Trust" was put on coins for the first time during the Civil War in an attempt to legitimate Lincoln's actions. The degree of the president's autocratic tendencies came out later during the war when he alone took on the task of reviewing military court death sentences. He did not want civilian courts to be involved, because they had jurisdictions and traditions, checks and balances, and appeals processes. In his system of martial law the courts, the legislatures, the newspapers, even his cabinet, and even foreign governments, and certainly the people, were kept far out of the picture and he alone took the stage.

14. Paludan, *Lincoln*, 115–16.
15. Ibid., 26, 141, 151, 308.

Lincoln turned the anti-central power history of the Whig party on its head and made it into what traditional Whigs and republicans hated, a "vigorous," "energetic," "active," presidency that usurped the powers of the legislative and judicial branches. One Republican newspaper openly pressed for tyrannical rule and sighed, "Oh, for one hour of Jackson." In Lincoln they got four years of Jackson times two or three. When General Hooker told Lincoln that the president was veering toward dictatorship, Lincoln responded sharply that the general should not worry about such things: "What I now ask of you is military success, and I will risk the dictatorship." But for Lincoln, dictatorship was not a risk, it was the only thing—both the means and the end. One historian summarized, "Certainly, Lincoln extended presidential power beyond any limits seen before his time." It took some time before an American ruler could touch what Lincoln touched. One historian writes, "For the rest of the century, no president came within miles of Lincoln's power."[16]

Lincoln saw to it that political image making, with his image in the limelight, would proceed apace under his command. He had his own picture placed on the higher denominations of treasury notes so as to exalt himself in the eyes of wealthy northerners who would finance his reelection campaign. It remained for a later central government devotee, Theodore Roosevelt, to place Lincoln's image on a particular coin destined to become the most mass-produced molten image of any human being in the history of the world. He thus gave a great assist to what in time would become near-deification of the man.

Lincoln was an economic elitist, one who would be called a member of "the one percent" in twenty-first century America. Many in both the north and the south believed that the northeast part of the country was filled with "spiritless, money-worshippers," devoted to "gross materialism." Lincoln's wife, for example, was a notoriously spendy woman, insisting upon all the trappings of high wealth, including the finest clothing and furniture. As president, Lincoln worked hard to supply the needs both of his own family and the needs of the northeast's financial and industrial aristocracy. He worked as a lobbyist and counsel for the Illinois Central Railroad before assuming the presidency, earning his largest fee representing that particular industrial interest. His access to railroad boardrooms and the railroad baron lifestyle was a continuing and developing journey for Lincoln. He chose as one of his most important

16. Ibid., 27, 29, 198, 316–17.

generals the previous president of the Mississippi and Ohio Railroad. Lincoln earned his stripes with the rich in the north by allowing the wealthy to get out of the Civil War draft, letting rich political dissenters out of jail, loaning government money to the rich at the start of the war, letting government contracts to corrupt wealthy corporations during the war, and asking his banker friends to bankroll the 1863 state elections in Illinois, Michigan, and Iowa. During the war, his railroad friends made train cars available to transport soldiers home to vote for his reelection in 1864. He enacted a national sales tax by which the "middle class and poor paid more than the rich." Even before the war started, he tipped off friends in industry in Massachusetts and New York to retool their factories for war business, featuring guaranteed income and profits. He helped make many "wartime millionaires" by using brokers to sell bonds and firms to sell artillery to support the north. Later on, he sold abandoned southern land in small lots to a few poor, newly freed blacks, but in large lots to northern white investors, who could in turn exploit both poor southern whites and blacks. In the north, "profits rose in almost every aspect of business." On the other hand, massive "inflation gobbled up wage increases" for the northern working man. Lincoln's open-the-flood-gates immigration policy created wage competition and increased profits for manufacturing. Lincoln even welcomed the Russian Czar's fleet into New York harbor to demonstrate European monarchist support for Lincoln's economic cause.[17]

If Lincoln's construction of the Constitution was loose in economic terms, his interpretation of the place of the judiciary in both war and peace was even looser. In the words of one historian, "The entire judicial system was set aside." In fact, he achieved "the obliteration of the traditional American system . . . of law . . . The Anglo-Saxon concept of due process, perhaps the greatest political triumph of the ages and the best guardian of freedom, was abandoned."[18]Historians justify the suspension of the right of habeas corpus, refusing to enforce decisions of the Supreme Court, and other things like shutting down newspapers, and raising armies without Congress, by noting that these things took place during war time. But the legal tyranny during the war set a precedent for permanent installation of some of these features in peacetime, like the national income tax and national standing-army conscription. Lincoln's

17. Ibid., 11, 85, 89, 111, 116, 118, 193, 210, 212, 263, 290.
18. DiLorenzo, *Real Lincoln*, 161.

intimidation of the judiciary during the war became a precedent for judicial kow-towing to the chief executive rather than respecting what the Constitution required.

Lincoln did not want Congress in town when he made his bold move to get the country into war. The Congress adjourned after his inaugural address, as was their custom. But, the fragile conditions in the states required that they stay in town, or come back after only a brief recess of a week or two. Presidents before and after Lincoln had called special sessions on matters of much less importance than secession and Fort Sumter. But Lincoln did not call them back for four months, until after he had broken a long string of laws and it was too late to stop him.[19]

Many intelligent observers were onto the president's tactics, however. The Providence Daily Post newspaper reported: "For three weeks the administration newspapers have been assuring us that Fort Sumter would be abandoned . . . [but] Mr. Lincoln saw an opportunity to inaugurate civil war without appearing in the character of an aggressor." The Jersey City American Standard wrote: "There is a madness and ruthlessness . . . [in Lincoln's behavior] which is astounding . . . this unarmed vessel . . . is a mere decoy to draw the first fire from the people of the South, which act by the pre-determination of the government is to be the pretext for letting loose the horrors of war."[20]

But there was another great irony of Lincoln's unilateral action to start the war. Secession happened because of America's great suspicion of central governmental power. Lincoln then proceeded to demonstrate the validity of that suspicion not only because he used illegal actions to start the war, but because over the next several years he jerked America into a degree of centralization she had never seen before and would never recover from. In taking these actions, Lincoln both learned from his predecessor Polk, who twisted the facts regarding a minor incident to start the Mexican War, and inspired other presidents after the Civil War, including William McKinley, Woodrow Wilson, Franklin Roosevelt, and Lyndon Johnson, who all provoked incidents or fabricated details of incidents to start or expand war. But Lincoln's War cost more American lives than most of these others' wars put together.

Lincoln's initial usurpations of law paint a dark picture of a tyrant betraying the electorate. "He took a leap, claiming powers that the

19. Paludan, *Lincoln*, 57, 80.
20. DiLorenzo, *Real Lincoln*, 120.

Constitution gave Congress." For example, "His blockade implied a declaration of war that only Congress could provide." He censored the mails
of opposition newspapers. He illegally raised men and money for his program. Specifically, he ordered generals to raise armies apart from the militia call-up process allowed in the law. He paid $2 million out of the U.S.
treasury to private citizens in New York to recruit his new armies, when
only Congress had the power of the purse. He committed government
credit in the amount of $250,000 for loans to jump start some of these
efforts. One mostly sympathetic historian writes, "He had no authority to
do these things." Further, "The Constitution gave the president no power
to raise taxes, to pay debts, to borrow money, or to coin it," but Lincoln
wanted to do all of this, so he did.[21] He worked his will while Congress
was out of town, disinvited by the president to be at their posts to debate,
give consent, and deal with resources.

One author indicates that Lincoln promoted "a new and remarkable
doctrine," that the president could exercise Congress's war power, its legislative power, its appropriations power, its habeas corpus power. When
the Congress, now further stacked politically by additional evacuation of
opposition voices during its recess, was finally invited back into session
to ratify his actions, what could they do? How does such a Congress,
any Congress, stop a war after the hard working president has already
provoked a second wave of secession, contracts have already been let,
mass arrests already made, a huge standing army already called up, an
international blockade already cordoned off, loans to war industries
already divvied out, the Supreme Court and state courts already shut
down, newspaper editors already arrested and in jail, and the south already tricked into firing the first shot?[22]

It remained only for Lincoln to tighten up the screws while the
Congress limply complied with his wishes. Lincoln set up the nation's
first ministry of repression in Seward's state department to handle "internal security," or secret police surveillance of the northern population
and its now treasonable free press. Its purpose was to strangle opposition
to Lincoln's dictatorial policies. Seward proceeded to employ thousands
of federal postmasters in towns across the country as informants and
spies, shifting their job descriptions away from facilitating free speech
and press, to suppressing free speech and press. Lincoln's patient but

21. Paludan, *Lincoln*, 71, 108.
22. Ibid., 80.

thorough party purge of the mail department now paid off for him. His minions responded like political hacks and legal ignoramuses by sending back to Lincoln letters, poems, songs, even scripts for plays, that they judged to be "disloyal." Northerners had to request permission to write to southern relatives. Soon enough, Lincoln would also use Chase's treasury agents as "field agents" to find candidates for jail. As to the results, it could be said, "There was not much pattern to such imprisonments." Some citizens were arrested on the basis of rumors, and many took oaths of allegiance in order to get out of jail. Others were paroled and rearrested, and some kept in jail long term. This was a matter of "partisan caprice." Lincoln had purged Democratic politicians from federal service, now he was purging average citizens from the safety of their civil rights. Newspapers were targets for blanket surveillance. Many northern papers were closed as a result. They could be closed for arguing that the war was wrong, or that war threatened American liberties, or that the war cost too much, or that the war enriched Lincoln's friends. Some newspaper editors had private mail confiscated and then were thrown in jail. State legislators in Maryland, who had not yet voted on whether to commit the state to the south, nevertheless were imprisoned for just thinking about taking such a vote. Lincoln arrested northern court officers who tried to serve writs of habeas corpus on the military authorities Lincoln had put in charge. In northern towns and cities not touched by war, dissenters were put in jail and Lincoln let them languish there. Lincoln's terrorist program set a precedent for Teddy Roosevelt, Kennedy, Nixon, and others to use the IRS as an instrument of repression later on. [23]

Lincoln enacted forced military servitude because he could not raise an army voluntarily for the purposes he intended to pursue. U.S. presidents historically called up volunteer state militias for short-term national service of six months or less and at the direction of Congress, as for example in the War of 1812. Lincoln started things out by paying his respects to this legal tradition. But after the Fort Sumter debacle, Lincoln combined state militias into a national army of 75,000 troops by executive order, deliberately failing, as we mentioned above, to call Congress into session to do their constitutional duty in this regard. Within short order, Lincoln called for 40,000 new state volunteers. After the loss at Bull Run in July, 1861 he called for yet 500,000 more volunteers.[24]

23. Ibid., 70–75.
24. Crenson and Ginsberg, *Presidential Power*, 230; Paludan, *Lincoln*, 82, 84.

After the horrific northern losses in the battle of Shiloh in April, 1862, the generals began calling for more cannon fodder. Lincoln felt certain he could not get more men by volunterism, as enlistments had already slowed down to a trickle. In part because of the financial demand that raising and equipping soldiers placed on the states and because not enough Americans were responding to his program of voluntarism, Lincoln took the first step in the nationalization of the militias by appointing federal recruiting supervisors in each state. He wanted 300,000 more "volunteers." However, "the lack of enthusiasm among potential recruits raised only one-quarter of the 300,000 men Lincoln asked for." The problem of desertion remained "formidable." By July of 1862, Lincoln directed the states to institute their own mandatory conscriptions. In order to finance the growing war and to support what would become, in due time, America's newly muscular standing army, Lincoln enacted a war tax on personal incomes, which came to be known as the national income tax.[25]

The anti-war movement blossomed as well. When the governor of New York denounced Lincoln, one reporter noticed, "Men whose lips had been sealed for months (except in their family circles) upon the great questions agitating the country, and dared not express their honest convictions in public for fear of arrest felt that the fetters had dropped from their limbs, and their tongues were loosed." Pamphlets were distributed protesting arbitrary political arrests of those protesting national tyranny.[26] Finally, in March 1863 Lincoln pushed through his military servitude law, which conscripted Americans directly into the service of the national government for the first time in U.S. history. Anti-war and draft riots broke out "throughout the North," from Albany and Boston to Chicago, Milwaukee and St. Paul. Then in July 13–17, 1863, New York City "exploded" and Lincoln had to move an army there to get the city under control.

The Lincoln tax measure also included a myriad of other national taxes on commodities, services, and occupations. These included inheritance taxes, excise taxes, stamp taxes (tax on paper), gross receipts taxes, and license taxes, many of which remained long after the war. The excise tax of July, 1862, hit manufacturers, distributors, sellers, farmers, miners, processors, and luxury goods makers. It was so broad it took in

25. DiLorenzo, *Real Lincoln*, 141; Miller Center, Lincoln—Domestic Affairs; Crenson and Ginsberg, *Presidential Power*, 233; Paludan *Lincoln*, 128–29, 142.

26. Paludan, *Lincoln*, 191, 193.

all professions except the ministry. "Everyone paid in some way and the middle class and poor paid more than did the rich." The tax bill was so lengthy it was the largest single bill introduced in Congress in terms of sheer size in U.S. history.[27]

Historically, tyrants have exiled specially targeted populations away from their homelands to destinations where it was felt those populations either would be morally, culturally, or economically better suited to live, could be better controlled, or would be ineffective in raising opposition to policies. Lincoln had long envisioned a final strategy for the population of African slaves in America. He would send them back to Africa from whence they came, or perhaps to destinations to the south of the country.

Lincoln was acknowledged to be "the leading proponent of black emigration" out of the United States. Eliminating the black population from the American south, he wrote, would be "a glorious consummation." He stated, "I cannot make it better known than it already is, that I strongly favor colonization." Even before the Civil War, he urged his colleagues in the Illinois legislature to appropriate money to remove the free blacks from the state. During the war, Lincoln took measures to prepare the freedmen for journeys east and south to Africa, and Latin America. The anti-slavery advocate William Lloyd Garrison denounced Lincoln for trying to deport "those who are as good as himself." He railed that Lincoln "had not a drop of anti-slavery blood in his veins."[28]

Thus, one historian writes that the Emancipation Proclamation was "manipulative, and opportunistic." In part, Lincoln's freeing of some slaves was a political tactic to keep Britain and France from intervening on the side of Confederacy, since they did not like Lincoln's racism any more than they did the South's pro-slavery stand.[29] Initially, Lincoln wanted merely to exile any slaves incidentally freed in the process of the war. Then, when forced soldiering did not produce enough bodies for the army, Lincoln began to believe he could use slaves to do his bidding and get the north over the top in the war.

One critic of Lincoln's two emancipation proclamations summarized his policies in harsh terms. The abolitionist Wendell Phillips said the first proclamation, finally issued in September, 1862, essentially said

27. Ibid., 111.
28. DiLorenzo, *Real Lincoln*, 17–20.
29. McDonald, *Presidency*, 197.

"Will you go away if I venture to free you?" And "May I colonize you among the sickly deserts or the vast jungles of South America?" The second proclamation, issued in January, 1863, acknowledged the usefulness of black soldiers and thus made a call for the freedmen to stick around for a while. It essentially said "Let me colonize you in the forts of the Union and put rifles in your hands."[30]

Lincoln's policies involved exile not just for blacks, but for whites as well. Lincoln's forced northern military conscription law in March, 1863, amounted essentially to a forced deportation measure, as 90,000 northerners fled to Canada to live. Lincoln also exiled white civilians from the Shenandoah Valley, principally because it was his aim, callously achieved, to lay the entire valley such a wasteland that there would be virtually no human shelter available for them even to squat and hide in. They could die, or move on. In Atlanta, he exiled virtually the entire remaining population of the city in his effort to depopulate the race of southerners from their beloved homes in the city. His general Sherman ordered the evacuation of the city by those still left in it after his merciless bombing of it. Lincoln was not as merciful as Greek and Roman tyrants, who often found alternative colonies for their exiles to live in. He left the southern whites to fend for themselves in the winter. He also did as ancient Assyrian kings did in order to discourage them from ever returning. His agents dug up graves in parts of the south to remove the last cultural traces of southern ancestral civilization there.[31]

Late in the war, when large areas of the south had come under Lincoln's control, he exiled those who refused to take loyalty oaths. And deportation was not merely a consequence of disloyalty to Lincoln in the south, but also in the north. Congressman Clement L. Vallandigham of Ohio was arrested without a civil warrant, thrown into a military prison, and exiled by Lincoln to the southern states because he criticized Lincoln's income tax proposal at a Democratic party rally.[32]

In his 1864 presidential reelection campaign, Lincoln called in his extensive presidential chits. He had made cabinet members of heads of diverse sections of the party and made them promise to deliver their sections and delegates to him in his reelection effort. Chase argued that Lincoln's political use of patronage was so effective in rigging the election

30. Paludan, *Lincoln*, 222–24.
31. Ibid., 45.
32. Ibid., 132, 153.

in his favor that the party ought to insist upon a one-term presidency for Lincoln. In fact, Lincoln kept up the pressure for his reelection and for continued military destruction. He succeeded in tightly controlling the Republican convention delegates and platform, which called for "unconditional surrender" of the south. One historian glibly remarks, "The platform reflected Lincoln's views."[33]

In order to win over the support of abolitionists in his 1864 reelection campaign, Lincoln proposed that he would support "absolute equality before the law" for blacks if it were ratified by constitutional amendment. In fact he knew that that would be an impossibility given the widespread racism in the country, but he did win over a one key abolitionist to his campaign. In fact, it was Congress, and not Lincoln, that initiated the constitutional amendment to overturn slavery throughout the land, and to do so in peacetime. It passed on January 31, 1865, and became the Thirteenth Amendment. Amendments do not require presidential signature, but Lincoln wanted to get credit for blowing with the winds of the people, so he signed it.[34]

Because of the Civil War, the national budget exploded to thirty times its yearly average; a national income tax was imposed on the people for the first time; the army grew to sixty times its previous level (from 17,000 to 1,000,0000); and the national debt bloated to forty-three times its pre-war level, from $65 million in 1861 to $2.8 billion in 1865. In the first year of the war, federal expenses jumped by 700 percent. In 1861 there were 40,651 civilian jobs in the federal government. By 1865 there were 195,000, a five times increase in national government employment. Lincoln set a precedent for fiscal irresponsibility as well. For some time, government contractors were not being paid, and neither was the army. The price tag of the war was $3.2 billion, most of it borrowed. This cost eventually tripled once veteran pensions and infrastructure rebuilding costs are factored in. In addition, hundreds of new regulatory laws were propagated out of Washington. Wartime centralization produced 428 public laws in the 37th Congress, the largest ever spate of national legislation to that time. The 38th Congress produced 411 bills. Each wartime Congress more than doubled the previous record of 201 bills set in 1841–43. "Clearly the war was creating a national government whose power reached throughout the life of the country."[35]

33. Paludan, *Lincoln*, 268–72.

34. Ibid., 262–64, 270, 272, 277, 282, 300, 302.

35. Flagel, *Guide*, 19, 118–19; Paludan, *Lincoln*, 36, 71, 100, 108–9.

Northerners were oblivious to much of the human suffering in the south during the war. One northerner explained, "The peculiar horrors of war have never reached our homes and firesides." Profit-taking had "a tendency to secure acquiescence in all measures demanded to carry on the war." Lincoln himself was giddy playing with taxpayer money. He exulted, "The national resources . . . are unexhausted, and, as we believe, inexhaustible."[36]

Long before the Lincoln cultists built up a reputation made of dishonest commentary, selective amnesia, and bluff and bluster, many of Lincoln's countrymen were striking much closer to the truth. Abolitionist Wendell Phillips blandly called Lincoln an "unlimited despot." Justice Benjamin R. Curtis charged that Lincoln established "a military despotism." Senator Charles Sumner noted that Lincoln's martial law was "a pretension so irrational and unconstitutional, so absurd and tyrannical" as to be dismissed completely as legitimate policy. Increasingly, modern historians are making judgments that earlier politicians and historians lacked courage to make. One, for example, has written, "Lincoln paid the largest army on earth to destroy half of the nation." Ultimately, Lincoln was assassinated by northerners who believed he was acting the part of a tyrant. In fact, had Lincoln not been assassinated, he might well have been impeached by the U.S. Congress. Only a tyrant genius like Lincoln could partially liberate a population, use them to help kill their masters, and convince them they would be turned over after the war to officials who would guarantee their rights and their safety.[37]

Andrew Johnson

Andrew Johnson had no formal education at all, hampered by the fact his parents were illiterate tavern employees. As a young man, he was somewhat of a delinquent. He ran away from his commitment as an indentured servant (working to pay off debt) after throwing stones at the house of an old woman, leaving Tennessee at age fifteen and moving to South Carolina, where he became a tailor. He was a follower of Andrew Jackson and a supporter of the plight of small farmers and craftsmen. He eventually served five terms in the U.S. House of Representatives. He also

36. Paludan, *Lincoln*, 207–9, 211–12. 215, 304.

37. Flagel, *Guide*, 118–19, 174; McDonald, *Presidency*, 400, 477; Paludan, *Lincoln*, 201.

supported Polk's unconstitutional war. As a national government representative and later as a senator, he pushed for homestead laws providing inexpensive land for those who would work and develop it. At each stage of his political career he used appeals for land giveaways to get votes. The giving of gifts to the people was the classical pathway to power for tyrants. As a senator, his homestead bill was finally passed, but was vetoed by Buchanan. To this, Johnson rightly complained about executive usurpation of the legislative prerogative. The people's representatives passed the land bill, and it was wrong for one person to undo that. However, Johnson later became the kind of autocrat he believed Buchanan was. For example, he usurped the role of the judiciary by trying Lincoln's assassins under a military commission, even though civilian courts were functioning at the time.[38]

Johnson was a "verbal bludgeonist" and somewhat of a "demagogue," seeking to move people to his side by emotional appeals. And he was easily drawn into insult-trading and unable to compromise. Desire for power was his passion. This stemmed from bitterness over the harshness of his boyhood and the haughtiness of the wealthy and educated who looked down on such as he. Politics was a way to elevate himself above the snobs. He once said, "I will show the stuck-up aristocrats . . ."[39]

The pro-union Johnson was the only senator from a rebel state to stay in Congress. Johnson then was Lincoln's military governor of Tennessee, the only seceding state to end slavery by its own action, that is, before the Thirteenth Amendment to the Constitution was passed. As governor of a state half north and half south, he had rammed through the anti-slavery law. Johnson could be the negro's best friend, if it was in his political interests. Speaking to a crowd of blacks in Nashville, he said he would be their Moses, leading them to freedom. The Republican party, admiring his pluck and perhaps thinking him an abolitionist, picked him to be Lincoln's running mate in the 1864 election. But Johnson supported the emancipation proclamation only as a way to win the war and to subvert the power of the southern wealthy class. "Damn the negroes," he said, "I am fighting those traitorous aristocrats, their masters!"[40]

Johnson inherited the presidency after Abe Lincoln was assassinated, only months into his second term. He then served in the presidency from

38. Flagel, *Guide*, 331; Castel, *Johnson*, 2, 6–7, 25, 34.
39. Castel, *Johnson*, 6.
40. Whitney, *Biographies*, 152–55; Castel, *Johnson*, 2–6, 8–9, 20.

1865 to 1869. Johnson called himself a Jacksonian democrat. It is said, "He possessed a Jacksonian concept of the president as the tribune of all the people." Congressmen represented, he believed, only small fragments of the electorate. In his inaugural address, he spoke of "popular rights," referring to local self-determination. Johnson, on the other hand, tried his best to implement Lincoln's system of reconstruction, which tilted heavily toward national control of the process. Lincoln initially called for presidential appointment of provisional governors in the seceding states. These governors would, in turn, set up state constitutional conventions to reorganize state governments and abolish slavery. These conventions were to be populated by at least ten percent of local citizens who took an oath of loyalty to the national government.[41]

For each southern state, Johnson issued proclamations, which basically required the states to renounce slavery by ratifying the Thirteenth Amendment, to renounce any future secession, and to limit the vote for a new state constitutional convention to those who could vote in 1861, that is, white males. To be admitted, the states also had to repudiate Confederate debt. This would punish those who financed the southern war effort. The newly constituted states would later decide their own policies about black suffrage and other civil rights for freed slaves. [42]

Under Johnson's program, leaders in the rebellion could apply to Johnson for pardon. He was suspicious not only of southern rebel leadership, but also of southern wealth, so those with estates over $20,000 had to apply for individual pardons in order to get the right to vote and hold office. In the meanwhile, power would essentially be transferred to the middle class. He passed out pardons liberally, as he wanted an early restoration of Democratic governments in the south, which would, in turn, support him for reelection in his own right in 1868. He also returned land to Confederates and declined to collect a cotton tax passed by Congress, both in order to purchase favor with southern voters. His overall policy was "restoration," not "reconstruction."[43]

Johnson encouraged the governor of Mississippi to allow voting for blacks who could read the Constitution or who owned $250 in property.

41. Whitney, *Biographies*, 154; Castel, *Johnson*, 21, 30; Morley, *Freedom and Federalism*, 79.

42. Boyer, *Oxford Companion*, 406; Castel, *Johnson*, 26, 44; Whitney, *Biographies*, 155.

43. McDonald, *States' Rights*, 210; Miller Center, *Johnson—Domestic Affairs* ; Castel, *Johnson*, 28–29, 50–51; Crenson and Ginsberg, *Presidential Power*, 102.

He said that voting was not a natural right but a political right that had to be earned through education. However, Johnson overturned the provision in the Mississippi "black code" of laws for freedmen that prohibited them from renting rural land. They could manage land without an education. He also allowed the re-organization of southern militias.[44]

On Christmas Day, 1868, Johnson granted an unconditional pardon of treason charges for all who participated in the rebellion except high ranking military officials and politicians. He said his goal with the policy was "to secure permanent peace . . ." Prior to his presidency he had said that southerners in the rebellion should "suffer . . . at the hands of the executioner." This about-face in post-war policy from prosecution as traitors to acceptance as citizens can be seen as a desire by Johnson to win political support for his presidency. Aside from granting general amnesties, Johnson had autocratically pardoned an additional 13,500 former confederates individually, until Congress took the power of pardon away from him.[45]

Johnson had six clerks working for him in the White House. Under his tenure, the treasury department staff grew from 6,333 in 1865 to 7,851 in 1867 and 8,168 in 1869. Despite the absence of southern states not yet readmitted to the union, his interior department grew from 1,342 in 1865 to 1,875 in 1869. Johnson removed 1,2000 postmasters in 1865, replacing them with political loyalists. He also went "on stump" to push candidates he wanted prior to the mid-term elections in 1866, the first president to make a whistle-stop tour around the country.[46]

Johnson abolished all restrictions on interstate trade in order to stimulate commercial relations between all the states. He also ended the blockade of southern ports. He generally opposed unconstitutional measures in reconstruction, such as the measures eventually passed by the Radical Republicans in the 1867 Reconstruction Act. He vetoed the first attempt at harsh reconstruction by saying it is "Unwise to . . . unite a very large section of the country against another section of a country." After harsh measures were later passed, he said the legislation "fails to consider the rights it transgresses, the law which it violates, or the institutions which it imperils." In his last message to Congress, he said, "Our

---

44. Castel, *Johnson*, 26, 44–46, 51–52.

45. Flagel, *Guide*, 153, 161; McDonald, *Presidency*, 308; Castel, *Johnson*, 49, 107.

46. Castel, *Johnson*, 36, 38, 90, 148.

domestic troubles are directly traceable to violations of the organic law [the Constitution] and excessive [national] legislation."[47]

The radicals refused to seat southern representatives in Congress. They feared that seating Democrats would interfere with one-party control of the nation, possibly even turn the balance of power to the other party, and lead to repeal of the high and discriminatory tariff. They also irrationally believed the southerners might cancel the north's war debt and possibly even try to assume, or pay, the Confederate war debt. After frequently speaking out against the protectionist tariff, Johnson flip-flopped and signed a protective tariff on wool and woolens.[48]

The Radical Republicans wanted national imposition of full liberal civil rights for blacks. They also wanted to shift the political establishment in the south away from plantation self-determination to nationalist determination, that is, to shift loyalty to the national government and president over loyalty to state government. They wanted black suffrage in order to ensure Republican control of the south, while at the same time treading lightly on the racist sympathies of many of their colleagues in the north. But under Johnson's plan, many of the planter class were reelected to the state legislature. Those legislators then enacted "black codes" denying civil rights. Radical republicans turned on Johnson with the rise of riots and killing of blacks in the south. Johnson defended the codes as protection for blacks. One code promoted black apprenticeship to white business owners, licenses for practicing a trade, and said that blacks could not own a gun or rent land outside a town. Such codes were typically modeled after black codes in the north. The rise of the codes moved Congress, increasingly controlled by radical Republicans, to propose a military reconstruction program to ensure greater sympathy from blacks. Johnson, vindictive like Jackson, in turn called for hanging of the three main radical Republicans.[49]

Congress passed an extension of the Freedman's Bureau and the Civil Rights Act, both in 1866. Johnson vetoed both of them, in part because they nationalized many aspects of reconstruction policy like land distribution policy and education and welfare programs (taking land and privileges away from whites and giving them to blacks), federalized law

---

47. DiLorenzo, *Real Lincoln*, 205; Whitney, *Biographies*, 155; Morley, *Freedom and Federalism*, 82, 89–90; Whitney, *Biographies*, 156–58.

48. Castel, *Johnson*, 58–59, 61, 65, 67, 83, 118–19.

49. Ibid., 47–48, 69.

enforcement, violated states' rights, and were unconstitutional in that they extended military rule into peacetime. The Freedman's Bureau, in fact, was located in the war department. The civil rights bill gave blacks the right to contract, and to sue and be witnesses in court. Johnson's cabinet supported the vetoes. Supporting the 1866 laws would have caused Johnson to lose southern support for his reelection bid, but they seemed radical to many people. One historian wrote, "The proposition that United States courts should assume jurisdiction of disputes relating to property and contracts, and even of criminal actions down to common assault and battery, seemed like a complete revelation of that diabolical spirit of centralization . . ." Johnson also wanted to win white southerners to his side by rejecting convulsive changes in race relations in the south. Overall, Johnson vetoed twenty-nine Congressional bills, and Congress overrode fifteen of them, including both the Freedmen's Bureau extension, the civil rights act, and one to allow the black vote in Washington, DC.[50]

Congress refused to recognize the new southern state governments set up under Johnson and in June 1866 drafted the Fourteenth Amendment to the Constitution to define national standards for citizenship and so that states could not reject civil rights of freedmen. The Fourteenth Amendment made permanent the protections of the civil rights act, so those protections couldn't be overthrown by simple congressional legislation, as they were first enacted. Congress intimidated the states to pass the amendment by threatening to reduce their national representation in Congress in proportion to the adult males disfranchised. This punitive provision outraged the south. The democratic principle of consent was ignored, as this particular constitutional amendment was forcefully enacted on unwilling participants. The military, for example, compelled Democratic legislatures to convene and to make a quorum for a vote. If a state ratified the amendment, it could be readmitted to the union. The amendment also dealt with northern fears about war debt of the north and south. It indicated that northern debt must be honored, and that southern debt could not be honored. Johnson himself wanted to quickly repay the northern war debt in order to get the government out of the clutches of wealthy financiers. However, Johnson lobbied against the Fourteenth Amendment. He said Congress should not promote an

---

50. DiLorenzo, *Real Lincoln*, 206–7; Castel, *Johnson*, 65, 67, 70–72; McDonald, *Presidency*, 321; Nelson, *Presidency*, 107; Flagel, *Guide*, 126, 132, 160.

amendment while at the same time denying eleven states admission to the union and representation in Congress. In sum, it could be said "less than three-fourths of states had expressed the will of the majority." But the amendment would allow enough blacks to vote, and take enough white votes away so as to help the Republican U.S. Grant win in 1868. That was its immediate purpose, to perpetuate one party rule.[51]

Radicals in Congress ultimately pushed through four successive military reconstruction acts. The first created five military districts and military courts in the south. State conventions elected by black voters and loyal whites (those who did not volunteer in the Confederate army) would write new constitutions that must guarantee the black vote. Collectively, the radical reconstruction acts are known by historians as "bayonet rule." The acts defied the Constitution by depriving Americans of habeas corpus. They also ignored a Supreme Court ruling that said disfranchisement of a hundred thousand or more whites by using a test oath is unconstitutional. It also noted that the acts ignored the Milligan ruling, which said military trials of civilians is unconstitutional both in peacetime as well as wartime. Johnson's veto, which was overridden, called the first law "absolute despotism." Subsequent acts required district commanders to register eligible voters, provide stricter test oaths, hold conventions under military supervision, deprive the president of administrative control over the district administrators, and provide for only a simple majority to ratify the state constitutions, rather than two-thirds (to overcome voter boycotts). Congress also passed an army appropriations bill that required the disbanding of the new southern militias and required Johnson to transmit all orders through the General of the Army, U.S. Grant. Both these last two provisions were unconstitutional "riders" to the funding legislation.[52]

Congress also passed other laws to restrict the power of the presidency. One of these, the 1867 Tenure of Office Act, required that an appointee should hold office for the term of the president who appointed him, and only removed upon the advice and consent of the Senate. This prohibited the president from removing federal officials, including the General of the Army, without Senate approval of the chosen successors. Johnson challenged the removal authority issue brought up by the 1867 Act by firing Secretary of War Edwin Stanton. The House then started

51. Flagel, *Guide*, 161; Castel, *Johnson*, 74–75, 82, 101–2, 104, 118, 206, 208.
52. Castel, *Johnson*, 75, 101, 108, 110–11, 113, 115, 131, 182.

impeachment proceedings against Johnson, in part because the Republican party thought it might lose control of the national government if it did not. Johnson was thus the second president to arouse impeachment sentiment in the Congress based on his asserting of executive supremacy over Congress. The first, of course, was Tyler. The Congress failed within one vote of impeaching him, in part because it became known Johnson was ready to give in on the tenure of office issue and in part because the radicals were afraid that the President Pro Temp of the Senate who would replace Johnson would not be favorable to northern business interests. Johnson subsequently stopped obstructing the new reconstruction law. The Tenure of Office Act remained on the books for decades until 1886, and Congress controlled federal patronage during this time.[53]

Johnson did not fail to consider the reelection implications of whatever he did. He used the popular General Grant to stand next to him on public occasions to improve his prospects. He enforced Congressional neutrality laws against Irish American Fenians, who made some armed attacks in Canada, trying to conquer and annex parts of the that land to the United States. But then he tried to court the Irish vote in the handling of the Fenians. He released arrested Fenians from jail. He tried to court the big city union labor vote in public at the same time privately saying the poor working class people should lose the right to vote. He courted big business interests by keeping business' man as treasury secretary and by enforcing a hard money policy rather than printing more greenbacks and causing inflation. Tellingly, the Republican platform in 1868 called for the black vote only in the south, not the north. Ultimately the Fifteenth Amendment called for voter rights across the entire nation.[54]

In foreign affairs, Johnson was a nationalist (one who wished to act independent of consultation with other nations) and an expansionist. Johnson's secretary of state William H. Seward had famously bragged during the Civil War while he was Lincoln's secretary of state, that he had more power than the monarch in England. This was the intoxicating atmosphere of power breathed in by men who stood near the Great Autocrat. Seward's ardor for land and power did not diminish during Johnson's administration. Johnson and Seward purchased Alaska from Czar Alexander II for $7.2 million. Johnson and Seward got into the

53. Boyer, *Oxford Companion*, 407; Nelson, *Presidency*, 107; McDonald, *Presidency*, 322.

54. Castel, *Johnson*, 86–88, 119, 192, 208.

swing of the Lincoln's sense of superiority over the darkened masses by not writing into the purchase arrangement a promise of statehood. This would send a message to ethnic enclaves like the Eskimos that they were not sufficiently civilized to be able to handle self-government. Johnson and Seward also tried to buy Iceland and Greenland, but Congress would not agree.[55]

Napoleon III invaded Mexico during the Civil War and installed an ally, an Austrian Archduke, on the Mexican throne, which was a brazen violation of the Monroe Doctrine. Seward, however, counseled Johnson not to intervene militarily even after the war was over. He pressed for the gradual withdrawal of France from Mexico, which the French eventually complied with. Seward also tried to buy Cuba, Puerto Rico, and Fiji. Johnson agreed to temper his claims of Civil War-based tribute owed by Britain to the U.S. for building Confederate warships that sank Union ships. In 1869 he consulted with the Senate, as required by the Constitution, over a naturalization treaty with Britain.[56]

Ulysses S. Grant

Grant is a study in great contrasts. Conventional wisdom says he won the Civil War, enforced reconstruction after the war, and helped save the plains Indians from destruction. But also he was known as a drunk, a war butcher, and the greatest presidential scandal-monger in history.

Grant was the ruthless implementer of the scorched-earth wartime policies of one of the most destructive tyrants in world history, and yet was kind to his horses, and despised hunting. Sherman carried out Grant's orders to destroy the entire agricultural "store-house" of the state of Georgia. His aggressive military policy was gleefully applauded by Lincoln. Winning battles and destroying property helped guarantee Lincoln's reelection. Lincoln elevated Grant even after his massive and unconscionable losses at Shiloh. One participant at Shiloh wrote, "The ground became moist and slippery with human gore . . . arms, legs, and heads were cut off." Another wrote, "Death . . . bloomed like a poison-plant on every foot of soil." Also, Grant is associated with 65,000 casualties in five weeks of fighting in Virginia in the spring of 1864. As a soldier,

55. DiLorenzo, *Real Lincoln*, 139; Miller Center, *Johnson—Foreign Affairs;* Castel, *Johnson*, 120–21; Herring, *Colony to Superpower*, 256–58.

56. Castel, *Johnson*, 41, 144; McDonald, *Presidency*, 386.

Grant said, "I have nothing to do with opinions." This was a convenient way of saying that morality is suspended when patriotism is needed. Indeed, Civil War casualties of two percent of the population of 1864 is comparable to 5,400,000 casualties in the United States of 2004.[57]

Grant was not repentant of the enormous political opportunism, nor of the cruelty, he displayed during the Civil War. Instead, he pronounced that all was well with the war: "It is probably well that we had the war when we did. We are better off now than we would have been without it."[58] This is the analysis of a man whose head was empty not only of contemporary world affairs, but of age-old written history as well. For example, the Civil War brought about a six-year-long depression beginning in 1873, during which 18,000 businesses failed, a quarter of railroad companies went bankrupt, and the nation saw fourteen percent unemployment. But this economic dislocation did not seem to diminish Grant's enthusiastic analysis of the war. Also, the ineffective emancipation program of the Republicans and their war, purchased at the cost of 800,000 lives, was borne out by a steady morbidity if not outright mortality in black civil rights for the next 100 years.

Grant loved horses and operated a livery service as a carriage driver at age 14. He wanted to make lots of money as a young man, so engaged himself in the lucrative trade of the tanning profession. He was taciturn, not talking much. He eventually went to West Point and got a military education. He was the best horse man at the academy. He was only five feet one inch in height at age 17. He liked and excelled in math and wanted to come back and teach math at West Point.[59]

Grant participated in Polk's Mexican War as an infantryman and quartermaster. Later, Grant referred to the Mexican War as "one of the most unjust [wars] ever waged by a stronger against a weaker nation . . . an instance of a republic following the bad example of European monarchies." However, war tends to beget and fuel more war, in spite of occasional negative evaluations published later. Junior officers in Polk's War later served as senior commanders in Lincoln's War.[60]

Grant was one of those who responded to Lincoln's call for 75,000 volunteers after Fort Sumter. Once he worked his way up to high

---

57. Flagel, *Guide*, 32, 36; Whitney, *Biographies*, 162; Bunting, *Grant*, 34, 41.

58. Whitney, *Biographies*, 166.

59. Bunting, *Grant*, 9, 11, 14, 16, 18.

60. Ibid., 19, 26, 30.

command, he faithfully followed Lincoln's General Order #1 to advance on all union fronts immediately, and never looked back. Grant came to be adored for his military feats and his subsequent political pronouncements in an almost cultic fashion. It was said, "To doubt Grant is to doubt Christ." Grant's lenient terms of surrender offer to Lee—allowing soldiers to return home with their guns, horses and other property—can properly be seen as the kick-off of his presidential campaign by encouraging southern voters to support him. But he had genuine respect for Lee. Later he fought to keep Lee from being tried for treason. He pledge to quit the government if president Johnson moved ahead, and Johnson backed off. As Johnson's General in Chief, Grant protested Johnson's desire to fire Sheridan and remove war secretary Stanton. He continued to oppose Johnson's rough presidential methods while he served as interim secretary of war.[61]

Grant and his supporters shamelessly trafficked in his image as a war hero. At the May, 1868, Republican convention, organizers hung a huge portrait of Grant with the label, "MATCH HIM." Grant ran on a Republican platform calling for a skinny national government, after Lincoln's and Johnson's enormously bloated administrations. They promised a reduction of taxes and a reduction of the national debt, which had grown from $64 million at the start of the war, to $3 billion at its end. Some 400,000 blacks voted for Grant, and his margin of victory in the popular vote was 300,000, proving that blacks could be used by Republicans for more than just cannon fodder. Grant called for payment of the war debt in gold and signed the Public Credit Act to pay back bondholders in gold and redeem greenbacks. Unfortunately, this policy led gold speculators in and around Grant's administration to try to corner the gold market and actually caused a financial scare.[62]

Grant initially followed in the footsteps of Lincoln's and Johnson's culture of party patronage appointments among the nation's 50,000 civilian and military employees. However, congressional party leaders soon made it clear they wanted him to consult with them on his appointments. Grant wanted to make his own patronage decisions. When he did not consult with them, Congress said they would hold him to the advice and consent requirements of the Tenure of Office Act. Grant pushed back and said he would then remove none of Johnson's people. The Senate caved

61. Nelson, *Presidency*, 109; Bunting, *Grant*, 43, 69, 73–74, 80–81, 86.
62. Bunting, *Grant*, 82–83, 85, 94–98.

in and allowed him to pick whom he wanted. He then changed his tune and deferred to his party's Congressional leaders to recommend appointments. This created loyalty to Congressmen rather than to the president. He wrote, "The advice of Congressmen as to persons to be appointed is . . . generally for the best interests of the country." Ultimately, he pushed for exams and for each department to have its own examination board and also wanted to stop political assessment of partisan appointees. Congress did not agree with this last, and reform had to wait for another decade.[63]

Grant appointed eastern financial magnates (who also served as party contributors) as secretaries of state, navy, and treasury, along with other appointees representing the greedy class. Post-war periods are traditionally hedonistic and corrupt periods. The Gilded Age after the Civil War was such a time, as would be the Roaring Twenties after World War I. Corruption in war management leads to corruption in government management. Some of those appointees then abused their positions. Grant disliked personal confrontations with federal employees and so he let ethical conundrums breed in his administration. He handled his personal financial affairs the same way, and got burned several times. There were so many Grant administration scandals historians had to give them handy monikers to keep track of them. The Credit Mobilier scandal revealed stock offered as bribes to Congressmen. The Sanborn Contracts scandal involved treasury department staff getting a cut of delinquent taxes collected. The Back Pay Grab involved Congress and the president working to give themselves a retroactive pay boost covering the previous two years. The Indian Trading Scandal involved the illegal use of money associated with an Indian post tradership. The Whiskey Ring involved bribes used to falsify quantities of liquor manufactured and distributed, and thus the evasion of $12–15 million yearly in taxes. Grant luckily was able to skirt responsibility for these personnel disasters. At the corruption trial of an aide, a defense attorney said of Grant's deposition, that he had spoken as plainly as Christ had in the Sermon on the Mount.[64]

Grant, like Johnson, had little interest in expanding executive authority in the manner Lincoln suggested could be done. He believed the legislature should be the policy-making branch, not the executive.

63. Crenson and Ginsberg, *Presidential Power*, 103; Craughwell, *Payola*, 31; Whitney, *Biographies*, 163; Bunting, *Grant*, 91, 122–16.

64. Bunting, *Grant*, 92, 94, 132–36.

He also said, "I shall have no policy of my own to interfere against the will of the people." In fact, at the start of his term the White House staff consisted of a private secretary, two executive clerks, a messenger and a steward, paid for by the people at a total cost of $13,800. He used former military officers as White House staff. After Grant's term, White House staff receded even further and did not return to this level until 30 years later in the time of McKinley.[65]

One historian dings Grant for assembling a cabinet "without any particular course of action in mind." Given this general restraint, he nevertheless still supported the mercantilist program of high protective tariffs of the Republican party. He also pressed for the voting rights and other civil rights for freed slaves that most in his party, the party of Lincoln, did not care much about. In his inaugural address, he called for quick ratification of the Fifteenth Amendment to give the vote to blacks. He proposed reforms to improve federal administration and refused to spend money for pork projects, which he called "works of purely private and local interests, in no sense national." For example, while he approved the rivers and harbors bill passed by Congress, he impounded some of its funds, declining to spend them.

Grant mimicked Lincoln's emergency tyrannies in a small way when he ordered federal troops to enforce martial law in South Carolina in 1871, when whites were terrorizing blacks there. He also signed the Ku Klux Klan bill in 1871 and indictments of 3,000 Klansmen for violence resulted. In 1876 he sent the military once again into South Carolina to allow state elections to proceed peacefully. He admitted in his memoirs that "much of" reconstruction legislation involving military administration "no doubt was unconstitutional; but it was hoped that the laws enacted would serve their purpose before the question of constitutionality could be submitted to the judiciary and a decision obtained." In other words, subverting the Constitution was okay if it could be done quickly and devastatingly before the slow-moving judiciary could catch on to it. However, Grant passed up other opportunities to interfere in state affairs, because many in his own Republican party had states' rights sympathies, and, after Lincoln, they were able to express themselves more openly.[66]

65. McDonald, *States' Rights*, 215; Miller Center, *Grant—Domestic Affairs* ; Crenson and Ginsberg, *Presidential Power*, 180; Bunting, *Grant*, 90.

66. Bunting, *Grant*, 113–14, 143; Morley, *Freedom and Federalism*, 91.

Grant was a Methodist who believed in separation of church and state. He was famous for stating "Not one dollar . . . shall be appropriated to the support of any sectarian schools."[67] In fact, there was a long-standing tradition in Washington that the national government "could not take money from one taxpayer and give it to another, except in payment for supplies and services." Beginning during the Grant administration, Congress nevertheless began to violate this sacred principle by enacting sending private bills (benefitting one person only) granting pensions to civil war veterans. These veterans had been rejected by the Pension Bureau for service-related disabilities, and then had appealed to the Congress to do what the executive would not do.[68] Although Grant did not want to take the lead in policy-making, he was not unwilling to use the veto. Grant resisted the violation of the Constitution that private legislation represented and vetoed forty private bills. He said, "I will always express my views." On the other hand, he made no pretense of only vetoing unconstitutional bills as other Constitution-oriented presidents before him did. He said he would also veto "measures which I oppose." He vetoed more than the previous seventeen presidents put together: forty-five regular vetoes, and forty-eight pocket vetoes. Only four were overridden. He also vetoed several thousand dollars for war-related damages to East Tennessee University, saying if he signed these kinds of bills, "the ends of the demands upon the public Treasury cannot be forecast." He also was the first of ultimately a dozen presidents to request a line-item veto. Grant vetoed a bill providing for $100 million in greenbacks in 1874, which Congress passed as a means of stimulating the economy during the Depression of 1873.[69]

The Depression of 1873 convinced northerners that their own expensive reconstruction program was costing the country jobs and elections in the north. In the 1874 Congressional mid-term elections, the Republicans were swept out of power by the Democrats. The situation was much like Vietnam a century later when the nation once again tired of its "costly commitments." Reconstruction had technically ended in February, 1871, when the last of the southern states had their Congressional delegates seated. But Congress had established a federal Department of

---

67. Miller Center, *Grant—Domestic Affairs* ; M. Nelson, *Presidency*, 110–11; McDonald, *Presidency*, 310; Flagel, *Guide*, 41.

68. McDonald, *Presidency*, 351–52.

69. Flagel, *Guide*, 138–39.

Justice to oversee compliance with ongoing reconstruction laws while the military was slowly withdrawn.[70]

Grant gained respect for problems of Indians while he served at forts in Oregon and California after the Mexican War. It was in the west that he started drinking, while away from his new family. As president he appointed Quakers to an Indian peace commission. He said, "Our superiority should make us lenient toward the Indian." However, Grant failed to protect Indian culture in his rush to offer white education and religion.[71]

The day after the South's surrender at Appomattox, Grant, wanting to keep his army in motion, exulted, "Now for Mexico." Grant also wanted to annex Canada, but could not win that battle either. Union soldiers, 1,000,000 of them, were tired at the end of the war. They also understood the rights of America's neighbors and America's tradition of non-interference. Polk's nasty war against Mexico had been an embarrassment to many. Some 750,000 mustered out within months.[72]

Still greatly interested in national expansionism, Grant tried to purchase Cuba from Spain so as to grant independence to the Cubans. Spain declined to sell. When he chose not to support or recognize Cubans rebelling against Spain (they had no army and no government), Grant sustained the long U.S. tradition of neutrality in these kinds of matters. He worked to stop a Congressional joint resolution calling for military intervention there. Grant envisioned Santo Domingo as an offshore colony where U.S. former slaves could go and live more freely than in the U.S. He thus negotiated an annexation treaty with Santo Domingo. However, he dropped the idea rather than implement it against the will of the people, when the Congress failed to approve the treaty.[73]In fact, he asked the Senate three times for advice regarding treaty matters.[74]

In 1871, Grant and secretary of state Fish signed the Washington Treaty in which Britain acknowledged its responsibility for outfitting a Confederate ship, the Alabama. That ship had gone on to capture sixty-four union merchant ships over a two-year period. The international

70. Bunting, *Grant*, 108–09, 142.

71. Bunting, *Grant*, 118–21.

72. Bailyn, *Great Republic*, 736, 776.

73. Miller Center, *Grant – Foreign Affairs;* Herring, *Colony to Superpower*, 259–60; Miller Center, *Grant – Foreign Affairs;* Boyer, *Oxford Companion*, 318; Whitney, *Biographies*, 164; Bunting, *Grant*, 102, 104.

74. McDonald, *Presidency*, 386.

commission set up by the treaty ordered Britain to pay $15.5 million in tribute to the U.S. Settlement of this issue seems to have set the U.S. and Britain on the road toward the entangling alliance that would develop in the first half of the next century.[75]

Historians lament Grant's term because he weakened the tyrannical presidency begun by Lincoln and sustained to a degree by Johnson. Grant's reluctance to continue seizing power kept the phenomenon from re-emerging until Teddy Roosevelt's philosophical revolution in 1900, called "progressivism." This was a political movement involving even faster usurpation of the legislative power of the states and concentration of it in Washington. Progressivism finally destroyed forever the Jeffersonian tradition of states' rights and democratic consent of the people begun in 1800.

After considering, but eventually deciding against a third term, Grant toured Europe, where he was treated like a conquering Napoleon. After such adoration, he flip-flopped in 1880 and allowed his supporters to push his nomination for a third term, but he lost that bid.[76]

Rutherford B. Hayes

Rutherford B. Hayes got a private education as a youth, then went to Kenyon College in Ohio, and Harvard Law School. He was an Emerson-style secularist—a believer in education more so than religion. Like so many Americans, when the south seceded at the start of Lincoln's administration, Hayes wanted the two sections of the country to peacefully part ways. He remarked, "Let them go." But then he was angered when southern forces "attacked" Fort Sumter, just like later anti-war Americans changed their minds after Pearl Harbor. In both cases, few Americans knew how their presidents were manipulating the action in order to get the war that they wanted.[77]

As a Congressman, Hayes worked to develop the Library of Congress. As governor of Ohio he helped get the Fifteenth Amendment passed in the state and also got Ohio State University started. His idea about government was that "The intelligence of any country ought to run it." Applied to the south, this meant he felt that educated whites and

75. Bunting, *Grant*, 106.

76. Craughwell, *Payola*, 47; Whitney, *Biographies*, 165; Bunting, *Grant*, 1, 50.

77. Hoogenboom, *Hayes*, 9.

educated blacks together should govern there. His philosophy was a capable antidote to the poisonous tendency of tyrants to give the vote to elements of the population who don't know what to do with it and then keep pandering to their votes by handing out benefits to them and taking more taxes and more power away from the people. He said that "ignorant voters" were "powder and ball for the demagogues." To counter the corrupt use of the vote, Hayes said, "Universal suffrage should rest upon universal education." He had been a radical Republican as far as black rights, and defended runaway slaves in court. But he wanted blacks, Indians, and even Mormons to get well-educated before being fully enfranchised (obtain public office). For Mormons, being fully educated meant giving up polygamy.[78]

Rutherford B. Hayes had studied the Constitution as a law student of Justice Joseph Story, a leading interpreter of the document. Hayes believed the Constitution necessitated a single term for the presidency, and as a consequence did not plan to seek reelection. He served in office from 1877 to 1881. In fact, in his inaugural address he called for a constitutional amendment limiting the presidency to one term of six years. Part of the reason he was opposed to additional terms was that presidential patronage power to pass out jobs was an extremely effective way to buy votes and keep oneself in office, and something needed to be done to balance that power. For that reason, he had heartily opposed Grant's run at a third term of office. While Hayes had few helpers in the White House (his son served as his unofficial secretary), there were still 170,000 federal employees, and 13,000 of them were in Washington, DC. Typically, just before election time, a president went on a hiring spree and also asked, or demanded, a political tithing of existing employees of a portion of their paycheck to help him get reelected. [79]

Hayes did not participate directly in his own campaign, though he wanted the nomination and the office. He told his organizers that "mum" was the word, especially concerning divisive issues like Catholicism, temperance (moderation or prohibition of alcohol), and free trade. He did, however, indulge in a degree of demagoguery (using fear and

78. Ibid., 10, 33, 53, 61–62, 66, 205.

79. Nelson, *Presidency*, 114; Boyer, *Oxford Companion*, 331; Whitney, *Biographies*, 172; Hoogenboom, *Hayes*, 11, 17, 54, 103, 116, 138.

emotionalism) by asking them to stress "the danger of giving the rebels (southern democrats) the government."[80]

Members of Hayes' Republican party controlled the counting of votes in the South, due to the inferior position southern whites were put in after the Civil War during forced "reconstruction." He was thus able to add back black votes in areas where blacks had been driven out before the election. After the election, there were 19 disputed electoral college votes total in South Carolina, Florida, and Louisiana. Whichever candidate won those votes won the election. A commission of the Congress made up of members of both parties finally gave the 19 votes to Hayes. Southerners referred to the campaign as "the stolen election." Part of the reason was that Hayes cut a deal to get the office by agreeing to withdraw troops from the south and thus re-instate a degree of states' rights, although he made clear he wanted the war amendments (13th, 14th, and 15th amendments to the constitution) to be enforced still. He said he "will not use the federal authority or the Army to force upon those States government not of their choice." This basically put an end to Lincoln's policy of forced obedience to the office of the president and re-instated the constitutional principle of the consent of the governed. As a practical matter, this meant white supremacy in state government. Hayes also promised a faction of Democrats in the south who voted for him that as president he would make sure some internal improvement money "of a national character" (i.e., for railroad development) would come their way, along with federal support for education. To his credit, he did not ask for much in the way of railroad subsidies, but he did sign legislation subsidizing the laying of a telegraph cable from San Francisco to Hawaii. Hayes became a strong advocate of civil service reform rather than merely passing out jobs to party faithful, but still could not resist giving a job in the government to the son of the Supreme Court justice who cast the deciding vote in the commission that gave him the election. He also gave a conservative southern Democrat from Tennessee the chief jobs-providing cabinet position of U.S. postmaster. Perhaps this was part of the backroom deal as well.[81]

Hayes promoted a number of policies favoring centralization of national government and executive department control of the country. For example, Hayes appointed John M. Harland to the Supreme court and

80. Hoogenboom, *Hayes*, 17–19, 21.

81. Crenson and Ginsberg, *Presidential Power*, 104; Hoogenboom, *Hayes*, 27, 33–34, 36, 42–43, 52, 144.

Harland then worked for the next thirty-four years to increase the power of the federal government. He was like John Quincy Adams both in his struggle against congressional participation in handing out jobs and in favor of federal support of education. He also did not allow senators to dictate appointments made to people living in their states. This policy diminished states' rights. He also moved away from his party's founding (Whig) ideal of a weak president who allowed autonomy to cabinet heads. He directed their activities himself. He was correct in asserting that "universal suffrage should rest upon universal education," but wrong in infringing upon states' rights to get that particular job done. Thus he was an early proponent of enlargement of federal power in the area of human services. In his last annual message to Congress he called for federal supplementation of state "free popular education." During his time in office, the Bureau of Education had only seventeen statisticians, keeping track of levels of education across the country. Hayes supported legislation to expand the Bureau's duties, but such legislation died three times in Congress during his term. One factor working against proper education was the phenomenon of pornography, or "obscenity" in literature. Hayes used the post offices to put pornographers out of business, saying obscenity exploited sex to make money for people.[82]

Hayes also disregarded the traditional use of veto only for constitutional reasons. He used the veto several times for policy reasons to stop attempts to end federal supervision of national elections. He vetoed a silver bill, and a cabinet member chastised him since that was a policy veto and not a veto based on a constitutional reason. Another cabinet member defended Hayes, saying the president should be able to make or break laws along with Congress. Congress overrode that particular veto. Hayes also supported the gold standard, and in particular the 1875 Resumption Act to undo Lincoln's paper money economy by reducing the supply of greenbacks and exchanging them for gold. He argued that printing money in the form of greenbacks was like forcing IOUs onto the population—like forcing the people to loan money to the government—and that government should pay back those debts with gold to show its good faith.[83]

82. Whitney, *Biographies*, 173; Miller Center, *Hayes—Domestic Affairs;* Hoogenboom, *Hayes*, 58–59, 119, 125, 135.

83. Hoogenboom, *Hayes*, 75–77, 92, 96–97, 99.

Hayes signed legislation in 1879, the Arrears Act, to allow the U.S. Pension Office to process service-related disability applications from civil war veterans instead of the method of using congressional legislation. This whole phenomenon made it clear that the costs of a particular war continued to plague society for a generation or more.[84]

Hayes insisted that the Thirteenth Amendment (ending slavery), Fourteenth Amendment (national standard for due process, reducing representation in Congress if deny voting rights, and repudiation of southern civil war debt), and Fifteenth Amendment (right of citizens of color to vote) be obeyed and enforced. Hayes was probably the last president of the nineteenth century to care about black suffrage in the south. He later called for money to protect black voting rights when state promises to that effect proved poorly founded.[85]

Hayes struggled against Congressional use of "riders" to subvert presidential veto power. Riders were pork-barrel projects tied to appropriation bills Democrats believed Hayes would have to sign to keep government functioning. Some of the riders were designed to subvert federal election law enforcement in the south. He vetoed five of these bills in three months and gave stirring veto speeches naming those riders as an unconstitutional attempt to force legislation on the executive branch by sidestepping the constitutional process of congressional override of the veto. He won the struggle and Congress removed the riders.[86]

When a general railroad strike broke out in 1877 as a result of recession and consequent wage cuts, Hayes refused railroad owner pleas to use federal troops to break the strike. The Constitution (Article IV, Section 4) provides the national government shall protect states from domestic violence only "on Application of the Legislature." When "application" finally was made, Hayes dispatched army troops and sent arms to state militias to suppress the strike. The rail operators later restored their cuts, and Hayes' states' rights position was vindicated.[87]

The removal of Indian tribes was essentially a long-term national embarrassment involving exile of subjugated populations that were once treated as independent nations and accorded the respect of international law. It was said Hayes was "a decent egalitarian." Hayes ended the Indian

---

84. Ibid., 82–83, 86, 88, 117, 137, 178, 192.

85. Nelson, *Presidency*, 114.

86. Ibid.

87. McDonald, *Presidency*, 295.

removal policy of his predecessor Grant because he felt it unjust and expensive. Hayes made some reforms in the Indian Bureau, including the appointment of Native American police and judges, and funded Indian schools. In 1879 he restrained the army from further inflaming the Ute Indians in western Colorado. But he fell asleep at the wheel when his administration betrayed and mistreated the Nez Perce Indians, illegally forcing them off their lands. The government spent a large amount of money to carry out this sad chapter in U.S.-Indian relations. He vetoed a bill to restrict Chinese immigration to fifteen Chinese passengers on any one boat, because he wanted good economic relations with China, and because the legislation would overthrow a treaty without negotiation and without notice.[88]

Hayes asserted U.S. domination in the Western Hemisphere with respect to any canal zone project. He invoked the Monroe Doctrine in opposition to France's attempt to build a canal across Panama. His position was "a canal under American control, or no canal." He said such a canal would be "virtually a part of the coastline of the United States." The canal would be, among other things, a "means of defense . . ." He warned European investors in Latin America that they should not look to their government for protection of their investments. Teddy Roosevelt later took credit for what was really Hayes' "corollary" to the Monroe Doctrine. Hayes also wanted to annex Canada into the U.S., but only if Canadians consented. He also kept the U.S. out of conflict with Mexico, unlike Polk before him, and Wilson after him.[89]

While setting the tone for future heavy handedness in Latin American financial affairs, Hayes nevertheless re-enforced the long standing rule of American non-entanglement in European wars: "Our traditional rule of non-interference in the affairs of foreign nations has proved of great value in past times and ought to be strictly observed."[90]

88. Miller Center, *Hayes—Domestic Affairs*; Hoogenboom, *Hayes*, 159, 161, 165, 179–80.

89. Flagel, *Guide*, 190–91; Hoogenboom, *Hayes*, 173, 176, 187, 189.

90. Herring, *Colony to Superpower*, 272.

4

The Gilded Age and America's One Party System

The period of time after Reconstruction is marked by advancing industrialization and increasing wealth of the industrialists, and to a lesser extent the people of the nation. It was even possible for politicians to talk of limiting or abolishing national taxes altogether in the early 1880s. It was also politically correct to rail against pork barrel spending (passing laws or budgets to direct government money to one's home district) and government surpluses. Republicans had a lock on political power, while southern Democrats were only gingerly and slowly re-assimilated into the political scene.

This was a time when presidents could still be proud of their own honesty, moral decency, and personal responsibility, and therefore set an example for the nation's citizens, as Grover Cleveland demonstrated. At the same time, a new political attitude was becoming manifest on the previously anti-imperial Republican side of the aisle. This bravado included a strong urge to expand trade by means of building and brandishing a muscular American navy, and to find a wide variety of rationales for that new policy. This new masculinity grew out of the force demonstrated by northern soldiers during the Civil War. Several young northern military leaders matured into politicians and then became presidents. While Republicans of this group like Teddy Roosevelt were becoming increasingly irritated with and excited about events in Cuba and Latin America, and interested in possibilities for mischief in the Pacific, the one Democrat president of the group, Grover Cleveland, loudly declined to enter into wars or alliances in Latin America. For example, he resisted taking an aggressive stand with Spain over events in Cuba.

The new manliness also manifested in enlarging the legislative role of the presidency and specifically the role it would play in economic and labor relations. Even Grover Cleveland succumbed to the temptation to involve the presidency in labor disputes. At the same time the presidents resisted welfare, retirement, and disaster spending by the national government and the taxation that would be required to implement such programs. A couple of the presidents in this group of eight were heavily affected by the Second Great Awakening taking place in the middle of the nineteenth century. Republicans Benjamin Harrison and William McKinley were two of America's most genuine and devoted Christians. While privately extremely devotional, they did not mind an occasional public display of affection for the Creator and conveying a sense that they understood the Creator's wishes for the nation. That Creator turned out to be decidedly blood-lusty.

Benjamin Harrison spoke a good game about being a national government minimalist in domestic affairs, especially with respect to regulation of the economy. On the other hand, his wish to stay out of the way of Congressional law-making placed him in the position of presiding over a spending spree that awarded the title of the "Billion Dollar Congress" on the national legislators during his term in office. Republican Harrison was an expansionist in foreign affairs and thus continued the trend set by Democrats in the age of Jackson.

William McKinley and Teddy Roosevelt shattered the traditional American mold of non-engagement by not only courting, but, in McKinley's case, provoking conflict with European nations while remaining somewhat aloof from bald political entanglement with them. At the same time, many of the nation's academic centers seemed to be in lock-step with them, promoting not only a new international destiny for America but a new "progressive" domestic destiny for the presidency as well. McKinley used the "big stick" in labor disputes and in the Caribbean and the Pacific before Teddy used it in Central America. McKinley was the first president to openly trash constitutional neutralism in foreign affairs, and if he hadn't pushed the nation into war and off-shore entanglement, Teddy would certainly have done it right after him.

At the turn of the twentieth century, the U.S. conquered and subjugated its first foreign colonies. Hereafter, participation in management of small Latin American and Pacific properties and cozying up to large European nations, became a positive credential and clear pathway for winning the American presidency, as William Howard Taft demonstrated.

McKinley took the nation into the modern era of campaign fund raising of the type where the office holder is essentially taken hostage by corporate giants who then used the presidency as an arm of their business marketing. Although some Republican presidents reacted at least marginally against large corporate "trusts," none was willing to do much more than talk about curbing their political and economic power.

Finally, this was a period during which even presidents who were able constitutional jurists thumbed their noses at the law and justified new theories of presidential power that enabled new and illegal national executive department roles, all based on manliness and popularity rather than on the consent of the governed and the rule of law.

James Garfield

Garfield is a study in the proper level of ambition for the presidency. He was busy running John Sherman's campaign for president when his name was placed in nomination at the convention. He quickly announced his objection to the nomination. However, because the two the main factions of the Republican party—Stalwarts and Half-Breeds—had stymied one another, the convention convinced Garfield to run because he was decent and unabrasive. The convention chose Chester Arthur as the vice presidential candidate in order to try to unify a deeply divided political party. Garfield favored civil service reform, but not as much as Hayes had, and Arthur (a Stalwart) favored the political patronage tradition. Garfield spoke of the "waste of time and obstruction to the public business caused by the inordinate pressure for place . . ." He also promised to win back some respect for the presidency after Hayes' hotly disputed election, although Garfield himself had helped arrange the secret bargain that brought Hayes to power.[1]

Garfield's election campaign is associated with the trend toward personal presidential "stumping" (active seeking) for office that occurred in the 1880s. But rather than traveling broadly across the country as the more popularity-oriented presidents after him, Garfield brought

1. Crenson and Ginsberg, *Presidential Power*, 108; Whitney, *Biographies*, 180; Hoogenboom, *Hayes*, 202; M. Nelson, *Presidency*, 115.

people to see and hear him as he spoke on his front porch. Thousands visited him at his home in Mentor, Ohio, before election day, many of them northern veterans of the Civil War. Garfield participated in a "political meeting" with other Republican chiefs, and even this amount of electioneering irritated some in his party. Also, even though he spoke against "political assessments" (forced campaign contributions from current Republican officeholders), he flip-flopped and quietly asked for as much as he could get.[2]

In fact, there was a step-wise progression in the inevitable push toward political idolatry in the United States presidency. During the 1820s, parties held rallies and parades while candidates remained invisible. In the 1840s parties and candidates moved to promotional novelties of the type William Henry Harrison used. In the 1880s came stumping from the front porch. In 1896 came the mobile/out-bound political campaign, corporate purchase of the election, and political policy tours just before elections, typified by William Jennings Bryan, William McKinley, and later Woodrow Wilson.

Garfield was devoted to hard money and an unregulated economy, like modern day Libertarians. He was willing to give up some executive independence in forming his cabinet "in order to secure good relations with Congress." But Garfield had time only to deal with some personnel matters before he died by assassination only months after taking office in 1881. One of Garfield's accomplishments was to save money for the government. He recalled government bonds that were paying a high rate of interest and refinanced them to pay a lower rate. In doing so, he saved about four percent of the national budget.[3]

Chester Arthur

As a young man, Chester Arthur taught school while studying law. In his annual messages to Congress, he anticipated modern education "block grant" programs by asking for federal aid to education to be distributed to the states based on the level of illiteracy in each state. During the Civil War, Arthur, like McKinley after him, served as a quartermaster. Arthur served as collector at the New York customhouse, and in addition to his government salary he took in as much as four times as much in legal

---

2. Flagel, *Guide*, 71, 80; Hoogenboom, *Hayes*, 203, 206.
3. Hoogenboom, *Hayes*, 214; Miller Center, *Garfield—Domestic Affairs*.

fees, from splitting up confiscated smuggled goods. Sometimes his staff undervalued goods, giving New York businessmen an advantage over importers in Chicago and elsewhere. This reduced the level of tariffs collected. Arthur violated his country's constitutional trust when he supported Grant for a third presidential term, which the people, more alive to tyranny than he was, denied to Grant. As vice president, he gave a speech in Indiana while slightly tipsy. He let it out that the Republicans had won over Indiana with "a great deal of . . ." and then stopped himself. The crowd knew he was speaking of money. Arthur served in the presidency from 1881 to 1885.[4]

In general, Arthur is viewed as upholding the authority of the presidency in an era of Congressional dominance, and as a transitional figure in what one author has called the "long movement toward enhanced federal activity." In fact, he also contributed to the growing trend of veneration of presidents by dedicating the Washington Monument on February 21, 1885.[5]

Arthur has been described as perhaps the "nicest" president the U.S. has ever known. It was has been said that he was so honest and conscientious that his own party, based as it was on political opportunism and manipulation, refused to give him a chance to run for the presidency in his own right after Garfield's term ended.[6]

Arthur went against the party by supporting a lower tariff. Arthur was concerned that high tariffs left large surpluses in the annual U.S. budget. He did not want the money spent on pork barrel projects as had been done in the past. Arthur spoke out forcefully to argue that budget surplus should be reduced by revenue reductions rather than spent as handouts to constituents back home. Arthur respected Congress by using the veto sparingly, but still he vetoed the $19 million Rivers and Harbors Act of 1882 because it was targeted to benefit one section of the country only. Congress then passed the rivers and harbors law over his veto. Congress overruled Arthur and passed only a symbolic and tiny tariff reduction, the patchwork law called the Mongrel Tariff of 1883. By this means, it also asserted its legislative primacy over the president.[7]

4. Boyer, *Oxford Companion*, 51; Whitney, *Biographies*, 183, 185; Hoogenboom, *Hayes*, 111, 136, 207.

5. Boyer, *Oxford Companion*, 51; Whitney, *Biographies*, 85.

6. Flagel, *Guide*, 55; Whitney, *Biographies*, 182.

7. Boyer, *Oxford Companion*, 51.

Arthur made an executive order to open the Winnebago and Crow Creek reservations in the Dakota Territory to white settlement, an action that could be deemed detrimental to the native populations, and which Grover Cleveland reversed when he took office.[8]

During his term the nation was so prosperous that Arthur wanted all national taxes to be abolished except those on tobacco and alcoholic beverages. He had a libertarian bent, as did many presidents of his day. He said, "I may be president of the United States, but my private life is nobody's damn business."[9]

Arthur was thinking more broadly than the American electorate, and somewhat imperialistically, when he vetoed the Chinese Exclusion Act, which called for a twenty-year ban on immigration from China. Arthur had in mind economic treaties to enrich the U.S. and felt the ban might harm the U.S.-China market. He later yielded to pressure from California and signed a compromise bill involving a ten-year exclusion, the 1882 Chinese Exclusion Act.[10]

Arthur was against political and military entanglement in European affairs but had fewer qualms about entanglement in treaty affairs in the Western hemisphere and Asia, especially of the economic type. He and his secretary of state James Blaine promoted commerce with Latin America and Korea. Arthur and Blaine also advocated a canal across Panama or Nicaragua. They negotiated a treaty with Nicaragua but Congress rejected it because it violated a treaty with Britain that forbade one nation's exclusive control of a canal project. Arthur's successor, Grover Cleveland, later withdrew Arthur's treaty. Arthur, in this case, was more of a mind to abandon treaty commitments when it suited U.S. interests than the people's legislative representatives were. His successor restored treaty honesty to the office.[11]

Arthur's inclination to reduce tariff protection was linked to his program of expanding U.S. economic interests abroad. He signed trade reciprocity treaties with Mexico, Santo Domingo, and Spain (relating to

---

8. Welch, *Cleveland*, 70.

9. Whitney, *Biographies*, 185.

10. Boyer, *Oxford Companion*, 51.

11. Herring, *Colony to Superpower*, 277; Boyer, *Oxford Companion*, 51; Miller Center, *Arthur—Foreign Affairs;* Cleveland rejected Arthur's treaty because in return for U.S. sole privilege in controlling the canal, the U.S. was required to provide protection for Nicaraguan sovereignty, a most European-like military alliance that the U.S. had historically avoided.

Cuba and Puerto Rico). This placed him at odds with Republican party business interests such as sugar refiners. This was part of the reason he was unable to get a second term. He also drafted reciprocity treaties with Columbia and El Salvador. Reciprocity treaties tied our southern neighbor economies to ours and reduced their ties to other economies. When such treaties were tightly written, they gave the U.S. "an almost complete commercial monopoly." Arthur promoted the African market for U.S. cotton. He wrote a trade treaty with Congo near the end of his term at the Berlin Convention, which also assured the perpetual neutrality of Congo, but Cleveland scuttled it. [12]

Arthur made a major effort to build a new and modern naval fleet. This was thought necessary because by the 1870s the Civil War navy had been largely destroyed or scuttled. Where there had been several hundred vessels in the service of the north, there were only six able navy warships by the time of his presidency. The U.S. fleet was ranked below the fleets of Turkey and Paraguay. He pushed for steam-powered, steel cruisers and had three of them built. He established the Naval War College, and the Office of Naval Intelligence. He also created an intelligence arm in the army. On the other hand, Arthur took measures to reduce illegal arms shipments to Irish nationalists and thus backed up his concern to avoid European entanglement.[13]

The American ethicist Mark Twain said of Arthur, "I am but one in fifty-five million . . . still in the opinion of this one-fifty-five-millionth of the country's population, it would be hard to better President Arthur's administration."[14] Arthur was honest personally, but willing to bend the Constitution when it came to the economic interests of the nation's corporations. He was luxury-minded in his personal life, but frugal with public money. And he was nice.

Grover Cleveland—The First Term

Grover Cleveland was a teacher before he studied law. But his formal education was limited, and the multitude of his extracurricular activities

12. Miller Center, *Arthur—Foreign Affairs*; Herring, *Colony to Superpower*, 288; Welch, *Cleveland*, 159, 178.

13. Miller Center, *Arthur—Foreign Affairs*; Herring, *Colony to Superpower*, 277, 280, 282.

14. Whitney, *Biographies*, 186.

in life insured that he had a "lack of intellectual cultivation." For example, like many, he believed that the nation's founding fathers had no flaws. He was irritable and sensitive. Although he was plucked out of obscurity for the presidency, he was ambitious enough to relish victory in obtaining the office, especially when he won a second term in 1892. He had been written off after his first term, which lasted from 1885 to 1889, and sat on the sidelines for four years sniping at president Benjamin Harrison. [15]

In a sense, "Big Steve" Cleveland was a real people's president. He was a beer drinker, cigar smoker, card-playing bachelor who in a day of lingering Puritan morality, succumbed to sex outside of wedlock. He owned up to having a child from that affair, and made arrangements for the child to be adopted. One preacher defended Cleveland by saying that if every New Yorker who had broken the seventh commandment voted for Cleveland, he would carry the state by a large margin. Early in his life he worked at the New York Institution for the Blind in New York City. As an anti-war Democrat, he hired a substitute for his military obligation in the Civil War for the expenditure of $300. This was the price of Lincoln's war exemption for the well-to-do. He got the exemption, he said, to be able to stay home and provide support for his widowed mother. He did not get out of debt until he was thirty-six years old in 1873. He did not plan to get married, let alone be president of the United States. He finally married a twenty-two-year-old at the age of forty-nine, when he was president. He observed the Sabbath if there was no opportunity for hunting or fishing that day. Religiously he was very tolerant, except of the Latter Day Saint (Mormon) faith, because he was opposed to polygamy. He also was a hearty eater, and weighed around 280 pounds, but after two terms as president he had lost sixty pounds.[16]

He followed the American democratic tradition of not campaigning hard for office in order to show he was not ambitious for power. He made only two speeches in his 1884 campaign. Like all politicians, he had the ability to flip-flop. In his acceptance letter upon his nomination for president, he had called for a constitutional amendment to limit the office to one term. Later on, however, he did not hesitate to run for a second term. Both Cleveland and his hero George Washington dearly wanted to stay away from an second term of office, but both succumbed to a desire

15. Flagel, *Guide*, 24; Welch, *Cleveland*, 18–19.

16. Flagel, *Guide*, 28–29, 111, 113, 135; Welch, *Cleveland*, 16, 23–24, 37, 39, 51, 74, 210; Whitney, *Biographies*, 187, 189.

to rectify their reputations by serving hopefully a better-received second term. He hated yes-men and an intrusive press, and refused to make appeals to popular opinion to build support for his positions. In taking aim at the partisan, mud-slinging press, he said, "I don't think there ever was a time when newspaper lying was so general and mean as the present, and there never was a country under the sun where it flourished as it does in this."[17]

Cleveland was a political party man and understood the importance of party organization and patronage. On the other hand, he did not really like politicians and their sycophants. Cleveland made a public announcement asking office-seekers to go to his cabinet members for a job, but he still took an active role in considering candidates. Eventually, after Republicans in the government were undermining his administration, he purged the customs office, the IRS and the post office by the thousands—those on the unclassified list. But still, Cleveland was a civil service reformer. Even after the Pendleton Act of 1883 (the merit system) was passed, the president and cabinet could still fill 100,000 out of 110,000 jobs in the federal government. By the end of his first term, Cleveland expanded the classified list from 16,000 to 27,000. But, on the other hand, seventy-five percent of 100,000 unprotected positions had been replaced by new appointments, mostly 4th class postmasters. Cleveland started a movement to keep office holders away from partisan campaigning, and advocated exams for promotion. By the end of his second term, he had added at total of 44,000 positions to the classified list, including 5,000 employees of the railway mail service. He thus increased employees under the merit system from twelve percent to forty percent. But not all of this was idealism. He also wanted to limit the patronage authority of his (likely Republican) successor and lock in Democrats to permanent service somewhat like what Adams did in the federal judiciary a hundred years before.[18]

Cleveland was not like Jefferson, who ran the cabinet like a democracy. Big Steve let the cabinet have a lot of independence, but when they met with him, he used them like personal servants. He took no votes, and used no special advisers outside of the cabinet.[19]

17. Miller Center, *Cleveland—Domestic Affairs*; Crenson and Ginsberg, *Presidential Power*, 112; Welch, *Cleveland*, 36; Flagel, *Guide*, 79; Nelson, *Presidency*, 118; Whitney, *Biographies*, 192.

18. Welch, *Cleveland*, 59–61.

19. Ibid., 49–50.

Unlike Arthur, the gentleman president, Cleveland was decidedly tactless, and easily offended others without always intending to. Critics accused him of "monarchical arrogance." He thought of tact as weakness. He was a stubborn man and when it came to doing what he thought was right and best, he could not be persuaded to change his mind. As the "Veto Mayor" of Buffalo, and Governor of New York, and even as president, he had veto-fever, refusing to implement policies that he felt were unethical or unconstitutional, or that resulted from corruption. He vetoed measures that he felt interfered with the constitutional right to contract, such as public assistance measures, and corporate welfare measures. If a debtor had made a contract to pay back money, he should have to work to pay off the debt rather than go on welfare. If corporations went bankrupt, the government shouldn't bail them out. As Governor of New York, it was said he read every word of every law passed by the legislature before signing or vetoing, often having to stay up late in the night to do so. He was called "His Obstinacy" by some, since he wielded the veto power like a sledgehammer. He vetoed 304 bills in his first term, more than all other previous presidents combined. While others of his generation rose for early morning prayer, president Cleveland spent his time dissecting fraudulent pension appointments. He did not take advantage of the opportunity to streamline or modernize the federal government. While the federal government had 110,000 employees, the office of the president had only fifteen. Cleveland had one private secretary. He also personally wrote checks to cover White House expenses. He wanted a frugal government. He put the presidential yacht into dry dock, paid his own expenses on vacations, and paid for hay for the White House horse carriage barn. He often answered the White House phone and door himself. It was said he was a one-man federal government. He wrote an inaugural address lasting twenty-five minutes and was the only president to deliver such an address from memory. He had no use for speech writers.[20]

Cleveland was like Jefferson, in the sense that he revered the separation of legislative and executive powers and functions. Like Jefferson, he wanted to be left alone by the Congress to carry out his duties. He wanted "executive independence," the ability to operate freely in his sphere. His was the most extreme assertion of executive privilege regarding a president's department files until the presidency of Richard Nixon. However,

---

20. Flagel, *Guide*, 134; Whitney, *Biographies*, 189–90; Welch, *Cleveland*, 10, 15–16, 25, 27, 47–51, 56, 222.

Jefferson revered separation enough that he did not use the veto power to try to control Congress. In the words of one historian, Cleveland's "use of the veto is not an example of executive restraint."[21]

Cleveland tested the strength of his independence from Congress, and his idea that he was responsible only to the people and not to the Congress, when Senate Republicans decided to not confirm Cleveland's appointments to office. They wanted him to give documentation regarding his firing of an employee before they would act to confirm a new appointment. The Tenure of Office Act of 1867 had given the senate veto power over presidential efforts to remove those who had been appointed with senatorial consent. In 1869 the law was softened so the president would not have to provide "evidence and reasons" for his firings. Cleveland thus had the upper hand, and outlined his arguments in his message of March 1886. He said he was responsible only to the people, not the Senate and they could impeach him if they thought he was overstepping his bounds. The senate retreated and then enacted a complete repeal of the original act of 1867.[22]

After his victory in the tenure of office battle with Congress, he gradually increased his effort to advise and direct members of Congress. He wanted to see Congress abide by his wishes. His political mentality was a version of the "tribune" or "plebiscitary" notion of government, first claimed by Jackson and Polk, and later that asserted by Wilson and the two Roosevelts. He believed that the president represented the people's wishes better than the other branches of the national government, and better than state governments. At a ceremonial event in New York, he cast the office he held in a spiritual context: "That the office of President of the United States does represent the sovereignty of sixty millions of free people is to my mind a statement full of solemnity; for this sovereignty I conceive to be the working out . . . of the divine right of man to govern himself and a manifestation of God's plan . . ." He felt that he represented the moral conscience of the people, whereas Congress promoted "popular excitement" and exhibited "political cowardice." His job was to protect the people from the "vicious paternalism" of a Congress bent on getting reelected by bestowing gifts and privileges on the people and on corporations. For example, he vetoed a bill to provide free seed for farmers hit by a drought in Texas in 1887. He wrote, "I can find

21. Welch, *Cleveland*, 10, 17, 202, 217.
22. Welch, *Cleveland*, 11, 53–56, 214.

no warrant for such an appropriation in the Constitution; and I do not believe that the power and duty of the General government ought to be extended to the relief of individual suffering . . ."[23] In his veto message, he said the people should support the government, but the government should not support the people by paying for their needs. The power of the federal government, he wrote, did not extend to "the relief of individual suffering," and that almsgiving ought to be done on local levels. The role of the national government, in his words, was not "direct and especial favors," but rather "exact justice and equality."[24]

Cleveland vetoed 228 private pension bills stemming from the Civil War, many of them dishonest claims. After these were first rejected by the executive branch pension department, their promoters went to the legislative branch, and when these bills came back to the executive for approval, Cleveland deep-sixed them. He was the first president to dare the wrath of the veterans' lobby. But he ultimately approved 1,871 out of 2,099 of such bills. He also vetoed the Dependent Pension Bill of 1887. This provided $12 per month to disabled vets. There was no requirement to show that the disability was war-related. The legislation also gave the same money to parents or widows of a dead veteran if they, too, were disabled. Cleveland said the legislation would make a national charity program. He called the measure a fraud and a raid on the public treasury for private gain. Congress eventually responded to his push for veteran's pension reforms, but veterans responded by voting him out of office in 1888.[25]

One historian writes, "Grover Cleveland was perhaps the last president of the United States who waged principled battles against unconstitutional usurpations of power by the centralized state." For example, he vetoed income tax legislation and welfare spending bills and sought to cut tariffs, and thus ease the discriminatory burden those tariffs cast across the states. Not surprisingly, he is dinged by historians for not being sufficiently "activist," "energetic," or "leadership oriented." These are all code words for tyrannical. He once said of the presidential office, "I did not come here to legislate." His legislative agenda in the first term consisted of only two initiatives: repeal of the Silver Purchase and Coinage

23. Healy, *Cult of the Presidency*, 84–85.

24. Ibid., 11, 13–14, 57, 80.

25. Flagel, *Guide*, 134–35; Nelson, *Presidency*, 117, Whitney, *Biographies*, 194, Welch, *Cleveland*, 62–64; DiLorenzo, *Real Lincoln*, 228.

Act of 1878, which he did not win; and reduction of tariffs, which he did win. He used his appointment power to try to force Congress to repeal the Sherman Act, by delaying appointments until he got his way. He won minor battles by reforming the office of the federal marshal and the U.S. attorney office. He also established the first federal penitentiary. He also signed other legislation not the result of presidential initiative: the Presidential Succession Act, the Hatch Act establishing agricultural experiment stations, and elevating of the Bureau of Agriculture to cabinet status. He decided that federal intervention was warranted in agriculture in order to provide information to stop "noxious insects," and contagious diseases of farm animals.[26]

Cleveland recognized the growing importance of labor relations as a professional field of endeavor, and tried to stick the federal government nose into that particular tent quite far. In 1886, there were hundreds of railroad strikes across the country as workers were demanding higher wages and an eight-hour workday. Cleveland was the first U.S. president to send an entire message to Congress on one issue. In his April, 1886 message he asked for voluntary arbitration of labor disputes. He asked Congress for the creation of a three-member commission to settle those disputes. But he didn't want to use "government by commission" to decide rates. He thought the federal courts should do that. Congress passed a bill restricted to railroad disputes, not all labor disputes. The bill provided that arbitration was to be established on an ad-hoc basis. The commissions were to be composed of railroad employees, not government officials. During his first term, Congress passed and Cleveland signed a bill to create the Department of Labor, including the provisions mentioned above. He also signed bills prohibiting importing contract labor, and legalizing national trade unions.[27]

Over the course of two terms working to restrain national government expansion, Cleveland vetoed two-thirds of all bills passed by Congress, 482 of them, two times more than all previous presidents combined. Only Franklin Roosevelt vetoed more after him.[28] Although he presented some bold legislative initiatives, he was unable to compromise either with members of his own party, or the opposition party.

---

26. DiLorenzo, *Real Lincoln*, 228; Crenson and Ginsberg, *Presidential Power*, 112; Welch, *Cleveland*, 9, 53, 81–82, 90.

27. Whitney, *Biographies*, 193; Welch, *Cleveland*, 13, 77–78.

28. Boyer, *Oxford Companion*, 135; McDonald, *Presidency*, 352, 354.

Cleveland pushed, like many presidents, for tariff reform, but only after he was elected. In 1884, he would not debate with his opponent Blaine on the issue. But in his 1887 message he demanded it and made it a high priority of his administration. He wanted a lower tariff, like Arthur. He saw that a high tariff was reducing foreign trade and creating a budget surplus that kept capital out of circulation. The $70 million surplus of revenues over expenses was a temptation to dishing out favoritism to certain industries and products. His insistence on tariff reduction was a factor in his reelection loss in 1888 and also resulted in the huge tariff increase in 1890.[29]

Cleveland used the State of the Union address in 1887 to explain how tariff protectionism made for higher prices "and generated more money for . . . government." He said high tariff protectionism is a "vicious, inequitable, and illogical source of unnecessary" taxation. Excessive import duties were paid by the American people "as if it was paid at fixed periods into the hands of the tax gatherer." In sum, a high tariff raised prices to the level of duties imports for consumers, increased the cost of living for working people, and increased corporate profits. Government surpluses generated by excessive tariffs were used for pork barrel projects, and thus were "schemes of public plunder." He said, "Our business men are madly striving in the race for riches . . . immense aggregations of capital outrun the imagination . . ." He wanted duty-free raw materials and reductions in tariffs on consumer items. This would enhance exports and reduce over-production. He urged passage of the Mills bill, which failed in the Senate. He did not undertake any barnstorming to get it passed, in order to respect the separation of powers. He did not think the current tariff was unconstitutional, but rather unjust because it was inequitable taxation and unjustified favoritism. He wanted to continue to tax tobacco and whiskey. His tariff legislation was his boldest effort to influence Democratic party policy.[30]

The Supreme Court in the Wabash case said states could not regulate interstate railway traffic. Cleveland thus blessed the nation's first, and minimal, federal controls on business by signing the Interstate Commerce Act of 1887, although he was not closely involved in its promotion. He believed in the sanctity of private property. Thus, he would not support

29. Boyer, *Oxford Companion*, 135; Welch, *Cleveland*, 10–11, 33; Whitney, *Biographies*, 193; Nelson, *Presidency*, 118.

30. Welch, *Cleveland*, 17, 77, 82–89, 107–9.

legislation to investigate abuses of business, like Wilson would do with the Federal Trade Commission (FTC). He did not believe the Constitution allowed frank business regulation, at least on the national level.[31]

Cleveland noticed farmer protests against expanding power of the railroads. Politics had freed big business, but now big business was attempting to capture politics and intrude in party policy-making. In a anti-internal improvement policy action, Cleveland recovered tens of millions of acres of public lands previously granted to the railroads and to cattle ranchers. These private business interests were protected and promoted by the national government under Republican party presidents. Cleveland's action ultimately had the tyrannical effect of nationalizing locally-controlled land. Had he returned the lands to the states, he might have had a cleaner constitutional record.[32]

Some historians are inclined to see Cleveland as a racially intolerant president, since he opposed integrated schools in New York, and he opposed federal efforts to bolster black suffrage. But this was because he supported states' rights to decide issues related to race. He seems not to have been racist, since he was horrified about California's treatment of Chinese workers and immigrants. Chinese were not as easily assimilated as European immigrants, since they had an entirely different cultural tradition. The purpose of American immigration law he said, was "to invite assimilation and not to provide an arena for endless antagonism," which is what was going on in the west. With the 1888 presidential election coming up, Cleveland threw a bone to the anti-Chinese west. He supported a policy which might diminish violent antagonism between white laborers and Chinese laborers. He found a sponsor for legislation to prohibit the return of Chinese who left the U.S. for whatever reason. He signed the bill October 1, 1888. Cleveland said the Chinese labor experience in America was "unwise . . . injurious to both nations." On the other hand, he took a liberal position with respect to European immigration. In his second term he vetoed a bill barring illiterates from entering the U.S., saying "ability to read and write . . . (is) a misleading test."[33]

The period of Cleveland's presidency saw the last of the Indian wars, which involved the Apaches under Geronimo. By now, U.S. policy was firmly set regarding the disposition of Indian lands and Indian

31. Boyer, *Oxford Companion*, 135; Welch, *Cleveland*, 15, 78–79.
32. Whitney, *Biographies*, 193; Welch, *Cleveland*, 45–46.
33. Miller Center, *Cleveland—Domestic Affairs*; Welch, *Cleveland*, 72–73.

assimilation into the white population. Cleveland saw Native Americans as wards of the nation and felt a responsibility to look after their welfare. Cleveland was a Native American "reformer," encouraging assimilation through education, and private land ownership. He believed Native Americans should be instructed in the English language, and move from tribal ownership, or communal agriculture, to individual land ownership and farming. Unfortunately, promoting private land ownership through the Indian Emancipation Act, or Dawes Act of 1887, ultimately meant that much tribal land reverted to the government domain. Indians could receive forty to one hundred sixty acres per person, which they could not sell for twenty-five years. Rights of citizenship would be extended to those who held land and got an education. All remaining native land was bought by the federal government and the money used to put in a special account for Indian education and assistance. The former tribal land not going into private ownership was put in the federal domain and was opened to white settlers and land speculators.[34] Cleveland also terminated fraudulent grazing leases on native American land. He revoked president Arthur's order which had opened up Indian lands to white settlers in the Dakota Territory. He vetoed a bill granting railroads right of way through Indian land in Montana.

Cleveland was a nationalizer of public lands before Teddy Roosevelt made it popular. Typically, for the progressive movement, "reform" was a code word for nationalization, or removal of programs from the power of the states. Cleveland wanted to reform a century of exploitation of the public domain, which he dealt with in his first term, and to enlarge the "forest reserve," which he tackled in his second term. Cleveland revised land laws so cattlemen and timber companies could not play rough with individual homesteaders by using cowboys and lumberjacks as paid agents to make pseudo-claims on the land. The original intent of the sale of public lands was to encourage home building and farming for five years, and to "discourage the massing of large areas." Cleveland issued executive orders to destroy fences cattle men put up to monopolize water and use the public domain as private grazing lands. Also, railroads were abusing their "indemnity lands," large acreages where railroads could pick and choose from at a later time. In many cases railroads did not know exactly where their rail lines would go, so they got "indemnity lands" to make up for the uncertainty instead. Railroads would wait until homesteaders had

34. Miller Center, *Cleveland*—Domestic Affairs; Welch, *Cleveland*, 69–71.

settled, then claim the land out from under them. Cleveland even forced some railroads to give up their land if they did not fulfill their obligations. By executive order, Cleveland turned 25 million acres in California into a national reserve (San Joaquin Forest), and by the end of his second term he had doubled the size of the national forest reserve.[35]

Cleveland was perhaps the nation's last anti-imperialist. He saw that the canal treaty Arthur negotiated with Nicaragua entailed not just co-ownership of a canal zone, but something more nefarious, a commitment to protecting Nicaragua militarily against any assault on its sovereignty. Thus the treaty made Nicaragua essentially a protectorate of the U.S. He said it made an "absolute and unlimited engagement" for military protection of that nation. This was the very definition of an entangling alliance, and he declined to submit it to Congress. He also wanted it clear that if he opposed U.S. expansion in the western hemisphere, he was even more opposed to European expansion here. On the other hand, Cleveland went along with a seven-year renewal of a reciprocity treaty with Hawaii in 1884, giving the U.S. exclusive right to a naval base at Pearl Harbor. This did not entail a military obligation to defend Hawaii, though, and Cleveland did not see the treaty as a prelude to annexation. Sanford Dole, an American businessman, overthrew the monarch in Hawaii in order to promote annexation and consequent tariff protection under U.S. laws for his sugar crops. Americans constituted twenty percent of the Hawaiian population, but eighty percent of the wealth. Cleveland learned that a large majority of Hawaiians opposed annexation, so he turned the issue over to Congress, and they decided not to annex. It was said, "[Cleveland] postponed the march of empire in the Pacific."[36]

Cleveland also rejected the previous administration's trade treaty with Congo and refused to submit it to the Senate. In the guise of free trade, it was a thinly-disguised method for exploiting West Africans. He also scrapped reciprocity treaties negotiated with Latin American nations, including the Dominican Republic and the Spanish Antilles, since these were essentially economic protectorate treaties. Some economists had argued that the U.S. needed exploitative reciprocity treaties to get America out of the economic difficulties she experienced in the 1870s. But famine in Europe in 1879 led to a large increase in U.S. exports in the

35. Welch, *Cleveland*, 74–76.

36. Herring, *Colony to Superpower*, 291–92, 296; Welch, *Cleveland*, 159–60, 169–75.

mid-1880s even without the treaties. The treaty would have assured the neutrality of Congo, but Cleveland said this violated the Monroe Doctrine, which indicated America could not meddle in colonial rivalries outside the Western Hemisphere, in the same way Europeans could not meddle here in ours. [37]

In February 1888, during a presidential reelection year, Cleveland signed a treaty to allow a commission to decide which Canadian bays were not open to U.S. fishing, a diplomatic success in an election year. However, the treaty was rejected by the Senate. The U.S. navy was now big enough to exert its will over vessels of other nations. Cleveland seized Canadian fur sealers in the Bering Sea and arrested some Canadians. At the end of his first term in 1889 he signed an annual proclamation against hunting seals there, because it was depleting the seal population.[38]

Cleveland wanted to remain neutral with regard to Cuba's nationalist rebellion against the Spanish monarchy. Congress wanted to recognize Cuban independence but Cleveland said such action would usurp executive branch authority in foreign affairs. He said, "There will be no war with Spain over Cuba while I am president." If Congress had declared such a war, he determined he would refuse to mobilize the army.[39] Thus Cleveland was perhaps the last president to use the presidency as a brake on war, when Congress had war fever. Subsequent presidents went to war when Congress did not want to go there.

Benjamin Harrison

After Garfield's election, Harrison declined a cabinet post in favor of election to the U.S. Senate by the Indiana legislature. His job in the national legislature was thus beholden to state rather than national interests. This power arrangement lasted from the time of George Washington to the time of Woodrow Wilson in 1913, when the Seventeenth Amendment was enacted. At that time the state legislatures lost the privilege of instructing national senators in the needs of local constituents across the state and became beholden to big money and national government interests instead. Harrison ultimately became perhaps the least activist

37. Herring, *Colony to Superpower*, 287–89; Welch, *Cleveland*, 159, 179.
38. Welch, *Cleveland*, 162–65.
39. McDonald, *Presidency*, 396.

president in modern U.S. history in terms of trying to grow the federal government domestically. He served in the office from 1889 to 1893.

Harrison was a devout participant in what has been called the Second Great Awakening (religious revival) in the 1840s and 1850s. He noted, "Civil society is no less an institution of God than the church." When he won the presidency, he remarked, "Providence has given us victory." He began each day with a short religious service and selected a cabinet nearly all of whom were Presbyterian like himself.[40]

As a Republican party member, Harrison was not ready for the militant high-handedness of later Republican presidents. He viewed the office of the president domestically as an administrative rather than legislative office. If the Congress passed legislation he didn't necessarily agree with, or didn't have a hand in formulating, he was likely to sign the measure into law anyway. Ben Harrison did not veto legislation. He let the people's will be done. He said that the president "should have no policy distinct from that of his party and that is better represented in Congress than in the executive." Harrison "viewed personal dignity a cardinal virtue and demagoguery a sin." He also gave unqualified support to federal action in favor of black voting rights.[41]

Congress passed the Sherman Antitrust Act expanding the powers of the executive branch and it did so without Harrison's involvement. Harrison signed it without objection, but took a full year before he published regulations, the only form of protest he felt he could register.[42] The law was the first to regulate large corporations on the national level, and was the basis for ongoing usurpations of state regulatory prerogatives undertaken later by Teddy Roosevelt, Woodrow Wilson, and Franklin Roosevelt. While Cleveland used a bad method to achieve a good end, Harrison refused even to do that. For him, the veto had to be a good one (for a constitutional purpose) if he was to use it against bad public policy. However, if money was made available by the Congress, he had ideas about how to spend it.

Benjamin Harrison signaled his intent to spend more than his predecessor in his inaugural address. At that time he asked for a liberalization of veterans' pensions and an enhancement of federal revenue via increased tariffs. He said, "There is nothing in the condition of our

40. Flagel, *Guide*, 51.
41. M. Nelson, *Presidency*, 118; Welch, *Cleveland*, 106, 108.
42. Crenson and Ginsberg, *Presidential Power*, 112.

country or of our people to suggest that anything presently necessary to the public prosperity, security, or honor should be unduly postponed." The vulnerability of Harrison's determination not to use the veto was demonstrated most obviously when he signed legislation, the Dependent Pension Act of 1890, to pay pensions to any Civil War veterans who could not work, whether or not the disability was military-related. The law also granted a monthly stipend to veterans' widows and children. This nearly doubled the amount of money paid for pensions, and the U.S. Treasury went from $100 million surplus, to a huge debt. On the other hand, his intention was not to overspend. He called on Congress to "adjust our revenue laws that no considerable annual surplus will remain . . ."[43]

In his last state of the union address in December, 1892, Harrison purred, "The general conditions affecting the commercial and industrial interests of the United States are in the highest degree favorable . . . so general a diffusion of the comforts of life were never before enjoyed by our people . . ." Harrison's prognostications about the "general conditions" were largely misplaced. His address was delivered only months before general panic and the depression of 1893, making of Harrison a very poor prophet indeed. The nation dumped Harrison in favor of a comeback for Grover Cleveland, whom they knew would stop the profligate spending.[44]

Regarding foreign affairs, it was said of Harrison, "He did more to move the nation along the path to world empire than any previous Presidents." For example, he signed the McKinley Tariff of 1890, which granted the president unprecedented powers to negotiated reciprocal trade agreements with other nations without consulting Congress. He was slow to send such treaties to the Senate, but ultimately sent a number of substantial ones for their approval. He talked Congress into expanding the navy in order to complement, or enforce, this revivified trade policy.[45]

Harrison jump-started a decade of naval expansionism, which culminated in McKinley's war against Spain and imperial re-colonizations of Spain's old colonies at the turn of the century. His naval program was partly in response to Captain Mahan's 1890 book *The Influence of Seapower on History*, which urged the U.S. to acquire colonies for raw

43. Flagel, *Guide*, 135–36; Whitney, *Biographies*, 205.

44. Whitney, *Biographies*, 207; Flagel, *Guide*, 135–36.

45. Miller Center, *Domestic Affairs—Harrison;* Crenson and Ginsberg, *Presidential Power*, 112; Miller Center, *Harrison—Foreign Affairs;* Nelson, *Presidency*, 118.

materials, and for the U.S. to become an "offensive power." Harrison expanded the navy into a world class fleet with seven armored war ships. Harrison, together with his Secretary of State James G. Blaine, pursued a belligerent foreign policy in the home hemisphere. He escalated a minor skirmish in Chile to the point of war, aggressively pursued naval bases in the Caribbean and Pacific, and gave approval to a coup in Hawaii.[46]

Harrison followed up his predecessors' involvement in the Samoan debacle with Germany by creating an entangling alliance with Germany and Britain to provide joint military protection for Samoa. This almost precipitated a naval war with Germany, and was the nation's first example of a U.S. protectorate, or colony. The U.S. had "interests' there since the time of the Hayes treaty, which U.S. presidents had been enforcing without Senate approval from 1878 through 1889.[47] The principle U.S. "interest" in Samoa was the excellent harbor of Pago Pago.

Hawaii is a textbook example of the consuming power of the reciprocity treaty. The treaty negotiated with Hawaii in 1875 had turned that nation into a satellite of the United States by the 1880s. When in 1887 the U.S. concluded an extension of the treaty, providing the U.S. with a right to a naval base at Pearl Harbor, a British official wisely predicted that the base deal would "lead to the loss of Hawaiian independence." Harrison and Blaine soon enough fulfilled that prediction by negotiating a treaty with Hawaii that made it another U.S. protectorate. However, the Hawaiians balked. Harrison then turned a blind eye while a group of Americans overthrew the monarchy there and, once in power, offered the U.S. a treaty of annexation. Harrison sent 150 Marines to protect the group of white settlers who overthrew the monarchy. The United States gave an apology to Hawaii a hundred years later, when it was too late to do anything about U.S. treachery.[48]

Grover Cleveland—The Second Term

Before his campaign for a second term in 1892, Cleveland let the voters know he opposed Harrison's spending on veterans' pensions, coinage

---

46 Herring, *Colony to Superpower*, 292–93, 303; Miller Center, *Harrison—Foreign Affairs*.

47. Whitney, *Biographies*, 206; Boyer, *Oxford Companion*, 329; Herring, *Colony to Superpower*, 296.

48 Herring, *Colony to Superpower*, 296–97.

of silver, and a proliferation of spending measures that made that group known as the "Billion-Dollar Congress." After winning his old job back, Cleveland called a special session of Congress to repeal the Sherman Act, when the nation was in the midst of depression. He withheld patronage appointments until Congress would pass his unconditional repeal bill. He was accused of being the first president to use patronage to influence legislation. His tactic worked and the repeal bill passed after a two-month-long debate.[49]

Cleveland promoted the Wilson tariff bill in 1894, which he had authored. The bill put coal, iron ore, wool, and lumber on the duty-free list, and lowered the general tariff level by fifteen percent. Once again he used the threat of withholding appointments to force action. In order to compensate for the decrease in revenue, the bill specified a two percent tax on personal incomes over $4,000, essentially the rich. Corporate profits, gifts and inheritances got the same two percent. Lobbyists fanagled to raise duties on hundreds of imports. Only wool and copper remained on the duty-free list after all the negotiating. This produced a real mongrel tariff. The average duty was forty-two percent, only a slight improvement over McKinley's average tariff of forty-nine percent. Cleveland, in protest, let it become law without his signature. Cleveland was a staunch supporter of corporate America, in spite of his desire for tariff reduction. He made a half-hearted attempt to prosecute the Sugar Trust, which controlled eighty percent of the manufacture of refined sugar in the country. He only challenged the monopoly in Pennsylvania, and lost that case. In his second term he prosecuted five cases against monopolies under the Sherman Anti-Trust Act, but won only one of them. During Cleveland's second term, the Supreme Court in the Pollock case declared the personal income tax unconstitutional because it was not like an excise (sales) tax, but was rather a direct tax levied only on a per capita basis.[50]

Some politicians and groups pushed for federal government jobs and relief projects to assist in recovery from the depression of 1893. True to voters' expectations of him, Cleveland did not support federal involvement in sponsoring jobs.[51] The citizenry blamed Cleveland for the ongoing depression of 1893 by electing members of the other party in the

---

49. Whitney, *Biographies*, 184; Welch, *Cleveland*, 119–23.
50. Welch, *Cleveland*, 131–37, 151–52.
51. Miller Center, *Cleveland—Domestic Affairs*.

Congressional elections of 1894. The Democrats lost badly everywhere except in the south.

Cleveland's devotion to the Constitution declined somewhat in this second term of office, at least with respect to his earlier reluctance to use the military in domestic disturbances. In 1894, labor unrest related to the depression tempted him to inject national power into a problem of local labor relations. The Pullman Car company had cut wages twenty-five percent in order to maintain profits. When Pullman workers walked off the job near Chicago, threatening rail traffic in twenty-seven states, railway workers from across the nation struck in support of them. The Governor of Illinois expressed "vehement opposition" to any use of federal troops to break the strike, but the President sent 4,000 troops anyway in July 1894. Cleveland said he was not anti-labor, just anti-labor violence. He used as an excuse his desire to protect federal property, principally the U.S. mails, but his purpose was really to break the strike. A district court in Chicago, with Cleveland's encouragement, made an unprecedented extension of the injunction powers of the federal judiciary to help end the strike. The injunction even aimed at arresting those who used "persuasion" to encourage railroad employees to strike, not just intimidation, threats, or force. It said that the federal judiciary could decide whether states had the capability to enforce the orders of the court. Cleveland issued an order mandating that Illinois citizens must return to their homes, and extended the order to nine other western states.[52]

The presence of federal troops provoked a retaliatory reaction that produced an increase in property destruction. Governor Altgeld said the crime wave was the consequence of Cleveland usurping the Constitution. The police power was reserved to the states, and Cleveland had turned the standing army inward to take that power away from the state. Many believed Cleveland crossed the line over to bald federal tyranny, and many northern Democrats withdrew their support from him, as did organized industrial labor.[53] In fact, this was the first domestic use of the army without the request of a state governor.

Cleveland held to his constitutional guns, however, regarding the illegality of extending the already large American empire westward across the Pacific Ocean. He killed the treaty of Hawaiian annexation

52. Miller Center, *Cleveland—Domestic Affairs*; McDonald, *Presidency*, 295; Welch, *Cleveland*, 141–49; Whitney, *Biographies*, 197.

53. M. Nelson, *Presidency*, 119.

championed by his predecessor Harrison, since the Senate had not yet acted upon it by the time he took office a second time. He did not buy the fear-hype that predicted Japan would seize the islands if the U.S. did not. In addition, Hawaiians opposed the treaty. He believed that the overthrow of the monarchy there was all about protecting U.S. economic investments. He asked for congressional help to restore the deposed queen to power, and was denounced by many newspapers for declining to expand the American empire.[54]

Cleveland declined a recommendation by the U.S. consul to Samoa to make an agreement with the Samoan ruler to put Samoa under the U.S. as a protectorate. He recalled the consul for making the suggestion. He wanted to negotiate with Germany to get mutual assurance of Samoa's independence. Cleveland also stayed out of the China-Japan struggle over control of Korea. He pointedly declined the invitation of his China ambassador to get more involved in that nation. [55]

Cleveland was, however, more hospitable to U.S. breast-beating hegemony in Latin America. His secretary of state Olny brayed, "The United States is practically sovereign on this continent and its fiat is law upon the subjects to which it confines its interposition."[56]

Cleveland softened the posture of his state department by objecting to pressure for America to interfere in Spain's affairs in the Western hemisphere, particularly in Cuba. Cleveland regarded politicians and editors expressing American fraternalism with the Cuban rebels of 1895 as warmongers. He did not recognize a belligerent Senate resolution passed in February, 1896, which encouraged the president to recognize the Cuban rebels and abandon pro-Spanish neutrality. Cleveland simply remained silent. He offered to mediate the dispute with the rebels, but Spain refused. If Congress passed a resolution to recognize Cuban independence, Cleveland said he would disregard the act as usurpation of the executive power in foreign relations. When his own consul in Cuba requested a man-of-war to be placed in Cuban waters, Cleveland did not take the bait, which was designed to provoke war. Thus he injected a moral dimension into foreign policy that his successor, William McKinley had

54. Herring, *Colony to Superpower*, 297, 306; Whitney, *Biographies*, 197.
55. Welch, *Cleveland*, 66–67.
56. Herring, *Colony to Superpower*, 307.

no compunctions about. Cleveland asserted the nation should not be seduced to "follow the lights of monarchical hazards."[57]

In his last state of the union message in December, 1896, Cleveland reported that the government had slid into a $25 million deficit. However, he said this was an appropriate time to dip into the national government's rainy day fund of $128 million. He likened this to a family simply dipping into a savings account. He said, "It is the palpable duty of every just government to make the burdens of taxation as light as possible" and appealed to the Congress "for the most rigid economy in the expenditure of the money it holds in trust for the people." This would be the last time an American president would keep the nation in such good financial trim, as the war presidencies of McKinley, Wilson, and Roosevelt were about to turn the nation into an immensely profligate spender in order to accommodate both presidential glory in war and reelection. To his credit, Cleveland turned down re-nomination for a third term by the Gold Democrats, as the monetary conservatives called themselves.[58]

William McKinley

McKinley's Scottish ancestors struggled for independence against British overlords. McKinley felt that combative blood within, but directed it in the opposite direction. He subjugated other peoples rather than freeing them. Several of McKinley's American ancestors were armaments workers, including his father. His father operated an iron forging business, and from him William learned to support the interests of manufacturers. His mother was a strict Methodist church woman and wanted William to go into the ministry. William came of age during the second great American religious awakening, and was a seriously religious man. However, he inherited more of the gifts of war from his father than the gifts of peace from his mother. He twice became "a child of Mars [the war god]," first by participating in the Civil War, and second by committing the country to the Spanish-American War.[59]

McKinley quit college before the Civil War, and that massive conflict further delayed his return to educational progress by several years.

---

57. Welch, *Cleveland*, 195–98; Boyer, *Oxford Companion*, 135; Healy, *Cult of the Presidency*, 44.

58. Whitney, *Biographies*, 199–200.

59. Morgan, *McKinley*, 2, 27.

Like many others pulled into the vortex of a militant political party and the pathway of an ambitious politician, William felt Lincoln's war cause was blessed by heaven. He felt he was "a soldier for my country, but also a soldier for Jesus." Back home, his father's iron works prospered greatly during the war.[60]

In his race for Congress, McKinley campaigned for a tariff that would keep foreign manufacturers from competing with domestic manufactures. Other than his steadfast support for protection, he found he could turn the other cheek, politically speaking, quite readily. He moved easily between support for business and support for labor, and from support from western interests to support for eastern interests, often consulting prevailing winds before taking a stand. When he spoke in a Republican area he spoke of the gold standard and when in a Democrat area he spoke of silver coinage. He was called "the prince of straddlers." McKinley embraced national government expenditures on infrastructure/internal improvements, government subsidies for railroads and other big business interests, government land giveaways to homesteaders, and monetary inflation to aid farmers. He also expressed sympathy for labor causes, including restriction of immigration. He spoke in favor of civil service reform—professional rather than political appointments—although later he was keen to promote patronage appointments for Ohio residents. McKinley supported other economic legislation to strengthen the national government. He voted for legislation creating the Interstate Commerce Commission and also the Sherman Antitrust Act. He also voted to override Cleveland's veto of veterans' pensions, but lost that battle.[61]

McKinley did not have a huge presidential political issue like secession with which to cement a huge concentration of power in his own right hand. To get elected, McKinley had to use the political mass marketing tactics pioneered by William Harrison, and used later by Woodrow Wilson and Franklin Roosevelt. The Democrat, William Jennings Bryan, announced he would make a national tour, thus breaking precedent. McKinley refused to go on campaign tour himself, and thus honored the

60. Ibid., 11–37.

61. Eastern creditors were robbing western debtors, demanding payment in dollars worth more now than when they got the loan. The answer for the west was the more volatile silver, or paper currency, both of which would encourage inflation. For the east, the answer was to stick with the gold standard; Morgan, *McKinley*, 45–47, 105–6, 146, 163.

tradition against excessive public display of personality and ambition. But by actively promoting himself through a campaign committee, he effectively subverted the 100-year old American tradition of non-active pursuit of presidential power. McKinley also broke the tradition of the presidential campaign starting in September, and started instead in July. Some 1,400 party speakers blanketed the nation in his behalf.[62]

McKinley and his railroad friends had a card in their hand that centrally located Ohio presidential candidates had used in the past. The railroads, using special low fares for McKinley supporters, brought thousands of people to McKinley's hometown to hear him speak from his front porch. He spoke to 50,000 people from the front porch in one day.[63]

McKinley also had wealthy and politically savvy businessmen running his campaign, with deep links to corporate America. Republicans raised a "staggering" $4 million for the campaign and outspent Democratic candidate William Jennings Bryan ten to one. McKinley's campaign manager, Mark Hanna, believed, with Alexander Hamilton, that those who owned big business should also govern the country. Hanna, using railroad baron James J. Hill, assessed banks, insurances companies, and other commercial enterprises a percentage of their assets or a percent of their revenue as a sort of political tithing for the McKinley candidacy. McKinley was thus the first American president to basically purchase the office rather than win it democratically. One influential Republican noted, "We have carried the Middle West . . . by an unprecedented use of money."[64] Such was the monopoly on politics that the Republican party enjoyed for 50 years after concentrating absolute power in the person of Abraham Lincoln.

Teddy Roosevelt remarked that McKinley was advertised like "a patent medicine." Freight cars full of campaign literature were sent out across the nation, differentiated into 275 different pamphlets, covering special interest groups like blacks, women, labor, and civil war veterans. Mark Hanna, a campaign manager who had a "genius for propaganda," bought up whole newspapers and devoted them to the campaign cause.[65]

McKinley had his profile emblazoned on silver tea sets, glasses, fans, Napoleon-style hats, handkerchiefs, and walking canes. His bust was cast

62. Miller Center, *McKinley—Campaigns and Elections.*
63. Morgan, *McKinley*, 168, 176–78.
64. Crenson and Ginsberg, *Presidential Power*, 119; Morgan, *McKinley*, 142, 173.
65. Morgan, *McKinley*, 159, 173–74, 180.

in tin, marble, terra-cotta, and ceramic. Poster photos of him were plastered everywhere. Hotels served a McKinley drink.[66]

Because McKinley wanted the aristocrats to govern, he understood it would be better if the political party stalwarts were pushed to the side, because they held constitutional scruples, whereas the money men did not. He proposed a populist-type national campaign that would marginalize local party bosses. He flattered the common people by using the slogan "The People Against the Bosses." In doing so, he set a precedent for the populist subversion of the party that Franklin Roosevelt used so effectively later on. McKinley could make fun of political popularity contests, so confident was he of success in the game he was playing. He privately told the story of a politician who turned down baptism by immersion because he didn't want to be out of the public eye for that long.[67]

McKinley displayed one of the must-have requisites of an autocrat. Secretary of State Elihu Root said of him, "McKinley always had his way." One Senator remarked, "I have never had any trouble to get the President to do what he wants to do." Another of his contemporaries, the centralizer Herbert Croly, said that McKinley pushed interests "as clearly national as could any political leader of his generation." Another said he was "the leading nationalist of the day."[68]

McKinley used his cabinet appointments to reward large financial contributors and political activists supporting him in the country's various geographic sections. He did not allow subordinates much opportunity to exercise patronage, but kept it for himself, and he made many of those appointments outside the wishes of big city party boss men. McKinley issued an executive order reclassifying jobs in 1899. Against his promise to advance the civil service, the order actually reduced the number of jobs subject to civil service coverage. McKinley initially worked with only six White House staff, but by the end of his time in office he had increased it up to eighty.[69]

McKinley dominated his cabinet, controlled Congress, and used the press to publish his agenda by holding regular press briefings, the forerunner of today's presidential press conference. He entertained the press socially, and gave them regular access to his staff. It was said of him,

66. Ibid., 160, 166.
67. Ibid., 124, 143–44.
68. Nelson, *Presidency*, 120; Morgan, *McKinley*, 159, 221.
69. Morgan, *McKinley*, 204, 222, 232.

"He made himself daily news." However, he instituted a rule somewhat like that used in monarchies. News reporters could not approach him unless he spoke to them first. It is rightly said that McKinley was the first modern president (that is, tyrant) because he used the press as a personal propaganda tool, traveled frequently to push his agenda, and used his contacts and experience to influence Congress.[70]

Unlike Cleveland, "[McKinley] did not regard legislating as off limits for presidents." He also held Congress hostage by withholding patronage appointments pending passage of his legislation. In addition, he was not bashful about vetoing legislation enacted by the people. He vetoed 14 bills, "but prevented many more from reaching light of day." He, like Lincoln, also achieved "integration of the political branches of the federal government" under the arm of one strong boss. Ironically, this was the type of imbalance in power he campaigned against! In 1898 he toured the country to solidify his control of Congress and campaign for Republican candidates. He thus interfered with State and local politics in an unprecedented way and set a precedent for presidents of both parties to do so in the future. He also overthrew a 100 year old tradition of state militias by signing the 1898 Volunteer Act, whereby general officers and staff of state militias would now be appointed by the President rather than by Governors. He thus finished the job started by Lincoln of nationalizing states' means of defense (against such aggressive agencies as the national government), and subjected the entire military to his personal control.[71]

McKinley understood that the tariff was an extremely potent vote-buying tool. He could promise protection for citrus products in Florida, for example, when he wanted their votes. Local protectionist interests provided local funds for his candidacies. He used "some tariff favors, a little patronage, and a lot of charm" to win over westerners. In 1897 he signed the highest U.S. tariffs ever. The Dingley Tariff Act gave discretion to the president to negotiate executive agreements with Europe and Latin America in the pursuit of lower rates negotiated reciprocally on certain items.[72] America was moving to overseas markets to handle its surpluses. The second part of the economic equation for Republicans like McKinley, and Teddy Roosevelt after him (after market protectionism), was to use

70. Herring, *Colony to Superpower*, 312; Nelson, *Presidency*, 120; Morgan, *McKinley*, 245; Boyer, *Oxford Companion*, 482.

71. Morgan, *McKinley*, 210–11; Crenson and Ginsburg, *Presidential Power*, 120, 122, 247.

72. Ibid., 84, 105, 213–14.

the U.S. military to enforce economic agreements with poorer countries to the south of the U.S. This would provide not only foreign markets for exports, but cheap raw materials for the protected home industries.[73]

McKinley subverted the American tradition, institutionalized by rule in the House of Representatives, against what would later be called "transfer payments," the taking of money from one taxpayer and transferring it to another. Payment for supplies and services were excepted. When the Congress transgressed its own rule, presidents would most often veto such measures. But McKinley initiated a request for funds for Mississippi River flood disaster relief in 1897, setting a precedent for many other future raids on the national treasury of that sort. In May of 1897 he also asked Congress to appropriate $50,000 to assist Americans living in Cuba.[74]

McKinley was firm in promoting the annexation of Hawaii. In order to make this happen, McKinley used Teddy Roosevelt to rile up anti-Japan sentiment. He needed to promote the idea that the U.S. should take control of Hawaii before Japan could do it. The fact that some Japanese were immigrating to Hawaii stoked this fear. This Hawaii policy made use of the very jingoism (national aggression) he spoke against during his inaugural. He pushed a joint resolution from Congress, which would require only simple majorities. This would bring about a sort of "cheater's annexation" because the Constitution required treaties to have a two-thirds majority. In his annual message December of 1897 he asked for Hawaiian annexation. McKinley argued that Hawaii was now apart of America's "manifest destiny." He could foresee using Hawaii as a base against the Spanish Philippines. In June, 1898, he got his joint resolution.[75]

McKinley came in to office promising to be a peace president. He told outgoing president Grover Cleveland that he would to "what lay in my power to avert . . . (a) terrible calamity." In his inaugural he said, "We want no wars of conquest." Also, he sermonized, "We must avoid the temptation of territorial aggression." Within a year, McKinley was warring against Spain. McKinley also appointed the hot head Teddy Roosevelt as assistant secretary of the navy, who in turn used his leverage to assist the charge into war.[76]

73. Ibid., 48–51, 102, 212.
74. McDonald, *Presidency*, 351; Whitney, *Biographies*, 214.
75. Morgan, *McKinley*, 223–25.
76. Ibid., 198–200, 205, 208.

McKinley, like Wilson and Franklin Roosevelt after him, deftly maneuvered the country into war with a European power. Presidents since Ulysses Grant had uniformly pronounced a resounding "no" to American military intervention in Cuba. But in 1895 Cuban natives had once again entered into rebellion against Spanish rule there. That new conflict disrupted the flow of profits to investors in America. Spain told the U.S. that the problem was an internal matter, and complained about the history of lax enforcement of American neutrality laws. The U.S. had looked the other way as private citizens had taken up arms and traveled to Cuba.

McKinley aggravated and provoked Spain by trying to dictate the outlines of Spain's colonial policy in the Western Hemisphere. He first demanded that Spain should end the rebellion in Cuba by giving the rebels a voice in the government.[77] He also demanded an end to the internal relocation program, called "re-concentration," and insisted that Spain provide relief for the population.

There were indications that things were improving in Cuba. The Spanish liberal party came to power in October, 1897. The British monarchy had given autonomy to Canada and the new Spanish government in fact promised to do the same for Cuba. In fact, they recalled their cruel governor, Weyler, from Cuba to start the process. They also revoked the re-concentration order, released American prisoners, and turned over the whole issue to a Cuban parliament to meet a month later.[78]

Rather than respond positively to the Spanish initiatives and buck up under the Spanish minister's leaked (and all-too-accurate) characterization of him as "a bidder for the admiration of the crowd," McKinley moved warships to Key West, Florida. He then went one step further and did what Cleveland refused to do. He placed a warship in Havana harbor. He said this would show that the U.S. did not fear Spain. One pro-empire historian provides another reason for the move. He writes that McKinley sent a naval vessel "into troubled waters to induce calm." However, as a practical matter, this particular navy maneuver would be akin to an intruder carrying an unconcealed weapon into a person's home and brandishing it in front of the family. It was a clear act of war, yet Spain did not bite. McKinley's naval provocation to war set a precedent that future presidents used over and over again to start foreign wars.[79]

77. Boyer, *Oxford Companion*, 482.
78. Morgan, *McKinley*, 281.
79. Ibid., 264, 272.

When the battleship Maine exploded in Havana harbor, sinking and killing 266 Americans, the press blamed Spain, while McKinley judiciously held back finding fault. In fact, his entire cabinet believed from the early evidence that it had been an accident. In retrospect, responsibility for the loss of American life, if not the sinking itself, can be pinned directly on McKinley's own lapel, since he ordered the ship and its mates into harm's way. He thus followed the pattern Lincoln set of taking an action that was essentially an act of war, and then displaying public shock and dismay that it actually did lead to war.[80] History has judged that the catastrophe was very likely the result of an internal explosion.

Once McKinley got his war resolution, he called for 125,000 volunteer soldiers, and he ultimately mustered 270,000 into the army and navy. Half were still in training camps by the conclusion of the war. McKinley wanted to increase the size of the permanent professional army to 104,000, but Congress cut his request to 60,000 to be sustained by two-year enlistments.[81]

McKinley had in mind a multiplicity of uses for the unrestricted war spending Congress gave him. After subduing Spanish forces in Cuba, he refused to recognize the Cuban rebels as the legitimate government of Cuba. In fact, he then committed the U.S. to a war against the newly liberated Cuban rebels, who turned their attention from Spain to the new American occupiers of their homeland. Following the pattern of an ancient Assyrian conqueror, McKinley took Puerto Rico as tribute, or compensation, for American inconvenience in going to war against Cuba. He also dispatched a fleet to the Pacific islands, since Spain had interests there as well. He wanted to take advantage of this opportunity to chasten Spain across the globe, and convert their interests to American interests wherever that could be made to happen. Thus he seized one of the Mariana Islands, Guam and Wake Island, and pushed forward onto the Philippines. He then committed the U.S. to a much longer-term war in the Philippines, where the same citizen aversion to occupation of their homeland resulted. [82]

The initial armistice plan called for Spain to cede Cuba, Puerto Rico, and the Philippines to the United States. Spain said no to giving up the

80. Flagel, *Guide*, 229; Morgan, *McKinley*, 274; Herring, *Colony to Superpower*, 313.

81. Morgan, *McKinley*, 290.

82. Morgan, *McKinley*, 286; Herring, *Colony to Superpower*, 319–20.

Philippines. They argued the Philippines did not belong to the U.S. by right of conquest under international law since Manila fell after the armistice. But McKinley was "as firm as a rock." Speaking to a group of ministers in 1899 about how he made his decision to "keep" the Philippines, he said "there was nothing left for us to do but to take them all . . . and uplift and Christianize them . . . as our fellowmen for whom Christ also died."[83]

With respect to McKinley's imperial agenda, there were dissenters not only in the cabinet but in the Congress. George Gray, a Democrat from Delaware, reminded that empire was alien and unconstitutional, since it involved government over people without their consent. Republican Senator Hoar argued against ratification of the Spanish War peace treaty because the Constitution forbade acquiring lands not destined to be organized into states. Teddy Roosevelt labeled Hoar a "traitor" for upholding this time-honored constitutional principle. But McKinley had a few cards up his sleeve. McKinley made deals with wavering Senators to give them jobs in exchange for votes on the treaty. The treaty was approved by a margin of one vote. A resolution for ultimate independence for the Philippines was later defeated by McKinley's vice president Hobart, who cast the deciding vote as president of the Senate. William Howard Taft, future president of the United States, had opposed taking the islands, but McKinley offered him the job of governing there. When McKinley promised him a position on the Supreme Court if he would take the colonial administrator job, Taft threw his constitutional scruples to the four winds and went to Manila.[84]

Some 4,500 Americans lost their lives in the Philippines, but the Philippine body count stood at anywhere from 200,000 to 600,000, mostly from starvation and disease associated with the U.S. colonial concentration camps.[85]

Having learned just how easy it was to bamboozle the American people and take tribute from a conquered people like an ancient imperialist monarch, McKinley moved on to take tribute from China after sticking his nose in affairs there too. In 1900 he signed a treaty without Congressional approval that allowed him to cooperate with European imperial powers to send troops to China to protect hardly significant U.S. interests there. A massive rebellion called the Boxer Rebellion had broken

83. Herring, *Colony to Superpower*, 315–16.
84. Morgan, *McKinley*, 313, 317, 320—21, 337.
85. Flagel, *Guide*, 252.

out there to try to kick out foreigners like the U.S., who were dictating Chinese trading policy to Chinese. Initially, McKinley sent 2,500 troops there. Like the early commitment of a small force to Vietnam some sixty years later, this action initiated a long-term, escalating, military commitment in China, a nation at peace with the U.S. China was miffed enough by this adventurist action that it declared war on the U.S. McKinley laid low and did not reciprocate, knowing China could not threaten the U.S. mainland. Operating by the seat of his pants again, he ultimately dispatched 6,300 troops and a number of gunboats to further interfere with the democratic nationalist movement, under the excuse of rescuing diplomats. In 1901, he signed the Boxer Indemnity Protocol, taking tribute from China in the amount of $25 million for the U.S. share, once again without Congressional approval. McKinley was now a big enough man that his second Open Door Note announced that he was personally inclined to commit U.S. resources to promote "permanent safety and peace to China." But his real interest was expressed privately: "May we not want a slice if [China] is divided."[86] Asian entanglement and colonization was the game that McKinley started, and others like Truman, Eisenhower, Lyndon Johnson, and Barack Obama expanded.

Theodore Roosevelt

One of his biographers cast Teddy Roosevelt's pursuit of arbitrary power in glowing terms. He wrote, "He had fought all his life for supreme power . . . that highest form of success which comes . . . to the man who does not shrink from power . . ." He had been a published author and historian, a New York State Assemblyman, a candidate for mayor of New York, all in his twenties. In his thirties he was a U.S. civil service commissioner, police commissioner of New York, assistant secretary of the navy department in McKinley's first term (at which position he lobbied for an expanded navy and for war with Spain), and colonel in the Rough Riders during the Spanish War. At forty he was elected Governor of New York. He served as vice president in McKinley's brief second term, after which

86. Boyer, *Oxford Companion*, 482; McDonald, *Presidency*, 395; Miller Center, *McKinley—Foreign Affairs*; Whitney, *Biographies*, 216; Ultimately, in a fit of guilt, the U.S. returned the tribute money to China, which used the money to educate Chinese students at American universities, so the money still got to the U.S. with the added benefit of tutoring Chinese in the American way of doing empire; Herring, *Colony to Superpower*, 321, 333–35.

he served out the rest of the three and a half years of McKinley's second term as president from 1901 to 1905, and a second presidential term of his own from 1905 to 1909. While the nation mourned McKinley's death by assassination, Teddy celebrated his accession to power privately. One historian wrote, "He laughed with glee at the power and place that had come to him."[87]

McKinley's chief of staff referred to Teddy as the "madman." He said that Roosevelt had "boundless ambition." A personal friend, the author Henry Adams, said of Teddy, "Theodore betrays his friends for his own ambition." While betrayal was the method for personal political progress, the goal of ambition was popularity and reelection. His financier friend, Charles Dawes, noted that "Everything . . . (is) subordinated to his desire to keep the approbation of the public." In psychological terms, he wanted to please, and to be loved. Unfortunately, he could not find a way to do that without subverting the rule of law. There were not a few who noticed this right away. One former Senator pointed out TR's "demagogical and dangerous tendencies." The Columbian ambassador to the U.S. spoke of his "impetuous and vehement character." The Philadelphia Record judged, "He is the most risky man the United States has had in the presidency."[88]

After finishing McKinley's second term of office, Teddy served four more years elected in his own right. Teddy believed he could decide not only how much power should be his, but how long he could be trusted to hold that power. Teddy was brazen in the attribution of extraordinary ability to himself. He overthrew the combined wisdom of a thousand founding patriots with one breezy pronouncement from his own throne room. He wrote, "I don't think any harm comes from the concentration of power in one man's hands." Teddy did add one caveat, "[as long as] the holder does not keep it for more than a certain, definite time." Then, he lectured, the president should "return to the people from which he sprang."[89] Apparently, it was up to Teddy to decide what that "certain, definite time" was. Teddy did that at the start of his 1905 term of office, the first term he was elected as president in his own right. He said he would not seek a third term. He would have changed his mind, certainly,

87. Morris, *Rex*, 7; Boyer, *Oxford Companion*, 677; Healy, *Cult of the Presidency*, 58.

88. Crenson and Ginsberg, *Presidential Power*, 125–26; Morris, *Rex*, 91, 216, 220, 238, 268, 276.

89. Healy, *Cult of the Presidency*, 58.

for "nine tenths of him wanted to run again," but he wanted to preserve the appearance of being "a disinterested public servant." But Teddy thirsted for more time in office than those seven and a half years. He believed there was a reason why he should continue in power. He finally lost interest in being disinterested and ran again in 1912 for a third term, which he lost.[90]

Early on, TR fleshed out his notions about the place of African Americans in American society. He charged a commission to explore the idea of wholesale transportation of blacks to the Philippines. Teddy asserted that blacks were "two hundred thousand years behind" whites in evolutionary growth.[91] Ironically, he started out his term in 1901 a hero to blacks by becoming the first president to entertain a black man, Booker T. Washington, in the White House. This helped him with election in his own right in 1904, as he needed the black vote.

Teddy had charted a big course for the nation in his mind. As vice president, he had announced that the dawning era would be "a new century big with the fate of mighty nations." He wanted the United States to be the mightiest of the mighty. He asked, "Is America a weakling to shrink from the world? No . . . Our nation . . . rejoices as a strong man to run a race." Teddy had been a weakling as a boy and overcame it by constant doses of manly exercise, called "exertion." He wanted America and its government to grow hairs on its weak-willed, and internationally neutralist chest.[92]

Only one of the agenda items mentioned in TR's first message was enacted, a permanent Census Bureau. Teddy succeeded in enacting this in the American republic while the folk hero David got in hot water trying to enact it in the republic of ancient Israel. Getting this legislation passed laid the foundation for an expanded permanent standing army of the sort that would allow the U.S. to fight gigantic wars abroad in the big, new century. Although TR could not get the U.S. into a European or Asiatic war so soon after the Spanish War, Woodrow Wilson was able to do so less than twenty years later. And sure enough, because of TR's legislative success, Wilson could effectively use a national draft for forced soldiering. Because of the census, Wilson would know exactly how many

90. Morris, *Rex*, 490, 527.
91. Ibid., 65, 70–71, 77, 198, 425.
92. Ibid., 8.

men were available for his war and where they could be found if they did not show up for service.[93]

It cannot be overemphasized how Teddy marginalized, diminished, or evaporated those cherished American institutions and agencies of representative democratic society—political party, state government, Congress, courts. In his many speeches he often forgot to mention those hallowed institutions. He promoted just one institution, the happy marriage of Roosevelt himself with his loving and admiring electorate. In a 1902 speech to the citizens of Massachusetts, he soared, "The government is us . . . you and me." In his 1905 inaugural, he did not use the word "I," but only "we" and "us," which he used a total of 71 times. And once the people gave him the election, he wrote that the president was "bound actively . . . to do all he could for the people . . . [he had a] duty to do anything the needs of the nation demanded." Propaganda was a personal matter with Teddy. How would his pupils learn unless they were taught by the master? He mused, "Iteration is necessary in order to hammer truths and principles I advocate into people's heads." He would merely teach the people what they should demand of him, and then he would do it for them![94]

Roosevelt had a phobia of Congressional power. Near the end of his second term he admitted, "I achieved results by appealing over the heads of the Senate and House leaders to the people." He initiated the "stewardship theory" of executive power and trashed the idea of enumerated/limited powers. He believed he could do whatever was not prohibited to him by the Constitution, rather than only those things that were specifically opened to him. On one occasion he crowed, "Is there any law that will prevent me from declaring Pelican Island a Federal Bird Reservation? Very well, then I so declare it." He candidly stated, "If I had the power to dissolve parliaments, and the will to override the constitution, I should be tempted to do the same." During his time, he demonstrated his legislative superiority over Congress by vetoing 42 bills and pocket vetoed nearly as many. He bragged almost royally, "I have the right to veto every bill." This new and absolute right to dictate the policy of the nation excited Teddy immensely. He brayed, "No other president ever enjoyed the presidency as I did.[95]

93. Ibid., 109.

94. Fagel, *Guide*, 69; Healy, *Cult of the Presidency*, 58, 61; Morris, *Rex*, 222.

95. Morris, *Rex*, 130, 432, 519; McDonald, *Presidency*, 294, 353; Flagel, *Guide*, 27–28, 140.

Teddy also pioneered the sly tactic of using executive orders to institute laws Congress was about to pass, so that he could get credit for the policy rather than Congress. For example, by executive order he gave veterans their benefits at the early age of sixty-two.[96] Teddy signed into law his Act for the Preservation of American Antiquities in 1906. This law allowed him to designate historic and pre-historic sites on federal ground without approval of Congress.

Teddy began running for election in his own right almost immediately after McKinley's death. He placed political loyalists into positions in his government, sending the Hill as many as thirty appointments per day. With this many worker bees doing his bidding, he had to crack the whip to keep them in place. He was not immune to scolding his appointees in public to properly humiliate them. One former aide wrote to former president Benjamin Harrison, "It is a horrible thing to realize that we have a bully in the White House." Roosevelt not only wanted to control his friends, but also his enemies, for whom he reserved harsher tactics yet. In fact, he pioneered the use of the Post Office to open and monitor the mail of his political opponents, Senators Tillman and Foraker. When Congress made noises about investigating Teddy's use of the Secret Service for illicit purposes, Teddy responded with insinuations that perhaps Congressmen had something to hide. Evidence had been mounting that TR had been using bodyguards for personal errands and for assisting with political campaigns.[97]

Teddy wanted all of America to know him intimately. He paraded himself before the public as much as he could. In fact, in April, 1903, Teddy traveled 14,000 miles around the country, visiting 150 towns, and giving 200 speeches, getting people ready for his race in 1904. One speaker at the 1904 Republican convention brayed, "Our President has taken the whole people into his confidence." Old Guard Republicans still worried a bit, however, about "the undignified spectacle of a President campaigning for his own office. He was supposed to put himself in the hands of party professionals." While McKinley had sat out two presidential campaigns at his home in Canton, Ohio, Teddy was campaigning from the White House, and all over the nation, and controlling every last detail of the convention, even editing speeches to be given there.[98]

96. Morris, *Rex*, 317.
97. Morris, *Rex*, 482, 547.
98. Ibid., 215, 328, 334.

Teddy demonstrated an easy willingness to take the place of the traditional institution of conflict resolution in American society, the courts, by stepping in to deal with issues before the law courts could do so. For example, he stepped in to negotiate a state-based mine worker issue in Pennsylvania. He had no constitutional or regulatory authority to do so. Teddy put 10,000 regular army troops on alert. He gave instructions to General Schofield to "pay no heed to any other authority, no heed to a writ from a judge or anything else excepting my command." This threat to invade the state of Pennsylvania was "the most aggressive presidential performance since the Civil War." Teddy took the side of the workers in negotiations. They were asking for an eight-hour work day and higher wages. When management demurred, Teddy threatened to have Schofield seize the mines and operate them as property of the federal government. Teddy's unabashed sense of concentration of power in the national government at the expense of the states came out in moments of giddy honesty. To Senator Joseph Bailey, he said "I don't give a damn for the Legislature of Texas."[99]

Liking his experience in Pennsylvania, Teddy used this precedent for presidential micromanagement of the economy to push for the establishment of a Department of Commerce and Labor. In order to grease the skids for this new operation, he suggested that a constitutional amendment be obtained if Congress did not think it had authority to set up the new department and endow it with new powers. In fact, corporations traditionally got their charters under state government, not the national government, and the nation had always understood that business corporations should be regulated by the states. Some would later suggest that TR understood in a way that the nation's founders did not the implications of commerce moving across state lines.[100] But in the days of the founders much of commerce moved not only beyond state lines, but beyond national lines, and still the framers did not think to regulate its production, rates, and transportation on a national level.

Teddy decided to regulate corporations from his office, but not to regulate them too closely, since many of them he counted on to pay his

99. Crenson and Ginsberg, *Presidential Power*, 127; Miller Center, *Roosevelt—Domestic Affairs* ; Healy, *Cult of the Presidency*, 59; Flagel, *Guide*, 69; Nelson, *Presidency*, 124; Morris, *Rex*, 66, 165, 490, 527;Later presidents would up the ante further and make peacetime expropriation of corporate property an actual fait accompli, once Teddy had first successfully gotten away with the mere suggestion of such a lawless act.

100. Flagel, *Guide*, 68; Morris, *Rex*, 422.

reelection costs. He picked out one of them, Northern Securities, a railroad combination resulting from the merger of Great Northern, Northern Pacific, and Union Pacific railroads, to make a half-hearted attack on. His own attorney general Knox suggested that if litigation against this great trust were successful, it would guarantee TR a second term. He would be seen as David stoning Goliath and it would propel his career as Goliath's death had propelled David's. He could then go easy on other corporations, and all would be good. Eventually, the court ruled against Goliath, and TR got his reelection. The big corporations clearly understood Teddy would be leaving them alone and so decided to reward him with a second term of office. For example, Standard Oil donated the fabulous sum (in those days) of $100,000 to his campaign. Two of three corporate barons involved in the Northern Securities merger whose knuckles TR had rapped in court still gave huge sums of money to him, an indication that his trust-busting had not harmed them much personally. Teddy let E. H. Harriman know he would be softening his future course regarding railroad rate reform, as long as Harriman would donate sufficient money in New York State to carry the day for Teddy and other Republican candidates there in 1904. In fact, Teddy notoriously flip-flopped back and forth between the public interest in muckraking and the private interest in money making, admirably demonstrating the "versatility of his principles."[101]

In order to secure his administration a majority on the Supreme Court, and thus secure long life for his legislative initiatives, Teddy had nominated a new judge, Oliver Wendell Holmes, Jr. Holmes could be counted on to support the new Republican party colonial empire and hopefully Teddy's domestic policies as well. In fact, on one occasion Teddy suggested that the judicial branch was a sort of "branchlet of the legislative" power, which power TR felt was best wielded, in turn, by the executive department. The judiciary's job was to interpret laws in the light of current conveniences and needs. Teddy's choices for the bench were drawn from those he felt would be respectful of the President's wishes, that is, those who would "keep in mind also . . . relations with . . . fellow statesmen . . . in other branches of the government." Holmes believed that the Constitution was whatever the people, or in reality, their leaders, wanted it to be, something he called "the felt necessities of the time." When Holmes wrote against Teddy's position on the Northern Securities

101. Morris, *Rex*, 59, 88, 90, 92, 355, 357, 359, 444.

case, Teddy fumed that Holmes had not acted like "a party man." Perhaps Holmes had noticed that Teddy rarely consulted the party before making decisions either.[102]

The president came to believe that the earlier Sherman Act and the Anti-Rebate Law were insufficient. Those two laws only allowed the Bureau of Corporations to study and monitor business malfeasance, but not to control or stop it. He wanted an Interstate Commerce Commission (ICC), one that would at least be a weak regulatory commission. It would not fix rates, but rather just set a maximum rate in cases of dispute. At first, he had proposed to undermine judicial review of individual rate cases and give it instead to an agency of the executive branch. When the Congress objected to this usurpation of power, he went on a speaking tour throughout the western states appealing over the heads of the people's representatives. He tried to teach the people what they should demand of him. But in the end he listened to the corporate barons, who taught him what their needs were, and their needs prevailed. They wanted a check on presidential power to regulate their livelihoods and they knew the courts could take years to get to cases. TR got business on board supporting his legislation when he agreed it would be the job of the courts rather than the executive branch to settle actual disputes, if and when the commission overstepped its bounds. This gave "broad review" authority to the courts, and it could be used to slow down regulation to a snail's pace. Teddy signed the Hepburn Act creating the ICC and allowing it to regulate shipping rates on railroads and examine financial records.[103]

Teddy also wanted other economic regulation: national child labor legislation, legislation establishing sanitary standards for food, and government supervision of insurance corporations. All of these were currently provided for under the sovereign police power of the states, and not the national government. Teddy knew this, for as governor of New York he had exercised the state police power to make laws in these areas. But now he wanted to usurp the power he once felt was lawfully exercised on the state level, and do it on the national level. In 1906, he succeeded in pushing through the Pure Food and Drug Act and the Meat Inspection Act. He also pushed through the Child Labor Act of 1908 for the District of Columbia. In addition, he won a workman's compensation law

102. Ibid., 129–30, 316, 542.

103. Miller Center, *Roosevelt—Domestic Affairs*; Crenson and Ginsberg, *Presidential Power*, 129; Morris, *Rex*, 423, 433, 443, 445.

for federal employees, which provided for taxpayer-funded liability for negligence-related job accidents occurring under the watch of agencies and common carriers. This Employers Liability Act of 1906, however, was struck down by the Supreme Court because it applied to intrastate corporations as well as interstate ones, thus infringing on states' rights. Teddy trekked further into the realm of state regulatory prerogative by demanding that Congress act on his proposals for federal inheritance and income taxes, national incorporation of interstate businesses, and wider application of the eight-hour workday. These and other demands contained in his last annual message of December 2008 constituted "so imperious a call for enhanced executive authority that it amounted to a condemnation of the doctrine of checks and balances."[104]

In his first term, Roosevelt carried out an agenda related to the state militias in peacetime beyond even what McKinley felt could be gotten away with during wartime. McKinley had acted merely to appoint state militia officers, but Teddy signed a bill in 1903 authorizing the president to entirely dissolve state guard units into the regular army at times of emergency. In 1904, Teddy moved the forest service from the interior department to the agriculture department, giving it more power to marginalize state decision-making in the matter of natural resources.[105]

In 1907, near the end of Teddy's second term, Congress passed a law relating to six states (Oregon, Washington, Idaho, Montana, Colorado, and Wyoming), which prohibited the federal government from setting aside national parks or wilderness areas "except by act of Congress." Over the course of his administration he had created five national parks, sixteen national monuments, twenty federal irrigation projects, thirteen new national forests, and sixteen federal bird refuges. He had expanded federal woodland by thirty-three percent in his first term alone. He also obtained control of grazing licenses, hydroelectric leases, and police summonses in the national parks. The Congress clearly had had enough of his one-man-rule and stood up to him in the same way a later Congress stood up to Richard Nixon, by putting legislative shackles on his feet. But Teddy blithely took the shackles off his feet and felt warm inside about doing so. Before getting credit for signing this anti-tyranny law, Roosevelt overturned it entirely by issuing presidential decrees creating

104. Morris, *Rex*, 423, 448, 506, 511, 541.

105. Crenson and Ginsberg, *Presidential Power*, 247; Miller Center, *Roosevelt—Domestic Affairs*.

21 preserves in those same six states and enlarging preserves in others, adding twenty million acres to the federal domain. There was no basis in law for what he did except the power of his own right hand and the use of his manly imagination.[106]

Teddy believed war nurtured the human spirit. He said, "No triumph of peace is quite so great as the supreme triumphs of war." As president, he directed Elihu Root, currently serving both as his secretary of state and secretary of war, to hire a general staff to plan for and conduct future wars. Teddy obtained authorization for two new battleships and two new cruisers as a result of his first message to Congress. Under McKinley, the U.S. navy was fifth in the world. By the end of TR's first term it was third, and by the end of his second term the nation had moved up to second. Teddy saw the Philippines as a captive market for American exports, in part by means of a forced economic reciprocity treaty like the one with Cuba. He also saw it as a good place to house a forward navy. Furthermore, he also could see good use for an expanded navy in Panama: "We must build the Isthmian Canal . . . which will enable us to have our way in deciding the destiny of the oceans of the east and the west." Teddy expanded the original Federalist notion of internal improvements on American soil to internal improvements on the soils of other nations in the Americas. He asserted, "This canal cannot be built by private enterprise, or by any other nation than our own; therefore it must be built by the United States." In the matter of the best place to build the canal, TR trumped the wishes of Congress, who had voted by a plurality of 308 to 2 in favor of Nicaragua. Teddy successfully pushed through Panama as the site.[107]

Teddy's delight in suppressing the darkened masses of his own nation as well as the world came out once again during the civil war between the Philippine people and their new American colonial master. He made it clear that he felt free speech was suspended stateside during America's foreign wars, although nowhere in the Constitution was such a limitation on speech mentioned. He said, "Once the country is at war, the man who fails to support it with all possible heartiness comes perilously near being a traitor." The Constitution, on the other hand, limited treason to only two conditions: "Treason against the United States shall consist only in levying war against them [the states], or in adhering to

---

106. Crenson and Ginsberg, *Presidential Power*, 131; Morris, *Rex*, 221, 227, 486–87, 519, 554.

107. Whitney, *Biographies*, 222; Morris, *Rex*, 23–26, 76, 83, 87, 180, 302, 455, 548.

their enemies, giving them aid and comfort (Article III, Section 3)." The Philippine people had certainly never been declared the enemies of any of the American states, so stateside citizens speaking in favor of Philippine independence from the U.S. could not be deemed treasonous by any stretch of the imagination. But TR's imagination was unique to himself, and he had no trouble stretching it to cover any disagreement with his exalted point of view. TR set the lawless example that Woodrow Wilson and Franklin Roosevelt happily followed when they cooked up treason charges against anti-war citizens in the twentieth century.[108]

Teddy pioneered the use of "executive agreements" in place of treaties. According to the Constitution, treaties needed approval by the Senate, but when Teddy made an executive agreement, he only had to get his left hand to agree with his right hand. While Teddy was deferential to the Senate in his first term, in his second term he used such unilateral agreements in major international matters and thus subverted the Constitution in foreign affairs. He used executive agreements to deal with the Dominican Republic's debt problems; to support Japan in establishing a military protectorate in Korea; to restrict Japanese immigration to the U.S.; to force the Open Door policy on China; and to recognize Japan's "special interests" in China. This last set a precedent for asserting both U.S. and European hegemonic spheres of influence after the great world wars.[109]

It might also be said of Teddy that not only did he not seek the consent of the people or of Congress, he often operated in foreign affairs in complete secrecy, moving players about on his chess board in a private game only he and his intimates knew about. For example, with the help of his successor in the presidency, William Taft, he made secret treaties with Japan in 1905 and 1908, which the public did not learn about for twenty years. These secret treaties gave Japan a free hand in Korea and violated the U.S.-Korea treaty of 1882. Root expressed the idea to Teddy that they perhaps ought to inform the Congress of the second treaty. Teddy responded, "Why invite the expression of views with which we may not agree?"[110] Indeed, the people's representatives might be less inclined than he to agree that the president had the power to unilaterally abrogate lawfully enacted treaties. No better or more revelatory statement of the

---

108. Morley, *Freedom and Federalism*, 148; Article III, Section 3, Paragraph 1.

109. McDonald, *Presidency*, 389–90; Nelson, *Presidency*, 124.

110. Herring, *Colony to Superpower*, 362.

thinking of a usurper and tyrant operating illegally in secret can be made than Teddy's admission.

Rather than respect Latin American national independence, Teddy enunciated a doctrine of preemptive control and even violence and invasion directed at Latin nations whenever they got into economic hot water. If they could not pay their debts to European nations, those nations might conceivably be tempted to make threats about forcefully collecting those debts. This would threaten U.S. hegemony over the hemisphere, and Teddy could not tolerate that. Teddy's statement became known as the Roosevelt corollary to the Monroe Doctrine. For example, in 1906 Teddy dispatched warships to Cuba to deal with rebellion there. Senator Foraker wrote, "Under our treaty with Cuba . . . Congressional approval was required before troops could be sent and local authority usurped." Teddy's banking friends wanted the troops there to guard the island's treasury to ensure Cuba stayed solvent.[111]

Teddy evidenced a "spectacular" show of bravado and personal manliness in Panama when he cleared out political and physical debris which had inhibited the American building of a cross-continent canal there. That debris consisted partly in the fact that Columbia exercised control over Panama as one of its provinces, and the Columbian Congress did not want the project to happen. Teddy sent warships and a landing party to Panama to overthrow the legitimate Columbian government there. Teddy later reminisced about the incident: "I took the canal zone without consulting the cabinet." He might have added that he did not consult the Congress, or the people either. Later, Roosevelt mused, "There was much accusation about my having acted in an unconstitutional manner . . ." by violating Columbian sovereignty.[112]

Near the end of his second term, Teddy pulled perhaps the most grotesque and provocative stunt the world to that point had ever seen from a megalomaniacal tyrant. In December, 1907, he sent a fleet of sixteen American battle ships on a ticker-tape military parade around the world trying to provoke war somewhere. The fleet's voyage was called "a sheer pageant of power." In the process, Teddy wasted untold amounts of fossil fuels and gave the lie to his conservationist self-image. After this provocative antic as a lame duck president, Teddy went on beating the drums of war for another decade or so, trying to get Woodrow Wilson to

---

111. Herring, *Colony to Superpower*, 371; Morris, *Rex*, 201, 459, 461.
112. Healy, *Cult of the Presidency*, 59; Flagel, *Guide*, 207.

allow him to lead a group of volunteers into World War I and charge up some German or French hill.

Teddy was a proud tyrant. He said, "I have not cared a rap for the criticisms of those who spoke of my 'usurpation of power' . . . I believe . . . (in) a strong central executive, and wherever I could establish a precedent for strength in the executive . . . I have felt . . . that my action was right in itself . . . I was establishing a precedent of value." While still president, he reminded his people, "I enjoy the White House; I greatly enjoy the exercise of power."[113]

William H. Taft

William Howard Taft was known for his political docility and loyalty. He was ambitious, gentlemanly, quietly manipulative, and ultimately politically astute. He became Teddy's best friend, did Teddy's bidding, and then got the king-maker's support for the presidency when Teddy got cold feet about trying for lifetime presidency himself. Before he was president, Taft was Teddy's Solicitor General (where he expanded presidential power by initiating the legal doctrine of mass pardons or amnesty), Governor of the Philippines, and Secretary of War. He was Teddy's yes-man, saying things like "I agree heartily and earnestly (with) . . . Roosevelt's policies"; "He and I view public questions exactly alike." In fact, he viewed many things very differently than Teddy, and that became clear after he became president. He made career decisions and political statements that would advance him to higher office the most quickly. After his one term presidency, which lasted from 1909 to 1913, he became Chief Justice of the Supreme Court of the United States, which was his ultimate goal. He was "as determined as McKinley and Roosevelt had been in getting his way."[114]

Taft presented the country with a judicial model of executive branch administration. He ruled like a chief justice, writing his own speeches without much political advice aimed at keeping him out of trouble. He opened his mouth too far and made political gaffes. He flip-flopped on his soft promise to keep Roosevelt's cabinet in place. He disliked partisanship, picked several Democrats for his cabinet, and made an effort to take partisanship out of the 1910 census employment process. Nonetheless,

113. Whitney, *Biographies*, 231; Morris, *Rex*, 540.

114. McDonald, *Presidency*, 307; Miller Center, *Taft—Life After the Presidency*; Gould, *Taft*, 5, 42.

he could hold a grudge and withheld some patronage appointments from rebellious Republicans as well. He was criticized for "slowness" to do government business, and ultimately admitted some laziness, a tendency to procrastinate, and liking to socialize too much. He quit work early, played a lot of golf, cruised around town in a motorcar, and took long vacations.[115]

Taft was a Unitarian, meaning he expressed doubts about the divinity of Jesus. One evangelical editor wrote, "Think of the United States with a President who does not believe that Jesus was the son of God, but looks upon our immaculate Savior as a common bastard and low cunning imposter." Taft alarmed evangelicals later when he opposed a measure to prohibit the shipment of alcohol to states which had gone dry by local law. He was not for political propaganda any more than he was for pushing conventional church wisdom. Although he benefitted from a campaign biography when running in 1908, he made it clear, "I don't want any forced or manufactured sentiment in my favor."[116]

Once Taft was free of Teddy's supervisory control and sat down in the seat of executive power, Taft expressed convictions that departed from those expected of him by the previous commander in chief. Taft, for example, did not subscribe to unrestricted executive power, like Teddy. He wrote, "The people have not any of them given into the hands of any one the mandate to speak for them peculiarly as the people's representative." Also, "Ascribing an undefined residium of power to the President is an unsafe doctrine . . . it might lead under emergencies to . . . irremediable injustice to private right." Taking direct aim at his old friend Teddy, he said "[The President] is [not] to play the part of a universal Providence and set all things right." Taft is bruised and battered by court party historians because he didn't want to make law from the executive branch, but just to administer law made by Congress. They do not like that he told the American people that presidents "cannot create good times . . . cannot make the rain to fall, the sun to shine, or the crops to grow." As a fairly strict constructionist of the law, Taft believed the Constitution ought to be consulted before radical action taken. He disapproved of Teddy's usurpation of the power to take state lands for national preserves and to exercise broad power over navigable rivers for hydroelectric power and

115. Gould, *Taft*, 13, 24, 26, 35, 40, 43, 48, 63, 93, 100, 118, 209.

116. Ibid., 15, 18, 45, 206.

irrigation projects. He believed the president needed legislative approval for this.[117]

During the campaign, Taft had said he would pursue limited campaign contribution disclosure. He defended the use of injunctions against the activities of organized labor. He wanted to push conservation, economy in government, and protection of rail workers. He also floated up a plan for "postal savings banks" as an alternative to William Jennings Bryan's call for government guarantee of bank deposits. The postal banks would allow poor people, especially new immigrants, to put money in a government-backed savings banks. Taft made good on this promise and signed such a bill into law. His economizing proposals included absolute cuts in the navy and army, but his own navy secretary lobbied Congress successfully to get two new battleships. He also wanted to implement a plan to convert some southern Democrats to the Republican party by playing to white prejudice. He ultimately phased out some black office holders to appease segregationists and uphold states' rights. On the other hand, he vetoed an immigration bill requiring a literacy test for citizenship, and Congress was unable to override it.[118]

During his inaugural address, Taft announced he would submit proposals for amendments to the Constitution to regulate trusts and interstate commerce, since, apparently, he did not feel existing clauses gave sufficient authority. Thus, Taft was, in one sense, an executive power guy in the overall tradition of Cleveland, McKinley, and Teddy Roosevelt, especially in his desire to expand the national and executive commitment to regulating the economy. But unlike them, he wanted to poll the will of the people and political parties before doing that. Another significant way Taft contributed to the present tyranny of the executive branch was by urging an amendment to the Constitution, authorizing an income tax. He said, "I do favor the imposition of an income tax." His rationale for the income tax was that it was needed to balance Congress's propensity toward spending. Taft sensed the need for more revenue during his own administration, as the administration operated in 1912 with a $22 million annual deficit, and the overall national deficit ballooned to $1.1 billion. Since the Supreme Court had said an income tax was unconstitutional, Taft supported a joint resolution of Congress to start the process

117. Healy, *Cult of the Presidency*, 8, 62;Miller Center, *Taft—Domestic Affairs*; Crenson and Ginsberg, *Presidential Power*, 131; Gould, *Taft*, 65–66.

118. Gould, *Taft*, 13, 20, 31, 33, 43, 47–48, 50, 95, 101, 123, 126, 128, 131, 207.

of amending the Constitution. His proposal finally became law as the Sixteenth Amendment during his successor Woodrow Wilson's term. When the amendment passed, it gave the national government virtually unlimited access to funds from the citizenry.[119]

Taft also supported the Seventeenth Amendment, which took the election of senators out of the hands of state legislatures. This allowed tyranny-leaning senators to seduce their constituents directly by means of outrageous political promises that the legislatures would have easily seen through. Taft also tried to take the traditional power of budget-making from Congress, which Congress duly rejected.[120] Congress was steadfast that cabinet department submit their financial needs estimates directly to Congressional appropriations committees rather than to the president.[121]

As president of the United States, Taft wanted to leave his mark on tariff laws, like presidents before him. He called Congress into special session to reduce rates from the McKinley/Dingley rates set in 1897, which he had promised to do during the campaign. But he ended up flip-flopping after he ran into opposition from business interests and because he needed income to help reduce the budget shortfall. Teddy had left him a budget deficit of $57 million in 1908, and the deficit rose to $89 million in 1909. In 1909 he signed the Payne-Aldrich bill, which had 847 amendments/exemptions penned into it. Observers were not sure whether there were more increases in tariffs, or decreases. An argument could be made for either side. This piece of legislation bolstered the national treasury, and therefore its institutional capacity, not only by means of its strong tariff revenue structure, but also by means of a two percent tax on net corporate income. It also kept consumer prices high and Taft reaped much of the blame for signing it.[122]

As president, Taft signed laws giving the national government more power to regulate the economy. He signed the Mann-Elkins Act of 1910, giving the Interstate Commerce Commission power to regulate telephones, telegraphs, and radio. He split the Department of Commerce and Labor into two cabinet-level departments to give more institutional clout to regulation of the economy. He also called a special session of Congress

119. Morley, *Freedom and Federalism*, 102; Gould, *Taft*, 56; Whitney, *Biographies*, 236, 238.

120. Miller Center, *Taft—Domestic Affairs*; Herring, *Colony to Superpower*, 289;.

121. McDonald, *Presidency*, 331.

122. Boyer, *Oxford Companion*, 760; Miller Center, *Taft—Impact and Legacy*; Nelson, *Presidency*, 27; Gould, *Taft*, 9, 50, 58, 123; Whitney, *Biographies*, 236.

to deal with Canadian trade reciprocity, which passed in July, 1911. He pushed many more successful anti-trust suits than the "trust-buster" Teddy Roosevelt. For example, Teddy had backed away from prosecuting International Harvester in 1907, but Taft went ahead against Standard Oil and American Tobacco.[123]

Taft appointed the first woman to head a federal bureau, Julia Lathrop. She headed up the Children's Bureau dealing with child labor problems beginning in 1912. His White House staff stood at eighty in 1909, most of them clerks and stenographers. He also appointed six justices to the Supreme Court. Disposing of any pretention that the judiciary should not be politically motivated, he quipped, "Damn you, if any of you die, I'll disown you." His picks made the court conservative for the next twenty-five years.[124]

Taft could not resist the temptation to travel in support of his reelection bid in 1912. His opponents were Teddy Roosevelt, who was finally now running for a third term, and Woodrow Wilson. He couldn't countenance campaigning in the election year itself, but took care of that little problem by going on an extensive traveling tour around the country in 1911, the "longest presidential tour up to that time." He spoke on "nonpartisan topics." Taft also continued the precedent that Teddy had set for traveling out of the U.S. while sitting as president. Like Teddy, he traveled to Panama to inspect the nation's newest colony, the Canal Zone. After losing the election, finishing third to Woodrow Wilson and Teddy Roosevelt, Taft came out in favor of a limit of one six year term for presidential office. Of Teddy, Taft said, "One who so lightly regards constitutional principles . . . and who has so misunderstood what liberty regulated by law is, could not safely be entrusted with successive Presidential terms. I say this sorrowfully, but I say it with the full conviction of its truth." He spoke disgustedly of Teddy's 1912 campaign as like those of "the leaders of religious cults who promote things over their followers by any sort of physical manipulation and deception." He mentioned "unscrupulous demagogues," "political emotionalists," and "a class of fanatical enthusiasts seeking short cuts" when referring to the new progressive candidates of both the Democrat and Bull Moose parties.[125]

123. Miller Center, *Taft – Domestic Affairs*; Gould, *Taft*, 144, 153, 165.

124. Gould, *Taft*, 121–22, 130, 134.

125. Ibid., 139, 148, 157, 163, 174, 177, 191, 202–3.

In foreign relations, Taft was anti-imperialism. He had been against the annexation of the Philippines, and was not much interested in European affairs. One author states, "Taft's instinctive tactic was to draft a note . . . rather than to mobilize a flotilla." This was especially true since the country was running a deficit. Interestingly, Taft had had as much foreign experience as any president since John Quincy Adams, due to his delight in foreign travel and his appointments during Roosevelt's terms. Taft said he had no interest in a course "which would prompt us for purposes of exploitation and gain to invade another country and involve ourselves in a war the extent of which we could not realize, and sacrifice thousands of lives and millions of treasure." One historian comments, "Taft's readiness to observe the constitutional limits on a president in foreign policy seems refreshing a century after his term in office."[126]

Taft pushed international arbitration for any kind of dispute between nations. Teddy had supported such arbitration as long as it gave the president plenty of room for war. Arbitration should not be binding, Roosevelt felt, if dealing with any vital national issue, or an issue of national honor, a code phrase for offense to the nation's manly leader. Of Teddy, Taft said, "He prefers the battle axe."[127]

Taft preferred to use the back door avenue to political hegemony, the economic carrot, rather than the military stick. He was noted for what was called "dollar diplomacy," a nice way of saying economic exploitation and control. Such diplomacy involved the encouragement of U.S. investment and loans in South and Central America, the Caribbean, and the Far East. He used government diplomatic officials to promote U.S. exports to the countries they were sent to. Those exports included military hardware. He encouraged U.S. banks to make loans to Central American countries like Honduras to pay off European creditors, and even used grants to help them switch their financial allegiance to the U.S.[128] The loans would then provide leverage for U.S. policy experts to impose American-style monetary, tax, tariff, and budget policies.

In Nicaragua, Taft used U.S. military power to stabilize the situation in America's favor. Taft allowed U.S. bankers to give the government there cash in return for control of the National Bank of Nicaragua and 51 percent ownership of the nation's railroads. When a rebellion arose, Taft sent

---

126. Ibid., 4, 25, 79, 81, 83, 208, 214.

127. Ibid., 160–61.

128. Miller Center, *Taft—Foreign Affairs*; Herring, *Colony to Superpower*, 373.

2,700 Marines to snuf it out, and left a contingent of troops to remind the little nation of U.S. intentions. Taft ultimately sent troops into six countries, and his occupation of Nicaragua lasted until 1933, effectively establishing a protectorate there. Taft negotiated a treaty with Nicaragua just before he left office, giving the nation $3 billion for a naval base and canal rights, but the treaty was not ratified until 1916.[129]

Taft was even more pushy about challenging existing economic power relationships in Asia than Teddy had been. He tried to gain access to Asian markets by achieving joint international ownership of railroads in China through U.S. financing of rail construction in Manchuria, but failed. This effort alienated both Japan and Russia.[130]

Taft ordered 20,000 troops to the Mexican border, where they were poised to enter and protect U.S. investments during an unstable political time there. When Congress expressed its displeasure, Taft backed off. This was perhaps one of the last times a U.S. president deferred to the will of the people's representatives in international relations. Taft believed that, overall, he had kept the U.S. out of war by "keep(ing) the army out of these disturbances in Central America." He wrote, "I am very sure that the course of self-restraint the administration has pursued in respect to Mexico will vindicate itself in the pages of history."[131]

129 Morley, *Freedom and Federalism*, 119; McDonald, *Presidency*, 396.

130. Herring, *Colony to Superpower*, 376; Nelson, *Presidency*, 127–28.

131. Miller Center, *Taft—Foreign Affairs*; Gould, *Taft*, 152, 194–95.

5

The World War Era Presidents

Democrat party presidents during the first half of the twentieth century took over the Republican program of international conquest, by extending the program beyond the Caribbean and Pacific islands to Europe and the Middle East. In doing so, they abandoned the return to neutralism bequeathed to the nation by two-term Democrat president Cleveland, and also abandoned all pretense of guarding the law and the interests of the people. They became unalterably committed to protecting the interests of favored segments of the American electorate and to satisfying their own lust for power in the process.

Democrat presidents during the period of the two world wars became obsessed with projecting an image of being mentally and physically competent, all the while hiding extraordinarily debilitating medical conditions that would have disqualified them from continuing in the job had the people known. So domineering and insecure in personality were they that they succumbed to the temptation to use emergency power to punish those who disagreed with them politically, by suppressing speech and assembly. Taking emergency power not only in wartime, but in peacetime, they refused to give it up after the emergencies had passed by. They regulated or nationalized private industry like Soviet commissars.

Woodrow Wilson initiated American entanglement in Europe for the first time, and Franklin Roosevelt established American hegemony there, after spilling the blood of hundreds of thousands and treasure of a nation of 131 million people who had little say in what he was doing. For this, the World War II generation is called "the greatest generation" by court historians. This accolade is meant to cover up the fact they were perhaps the most gullible, disinterested, and socially dissolute generation the American republic had ever known to that point.

The world war presidents adopted the methods of ancient tyrant despots by exiling internal populations, taking tribute of conquered nations, forcing alliances on tributary nations, and conducting policy-making in secret, elaborating new constitutional theories to justify their depredations. Republican presidents coming into power between the two world wars enjoyed much of the idolatry, used some of the methods, and tilted toward many of the policies embraced by the two Democrats they were sandwiched between.

Woodrow Wilson

Woodrow Wilson was the earthquake that shook the American political foundation to its core. He single-handedly un-tethered the United States from its anchor in the rule of law and set it swirling about on a sea of crude despotism, at least for his lengthy term of office. There have been few presidents before or since who wielded such a panoply of the tools of tyranny, all the while convincing the citizenry and biographers that he was good for America. Wilson tutored those who came after him in the wiles and guiles of the accumulation of power. He was an insatiable glory-hound. In many ways he resembled the Great King rulers of the ancient world who craved and abused power, co-opted religion into the service of his ambition, and hurt many people.

Those who knew Wilson did not hesitate to call him a "liar" and a "demagogue." For example, he announced that he was descended from "old Revolutionary stock." The press corrected him and reminded him that his four grandparents had all been born in the British Isles. Grover Cleveland called him "volatile" and "vindictive." He was noted for ego-tism, inability to accept criticism, and stubbornness. Much of his ability to seduce the American people intellectually came from his academic training, which he used to propound a quack political science that junked many of the constitutional values Americans and their leaders held sa-cred before him. Even while at Princeton, he began to denounce his op-ponents on the faculty as "traitors," using the language he would later direct at opponents in the political arena and at average Americans.[1]

---

1. Fleming, *Illusion*, 3, 41c.

Wilson was a top-drawer propagandist. He pioneered the practice of presidential publicity hounding and spin-doctoring. He used deceit, disinformation, and political dissembling to achieve his ends. He wanted to use his education to inspire what he called "a great movement of opinion," and to "interpret great events to the world." In other words, he wanted to disseminate propaganda on the world scene, not just the national scene. This ambition led him to be one of the greatest political flip-floppers of all time. His critics said that anyone who followed Wilson down a political path was almost certain to meet him coming in the opposite direction. Teddy Roosevelt, for example, was sure that Wilson had changed his mind about almost every important political issue. For example, at first he promised to stay out of war, and then led the nation into war. At first he praised the constitutional amendment process as the way to produce change in the system, and then junked that method in favor of autocratic decrees. He changed from a conservative, pro-business, pro-trust, anti-union position to a liberal, pro-union position. He opposed conscription during the reelection campaign, then embraced it. He promised the nation "full information" about the nation's affairs, and then imposed an iron curtain of secrecy and disinformation about the war.[2]

Wilson enrolled in law school, but he hated the tedious, laborious study of law, withdrawing from University of Virginia law school after a year. Like Teddy Roosevelt, he thought it "monotonous," and compared it to Prussian-style legalism. Accordingly, Wilson persuaded the law school, and also the government affairs graduate program he enrolled in later, to give him degrees without completing requirements that others had to go through.[3]

As a political scientist, Wilson praised the British ministerial system, whereby the Prime Minister not only administered the laws, but initiated the laws. Wilson seemed to forget about the other two branches of the national government when he wrote: "[The President's] is the only national voice in our affairs." He projected his own fantasy upon the entire citizenry and believed they wanted what he wanted: "[The people's] instinct is for unified action and it craves a single leader." The President was free to use force during emergencies like wartime, but he ought to be

2. Ibid., 4, 13, 19.

3. Napolitano, *Theodore and Woodrow*, xvi; Whitney, *Biographies*, 242–43.

so free at all times: "[The President's] office is anything he had the sagacity and force to make it."[4]

Such a president must have "the attitude of originator of policies." The national executive branch would be "the people's direct and exclusive link to the single man in the white House as their only national representative." He wrote that the power of the President "was very absolute." The greatness of the office would manifest to all and give him "liberty . . . to be as big a man as he can." In his book *The State* he wrote that "government does now whatever experience permits or the times demand." He meant, essentially, that government must give a tyrant plenty of room to operate. [5]

An aristocratic snob, he was prejudiced against blacks and also against lower and middle class whites. He wrote, "We want one class of persons to have a liberal education, and we want another class of persons, a very much larger class of necessity in every society, to forgo the privilege of a liberal education and fit themselves to perform specific difficult manual tasks." It is instructive that Wilson wanted to dumb down a certain portion of the citizenry. This new class could be more easily manipulated by means of their ignorant passions to support an assault on the Constitution and the rule of law. He wrote that the uneducated masses "are much readier to receive a half truth which they can promptly understand than a whole truth which has too many sides to be seen all at once. The competent leader of men . . . supplies the power; others supply only the materials upon which that power operates . . . it is the power which dictates, dominates; the materials yield. Men are as clay in the hands of the consummate leader." No clearer boast of intent to tyranny could perhaps ever have been written.[6]

Woodrow Wilson was a predestination Presbyterian, which allowed him to see God's specific purpose fulfilled in every victory or defeat. Earlier in his life, he worried that "I have done almost nothing for the Savior's Cause here below." He went to prayer meetings every Wednesday, and read the Bible nightly. The French President Clemenceau later said of him, "He thinks he is another Jesus Christ come upon the earth to reform men." In fact, Britain's Lloyd George saw Wilson's great war as the first

4. McDonald, *Presidency*, 331; Genovese, *Power*, 119.

5. Healy, *Cult of the Presidency*, 55; Herring, *Colony to Superpower*, 381; Genovese, *Power*, 118–19; Clement, *Wilson*, 45.

6. Napolitano, *Theodore and Woodrow*, 23, 77.

great American crusade against "the poor European heathen." Back at home, Wilson issued an executive order for American's to work and fight as little as possible on Sunday, to show "due regard for the Divine will."[7]

Privately, Wilson told the Democratic national chairman, who had made an appointment with him to talk about patronage appointments, "Before we proceed, I wish it clearly understood that I owe you nothing. Remember that God ordained that I should be the next President of the United States." Even Herbert Croly, the apostle of government central-ism, wrote "Mr. Wilson . . . write(s) only upon brass, and for nothing shorter than a millennium," since he presented all his programs in the packaging of a great moral crusade.[8]

Wilson's domestic religious politics, like his international religion, however, were not exactly mainstream Bible. During the first inaugural speech, Wilson took direct aim at the early Israelite system of local liber-tarian government characteristic of the period of Judges. Wilson chided, "Our thought has been 'Let every man look out for himself . . .'"[9] He was a biblical Saul pushing for strong kingship to take the place of individual liberty.

Previously, Presidents sent only written messages to Congress, rath-er than communicate in person. Jefferson had called for the delivering of messages to Congress in written form and this had been followed until the time of Wilson. One Senator called Wilson's breaking of republican tradition a "cheap and tawdry imitation of English royalty." Wilson also held the first Presidential press conference ever. Soon enough, reporters saw Wilson as dictatorial in his control of the news.[10]

Wilson made unprecedented direct appeals to the public and to Congress to influence and control the legislative process. He went per-sonally to the Capitol to address Congress and made many other public speeches. One historian writes, "No president had ever appealed so open-ly to public opinion to put pressure on a sitting Congress as Wilson did." Wilson called Congress into special session soon after his election to have them hear the details of his tariff program, as if that agenda constituted the kind of emergency basis that the Constitution wording, "on extra

7. Flagel, *Guide*, 49–50.

8. McDonald, *Presidency*, 359–60.

9. Whitney, *Biographies*, 247.

10. Healy, *Cult of the Presidency*, 63; Nelson, *Presidency*, 129; Genovese, *Power*, 119–20; McDonald, *Presidency*, 437.

Ordinary occasions," suggested. (Article I, Section 3). He went to the Capitol to meet with Democratic members of the Senate finance committee in April, 1913. He later set up joint sessions on banking and trusts in 1913 and 1914. He also called another joint special session in 1916 to ramrod through an eight-hour day for railroad workers. In fact, Wilson was the first president to bring a "clear agenda" to the presidency. He said at this time that the president should not have to "hail . . . congress from some island of jealous power . . . not speaking naturally with his own voice . . ." One scholar suggested the Wilson single-handedly turned the U.S. Presidential system into the British Prime Minister system, with the President as leader of party, of legislature, and of the public. In fact, Wilson wrote the year of his first election that the president "must be the prime minister, as much concerned with the guidance of legislation as with the just and orderly execution of the law, and he is the spokesman of the Nation in everything."[11]

Wilson's autocratic nature was on display during the tariff debate. He noted that food, sugar, leather, and wool must be made duty free or he would veto the entire effort so that there would be no tariff reform at all. He told the press, "I am not the kind that considers compromises when I once take my position." As if to prevent any further talk by the press of compromise, and foreshadowing his future repression of them and the citizenry at large, he took a dictatorial tone and told a group of them, "There will be nothing more of that sort . . ."[12]

Wilson signed legislation (the Underwood Act) to lower tariffs to promote international enterprise. The new law dropped tariffs to their lowest levels since before the Civil War. Wilson stood philosophically with Southern democrats, stating that to collect import duties for any other purpose than to raise necessary revenues was "to tax one man for the benefit of another." In fact, the tariff reduction law necessitated for the first time a peacetime federal income tax law, in order to shore up lost revenues from tariff decreases. The Constitution had made it clear that the founders did not wish the national government to have a financial relationship with individual citizens. Article I, Section 2 required that direct taxes should be "apportioned among the several States . . . according to their respective Numbers." The federal government could only

11. Clements, *Wilson*, 35–37, 42, 47; Whitney, *Biographies*, 250, 252; Genovese, *Power*, 121; McDonald, *Presidency*, 342, 359.

12. McDonald, *Presidency*, 360–61.

tax the states as a whole, and could not sidestep the states and directly tax people living in those states. But the Sixteenth Amendment stated, "The Congress shall have power to lay and collect taxes on incomes . . . without apportionment among the several States, and without regard to any census or enumeration." The legislation allowed a personal exemption of $3,000 for individuals and $4,000 for married couples. There was a one percent tax on income below $20,000, going up to seven percent on income above $500,000. Wilson agreed to make the new income tax less progressive by dropping the top income tax rate from ten percent to seven percent, and signed the tariff/tax bill in October, 1913.[13]

Wilson also favored the Seventeenth Amendment for direct election of Senators, since it would diminish states rights and increase national power.[14] The Constitution, in Article I, Section 3, said, "The Senate of the United States shall be composed of two Senators from each State, chosen by the Legislature thereof . . ." For the nation's first 120 years, the states selected Senators based on their willingness and ability to represent the interests of the localities, so that those interests as defined by the body of the duly elected state legislature would be represented in the national government. Pushing for the Seventeenth Amendment was in Wilson's immediate interest to do, since a Senate elected by state legislatures had barely fell short of disgorging America's new Spanish War colonies, and in fact had refused to allow Grant's Santo Domingo annexation. The Seventeenth Amendment was therefore as much a pro-empire amendment as a pro-popular-tyranny provision. It would serve well as legal support for his autocratic and internationalist agenda.

Like Franklin Roosevelt after him, Wilson flip-flopped on labor issues. His early position was that he wanted laws to regulate corporate-labor issues rather than collective bargaining between the two private parties. But at election time in 1912 he changed his mind to purchase favor with organized labor. He signed the Labor Department Act in March, 1913, and later increased appropriations to the department during the war to mediate labor disputes. He sent federal troops to Colorado and kept them there for nine months after the governor had requested some temporary assistance.[15]

13. Nelson, *Presidency*, 129; Whitney, *Biographies*, 250; Clements, *Wilson*, 39; Napolitano, *Power*, 236, 239.

14. Whitney, *Biographies*, 255.

15. Clements, *Wilson*, 74–75, 78–79.

Wilson used the department of agriculture as a model to re-fashion the long-time system of dual legislative-executive branch control over executive department operations specified in the Constitution into a system of exclusive control by the president. He cut off department bureau-level connections to Congress by having bureau directors report to a new assistant director of the department. More assistant directors were hired during the war and the department budget increased by fully fifty percent even before its outbreak. The "enormous expansion" of federal employment in the department was evident in the growth of department employment from 14,500 in 1913 to 25,300 in 1918. Its budget grew from $20 million in 1913 to $47 million in 1918, but as became the norm in national government expansion, the war-time budget continued at only a slightly contracted level ($42 million) in peacetime.[16]

Many were mystified by Wilson's twists and turns on the corporate trust question. Before taking the presidency, he argued against a federal commission to regulate business. But he changed his mind and promoted and signed the Federal Trade Commission (FTC) Act in September, 1914. The FTC was created to regulate business by issuing cease-and-desist orders curbing unfair trade practices. However, its orders could be set aside in the courts and it did not have power to determine in advance if a practice was unfair. The FTC ruled on 224 restraint of trade cases from 1915 through 1920. Wilson also signed the Clayton Act the same year. Its purpose was to strengthen the Sherman Act by outlining specific kinds of anti-competitive practice like interlocking directorates, discriminatory pricing, tie-in selling, exclusive dealing, and corporate raiding. But the Clayton Act left loopholes. It exempted labor unions and farm organizations from prosecution under the law. During the war, Wilson postponed anti-trust activity because break-ups would cause private borrowing that would compete with the government's own massive war borrowing activity.[17]

Woodrow Wilson wanted to reform banking and monetary policy, and dominated the debate over the shape of the new law. He openly opposed Jackson, the founder of his party, with respect to the danger of a national bank. He said, "The control of the system of banking . . . must be vested in the Government itself." His use of the term "must" is symptomatic of his view that all his legislative initiatives are essentially mandates

16. Ibid., *Wilson*, 53–71.

17. Napolitano, *Theodore and Woodrow*, 46, 150; Clements, *Wilson*, 48–52.

and must be enacted. His new Federal Reserve system was aimed at "reform" of banks and currency. Its real intent was to control 7,000 banks so that capital could be raised for the national agenda, and especially for war, and to expand or contract the currency to suit the interests of government, big business, and special political factions. The act ultimately created twelve national banks owned by the national government, rather than set up private banks as suggested by Congress. The stated purpose of the national banks was to regulate the supply of soft money, control the flow of credit, and get a handle on the "money trust" which had been associated with the Panic of 1907. But its purpose was also to bail out the money trust when it shot itself in the foot. In fact, the act was creating a new nationalized money trust, with more power than the private banks. The president controlled the nation's banking by appointing all members of the board of the central Federal Reserve and three of nine members of each of the regional boards.[18]

Wilson signed bills for other vote block segments he believed would help him get reelected. He signed the Seaman's Act of 1915, increasing wages and dealing with working conditions of those who worked the high seas. Before the 1916 election he made a sudden decision to support federal child labor regulation. In 1914 he had said, "No child labor law yet proposed has seemed to me constitutional." In 1916 he supported the nationalization of child labor law "with all my heart." He signed the Federal Workmen's Compensation Act in 1916. In 1916 he signed the Adamson Act to provide shorter hours and higher pay for rail workers, so there would be no economic disruptions interfering with his reelection campaign. In order to get the southern vote in 1916, he staked out a position against farm price controls, but after winning, then hypocritically went on to establish wheat price controls in 1917. In all, Wilson's vote buying efforts were so far left for the times that the Socialist Party endorsed him for president.[19]

Wilson had a tendency to humiliate or ignore the cabinet. Unlike previous presidents who shared drafts of important speeches with the cabinet, Wilson did not even share his war speech with them. Wilson had said he was above party patronage, but then refused to appoint Republicans to the War department. In fact, he appointed his own son-in-law as

---

18. Boyer, *Oxford Companion*, 831; Whitney, *Biographies*, 250; McDonald, *Presidency*, 360; Clements, *Wilson*, 42–43, 64.

19. Clements, *Wilson*, 44, 70, 81.

secretary of the treasury. This relative later resigned and intrigued against his father-in-law for the presidential nomination in 1920 like a European royal family member would.[20]

Wilson, an immensely stubborn man, did not like Congress making laws and intruding on his domain, so he vetoed more than twenty "public" bills (bills affecting broad public policy). Congress did not like Wilson vetoing measures passed by the mandate of the people, and so overrode six of those twenty. Wilson vetoed an immigration restriction bill advocated by organized labor, the constituency he vowed to support. He also vetoed bills promising benefits to farmers and veterans. Wilson wrote that the veto is a president's "most formidable prerogative." In fact, presidents have usually had about a ninety-five percent success rate for their vetoes, so Wilson's much lesser rate reflects their extreme unhappiness with him. In fact, Ben Franklin had long since reminded that if one person could override Congressional legislation, "the Executive will always be increasing here, until it ends in monarchy."[21]

Wilson shocked the American public and many political scientists and historians with the historic number of presidential decrees, or executive orders, he issued while in office. He issued 1,791 of these executive department laws before, during, and after World War I. In so doing, he essentially relegated the Congress, and the Constitution, to his own personal dustbin. The executive branch, by clear constitutional assignment, had the duty only to implement or administer what Congress passed in the way of legislation, but not to enact legislation itself. The Constitution read "The Congress shall have the power to . . . make all Laws . . ." During war time the President could be expected to exercise some discretion in issuing executive orders for the military, but it was unprecedented to exercise them for the civilian population. One study showed that his "land orders" outstripped "military directives" one hundred and two to seventy-six. Indeed, orders affecting individuals, and amounting to a version of the hated discriminatory private legislation known as attainder (prohibited by the Constitution), numbered sixty-nine, almost as many as war orders.[22]

In 1898, Wilson had revealed his imperialist mindset when he wrote that the "impulse of expansion" was "the natural and wholesome impulse

20. Fleming, *Illusion*, 9, 91, 455.

21. McDonald, *Presidency*, 353; Flagel, *Guide*, 131–32.

22. Article I, Sections 8, 9–10; Cooper, *Order*, 3, 7 note, 8, 72.

which comes with a consciousness of matured strength." This was exactly the mentality he found offensive, or pretended to find offensive, in big business. It was also the opposite of the propaganda he eventually put out in the form of his war-time Fourteen Points, which condemned imperialism and championed self-determination. Indeed, Wilson promised in 1913 that the U.S. will "never again seek one additional foot of territory by conquest [like Puerto Rico and the Philippines]." He also said, "If I want to serve the lowest of human beings I have got . . . to put myself . . . in his place . . ." However, Wilson returned to his earlier mindset at the peace conference at Versailles when he supported the imperial spoils system in Europe. Ultimately, the president had an "inability to see the world through others' eyes."[23]

Prior to the Great War, while loudly trumpeting the anti-imperialism position, Wilson did quite something else. He sent troops into a half dozen Latin American countries in a "remarkable number of interventions" during his first term. One author remarked that the incursions seemed very much "like overt imperialism" to Latin America. But Wilson did not think of military occupation as "intervention." Intervention to him was total conquest, but anything else short of that was fair game, even the imposition of a military government on the Dominican Republic. Wilson's military interventions in Latin America in his first term exceeded that of even his militaristic predecessors Teddy Roosevelt and William Howard Taft. He intervened in Cuba, Panama, Haiti, and Dominican Republic and sent troops to Honduras five times.[24] He tried to make Nicaragua officially into an American protectorate colony.

The United States already controlled about ninety percent of Mexico's wealth, and the U.S. had intervened in Mexico by supporting one dictatorial usurper of power after another there since 1910. Wilson supported the latest of the Mexican usurpers, the lighter-skinned Carranza over the darker-skinned Huerta, who was currently in power. While Wilson was waiting for Congress to give him permission to aid Carranza, he jumped the gun and sent the navy with 15,000 troops to seize the port of Vera Cruz. The dead after one day of fighting included 126 Mexicans and 19 Americans. Carranza himself denounced the invasion. Anti-American riots erupted in South America. Wilson then occupied Vera Cruz militarily for seven months, which produced a tremendous amount

23. Clements, *Wilson*, 93, 95–96, 101, 177.
24. Clements, *Wilson*, 95, 98, 106; Herring, *Colony to Superpower*, 386.

of political "blowback" against the United States. Like Andrew Jackson and James Buchanan before him, Wilson inexplicably asked Congress for the go-ahead to occupy all of Mexico. He instigated so many treaty violations that his own secretary of state William Jennings Bryan resigned his office in protest, the first American secretary of state to do so. Wilson also mobilized the National Guard in forty-eight states in preparation for war with Mexico. U.S. troops entered Mexico ten times in two years under Wilson.[25]

Wilson made a unilateral change in U.S. China policy that shocked experts. He extended recognition to a shaky Chinese republican government, and created a serious strain in relations with Japan, which contributed to later Japanese dislike of Americans leading up to World War II.[26]

Woodrow Wilson engineered a stunning stumble of the nation into world war and an alliance with western European imperial monarchies at war against central European powers. He did this by a deft combination of economic warfare, political philosophy, cultic appeal, secret foreign affairs manipulations, skillful use of propaganda and disinformation, and direct provocation by endangering and sacrificing the lives of U.S. citizens. Wilson won a considerable amount of acclaim in his first term by keeping America out of the war that had erupted in Europe. In fact, he was reelected in 1916 under the slogan "He Kept America Out of War." At the same time, Wilson showed his real hand when he went on a nationwide speaking tour stumping for an increase in military spending. He won a large increase in 1916 in the form of his National Defense Act. How anyone could worry about the danger of the "Hun" invading America after suffering such huge casualties in Europe early in the war, Wilson did not explain. This law authorized an increase in the regular standing army to 223,000 over the next five years. It also increased the National Guard to 450,000 and expanded federal controls over the Guard. By this means, Wilson sent an early signal to Britain that he would be moving the nation toward war. His Revenue Act of 1916 financed the new peacetime standing army with the income tax, an estate tax, a corporate tax, and a munitions profits tax. However, Wilson made little provision for housing, clothing, moving or equipping the massive new army.[27]

25. Flagel, *Guide*, 253; Herring, *Colony to Superpower*, 391, 396, 403; McDonald, *Presidency*, 397.

26. Clements, *Wilson*, 107–09.

27. Fleming, *Illusion*, 481; Herring, *Colony to Superpower*, 405; Clements, *Wilson*, 81.

The British ambassador to the U.S. saw how difficult it would be to draw the U.S. into the war and wrote: "For certain . . . the vast majority of the country desire peace . . ."[28] The best way to stay out of Europe's new war was to tread lightly on the shipping lanes of European combatants, and stick firmly to political, military and economic neutrality, as Washington, Adams, and Jefferson had done a century before. European nations at war typically blockaded their opponents' ports and were doing so again, scaring off neutral nation shipping. Wilson knew that continuing regular trade relations with nations at war was the best way to get the U.S. into war and win for himself a role as decider of world events.

Wilson thus insisted upon continuing U.S. trade with the warring nations, particularly with Britain and Germany, knowing that this would deeply offend both sides in the conflict. He put U.S. merchant vessels in harms way, tilted trade traffic toward the allies and away from the central powers, sidestepped laws prohibiting loans to belligerents, and started selling weaponry to the allies. He also took a stand against the type of warfare waged by the Germans, saying submarine warfare was immoral, while at the same time saying little about Britain's policy of starving German civilians.

Churchill stated what was already obvious to Wilson: "It is most important to attract neutral shipping . . . to embroil the U.S. with Germany." Wilson deliberately declined to stop Americans from obtaining passage on the British ship Lusitania, and Britain deliberately loaded the ship with war material and plowed it straight into German submarine-controlled waters, with the result that 128 Americans lost their lives.[29]

Wilson then broke off relations with Germany, and asked Congress for a declaration of war, with the idea the war appropriation would be for arming the American merchant marine for self-defense and for helping the navy deal with German submarines. He derailed any notion the U.S. would get involved in a ground war, but secretly ordered ground weaponry without an appropriation from Congress.[30]

Wilson initiated a barrage of propaganda to assure Europe and the world that America had only the highest interests and would condition the peace settlement upon Fourteen Points that would bring peace and independence to all the nations of the world. These points included free

28. Fleming, *Illusion*, 82.
29. Fleming, *Illusion*, 33, 41–42, 67; Nelson, *Presidency*, 131.
30. Fleming, *Illusion*, 7, 37, 114, 122, 125, 409.

trade, self-determination, and a League of Nations to enforce ethical conduct among nations. Back home, Wilson's Committee on Public Information made as its goal something less than the highest ideals: to create "a passionate belief in the justice of America's cause . . . meld the people into one white hot mass with . . . deathless determination." The agency accomplished this by using 75,000 speakers to deliver mini-propaganda speeches at venues across the country.[31]

Wilson set war-time agricultural policies from the top rather than consult farmers. He gave his new wartime Food Administration leader Herbert Hoover "near dictatorial powers" to control production, distribution, imports, exports, pricing, and food hording. His policy was "revolutionary in the extent of control of private business." As another example, by executive order Wilson announced in December 1917 that the nation's railroads would be taken over and operated by the national government by means of a new Railroad Administration czar. Congress later gave up its power to reorganize executive agencies and to conduct war mobilization when Wilson signed the Overman Act in May, 1918.[32]

Wilson knew he could not conduct a foreign war against the will of the American people without undertaking significant repression at home. He therefore arrested draft protesters and cracked down on ethnic communities, which he believed were allied with the unpatriotic German citizens of the U.S. He censored newspapers "for public safety." His Sedition Act of 1918 was used for surveillance, arrest and imprisonment of many who might "utter, print, or publish disloyal, profane, scurrilous, or abusive language . . . [about] the constitution, soldiers and sailors, flag, or uniform of the armed forces." His federal Bureau of Investigation grew significantly. He used some 300,000 citizens as deputized spies by means of the American Protective League, who reported 1,500 disloyal acts per day.[33]

During war time, Wilson reversed both liberal labor reforms establishing shorter work days and civil service reforms. He issued a personal decree reversing the eight-hour work day not only for railroad workers, but for the entire American workforce. He also issued a decree suspending civil service hiring rules (Executive Order 2600), and thus trashed the federal merit-based hiring system and replaced it with a patronage- or

31. Fleming, *Illusion*, 93–94, 290, 298.
32. Clements, *Wilson*, 55, 65, 67–68, 88, 209.
33. Flagel, *Guide*, 63; McCoy, *Policing*, 301.

crony-based system. In addition, Wilson refused to raise wages for telephone workers after rates were raised to help increase corporate profits. Some 20,000 operators went out on strike. War industries predictably did well during the war. Dupont's assets tripled. Bethlehem Steel's profits increased by a factor of eight times. Wilson shored up his political support in seven key east and mid-west states by awarding three-fourths of defense contracts there. Many corporate CEOs and CFOs sat on government agency boards, helping their industries out. Wilson tried to continue this pattern even after the Lever Food and Fuel Bill prohibited executives from signing contracts with companies they had an interest in by creating a War Industries Board agency outside of government. But many executives stayed on the Board anyway. The War Industries Board was organized into commodity sections where CEOs bought from their own companies in what was called a corrupt "whol[ly] extralegal system." U.S. Steel had huge profits, but refused to negotiate with its 250,000 workers. By the end of 1919, twenty percent of American workers had gone on strike, in part because the war stopped immigration and because the labor shortage due to the siphoning off of workers into the military gave labor more power. Wilson's promised cooperation between labor and industry did not materialize. Wilson nationalized Western Union and threatened Smith and Wesson workers they would lose their draft exemptions if they did not go back to work. In addition, Wilson's government gave war loans to Europe, whose nations turned around and bought food and other products from big farm enterprises at inflated prices, bringing in large profits to American agri-business. Some eight months after the World War I armistice, Wilson's government was still running railroads, and telephone and telegraph companies under an ongoing emergency power. Congress begged him to return the private sector to its rightful stewards, but Wilson refused.[34]

At the peace conference in Paris, Wilson embarrassed the United States and the world by giving away all fourteen of his principles of political ethics and throwing in his lot with a mandate system protecting European colonial imperialism, a winner-take-all spoils system by which seventeen million people and their lands were handed over to the allies. He associated himself and the U.S. with secret treaty-making, a forced and unfair acknowledgement of German unilateral guilt for the war, and

---

34. Cooper, *Order*, 72; Fleming, *Illusion*, 395–96; Clement, *Wilson*, 65, 81–82, 85–89.

a horrendous burden of tribute payments imposed upon the defeated parties. Herbert Hoover said that the treaty "contained seeds of another war." The American Congress, worried about turning over American sovereignty to an international body, refused to ratify Wilson's plans for the League of Nations. The American people had a bad taste in their mouth about any further involvement in European alliances or wars. Some 53,000 Americans died in combat, 198,059 were wounded, and 63,000 succumbed to disease after only six months of fighting.[35] Ultimately, Wilson's war increased the national debt from $1 billion to $26.6 billion, an increase of twenty five times.

Senator Henry Cabot Lodge wrote that Wilson was "one of the most sinister figures that ever crossed the history of a great country." One critic spoke of Wilson's "bizarre attempt to perfect the world without the consent of Congress or the American people." John Maynard Keynes, who helped represent Britain at the peace table, said Wilson lacked the "intellectual equipment" to negotiate peace, and "was not a hero or a prophet." He added, "There can seldom have been a statesman of the first rank more incompetent than the President."[36]

Warren G. Harding

Warren Harding, a handsome and charming man, received more than twice as many votes for president as any previous presidential candidate, many of these coming from women who were voting for the first time under a new suffrage amendment to the Constitution. His election, based as it was on personal physical attraction, highlighted the new kind of electoral normalcy by which citizens appreciated externalities more so than constitutional intelligence. But while clean and apparently healthy on the outside, Harding was a sick man, having quite high blood pressure.[37]

Harding was incensed by Wilson's power grabs and promised he would shun what he called "executive autocracy." He wanted a return to "normalcy," which included not only ending the restrictions and hardships imposed by the war, but placing confidence in political parties and a diversity of people rather than an individual leader. Harding's statements on civil rights made him look good in comparison with Wilson's.

---

35. Fleming, *Illusion*, 307, 384.
36. Ibid., 406, 413, 486.
37. Whitney, *Biographies*, 256; Ferrell, *Coolidge*, 17.

If Republican normalcy involved limiting military plundering of the globe, it did not mind domestic commercial plundering and moderate economic regulating. Republicans also wanted to limit national spending somewhat and get a handle on Wilson's humongous war debt. In fact, Harding and his Republican successors were able to trim Wilson's war debt from $26 billion to $16 billion in under a decade. When Congress passed an expensive World War I soldier's bonus bill, for example, Harding vetoed it, since the bill did not provide for additional revenues to pay for it. He also vetoed bills to subsidize the marketing of farm products. His basic program of tax cuts, spending cuts, and debt reduction seemed to have fueled prosperity. He balanced the budget and obtained a surplus until the time of his death in office.[38]

Harding, who served in office from 1921 to 1923, presented an ambitious policy agenda to Congress, but left it to them to accept or reject it. He did not lobby for it. Harding's policy agenda included tariff and tax reform, federal regulation of transportation (air, roads, merchant ships), aid to farmers, federal money for highways and veterans hospitals, federal regulation of radio and cable, creation of a national public welfare department and administration, and an executive department consolidated budget process. Harding signed the 1921 Federal Highway Act, which built upon a 1916 law. The 1921 legislation providing matching grants to states for construction, but left road maintenance to the states. Harding's commerce secretary, Herbert Hoover, took initiative to regulate air travel and radio. But Hoover and Harding implemented their regulatory ideas only after extensive consultation with the full cabinet, Congress, and business leaders. Harding's basic approach involved pushing for further breadth in regulation of the economy, while easing off on the depth of that regulation. For example, he encouraged the Federal Trade Commission to ease up on regulating businesses.[39]

This ambitious agenda a court historian group calls "ceremonial," because it reflected a lack of grandiose executive vision. From the point of view of this essay, however, Harding must be categorized as at least a halfway tyrant, wanting to mold the world in the image of his backers and friends. He presented the outlines of his plan, and won approval on the

38. Crenson and Ginsberg, *Presidential Power*, 20; Flagel, *Guide*, 304; Whitney, *Biographies*, 259, 264; McDonald, *Presidency*, 353; Boyer, *Oxford Companion*, 327; Ferrell, *Coolidge*, 167.

39. Nelson, *Presidency*, 136; Crenson and Ginsberg, *Presidential Power*, 143; Flagel, *Guide*, 319; Miller Center, *Harding—Domestic Affairs*; Ferrell, *Coolidge*, 99, 109.

basis of his personality and popularity. He was the antithesis of Wilson, who touted the idealistic merits of his proposals above all other concerns, and enforced total loyalty to his program. Harding served notice that he did not feel the level of repression Wilson got away with during the war was warranted. For example, he granted a presidential pardon to Eugene Debs.[40]

Harding did not affirmatively reject the imbalance of power between the executive and legislative branches that Wilson produced, or even Wilson's new internationalism. In fact, he solidified the relationship between business and the executive branch, giving corporate America the power over the government that Wilson held for himself. It was said that he supported a business-government partnership, with "the government as the junior partner." His campaign slogan was "Less government in business, and more business in government." Harding operated the White House with a small staff: twenty-one clerks, two stenographers, a records clerk and an appointments clerk, a chief clerk, an executive clerk, and a secretary. This was, nevertheless, quite a large increase over the staff Grover Cleveland had in the White House only a generation before.[41]

One of Harding's executive department-bolstering initiatives was his support and signing of legislation, the Budget and Accounting Act of 1921, creating the Bureau of the Budget, and the General Accounting Office. Before this bill, there was no good way to sort out budget proposals made by departments and agencies or calculate the effect of legislation being developed by Congress. But the legislation curbed the departments' ability to deal with Congress independent of the president. It therefore surrendered a good deal of Congress' constitutional duty to regulate the national public purse to the president. The Constitution, in fact, read, "No Money shall be drawn from the Treasury, but in consequence of Appropriations made by Law . . ." Further sealing its power, Congress had power to exercise "all other Powers vested by this constitution in the Government of the United States, or in any Department or Office thereof." The transfer of budget power to the executive branch was promoted by corporate giant Andrew Mellon, Harding's treasury secretary. Harding then asked agencies with legislative proposals costing money to submit them to the new Bureau of the Budget for clearance, rather than to the Congress. Further implications of such a transfer of authority could also

40. Miller Center, *Harding—Impact and Legacy*; Flagel, *Guide*, 162.
41. Crenson and Ginsberg, Presidential Power, 180; Nelson, *Presidency*, 134, 136.

be detected in the statement by Harding's new budget director, Charles G. Dawes, who argued that Congressional appropriations were not mandatory on the executive branch to the extent the work could be done for less.[42] The executive department fiscal impoundment revolution can be traced to the Mellon/Harding brash act of constitutional sorcery.

Harding's commerce secretary, Herbert Hoover, promoted foreign trade on behalf of his boss. But Harding was not inclined to entangle America politically in Wilson's League of Nations, although he had loyally supported Wilson's war effort. At his inaugural, Harding said, "A world super-government is contrary to everything we cherish and can have no sanction by our Republic." He did, however, support U.S. involvement in the World Count, which would hear cases only with the consent of both parties. He submitted the Court "protocol" (treaty) to the Senate.[43]

Harding, together with his Secretary of State Hughes, began to back off the military protectorate commitments created by Roosevelt, Taft and Wilson in Latin America. For example, they terminated the military occupation of the Dominican Republic. Hughes, representing Harding, stated, "I utterly disclaim . . . [supervision] of the affairs of our sister republics to assert an overlordship . . ." He also avoided entanglement in Europe in Germany's border dispute with Poland." On the other hand, Harding reversed the increased level of independence given to the Philippines by Wilson.[44]

Harding preferred more subtle control, like Taft, via economic measures. He pushed U.S. bank involvement in foreign affairs by establishing a corp of commercial attaches to foreign service offices. Those new officers could pursue foreign markets, while the ordinary diplomats dealt with political issues. Harding used the reciprocity provision of the Fordney-McCumber Tariff Act to secure "open door" economic concessions on oil in the Middle East. He thus set the stage for later ratcheting-up of exploitation of the Middle East after World War II. He also got the U.S. into rubber concessions in Malaysia.[45]

Harding refused to write off the U.S. tribute demand of Germany resulting from World War I, but instead reduced it. U.S. bankers got a cut

42. Ferrell, *Coolidge*, 27–28; Article I, Section 9; Article I, Section 8; Flagel, *Guide*, 303–04; McDonald, *Presidency*, 311, 364.

43. Crenson and Ginsberg, *Presidential Power*, 143–44; Whitney, *Biographies*, 260; Herring, *Colony to Superpower*, 450.

44. Herring, *Colony to Superpower*, 472–73; Ferrell, *Coolidge*, 53.

45. Miller Center, *Harding—Foreign Affairs*.

of the action by loaning Germany the money to pay off the remaining owed to the U.S. government. Germany also used the money it received from U.S. bankers to pay off British and French tribute demands, which those nations then used to pay off the tribute the U.S. had demanded of those two allies. U.S. bankers got rich, and the U.S. government, raking in some cash, paid off, presumably in government services, some of the war money it taxed from the American people to finance Wilson's adventure in tyranny and imperialism.[46]

Calvin Coolidge

Calvin Coolidge served as president from 1923 to 1929. Elected vice president in 1920, he became president when Harding died in office. He won election to a full term in his own right by an overwhelming margin in 1924, but chose not to run for another term, thus setting a model example of self-limitation on the accumulation of dangerous national power.[47]

Calvin Coolidge was a spoiled and angry child, a result of lack of maternal discipline, having been raised by his grandmother. Raised in Vermont, he was well educated at Amherst College, and studied law in a legal office in Northampton, Massachusetts. Coolidge had one qualification rare in presidents. He had served in local government on the city council of Northampton, Massachusetts, and also worked in that city's executive department. It is no wonder he carried with him a belief that much of government rightly happens on local levels. Coolidge is remembered as a national government "minimalist" even more than Warren Harding. He noted that the country already had a great number of laws, "and we would be better off if we did not have any more . . . the greatest duty . . . of government is not to embark on any new ventures." Coolidge also served as state senate president, lieutenant governor, and governor of Massachusetts.[48]

Coolidge was a religious man, keeping a Bible on the table next to his bed in the White House. He became a member of the First Congregational Church of Washington, DC. His religion manifested, perhaps,

46. Ibid.
47. Nelson, *Presidency*, 137.
48. Whitney, *Biographies*, 268; Crenson and Ginsberg, *Presidential Power*, 144–45.

in his support for prohibition, and for female voting rights, which were achieved in 1920.[49]

As president, Cal Coolidge followed the path of government frugality. He reduced the national debt from $22.3 billion in 1923 to $16.9 billion in 1929, over the course of his five years and seven months in office. He also produced a budget surplus each year he held office, keeping spending flat with the help of the new income tax. He said that retiring the debt was "the very largest internal improvement . . . possible to conceive."[50] He prevented a wage increase for post office employees. During his term federal employment still grew from 436,900 to 479, 559, and the military budget from $730 million to $789 million.

But his record was not perfect in terms of traditional constitutionalism. He had supported the 17th Amendment side-stepping state political power. In 1925 he promoted a program of public building worthy of an ancient autocratic king. The new granite public buildings housing government departments had "ceilings twice as high as necessary" and due to other "excesses of ornament" necessitated budget-busting levels of maintenance. In addition, he made an amazing, if not fully serious, assertion of executive privilege when Congress proposed to investigate his administration's devotion to prohibition enforcement. He sent a letter to Congress stating, "I enter my solemn protests and give notice that in my opinion the departments ought not to be required to participate in it . . ." A Democratic senator said the message was "the most arrogant sent by any executive to a parliamentary body since the days of the Stuarts and Tudors." Another called it "the most extraordinary breach of official etiquette that has ever occurred in the history of the Republic." Coolidge truly did have Jacksonian tendencies.[51]

Coolidge gave only one annual message in person to Congress out of his six years in office. He remarked, "I never felt it was my duty to attempt to coerce Senators or Representatives, or to make reprisals. The people sent them to Washington." He added in his 1929 autobiography an insider's statement of the problem of executive arrogance and idolatry that infected presidents before him and after him: "It is difficult for men in high office to avoid the malady of self-delusion. They are surrounded

49. Ferrell, *Coolidge*, 3, 5, 7, 10, 22, 38, 106.

50. Flagel, *Guide*, 123; Wilson's war saddled the nation with debt that took 50 years to pay off; Ferrell, *Coolidge*, 21, 43, 167–68.

51. Whitney, *Biographies*, 271; Ferrell, *Coolidge*, 10, 26–27, 172–74.

by worshippers . . . They live in an artificial atmosphere of adulation and exaltation, which sooner or later impairs their judgment. They are in grave danger of becoming arrogant or careless."[52]

Coolidge seems to have been speaking from real experience. He was regularly seen on newsreels because he was enormously popular. Indeed, he also continued Taft's and Harding's regular press conferences, meeting with them twice weekly to answer pre-selected questions. However, he only answered pre-submitted written questions. By the end of his presidency, he had held more press conferences than any other president before him. He was also the first president to speak on radio, doing so once a month. He agreed to an early "talkie" movie made of a speech he made on the economy. Although he maintained an air of indifference to power, he actually was extremely ambitious. Once he took over after Harding died, he immediately began making arrangements for winning the presidency in his own right. One senator who knew him well said, "I really believe there never was a man in high position so politically minded. I do not think there is any principle or policy of government that for one instant will sway him when he believes his personal political fortunes may be influenced."[53]

Coolidge used executive orders but limited them to non-policy matters. No more than ten percent of them were policy specific. Thus he somewhat honored the founders' Constitutional commitment to Congressional lawmaking. He also kept White House staff at a minimum (some thirty-eight), compared to the immense explosion about to occur in the term of one of his successors, Franklin Roosevelt.[54]

One of the natural consequences of imperial war-making is the immense pressure to bring about centralized efforts to care for returning war veterans, who are, after all, temporary employees of the central government while at war. For many of them, their ruined lives become apparent to those who care to inquire. However, in a nation like the U.S., a large number of resources existed at the local level to deal with such ruined lives. Coolidge used the presidential veto to keep the national government out of corporate welfare and worker pension programs. He is among the top ten veto presidents, having issued twenty regular vetoes,

52. Healy, *Cult of the Presidency*, 70, 83, 247.

53. Flagel, *Guide*, 136, 143; McDonald, *Presidency*, 444; Ferrell, *Coolidge*, 19, 23–24, 27, 33, 40.

54. Healy, *Cult of the Presidency*, 100, 248.

and thirty pocket vetoes. He vetoed the 1924 Bonus Bill for relief/pension money for World War I veterans. The idea was to make up for low military pay compared with civilian wages during the war by using paid-up insurance. The plan allowed vets to borrow up to twenty-five percent of the value of the insurance policy. Congress overrode that veto. Next, he vetoed a bill allowing for a general increase to the pensions of veterans of earlier wars, including pensions for war widows and dependents of the War of 1812. That veto was upheld. He also twice vetoed farm subsidy bills asking for purchase of surpluses and raising agricultural prices, and supported farm co-ops instead. About nationalization of farm policy he said, "No resort to the public treasury will be of any permanent value in establishing agriculture." He once had four vetoes overridden in one day. He pocket vetoed an early TVA (Tennessee Valley Authority) plan called the Muscle Shoals project, because it would have had the federal government compete with private development. He also cut income taxes used to strengthen the federal government at the expense of the states. He especially targeted income tax cuts for the wealthy, by means of the Revenue Acts of 1924 and 1926, but also cut gift, excise, and inheritance taxes. The 1924 tax cut lowered the maximum tax rate from fifty percent to forty percent, just in time for Coolidge's reelection effort. The 1926 tax act cut the maximum rate from forty percent to twenty percent, and abolished the gift tax.[55] Coolidge also raised tariffs to benefit industry and suppressed labor unions.

There is no question that the Coolidge tax cuts helped accelerate the disparity between the poor and the wealthy. It was said that Coolidge followed the scripture closely in his economic policy, since Mark 4:25 read, "For he that hath, to him shall be given: and he that hath not, from him shall be taken that which he hath." Even with the tax cuts, he was able to balance the yearly budget, run a surplus, and cut the national debt. This was possible since the economy was booming as a result of forced wartime production. His business- and wealth-friendly policies had negative effects as well, since they encouraged financial speculation by means of margin trading in the stock market and easy installment credit. Coolidge did not use the ICC, FTC, the Federal Reserve, or the Treasury to regulate the economy much. For example, as the depression neared, he did not use his influence to make a significant restriction of credit or to set margin

55. Flagel, *Guide*, 143–44; Whitney, *Biographies*, 272; Nelson, *Presidency*, 138; McDonald, *Presidency*, 353; Boyer, *Oxford Companion*, 161; Ferrell, *Coolidge*, 41–42, 85, 88, 93, 119, 170.

requirements or to deal with the rising number of "call loans." He did little on the federal level to regulate management-labor disputes or to inspire state and local efforts to deal with the forty percent of wage earners who could not buy consumer items, unless on installment credit. He failed to encourage capitalists to share their profits with wage earners. He failed to regulate holding companies and investment trusts, which were engaged in "essential chicanery," and did little with anti-trust. He put a protectionist majority on the Tariff Commission.[56]

Coolidge contributed to the upcoming depression in another way other than through turning a blind eye to financial speculation. While it may have been appropriate to keep the national government out of too great involvement in the plight of farmers—particularly production and pricing issues—he might better have encouraged the states and localities, and voluntary cooperative agencies, to do more. During his presidency, the Federal Reserve kept interest rates low, thus providing easy credit, which then produced a "bubble" which burst in a stock market crash. Coolidge twice vetoed the McNary-Haugen bill, which called for the national government to buy surplus crops at artificially high prices to be held or sold abroad when prices rose. He did, however, sign a bill that allowed Hoover to regulate the new radio industry via the Federal Radio Commission, later re-named the Federal Communication Commission. Under his administration, the FTC became a counselor to big business, and the ICC was staffed by railroad people. Thus, the precedent was set for national government to become a tool of big business.[57]

Coolidge also famously refused to visit and inspect the Mississippi River flood of 1927, the worst natural disaster in America up until Hurricane Katrina in 2005. Congress wanted legislation, but Coolidge believed states, counties and cities should pay the costs to bail out individual citizens, not the federal government.[58] He said that he did not want "to surrender to every emotional movement" seeking funds for what other units of government could handle. He ultimately sent Hoover to coordinate some federal relief.

Regarding race matters, Coolidge signed the Indian Citizenship Act in 1924, which made the remaining third of Indians full citizens. He

---

56. Miller Center, *Coolidge – Domestic Affairs*; Ferrell, *Coolidge*, 68–70, 72, 75, 77, 171, 175–79, 183, 186–87, 207.

57. Boyer, *Guide*, 161; Nelson, *Presidency*, 137.

58. Healy, *Presidential Power*, 71, 85.

signed a permanent immigration law in 1924 restricting immigration to two percent more of each immigrant group per year. That law lasted until the time of the Truman administration.[59]

In foreign affairs, Coolidge was a half-way imperialist. He continued the post-World War I American retreat from military intervention in world affairs, favoring economic intervention instead. He said little about possible membership in the League of Nations, although his secretary of state said of the citizenry, "They want us to stay out of Europe." He favored membership in the World Court. He opposed cancelation of World War I debts, although he agreed to revise the debt level downward. In fact, in his inaugural address in 1925, he gave his anti-imperialist sentiments a religious cloak, stressing service to the nations, saying, "America seeks no earthly empire built on blood and force . . . the Legions which she sends forth are armed, not with the sword, but with the cross. The higher state to which she seeks the allegiance of all mankind is not of human, but of divine origin." In China, Coolidge threw water on American war fever after the Nationalists killed Americans and burned missionary buildings in Nanking. He said, "It is impossible to make war on 400 million people."[60]

Coolidge nevertheless maintained a strong military and economic presence in Latin America. U.S. investments there rose almost triple during his term. For example, U.S. Fruit and Standard Fruit controlled most of the economy of Honduras. Also, U.S. companies dominated Venezuelan oil production. Coolidge followed earlier presidential policy in treating Latin America as a protectorate, whether or not the locals wanted that, or had agreements validating it. Coolidge, in a gesture of harmony, withdrew marines from the Dominican Republic in 1924. However, he sent 5,500 marines to Nicaragua and positioned eleven cruisers and destroyers at Nicaraguan ports until the first free elections were held in 1928. The U.S. continuously occupied Nicaragua and Haiti with U.S. troops throughout the 1920s, and brokered elections in Nicaragua. The U.S. also continued to control the Cuban economy.[61]

The U.S. and Mexico almost came to blows over $1.5 billion in U.S. interests there and also over Mexico's involvement in Nicaragua.

59. Ferrell, *Coolidge*, 110, 113–14.

60. Boyer, *Oxford Companion*, 161; Whitney, *Biographies*, 273; Ferrell, *Coolidge*, 41, 146–52, 156, 164.

61. Herring, *Colony to Superpower*, 473; Miller Center, *Coolidge—Foreign Affairs*; Ferrell, *Coolidge*, 122, 135.

Coolidge provided arms and military equipment to control rebels fighting president Obregon, whom the U.S. supported with loans. Obregon's successor Calles nationalized U.S. oil interests, but Coolidge negotiated rather than intervene militarily. He lifted the U.S. embargo on arms to Mexico in 1924, and requested that the Senate consider payment for Mexican claims arising from Wilson's occupation of Vera Cruz in 1914. Ultimately, he prevented the seizure of U.S. assets by non-violent means. In the process he announced the Coolidge Doctrine: "The person and property of a citizen are a part of the general domain of the Nation, even when abroad." In 1928, Coolidge backed off his policy of military intervention in Latin America, disavowing Teddy Roosevelt's policy of using a big stick with our neighbors to the south, thus bringing his actions more in line with his stated intentions. In 1927 he backed the Kellogg-Briand Pact that said the signing nations "condemn recourse to war . . . (and that) . . . solution of all disputes . . . shall never be sought except by pacific means." One author wrote that "The only effect . . . was to make wars in the 1930s undeclared." [62]

Herbert Hoover

Herbert Hoover served as president from 1929 to 1933. Like so many pre-World War II presidents, he had conflicting political currents running within. He was extraordinarily ambitious for power, and was a progressive centralizer earlier in his career and at the end of his career. And yet he still understood the nineteenth century sense of restraint about too much aggressiveness in the executive branch. He was perhaps the nation's last somewhat aggressive rhetorical supporter of states' rights, since he encouraged states to make the main effort to solve the depression. In his inaugural, he warned against a large and activist federal government and also against large corporations.[63] He was also perhaps the first truly anti-war president since founders like Adams and Jefferson, and possibly Grover Cleveland, and the last one the U.S. has had the distinction of having.

Herbert's father died when he was six, and his mother often traveled to spread the Quaker religion, leaving Herbert and two siblings in the care of other Quakers. He read the Bible daily, participated in silent

62. Herring, *Colony to Superpower*, 476–77; Ferrell, *Coolidge*, 124, 128, 161.
63. Miller Center, *Hoover—Domestic Affairs*.

prayer before meals, and watched the Friends participate in service to others. Quakers opposed war, alcohol, musical instruments, luxury, gambling, paid ministry and capital punishment. They promoted prison reform, education, rights for labor, better treatment of Indians and African Americans, equality of the sexes, and religious freedom.[64]

After graduating from Stanford in engineering, Hoover worked in mining in Australia, China, Burma, Peru, Russia and Mexico. In 1914 he headed the American Citizen's Relief Committee, which helped Americans return to the U.S. from war-ravaged Europe. He also headed the Commission for Relief in Belgium. In both jobs he worked in the capacity of a neutralist to aid the needy. Before America's entry into the war, he asked consumers to limit consumption to help provide food for Europe. Wilson later appointed him U.S. Food Administrator, so he was perhaps the first U.S. "czar," having almost dictatorial power to regulate the distribution, export, import, purchase and storage of food. Overall, he fed both military and civilian populations in America and Europe. At times he was feeding nine million people per day. At the end of the war he headed the American Relief Administration and the European Coal Council.[65]

Hoover admired Wilson, calling him a "born crusader" and writing a book about his efforts to enact the League. John Maynard Keynes said that when the World War I peace treaty was signed, Hoover was "the only man who emerged ... with an enhanced reputation ... (having) precisely that atmosphere of reality, knowledge, magnanimity and disinterestedness which, if then had been found in other quarters would have given us a Good Peace." In other words, if Wilson had been Hoover, the world would have been in a much better place as a result of the peace activities. At the end of the war, Hoover was vice-chairman of the Second Industrial Conference, where he endorsed the forty hour work week, a minimum wage, prevention of child labor, and equal pay for women.[66]

Hoover unsuccessfully sought the nomination for president in 1920 and was appointed secretary of commerce under Warren Harding. Fifty years later, the nation's new commerce building was named after him. Harding allowed him a voice in treasury, agriculture, and foreign affairs

---

64. Fausold, *Hoover*, 2–4, 7, 27.

65. Bailyn, *Great Republic*, 1021; Herring, *Colony to Superpower*, 443; Fausold, *Hoover*, 9–10.

66. Cooper, *Order*, 122 note; Flagel, *Guide*, 50; Hoover supported the League, but only with modifications that Wilson was unwilling to allow; Fausold, *Hoover*, 10, 13.

matters. In 1928 many Democratic wanted Hoover as their candidate, but he announced he was a progressive (big government) Republican.[67]

Hoover was a born crusader as well, and about as good a prophet as Wilson in predicting the future. During the presidential campaign he gave an almost delusional speech, which said, in part, "We in America are nearer to the final triumph over poverty than ever before in the history of any land . . . given a chance to go forward . . . we shall with the help of God be in sight of the day when poverty will be banished from the nation . . ." These words he spoke only months before one of the worst depressions to hit the planet. He also spoke of "the growth of religious spirit and the tolerance of all faiths; the strengthening of the home; the advancement of peace . . ." All this he said only a few years before the beginning of the most destructive war the planet has ever seen, attended by the dismembering of limbs and families and properties across the globe. Hoover thus positioned himself as a secular messiah promising great things, but without much ability to produce them. In other words, he was a philosopher tyrant. He actually expanded the reach of the federal government by quite a bit. It is only against Franklin Roosevelt's all-encompassing despotism and expropriation of the property of the people that Hoover's administration can be labeled by some as "do nothingism."[68]

Hoover was inexperienced not only in electoral politics but in Congressional relations. His campaign race in 1928 was his only election to public office. He scorned political methods like manipulation and force, and preferred administrative efficiency and Quaker methods of conciliation and agreement. He was critical of the press, saying they seemed "to have a Divine mandate to invent something sensational each day." He wanted their questions in advance so he could give them "mature thought," and if he didn't get them he would say at the press conference "There is a famine again today." The Republican platform supported some of his positions, such as the continuation of prohibition, and relief for agriculture in the form of cooperative local planning. Early on, he called for development of water power, collective bargaining, and curbing use of the injunction against labor. In March, 1932, he signed the Norris-La-Guardia Anti-Injunction Act to limit injunction use to restrain strikers, a foundational liberal labor law. He also signed two of Senator Wagner's bills on labor in 1930 and 1931, the first on gathering labor statistics, the

67. Fausold, *Hoover*, 14–15, 17.
68. Whitney, *Biographies*, 281; Boyer, *Oxford Companion*, 346.

second on planning (rather than implementing) public works. A third bill to fund state and local employment agencies he vetoed, saying it would embroil labor problems with big city political machines like Tammany Hall in New York city and would shut down the federal government's own employment service. This was "inconsistent with his commitment to de-centralization."[69]

In 1928 he promoted a $3 billion rainy day fund to be provided by states and the federal government, to be built up during prosperous times and held by the federal government to relieve unemployment during hard times. Unfortunately, the rainy day hit before the rainy day fund idea could catch on. In the meanwhile he wanted departments to cut their budgets to keep the deficit down. In 1930 he anticipated a $20–30 million deficit, but the onrushing depression added another $720 million to that in 1931. He was reluctant to have the federal government feed drought victims with surplus wheat. He pushed for the Red Cross to handle it. He had a copy of Cleveland's veto message in his files should he have to use it. But he finally signed a $65 million congressional relief package. He turned down an opportunity for setting a national policy precedent for private systems to assist with unemployment, health care, retirement, and disability, when American trade associations offered to handle these social issues in exchange for government restraint in anti-trust action. Hoover's reluctance to get the private sector into these policy areas set the stage for Franklin Roosevelt's nationalization of social welfare soon after.[70]

Hoover left many of Coolidge's appointees in office, but this denied him the use of patronage power to help get what he wanted through Congress. For his major appointees, he picked wealthy businessmen known for loyalty, conservativism and minimal partisanship. In contrast, Franklin Roosevelt obtained resignations and then delayed filling those important positions until he got his early legislation passed. As his navy secretary, Hoover appointed Charles F. Adams, a non-partisan who favored disarmament and descended from former presidents. Hoover wanted even more cuts in the navy than Adams and got them. He wanted to convert swords into plowshares—that is, direct the money for domestic needs.[71]

69. Fausold, *Hoover*, 22–25, 28, 30–32, 120, 122.
70. Ibid., 33, 72, 98, 111, 117, 141.
71. Ibid., 34–35, 40, 44–46, 58.

In his inaugural address, Hoover promoted "absolute integrity in public affairs," "freedom of public opinion," a jab at Wilson's red baiting (later he told his attorney general that communists could picket peacefully even in front of the White House), "the advancement of peace," "denial of domination by any group or class," "growth of religious spirit," "strengthening of the home," "self-government," "justice," "ordered liberty," "equality of opportunity," and "stimulation of initiative and individuality." This was almost the ten commandments in secular language. He wanted progressivism to build "a new economic system, a new social system, (and) a new political system." In spite of his optimism here, he was a pessimist and often saw backsliding more so than improvement.[72]

Hoover pushed open government. He instructed his attorney general to publish a list of backers of all judicial appointments in order to expose partisan pressure for these "non-partisan" jobs. He ordered the treasury secretary to publish all government refunds of taxes. He also asked Congress for a more progressive income tax, reducing taxes on lower incomes to a greater degree than middle or higher.[73]

Like Wilson, Hoover came into office with an agenda he wished to accomplish in his first year. For example, he made reforms in the Bureau of Indian Affairs to improve conditions on government-coordinated reservations. He eliminated the practice of segregated Indian boarding schools and promoted a policy of Indians retaining their culture. He doubled federal expenditures for Indians.[74]

Hoover made reforms in the crowded federal prison system. He won legislation to create the Boulder Canyon Project (Hoover Dam), destined to provide electric power in California. He thus fit well into the traditional Republican political system of promoting national internal improvement projects. He placed two million acres of federal land into the national forest reserve, demonstrating his commitment to conservation not so much of the environment but of federal hegemony over western lands. He rejected a proposal to build a dam in the naturally beautiful Cumberland Valley and also vetoed the Tennessee River Muscle Shoals dam project. He wanted a massive internal improvement project to dredge and modernize the Ohio, Mississippi, and Tennessee rivers, and thousands of miles of other rivers and canals, the sort of plan that

72. Ibid., 39–43.
73. Ibid., 56, 159.
74. Miller Center, *Hoover—Domestic Affairs;* Fausold, *Hoover,* 57.

James Polk eighty years earlier said would bankrupt the nation. Hoover also initiated the Federal Home Loan Bank System.[75]

Hoover signed the Agricultural Marketing Act of 1929. This legislation created a federal Farm Board to administer loans from a fund of $500 million to aid agricultural coops in marketing crops through national commodity organizations. Like Harding and Coolidge before him, he did not want peacetime direct federal control of surpluses through price supports, or federal purchase and storage as there had been during wartime. He was against paying farmers to reduce acreage under production.[76]

Hoover was clearly more active in legislation initiation than Harding or Coolidge. In fact, in December, 1931, he proposed sixteen major pieces of legislation. Only four were enacted, since the Democrats had gained control of the House in 1930. He proposed a large reduction in income tax rates, which Congress approved.[77]

Hoover convened the White House Conference on Health and Protection of Children in July, 1929. Some 2,500 delegates gathered to study child welfare. The result was thirty-five volumes of published findings. Hoover did not want the federal government to directly administer programs for children, or adults, for that matter. He said, "Shall we abandon the philosophy and creed of our people for 150 years . . ."; "shall we establish a dole from the Federal Treasury? Shall we undertake Federal ownership and operation of public utilities . . .?"; "Shall we regiment our people by an extension of the arms of bureaucracy into a multitude of affairs?" But he focused enough federal attention on the problem that later administrations moved more easily to usurp health and welfare policy-making from states and localities. He appointed Ray Lyman Wilbur, president of Stanford University, as secretary of the interior, where he wanted to carry out studies and encourage reforms for children, the sick, aged, homeless, and Indians. He called together conferences on housing, public land policy, oil conservation, federal involvement in education, and waste management. He also sponsored commissions like the Wickersham Commission on Law Enforcement, which reported that the Eighteenth Amendment (prohibition) was not being effectively enforced. Hoover thought there was some progress and was opposed to repeal.[78]

75. Crenson and Ginsberg, *Presidential Power*, 148; Miller Center, *Hoover—Domestic Affairs*; Boyer, *Oxford Companion*, 345; Fausold, Hoover, 57, 73, 136.

76. Fausold, *Hoover*, 50, 52, 112.

77. McDonald, *Presidency*, 364–65; Whitney, *Biographies*, 282.

78. Fausold, *Hoover*, 36, 59–60, 127, 142.

Hoover was concerned about attracting well educated young social scientists to federal government and to his commissions. He believed it was the role of the executive branch to study problems, and then recommend solutions to Congress, to the states, and to private institutions. He was like Harding in that he would not lobby Congress to get what he wanted. He kept his distance from Congress. In this spirit, Hoover did not use the veto often. It was said "No activist president in this century has kept his distance from the Congress as did Hoover." His approach was educational and apolitical. He even refused to comment on legislation when Congress was deadlocked on bills. In fact, once out of office he gave a spirited defense of separation of powers in the national government. He recalled, "I had felt deeply that no President should undermine the independence of legislative and judicial branches by seeking to discredit them. The constitutional division of powers is the bastion of our liberties and was not designed as a battleground to display the prowess of Presidents."[79]

In this spirit, Hoover gave little input to formulation and passage of the Smoot-Hawley Tariff. He personally wanted to protect agriculture and to see a "limited revision" of other tariffs. Initially, manufacturing tariffs were slated to rise nearly ten percent under the legislation. Congress withdrew most presidential flexibility to modify tariffs, a delegation of legislative power to the executive which Hoover wanted. Ultimately, the bill he signed increased agriculture schedules by ten percent and manufacturing schedules by only three percent. The raising of tariff barriers in the U.S. and worldwide was an early hint of the kind of economic and political nationalism that allowed tyrants to take their countries into war.[80]

The Depression unfolded in stages in the Hoover administration. Business people had become adept at creating and exploiting the "business cycle." In this latest cycle, first came a stock market crash, which followed years of unregulated speculation, the easy money policies of the Federal Reserve from 1925 to 1927, and ever more frequent purchasing of stocks on margin. In addition, wealthy Americans had money, but were not spending it, while middle and lower class Americans lost jobs and therefore could not spend to stimulate the economy either. In 1929,

79. Whitney, *Biographies*, 148, 285; Fausold, *Hoover*, 48–53.
80. Fausold, *Hoover*, 93–97.

five percent of Americans held thirty-three percent of the wealth. Some eighty percent of Americans had no savings at all.[81]

Then the financial outfall of World War I came home to roost in the form of world-wide depression. Wilson and the allies had placed a heavy burden of tribute on Germany. That nation could no longer make the war reparations payments to Britain and France. High tariffs meant the U.S. experienced a decrease in European imports, so Europeans did not have enough money to pay off American loans, and wanted to borrow money from the U.S. to make the payments. Hoover did succeed in procuring a one-year moratorium on all inter-government debts owed by major nations one to the other in order to help out the international economy. Germany had to make an annual debt payment of $400 million to France and England, and two-thirds of that was normally turned over by those two countries to the U.S. However, cash in the U.S. was drying up. France and Britain also could not make the payments they owed to the U.S., putting further pressure on banks in the U.S., which began to fail. Europe was still dealing with costly war reconstruction to get back to where they started before world War II. There were revolutions, unbalanced budgets, increased arms expenditures, inflation, and overproduction of certain commodities. In wartime, no one dreamed of balancing budgets, so European perpetual war, together with perpetual deficits brought inevitable recessions and depressions. The great drought in the American west also hurt the world economy. In the election year of 1932 Hoover declined to support forgiveness of Germany's debts, since he needed bank contributions to his campaign.[82]

In America, farmers were earning less, and could not pay bills and mortgages, so farms went into foreclosure and rural banks failed. Farm mechanization had increased production, but a falling population meant a reduction in the domestic market. There was a glut of agricultural production in Europe after World War I as well. Durable products were at a saturation point in the U.S. as well. These were the kinds of crisis economic conditions that historically invited a politician with less ethical fiber than Hoover to make grandiose promises, institute unsustainable programs, take great liberties with the law, and gain a good deal of glory for himself. Such tyranny would not have to wait much longer, but Hoover

81. Nelson, *Presidency*, 139; Miller Center, *Hoover—Domestic Affairs;* Fausold, *Hoover*, 68, 75–76.

82. Herring, *Colony to Superpower*, 481; Fausold, *Hoover*, 66–67, 78, 102, 110, 140, 143–44, 188, 191.

was not to be the one to instigate it. Hoover was a student of economic cycles and believed if production and inventories were controlled during good times, and good relations were maintained between capital and labor, planning by trade associations could prevent depressions. He now urged industry to maintain their labor forces intact and maintain wage levels, while he asked labor to withhold wage demands. But all of this was an uphill battle. Hoover resisted the urge for the central government to solve all the economic problems, and called for the states to dig their own citizenry out of the mess by enacting public works programs (internal improvements) to help create jobs, and asked private industry to hold the line on payroll even if it curtailed production. Hoover's efforts increased private relief programs by a factor of eight times previous levels.[83]

Hoover rejected federal relief bills and bond sales to fund unemployment benefits. He stated, "Legislat(ing) out of a worldwide depression . . . [is as easy as] exorcis(ing) a Caribbean hurricane by statutory law." He vetoed a "Bonus Bill" in 1931 which would have increased the loan value of veterans' federally funded life insurance policies, their "bonus certificates," from twenty-two percent to fifty percent. Congress overrode the veto and gave almost a billion dollars to veterans. Hoover, on the other hand, established the Veterans Administration, supported federal money for vet housing and hospitals, and increased veteran disability payments. Liberals in Congress won passage of bills collecting unemployment statistics on a national level and planning for possible public works programs. These baby steps led quite naturally to later federal commitments in the economy based on the statistical findings and plans. Hoover vetoed a bill that would have set up federal unemployment agencies at the state level.[84]

The Glass-Steagall Act was one of the pieces of Hoover's legislative program that Congress passed. The act initiated a federalization of parts of the credit system, and was modeled on Wilson's wartime federal lending agency. It substituted government bonds for gold as partial backing for currency. It was designed to deal with the contraction of credit and currency by authorizing the expansion of credit, and broadened the kinds of commercial paper acceptable for re-discount and use as money in the Federal Reserve System. It made government debt acceptable for re-discount, so the more the federal government borrowed, the greater

83. Crenson and Ginsberg, *Presidential Power*, 149; Miller Center, *Hoover—Domestic Affairs*; Fausold, *Hoover*, 64–65, 72, 76; Bailyn, *Great Republic*, 1076.

84. Crenson and Ginsberg, *Presidential Power*, 149; Whitney, *Biographies*, 282; Fausold, *Hoover*, 8, 134, 200; Miller Center, *Hoover—Domestic Affairs*.

the possible money supply. It also reorganized the railroads and ratified his proposal for the one-year international debt moratorium. The Glass-Steagall Act, together with the Sixteenth Amendment establishing a permanent national income tax on personal and corporate wealth, set the stage for the subsequent astronomical growth in the size of the national government. The legislation strengthened Lincoln's and Wilson's attempts at nationalization of monetary policy, as it enabled overnight regulation of credit and gave a huge infusion of power to the president. In fact, Hoover used the income tax provision to recommend a tax increase when the budget could not be balanced. He signed the Revenue Act of 1932 raising corporate taxes, incomes over $100,000, estate taxes, and excise taxes on certain items. A manufacturer's sales tax was taken out of the measure. His budget included savings from proposed government reorganization, but Congress said that reorganization was a legislative responsibility.[85]

Hoover next got a large dose of Potomac fever, as he pushed the national government deeply into the economic rescue business. In the fall of 1931, because the Federal Reserve was moving too cautiously, he got large banks to set up the National Credit Corporation and use their $500 million reserve fund to help small banks. He then drafted legislation for the Reconstruction Finance Corporation. When Congress capitalized it with $2 billion, Hoover vetoed it, saying it would make it a "gigantic banking and pawn-broking business." Some months later, after the voluntary concept was not working well, he caved in and signed a bill providing $3.3 billion in new credit. It was a central government-run and funded agency to provide credit to banks, railroads, agricultural, and insurance organizations, essentially a federal bailout agency.[86] This corporate welfare agency "saved" many larger banks from failure, and thus served as an early version of the "too big to fail" bailouts which came about in the 2008 recession. Thus the pattern was set for a profligate central government run by a few power-hungry bureaucrats to bail out profligate industry barons so that they could in turn keep the politicians in power. Business and government became two sides of the same dissolute coin.

In the summer of 1932, Hoover also signed an act creating an emergency federal relief program, the Emergency Relief Construction Act,

85. Boyer, *Oxford Companion*, 345; McDonald, *Presidency*, 365; Fausold, *Hoover*, 155–56, 158, 161–62.

86. Whitney, *Biographies*, 383; Fausold, *Hoover*, 145, 153–54, 163; Nelson, *Presidency*, 140.

which he had previously rejected because it would require deficit financing. This legislation provided $2 billion for federal public works projects and $300 million for direct relief programs run by state governments. Hoover saw the act as a temporary measure, and remained opposed to large-scale and permanent national government welfare expenditures.[87]

Hoover's Quaker upbringing had a decided effect on his foreign policy positions and actions. Once in the White House, Hoover worked hard at disarmament agreements. His Secretary of State hammered out an agreement with Britain and Japan to make limits in the number and size of naval cruisers. The Senate approved the treaty in July, 1930. In 1932 Hoover sent an envoy to a conference in Geneva to make a startling proposal for the abolition of submarines, airplanes, and tanks. When France made reductions contingent on the U.S. entering into a treaty to consult with France in the event of a military threat to them, Hoover rejected the deal, because it was too close to military protectionist entanglement in European affairs. Hoover negotiated an eighteen month moratorium on repayment of tribute from World War I, which took the edge off U.S. and allied economic imperialism in Europe. But Congress rejected his idea for a World War Foreign Debt Commission because they thought it was a prelude to total forgiveness of the tribute demanded by the U.S. Hoover negotiated later reductions in the tribute burden, but even so, France and Germany defaulted.[88]

Right after his 1928 election victory, Hoover made a ten week tour in Latin America stressing his plans to reduce U.S. military interference there as a method of forced debt collection. But then he went on a costly battleship because a cruiser did not have enough room for his press contingent. He encountered demonstrations against the "Colossus of the North." He also ruled out the U.S. becoming the international lender of last resort, applying economic sanctions against aggressors, and cancelling World War I debt. He essentially disavowed Teddy Roosevelt's corollary to the Monroe Doctrine, which allowed for military intervention to protect U.S. investments. He used what came to be called the J. Reuben Clark Memorandum detailing the recent history of U.S. involvement in Latin America to accomplish this turnabout. Hoover walked the talk. When the New Orleans Banana Company wanted military protection for U.S. citizens living in the interior of Nicaragua, Hoover declined. He

87. Crenson and Ginsberg, *Presidential Power*, 150.

88. Herring, *Colony to Superpower*, 479–80; Miller Center, *Hoover—Foreign Affairs*.

also removed the Marines out of Nicaragua in 1933 and promised to get them out of Haiti by 1935. He said that regardless of the consequence of leaving Haiti, "We should get out anyway." He personally arbitrated a dispute between Chile, Peru, and Bolivia. He established the genuine Good Neighbor policy that Franklin Roosevelt later felt was politically helpful for him to continue and get credit for.[89]

Japan invaded China in late 1931 to dislodge Russians from the Central Eastern Railway across Manchuria, precipitating the second Manchurian crisis (the first was between Russia and China in 1929). This made clear to Hoover that the Wilson-oriented view of world organization, which he had supported, was not working. Hoover opposed economic sanctions against Japan, and refused to intervene militarily, even though his secretary of state wanted to. Secretary Stimson wrote in his diary, "an embargo [is] an attempt to put on economic pressure [and the president] ruled it out on the ground that it . . . would be provocative and lead to war." When Japan marched into Shanghai, Hoover did send some troops to protect 3,500 Americans there. His most hawkish proposal, actually quite dovish, was to support the so-called Stimson Doctrine to not recognize Japanese territorial gains if a peace treaty should be signed, since Japan had signed the Kellogg-Briand Pact outlawing war, and a new treaty would violate that earlier pact. Japan left the League of Nations after the League condemned Japanese action. Hitler withdrew from the League of Nations not long after, demonstrating the frail nature of international associations. However, Japan eventually left Shanghai. In the Philippines, Hoover was against independence because that would hurt foreign trade for both countries. Colony status for the Philippines meant there could be no tariff barriers between the two. Thus economic concerns trumped political concerns. Hoover opposed a "consultative" pact with France to morally commit the U.S. to defend France if attacked, since this was a serious step to actual European alliance.[90]

After retiring from the presidency, Hoover advocated that the U.S. should stay out of World War II. He denounced the expansion of government under his successor FDR in a book titled *The Challenge to Liberty*. He wrote, "We cannot extend the mastery of government over the daily

89. Boyer, *Oxford Companion*, 345; Miller Center, *Hoover—Foreign Affairs*; Herring, *Colony to Superpower*, 497; Fausold, *Hoover*, 32, 184–85.

90. Bailyn, *Great Republic*, 1166; Herring, *Colony to Superpower*, 489–90; Miller Center, *Hoover—Foreign Affairs*; Fausold, 58, 175, 179, 182, 190.

life of a people without somewhere making it master of people's souls and thoughts. That is going on today."[91]

Franklin D. Roosevelt

The generation that fought World War II is today called The Greatest Generation. That generation's Commander in Chief is often judged to be the greatest U.S. president, or second greatest, next to Lincoln. Both those judgments can be partly written off as partisan reveling in self-congratulation by recent or still living generations of Americans. Indeed the glorifying of Roosevelt's expansion of central and executive power, his depression-era relief policies, and his "victory" in World War II have begun to subside a bit.

This book sees Roosevelt at or near the top of the list of bad presidents. His life was filled with unbridled ambition for power, and such ambition usually means that decisions are made contrary to the long-term interests of the people. Roosevelt began active planning for obtaining the presidency in 1920, some twelve years before he won the prize. FDR's activities while in office were marred by manipulative duplicity, bald dishonesty, secrecy, corruption, and repression. British philosopher Isaiah Berlin called FDR a "perfect chameleon," since he changed his colors so often. [92]

Roosevelt was the master of mischievousness and vindictiveness. He was known as one who would treat a man warmly in person, then stab him in the back later. His policies were often poorly designed and administered. His overall domestic program was tyrannical, and his foreign policy blood-thirsty and imperialistic. Tyranny is a function of vote-buying at election time, expansion of central government power, propaganda in place of information, purging of political intimates, marginalization or repression of populations, illegal use of power, and extension of the time of office-holding. Imperialism is a function of provoking war, expanding the standing army, forcing peace-minded citizens to be soldiers, forming ill-advised personal and political alliances, and the annexation

---

91. Bailyn, *Great Republic*, 1163; Boyer, *Oxford Companion*, 345; Whitney, *Biographies*, 284.

92. Fleming, *New Dealers' War*, 558.

or allocation of foreign lands as spoils of war. Of all of these practices, domestic and foreign, Franklin Roosevelt is guilty in spades.[93]

While FDR can be credited with helping to stop German and Italian fascism, at the end of World War II he unleashed Soviet totalitarian communism, a force more virulent than those other two combined. He did that by befriending Stalin and propping up Stalin's brutal regime with the tax proceeds of U.S. paychecks. He also committed the children of the Greatest Generation to the management of hundreds of nations by means of a "level of global supremacy unique in world history." This supremacy required an unprecedented level of wealth transfer from the paychecks of the American people to some 800 American military bases overseas and into the pockets of shady governments and government leaders who more often limited local freedoms than liberated them.

Roosevelt's habit of lying was widely known both within and without his administration, and it included social lying as well as political lying. For example, he lied to his lover Lucy Mercer, telling her that his wife Eleanor would not agree to a divorce, when Eleanor had already offered him the divorce. It has been said he "never developed a capacity for real intimacy . . . he needed people, but he needed them to help him accomplish his purposes." Divorce, for example, would have derailed his political career. He wanted personal power above all else, and "his world was filled with people used to getting their way." His own vice president Henry Wallace said, "The President certainly is a waterman. He looks one direction and rows the other with the utmost skill." FDR once said, "I never let my right hand know what my left hand is doing." This was a cute, yet arrogant, way of saying nobody could figure out what he was really going to do in spite of what he might have said, since his political calculations kept him busy right up to the moment of decision. He flip-flopped so often due to his evolving power calculations that one cabinet member made sure to have his approval twice before moving ahead with any project.[94]

Franklin Roosevelt set a precedent for hogging the limelight when, after winning the Democratic nomination, he was the first presidential nominee in American history to travel to the convention center to accept in person. He campaigned as a unifier, "a national healer." He had in mind

---

93. Ibid., 100.

94. Fleming, *New Dealers' War*, 360; Genovese, *Power*, 131; McJimsey, *Roosevelt*, 13, 16, 130.

a balm for everyone's ailments. He championed himself and the federal government as the only force that could unify "a division between different regions of the country." One historian writes, "Roosevelt's willingness during the campaign to appeal to all factions and ideological positions served the political purpose of attracting the largest possible-following." But with that popularity, unity for Roosevelt took on more the aspect of national "heeling," as he wanted people to follow him like a loyal pet wherever he might go. One author argues, "As long as he remained popular, he could afford to manipulate the people around him."[95]

In order to implement his constantly changing directions in policy, Roosevelt needed to gather sycophants (yes-men) around him. From his advisers and cabinet members he valued loyalty above any other value, including respect of the law. Agencies of his government could not hire anyone or keep anyone employed who worked against him or his programs. He told cabinet members what to include in their speeches. His relief administrator, Harry Hopkins, typified many of his administrators. Hopkins said he was going to be "all political" in running his agency and hire only loyal New Dealers to give out New Deal relief. He purged (fired) many employees to punish them, and the firings provided him with new jobs to offer Congressmen to help manipulate their votes.[96]

It is fair to say, as one political commentator did, that the "Depression created a constituency for active government . . ." A more forthright way of saying this is that Roosevelt took advantage of the American people in a time of great sadness, hunger, joblessness and emotional vulnerability, and used the office of the president to concentrate power in the central government and in himself. His coalition of supporters included, tellingly, the uneducated (young voters and new immigrants), the unemployed, and those on relief. The vast majority of all of these registered as Democrats. But FDR brought the middle class into his coalition by insuring their bank deposits, providing credit insurance to protect their homes, unemployment compensation to protect their employment, and government loans to buy their homes. Because of his popularity, it could be said, "No president since Abraham Lincoln had so dominated national party politics." But over the time of his four electoral victories, his popularity went steadily downhill, as his hastily thought-out policies and

95. McJimsey, *Roosevelt*, 19, 21, 23–25, 29, 36, 126, 131.
96. Ibid., 131, 133.

programs failed to meet expectations. They were good for him, but not necessarily for the people.[97]

The programs he enacted to court voters not only seduced the citizenry, but were "a magnet around which politicians arranged themselves." They saw that they could enhance their own stature as Roosevelt did his, if only they played ball with him. As one writer mused, "He brought security to the aged, relief to the unemployed, and shorter hours and higher wages to workingmen." What's not to like about that? He forever changed the face of government in America. In the words of one author, he expanded government "beyond anything imagined even by most Progressive reformers a generation earlier."[98] FDR was also the magnet that attracted big business to central government during the war. Business and industry saw clearly they could reap immense profits if only they followed the president's instincts.

Before Franklin Roosevelt's term of office, citizens had contact with the national government only through mail delivery or army service. Now they interacted with the national government by means of their transportation and communication patterns, their retail purchases, their employers and their labor unions, and their education systems. FDR's Works Progress Administration even built playgrounds, schools and hospitals. Federal employment increased five-fold during his lengthy term of office.[99] Most decisions that affected their lives now came from Washington, DC, and more specifically, from FDR's desk, rather than from local and state government and from private institutions.

Roosevelt came into office in 1932 in the midst of a banking, stock market, and industrial crisis. He dishonestly proposed deep spending cuts, knowing that Congress would not go along with such cuts as he proposed, which included veterans' pensions. As soon as blame for wanting increased spending could be placed on Congress, he shifted gears and asked for $300 million for his proposed civilian "forest army," in order to pay Civilian Conservation Corp men to work on conservation projects. His budget director was astounded at Roosevelt's change in fiscal philosophy and said he could not go in two directions at once. The Civilian Conservation Corps gave work to 250,000 youths in national forests and

---

97. Ibid., 140–45.

98. Boyer, *Oxford Companion*, 676; Whitney, *Biographies*, 286; Nelson, *Presidency*, 143.

99. Crenson and Ginsberg, *Presidential Power*, 292.

parks. In his first 100 days he launched many other new national agencies. He started with the Federal Emergency Relief Administration (FERA), which distributed $500 million in both matching and outright grants to woo the states and help them assist thirteen million unemployed. FERA, among other things, started twenty-eight new towns supplied with 2,400 housing units, and asked for volunteers to move to these planned communities.[100] The Home Owners Loan Corporation (HOLC) made several billion dollars available to help forestall foreclosure.

The Agricultural Adjustment Administration set production quotas in an effort to raise farm prices. It gave the president unilateral authority to increase agricultural tariffs, essentially the power to initiate trade war and set up the conditions for hot war. Roosevelt increased duties on cotton imports and cut checks to reduce domestic cotton, corn, and wheat acreage as well as hog production. FDR's Soil Conservation Service reorganized western rural farm lands and placed them in the hands of large landlords. Those landlords retired acreage, moved off renters, collected on AAA payments, purchased more machinery, and kicked out more renters. In 1934, FDR signed the Taylor Grazing Act, which nationalized all rangelands and established grazing districts. The federal government then rented back their own lands to former users and limited their grazing rights. The western states had always been "little more than a colony of the rest of the nation." As a result of the AAA, the SCS, and the Grazing Act they were now allowed to put on big boy pants and get some economic development for themselves if they agreed with Roosevelt's concentration of power in big agriculture, big business, and big government.[101]

The Public Works Administration (PWA) initiated huge construction projects such as the Boulder (now Hoover) Dam. The Civil Works Administration (CWA) set out to employ four million workers over a concentrated period in early 1934, doing work on roads, sewers, public buildings, and producing public art, editing and translating services.[102]

The Tennessee Valley Authority was aimed at bringing national planning and stimulation of employment to one of the poorest regions in America, the farms and small towns in the seven states bordering the Tennessee River. Lacking electricity in the area, the project provided dams, recreational facilities and a model community of racially segregated

100. McJimsey, *Roosevelt*, 37, 39, 47, 95–96.

101. Ibid., 49, 55, 58–59, 115, 117.

102. Ibid., 43, 98.

homes. It strove to tie industry and agriculture together in a huge public option-type project to supplant private interests. It set a precedent for European-style centralized industrial planning and nation-wide river watershed internal improvement programming of the type the founders worried would bankrupt the nation. FDR announced dishonestly, like a giant tooth fairy, "This is not coming from Washington. It is coming from you. You are not being federalized." The project displaced many families who were not adequately compensated, especially tenant farmers, and it became known for heavy environmental pollution. TVA became the prototype in 1937 for seven other such projects across the country, including the Grand Coulee and Bonneville projects on the Columbia River in Washington state. These later projects were coordinated through the National Resources Board, whose job it was to plan population settlement patterns in western states. FDR successfully placed public power production in the hands of the war department and distribution of power in the hands of the interior department. Public power was then used to support the huge public war machine FDR was planning to develop in the country. [103]

Roosevelt continued Hoover's Reconstruction Finance Corporation and pushed it to sublime lengths. Jesse Jones, its administrator, said, "We can lend anything that we think we should . . . any amount, any length of time, or any rate of interest . . . to anybody." The alphabet soup agencies were aimed at sealing the loyalty of and providing votes from the unemployed, homeowners, farmers, engineers, American youth, and southeastern Democrats, and many others. In fact, Harry Hopkins, FDR's head of the WPA, said in an unguarded moment, "We shall tax and tax, spend and spend, elect and elect." By means of the alphabet agencies Roosevelt thus became commander in chief of the entire economy in peacetime, as Wilson had been in wartime. Many of the agencies boasted of great goals, but achieved little. The Resettlement Administration, promising to relocate a million families from city slums to small forms, ultimately relocated only 11,000. In spite of hundreds of new agencies, and billions in new expenditures, FDR failed to bring the U.S. out of the depression into full employment, and by 1937, after four years of economic legislation, the nation slid back into deep recession once again. Unemployment in America remained about ten percent until 1941. In fact, Hitler was more

103. Ibid., 40–41, 43, 88–89, 112–13, 171.

successful in cutting unemployment, raising productivity and national income.[104]

Roosevelt's most ambitious project of all was the National Recovery Administration (NRA), which implemented his industrial policy for the nation. It regulated peacetime production and set prices across major industries. It created a huge amount of red tape, releasing hundreds of regulatory codes and 2,998 administrative orders modifying those codes in an "endless attempt to control the economy." It fostered monopoly and "cartelized the economy." It also published 6,000 press releases, some of which had actual legislative effect. One historian indicates "Department officials were sometimes unaware of their own regulations." The NRA was managed by the director of Wilson's wartime War Industries Board. It essentially licensed the existence of companies on the national level. Its appointments, structure and functions were the responsibility of Franklin Roosevelt alone, not subject to any checks and balances. Franklin wanted industry giants to bid for his favors. Benito Mussolini, the Italian fascist tyrant, called the National Industrial Recovery Act (NIRA) creating the NRA the "act of a dictator."[105]

The NRA had a rule, for example, that a customer could not take his pick of a coup of chickens, but must choose at random. The four Schechter brothers, New York City kosher chicken merchants, went to jail for allowing their customers to pick the best of the coup. About this sort of fulsome executive micromanagement and rough-riding, the Supreme Court agreed with Mussolini and said in the Panama Refining case, "This is delegation [of legislative power] running riot." The court reminded that the legislation gave FDR "unlimited authority to determine the policy" for transportation of excess production. The court also said that "disobedience to his order is made a crime punishable by fine and imprisonment." The court overturned the Schechters' prison sentences and declared the NRA unconstitutional by a vote of nine to zero.[106]

FDR's second wave of legislation created the Securities and Exchange Commission, the Works Progress Administration, the Rural

---

104. Boyer, *Oxford Companion*, 773; Healy, *Cult of the Presidency*, 72; Fleming, *New Dealers' War*, 50–52, 63, 82, 478.

105. Boyer, *Oxford Companion*, 676; Genovese, *Power*, 132; Whitney, *Biographies*, 292; McJimsey, *Roosevelt*, 45–46, 68–71, 83, 135; Fisher, *Constitutional Conflicts*, 95; Healy, *Cult of the Presidency*, 71–73.

106. Fisher, *Constitutional Conflicts*, 95; Cooper, *Order*, 22; Fleming, *New Dealers' War*, 56–57.

Electrification Administration, the National Labor Relations Board, Aid to Dependent Children, the Social Security Act, and the Fair Labor Standards measure, among others.

The Securities Act establishing the Securities and Exchange Commission preempted state securities regulation. The Works Progress Administration (WPA), larded with $4.8 billion, created jobs using somewhere between one and half to three million unemployed to build roads, bridges, drainage facilities, public buildings, parks, airports, and hospitals. It created fine arts employment through such means as the Federal Arts Project, the Federal Theater Project, and the Federal Music Project. The WPA didn't contribute much to recovery because it spent money for wages rather than materials, which would have created jobs in the private sector. However it was of great political value to Roosevelt because some eighty percent of WPA workers voted Democrat, much like Lincoln's Grand Army of the Republic soldiers voted for their Republican employer. One mayor noted, "Who is going to vote against Santa Claus." The WPA also did not cost the government much in current taxes, since it was done by deficit spending.[107]

In 1935 the Supreme Court invalidated the AAA, saying it was an attempt to give the federal government "uncontrolled police power in every state in the union." While this agency was going down, FDR and his Democrat controlled Congress passed the Social Security Act, the Wagner Act giving labor unions more power, and the graduated income tax.[108]

In June, 1934, Roosevelt had pushed the nation to go much faster than states and corporations were willing to go on old age security. Only six states had old age pension laws and few companies had programs. There was thus no real experience in or consensus around such a nationalized program. In fact, labor opposed the program because it wanted social security type programs to be establishing through collective bargaining. But Roosevelt seduced the nation in a time of crisis and irrational thinking. The Social Security Act was enacted in 1935, timed as a massive vote-buying program for a president up for reelection in 1936. Roosevelt unilaterally prohibited means-testing for the new Social Security Administration (SSA), which would have provided higher benefits for the elderly poor. He also allowed business to compensate for employer contributions by raising prices. He thus essentially enacted a

107. McJimsey, *Roosevelt*, 100–104.
108. Fleming, *New Dealers' War*, 57.

national sales tax on consumers to finance the program through the back door.[109]

The third phase of the New Deal was marked by the variety of executive department reorganizations he conducted after the winning of his second term. He also proposed national housing legislation, flip-flopping before the 1936 election on his earlier contempt for such a program, national wages and hours standards calling for a forty hour work week and a minimum wage, farm legislation, and tax reform. In 1937 he once again returned to the position of being a budget-cutter during a time of recession, as it suited his purposes then. Only a year later, with the recession still going on, he proposed huge increases in spending, a pattern Barack Obama would use to achieve political success some seventy years later. He authorized $2 billion in new spending and $1 billion in new loans. Nevertheless, it was not FDR's New Deal that got the nation out of depression and double dip recession, but rather the forced economic mobilization of World War II that did, as many historians now judge.[110]

When FDR implemented the several legislative waves of the New Deal, he sealed the loyalty of his constituents with "hundreds of thousands of federal jobs and millions of dollars in loans and benefits." The Works Progress Administration (WPA) and Social Security were directly administered by the federal government, that is to say, nationalized from the beginning. The federal government also wooed voters by extending low-cost electricity to rural America, and made other internal infrastructure improvements like paved roads, irrigation, and flood control. His reward for all this patronage vote-buying was a landslide reelection in 1936. By the time of running for reelection for a third term in 1940, Roosevelt was turning up his nose at political ethics entirely. For example, he wooed Chicago Democratic boss Ed Kelly by eliminating federal prosecution of Chicago mob bosses Kelly was protecting. In turn, Kelly gave an election speech entitled, "Roosevelt is my Religion." FDR channeled huge amounts of federal money to Chicago. In addition, FDR refused to prosecute a New Jersey postmaster appointed by New Jersey political boss Frank Hague. Hague was opening labor union mail to determine

109. McJimsey, *Roosevelt*, 105–8.

110. Crenson and Ginsberg, *Presidential Power*, 167; Miller Center, *Hoover—Impact and Legacy*; McJimsey, *Roosevelt*, 171, 178–181.

friends and enemies. FDR announced simply, "We need Hague's support if we want New Jersey."[111]

In 1938 FDR made "the most energetic effort by a president to influence off-year Congressional elections since Andrew Johnson's 'swing around the circle' in 1866." He used threats to reduce federal WPA spending in districts where senators were opposing his break-up of utility holding companies. He also pushed measures to reorganize the executive branch to give him more control over all aspects of national policy.[112]

Beginning in 1932 FDR got major grants of emergency power from Congress. He did this by calling an emergency session of Congress in March, 1933. In March, 1933, FDR called an emergency session of Congress and it gave him war powers in peacetime, saying that virtually anything the president had done so far was "hereby approved and confirmed." Then after his executive orders on banking and gold, Congress met again to ratify his actions. Also in 1933, Congress gave FDR broad power to reorganize the executive branch without the threat of a legislative veto. This authority lasted two years. In 1937 he asked for renewed authority to do so, as we mentioned above, subject only to a joint resolution of disapproval from Congress, and got this authority. But he persuaded Congress to enforce any disapproval in the form of a legislative veto instead. FDR declared thirty-nine emergencies in his first six years in office, all during peacetime. Many were not genuine but "because of neglect or contrivance." Congressman Barton quipped, "Any national administration is entitled to one or two national emergencies in a term of six years. But an emergency every six weeks means plain bad management." In hindsight, Barton might better have characterized such a string of emergencies as bald despotism. In 1971, Congress discovered that the United States had been in a continuous state of declared national emergency since March 9, 1933 when FDR proclaimed a banking emergency. A measure controlling the expiration of national emergencies was finally enacted in 1976, but has fallen into disuse as yet later emergencies were enacted by Presidential fiat.[113]

In his First Inaugural Address, Roosevelt tutored Congress in constitutional law, or at least his own new brand of it. He said, "[The

111. Crenson and Ginsberg, *Presidential Power*, 32–33, 165; Fleming, *New Dealers' War*, 70–73.

112. McJimsey, *Roosevelt*, 146–49.

113. McDonald, *Presidency*, 297; Cooper, *Order*, 41; Fisher, *Constitutional Conflicts*, 139–40, 264, 264–65, 267.

Constitution] is so simple and practical that it is possible always to meet extraordinary needs by changes in emphasis and arrangement without loss in essential form." One of the simple "arrangements" Roosevelt planned in 1937was to pack the Supreme Court with his stooges, so that they would not overturn his decrees. Within two weeks after his landslide victory in 1936 he pounced on the electorate like a cheetah. He drew up a bill in "total secrecy" and padded it with bogus statistics about federal court workload. The legislation would have given him power to appoint fifty new judges, and six or seven alone on the Supreme Court. The public and members of both political parties saw it as a transparent grab at additional power and a naked attempt to subvert the Constitution. The country declined to sign off on his plans. During the next mid-term Congressional election, Roosevelt sought to purge thirteen southern and western Democrats who had objected to his court-packing scheme. He travelled to their home states and spoke against them, in an unprecedented purge of his own party members. But even now, only half-way through his lengthy term, the nation was beginning to push back against his depredations. All but one of the thirteen Democrats was reelected in 1938. Republicans doubled their numbers in the House. Byrnes and Wallace called it the worst blunder of Roosevelt's career.[114]

Interestingly, during the 1930s the Supreme Court was against delegation of legislative powers to the president, but after Roosevelt's intimidation of them, and after making eight appointments to the bench, by the mid-1940s they gave way to his program of presidential usurpation.[115] All of this is rather ironic, and instructive, in view of the fact Roosevelt made a radio speech during the campaign in which he called for national recovery plans "that build from the bottom up and not from the top down, that put their faith once more in the forgotten man at the bottom of the economic pyramid." Roosevelt's top-down direction of the recovery and his coddling of institutional interests in his first term once he gained the White House thus makes of Roosevelt an immense hypocrite and an electioneering liar. As a result of this deluge of Rooseveltian first and second term legislating, spending and court appointing, it was said that he had "reached the pinnacle of legislative power," and that "he ran the country like a city government." One can see how a single dictatorial precedent

114. Whitney, *Biographies*, 294; Morley, *Freedom and Federalism*, 158; Fleming, *New Dealers' War*, 59, 61–62, 516.

115. McDonald, *Presidency*, 366–67; Healy, *Cult of the Presidency*, 75; Flagel, *Guide*, 152; only George Washington made more appointments at ten.

sets the stage for another, yet more outrageous usurpation. The Constitution makes clear that all legislative powersare vested in Congress, but in his first 100 days, Roosevelt wrote a new constitution for the country, making himself both the author the executor of it.

Roosevelt made continual effort to give himself maximum flexibility to run the executive branch as he saw fit without congressional input. He presented a reorganization plan which would allow him to consolidate agencies into new departments like a department of conservation and a department of welfare, and to re-direct functions. His proposed plan would break off relationships of the existing fairly independent agencies with their congressional committee and budget counterparts. He presented his reorganization plan in finished form without consulting Congress. Congress was not impressed and failed to act. But in 1939 Congress gave him a watered-down version requiring him to submit reorganization plans to Congress. It also gave him six new administrative assistants and gave him a window of two years to reorganize the executive branch, subject to Congressional veto if they did not like his plan.[116]

This turned out to be a huge mistake from the point of view of Congressional power, because FDR used the time and latitude given him to create the Executive Office of the President in September, 1939. One public administration expert called it an "epoch-making even in the history of American institutions." By means of the EOP, Roosevelt usurped power in three new and different ways: he enhanced presidential influence over Congress; he enhanced presidential control over the federal bureaucracy; and he expanded the purview of "direct presidential action" by means of executive orders, the rule-making process, and such things as presidential proclamations. Roosevelt also took away the independent litigating responsibilities of federal departments and centralized it in the Department of Justice. He did this by Executive Order 6166, even though dispersion of litigatory responsibility had been established by Congress.[117]

This reorganization started in 1939 and effectively gave Roosevelt a bill of divorce from Congress. He used it to start a new life for the presidency by building up a vast new bureaucracy under his personal control. Whereas in 1923 the president had thirty White House staff, by 1945 Roosevelt managed to build five divisions into his Executive Office

116. McJimsey, *Roosevelt*, 182–83.

117. Crenson and Ginsberg, *Presidential Power*, 178, 180; Krent, *Presidential Powers*, 63–64.

of the President, one of which, the Bureau of Budget, had grown from forty staffers in 1939 to 500 staffers in 1945, at which time Warren Harding was understood to have rolled over in his grave. FDR also employed unelected, and unsanctioned "unofficial advisers" like Thomas Corcoran and Benjamin Cohen, who operated "beyond the rules" and made legislation on their own.[118] In addition, Roosevelt borrowed staff from the executive agencies to help him consolidate control. By these means of enhancing the political autonomy of the White House, FDR could make policy without venturing outside the White House, consulting Congress, or listening to the wishes of the public. Rather than listen to the public, he chatted with them unilaterally and explained why he thought they wanted him to do what he had already decided to do.

The most potent vehicles that Roosevelt used to execute his one-man emergency rule and to marginalize his own party and also Congress were the use of executive orders and the veto. In the first two years of office, FDR unilaterally created sixty-five new executive agencies to administer his programs of banking relief, public works, farm policies, securities regulation, home loans, and farm credit. During his first fifteen months in office he issued 674 executive orders. By the end of his four terms of office, he had issued 3,723 such unilateral orders. Franklin Roosevelt's legislative unilateralism is also seen by the fact he exercised the veto more than any other president in history, some 635 times, which is astonishing considering he had huge Democratic majorities in Congress. He used the veto to discipline Congress as if they were his own advisers and also to win favorable publicity for his personal needs and ends.[119] Vetoes were weekly events.

In order to win support for his unprecedented policy measures, Roosevelt used extraordinary propaganda measures. Once he had warmed up to the entire process of tyranny after his two terms of legislative success and his third term of successful war-time engagement of the nation in the affairs of monarchs, tyrants and communist dictators in Europe and Asia, Franklin Roosevelt began to see the full range of possibilities of the power that he held. His Economic Bill of Rights, announced early in March, 1943, urged Americans to believe that their national government ought to provide them with a right to medical care, clothing,

118. Crenson and Ginsberg, *Presidential Power*, 180–82.

119. Ibid., 291; Fisher, *Constitutional Conflicts*, 95; Flagel, *Guide*, 133; McDonald, *Presidency*, 354.

recreation, education, a job, a home, and a pension—basically cradle to grave government giveaways. The Wall Street Journal called the program a "totalitarian plan," but that did not stop Harry Truman from using it as his platform for action after the war. The report also called for the creation of a national transportation agency, consolidation of the nation's railroads, and government-planned air transportation. His policy wonks also called for rivers and harbors public works projects, and an immense investment in public housing. Roosevelt brayed in his October 28, 1944 campaign address, "I know [that the American people] . . . agree with those objectives—that they demand them—and that they are going to get them." FDR also began to lay plans for extending the New Deal to allies in Europe by proposing a huge electrification project for Central Europe, where the communists had already taken power but needed a large assist in order to hold on to that power.[120]

In these middle and later years Roosevelt was exhibiting a "growing messianic complex" which convinced him that "his and the nation's interests were identical." Some of his admirers, and especially those seeing a lot of federal money, respected the man more than the law. For example, Chicago police arrested and fined a young man $2,000 for booing an FDR newsreel. When Roosevelt did his fireside chats on the radio, he was able to speak directly to the people over the heads of party and Congressional representatives. He thereby "educated," and ruled, independent of party, and encouraged the people to come to him for the benefits they sought. In the words of one author, "The party had become prisoner of a personality." He adopted all the weary and ailing adults of the nation and made them his children, providing them with benefits at his say-so. When the Congress sent him a tax bill he did not like, he vetoed a major tax bill for the first time in the history of the nation in 1944. This was seen as a transparent attempt to deprive the House of Representatives of its constitutional power of the purse.[121]

During the time from McKinley through Hoover, there was somewhat of a balance of power among the three branches of the national government, but that all ended with Franklin Roosevelt's control of both Congress and the court. He thus succeeded in "casting aside the long-standing commitment to states' rights and forcing acceptance of

120. Morley, *Freedom and Federalism*, 170; Fleming, *New Dealers' War*, 200, 326, 501.

121. Crenson and Ginsberg, *Presidential Power*, 36, 42, 171; Fleming, *New Dealers' War*, 84, 91, 341.

Hamilton's belief in a strong central government." "Political power was drained both from the State governments and from the Congress of the United States."[122]

One historian lists Roosevelt as the number one Machiavellian (strong-armed) president in American history for four reasons: his sense of superiority, his preference for force over mercy, his use of secrecy, and his fixation with his own legacy. These characteristics combined to make him emotionally detached, not caring what happened to people, or worrying about their welfare or interests. Franklin Roosevelt's successor, Harry Truman, at age eighty-six, finally commented on the essential personality of the man he served as vice president and succeeded as president: "Inside he was the coldest man I ever met. He didn't care about you or me or anyone else in the world on a personal level." For example, he did not worry about the implications of his decision to put Japanese Americans into concentration camps from 1942 through 1945, which he did by Executive Order 9066. He needed the political support of the west to successfully run for a fourth term, so he went against FBI intelligence that pointed out Japanese-Americans posed no espionage or sabotage threat. He detained 111,000 living in California, Oregon, and Washington in concentration camps. They lost jobs, homes and possessions. The FBI and Attorney General denounced the idea, since there was no evidence of disloyalty. He relied on no specific authority under law. The secretary of war said the whole idea would "make a tremendous hole in our constitutional system." The ACLU called it "the greatest deprivation of civil liberties in this country since slavery." Justice Jackson said that the Supreme Court decision to uphold his actions was a more dangerous blow to liberty than the action itself. FDR wanted to intern 140,000 more Japanese in Hawaii, who constituted a third of the population there. But he did not need the votes of white Americans there to get reelected, and, besides, the Japanese there could be used in the war effort.[123] This action gave the lie to the idea of Roosevelt as a "liberal" president.

In addition, during World War II Roosevelt adopted and played out the kind of ruthless racism and feud hatreds that European autocrats had long demonstrated for neighboring cultures. He made his personal hatred of Germans essentially the nation's own military policy and enforced

122. McDonald, *Presidency*, 277; Whitney, *Biographies*, 287; Morley, *Freedom and Federalism*, 151.

123. Flagel, *Guide*, 56; Fleming, *New Dealers' War*, 109–12, 560; Krent, *Presidential Powers*, 142.

it by means of his brutal policy of unconditional surrender. He prolonged the European war well beyond what needed to be. He wanted to exile European-based Germans between the ages of twenty and forty to Central Africa after the war, but dropped the plan because he was not sure what to do with their children. He even contemplated deporting Germans residing in America until he realized there were 60 million of them.[124]

A 1937 opinion poll, taken just before Germany's invasion of Czechoslovakia, showed that ninety-five percent of Americans opposed any further involvement in European war after the nation's experience in World War I. Most Americans, looking back, believed that the U.S. had had no real stake in the outcome of World War I, and that it had been bamboozled into participation by bankers, munitions makers, and Wilson. In fact, Congress nearly passed a Constitutional amendment, the Ludlow Amendment, that would have prevented U.S. participation in a foreign war without a popular referendum. Another poll indicated eighty percent of Americans were opposed to entering into war if no hostile act were committed against the U.S. FDR spoke continually out of both sides of his mouth as European events unfolded. In 1932 he called for the international abolishment of offensive weapons, but by 1942 he was building the largest offensive military machine the earth had ever known.[125]

Roosevelt provoked war with Japan by various means. His neglectful handling of intelligence intercepts in the fall of 1941 saying that an attack was coming somewhere in the Pacific was only the last of his deliberate provocations to war. In 1939, he indicated that the 1911 commercial treaty with Japan would end. He thus unilaterally nullified the Treaty of Commerce, Friendship, and Navigation without the consent of the Senate. In 1940 he embargoed U.S. aviation gasoline and high-grade scrap iron to Japan, and soon expanded this to all scrap iron and steel, and later yet to copper and brass, leaving oil as a bargaining tool in late 1940. He froze Japanese assets in July 1941, which turned into an embargo of not just oil but all trade with Japan. His treaty revocation and embargos were essentially acts of war. Commander in Chief Richardson had asked FDR to maintain the U.S. fleet at San Diego. He said the fleet would be vulnerable out in the Pacific, since they lacked oilers and supply ships. FDR insisted they be kept at Pearl Harbor and he fired Richardson. The

---

124. Fleming, *New Dealers' War*, 430; Flagel, *Guide*, 56–57.

125. Herring, *Colony to Superpower*, 503–504; McDonald, *Presidency*, 404; Fleming, *New Dealers' War*, 5, 66; McJimsey, *Roosevelt*, 48–49, 53.

Japanese assault on Pearl Harbor happened on December 7, 1941. The U.S. declared war on Japan on December 8. Germany, bound by treaty to protect Japan, declared war on the U.S. three days later on December 11. The dominoes that FDR expected to fall had now fallen. FDR's hot interest in warring against Japan ensured that 20,000 U.S. army were killed or captured in the Philippines early in the conflict.[126]

The Selective Service Act had enacted the first peacetime draft in U.S. history. Ultimately, some ten million were drafted, five million to the armed forces, and five million deferred to work in war industries. In June, 1941, before Pearl Harbor, FDR by executive order seized the North American Aviation plant in California. He also seized ship factories, cable companies, shell plants, and 4,000 coal companies. But not until 1943, under wartime duress, did Congress retroactively give him authority to do what he did in 1941. Thus Roosevelt made use of Lincoln's precedent of shooting first, and asking for permission later.[127]

Roosevelt served as propagandist in chief of his own army. He said, for example, that only three ships had been permanently put out of commission at Pearl Harbor, when the actual count was eleven. Soon after Pearl he also said America had destroyed more Japanese planes than the Japanese had destroyed American planes there. In fact, at Pearl, the U.S. lost 180 planes, and the Japanese only 29.[128]

FDR used Wilson's FBI to monitor not only subversives, but to get information about those who simply opposed the war as political non-interventionists. He viewed their opposition to the war as opposition to him and would not tolerate that. FDR used warrantless wiretaps on his own colleagues, thus encouraging later presidents like Kennedy, Johnson, and Nixon to think they could survive such raids on constitutional government. He surveilled those who sent him letters criticizing his policies. He created the OSS, his own secret police, by executive order in 1941. Roosevelt also authorized use of military courts, where evidentiary requirements are lax, for American citizens of German ancestry who attempt to commit "hostile or warlike acts . . ." These citizens were not given access to the Constitution's Article III civilian court system.[129] He

---

126. Herring, *Colony to Superpower*, 530-31, 534, 536; Fleming, *New Dealers' War*, 1, 12–13, 16–18, 20–23, 26–27, 30–31, 33–37, 42, 46, 88, 280.

127. Crenson and Ginsberg, *Presidential Powers*, 233; Fisher, *Constitutional Conflicts*, 106.

128. Fleming, *New Dealers' War*, 129.

129. Healy, *Cult of the Presidency*, 73; Herring, *Colony to Superpower*, 520; Crenson

thus set precedent for George W. Bush and Barack Obama to use of the same suspension of rights later on.

Roosevelt told his son Elliott that he thought the Soviet Union would be a "constructive force" once it got eastern Europe under its control. Roosevelt's view of the world was essentially imposed on his party and the literary organs of the party, including the media partial to the New Dealer's program. There were unmistakable signs of a huge body count associated with Stalin's methods both inside and outside Russia, but that didn't move Roosevelt in the least. Roosevelt took care to cover up Stalin's atrocities from public view in the United States, as he did his own humanitarian disasters. And he got big media complicity in his efforts.[130]

In 1943 Roosevelt hired a full-time pollster who urged him to make a show of cooperation with Congress, to take credit for battlefront good news, not to mention domestic politics—in other words, get elected by being a war glory president. Roosevelt's pro-Soviet propaganda was so effective that ninety-three percent of the American people in 1943 believed Russia would be a friendly partner of the U.S. in creating a democratic world after the war. But, in fact, there were many indications that Roosevelt's political marriage to Stalin was a marriage made in hell. In fact, Churchill said an alliance with Stalin was like "shaking hands with murder."[131]

American tax rates before the war began at as low as three percent and were increased to as high as ninety-one percent as a result of the war. Citizens once paying seven percent federal income tax, soon were paying twenty-eight percent. Federal government tax revenues went from $1 billion in 1940 to $45 billion by 1945. FDR broadened the number of households subject to the income tax from thirteen to twenty-eight million by means of the Revenue Act of 1942. In order to finance his war more effectively, he signed legislation in 1943, the Current Tax Payment Act, which called for automatic and involuntary withholding of taxes by employers amounting to twenty percent of wages. Previously, tax contributions depended upon the honesty of the taxpayer.[132]

FDR also developed the atomic bomb and allowed so much infiltration of Soviet agents into high levels of government, than soon many

and Ginsberg, *Presidential Power*, 247; Krent, Presidential Powers, 148.

130. Fleming, *New Dealers' War*, 280–81.

131. Ibid., 305.

132. Flagel, *Guide*, 122.

nations were capable of destroying entire populations with the push of a button.

Franklin Roosevelt is in the top three of American presidents as far as increasing the national debt. The national debt started at $19 billion when he came to office, and rose to $271 billion during his time, an increase of 1,326 percent. By the middle of the war, Roosevelt had not only increased the military to ten million persons, but had increased the number of federal bureaucrats to 172,736. This rates puts FDR high on the hypocrisy scale as well when one considers that he earlier said, "I accuse the present administration [Hoover] of being the greatest spending administration in peacetime in all our history . . . It has piled bureau on bureau, commission on commission." National spending went from forty percent of GDP to 120 percent of GDP during his administration. A large part of the national debt in 2008 consisted of principle and interest owed since 1945. Lend-Lease nation-building involving food, fuel, and munitions that were sent for free to forty allied countries cost the taxpayers $50 billion, greater than the entire national debt amassed in the U.S. in the first 150 years of its existence. And there was no repayment plan to reimburse the American people.[133]

133. Fleming, *New Dealers' War*, 197; Flagel, *Guide*, 121, 123.

6

The Era of the Expanded
Executive Office of the President

While Harry Truman wrapped up Roosevelt's war with some pyrotechnics of his own, he is best remembered as inaugurating the Next Big Step—the huge expansion in the staff of the president, which enabled post-World War II presidents to build vast domestic and international empires and place them under personal command. Truman tried to extend FDR's already bloated national welfare programs, but an exhausted and impoverished nation could not bear up under the thought of it, especially after he committed the nation to a new war of conquest in Asia only five years after World War II ended.

Truman milked U.S. taxpayers in order to rebuild Europe and to remobilize a humongous standing army which he then positioned in hundreds of foreign bases across the globe. He established a new national security and diplomatic apparatus that he used to overshadow the departments of government legally empowered by the Congress to carry out those functions. He used this National Security Council (NSC), and its associated police agencies, to conduct secret negotiations and covert activities across the globe.

While Franklin Roosevelt thought the Soviets were amiable democrats and therefore suitable U.S. allies during the war, Truman flip-flopped and made them into vile enemies who wanted to divest the U.S. of her new found European vassals and make those countries her own. He precipitated exactly what he supposedly didn't want to happen after he committed the U.S. to a taut military alliance in Western Europe. His action in forming NATO drove the eastern European countries into an alliance themselves. He developed the art of making domestic laws and secret international treaties that served as a precedent for the actions of autocrats of both parties following him.

Dwight D. Eisenhower, who sat in the chief executive's chair after Truman, used the executive office of the presidency to advance new nationalization programs. Not having access to life-long ruler-ship once the Twenty-Second Amendment passed, limiting the president to two terms of office, presidents resolved to speed up the process of usurping Congressional functions and carrying out what were once the social regulation functions of the states. They did this by using executive decrees, vetoes, and signing statements, rule-making, impoundment of lawfully appropriated funds, preemption of state law and policy, and use of the palace guard to intimidate political opponents and American citizens who awakened to their tyrannies and protested them.

Eisenhower and his successors, like Kennedy and Johnson, used the NSC to unravel democratic governments the world over and set up in their place largely fascist governments that would kowtow to the U.S. presidency. Presidents like Carter and Reagan saw the glory that World War II gave Franklin Roosevelt, and tried to convince the American people to go to war against freedom movements that might have a handful of communists in their midst wherever such movements could be found. They implemented massive buildups of the military as though the U.S. was still engaged in the heat of world war battles. But, in fact, the U.S. was in the heat of world hegemony instead, which necessitated enormous numbers of troops to be used as colonial police rather than as warriors. Their job was to guard new colonies and new oil fields and intimidate local populations.

On the other hand, Kennedy, Johnson, and Nixon committed the nation to traditional uses of the standing army as well, miring the U.S. in the military swamp of Vietnam for a decade. Carter, Clinton, and the first Bush committed the nation to additional hot wars in Europe and the Middle East. In order to dumbfound the American people, and extort their paychecks, the presidents had to convince them that the communist countries in Europe and Asia were capable of overrunning, converting, or destroying virtually every nation on earth, including the U.S. In fact, the Soviet Union was a house of cards, and once Reagan curbed the use of American money propping up the Soviet regime, it fell apart of its own accord. Learning very little from the Soviet experience, the presidents built up communist China into a fledgling new superpower in order to justify continuing military increases after the Soviet Union had melted away. In the meantime, the U.S. continued the laborious process of knocking off petty war lords and replacing them with other war lords in the Middle East, Africa, Eastern Europe, and Latin America. This necessitated only paltry numbers of troops but lots of foreign military and economic aid.

Harry Truman

Harry Truman, like Calvin Coolidge, first distinguished himself by serving in local government. He served as a road overseer. He then worked as a local postmaster, a federal government appointment. Perhaps the latter job instilled in him a love of the functions of national power. During World War I, Harry served as Captain of Battery D in the 129th Field Artillery. He was aggressive and salty. He discovered, "A leader is a man who has the ability to get other people to do what they don't want to do . . ." Later, as civilian president, he applied the same philosophy. He told his cabinet on May, 1945, "when the President [gave] an order they should carry it out." This governing philosophy didn't pay much heed to the time-honored democratic principle of obtaining the consent of the people. Early on, he had learned to play the political blame game. By a great stretch of imagination, he blamed president Harding for the failure of his own tiny haberdashery business in 1921. While he was in political office with the county government, he tried his hand at the study of law from 1923–25, but, like other presidents who chomped at the bit for unregulated power, dropped out before he could earn a degree. In fact, Truman was the first president in fifty years to not possess a college education. Truman became a professional politician. For 26 continuous years he held elective office, starting in 1926.[1]

Truman was a champion of Roosevelt's New Deal during his race in the primary election for U.S. Senate. He liked to read history, but his was an uncritical reading, opting for books that glorified the subject matter and the historical figures. In the Senate, he consistently voted for Roosevelt's New Deal programs and seemed to forget the constitutional powers of local government altogether. Truman was then selected as the

1. Whitney, *Biographies*, 303; McCoy, *Truman*, 3–4, 16.

vice presidential candidate in Roosevelt's successful, but sham fourth presidential run and served as vice president for eighty two days. FDR, concerned only about keeping power for life and not about a smooth succession, "told Harry nothing," in the words of Truman's wife Bess. But Harry had the Bible to turn to when he needed inspiration and advice. He regularly read the Bible. He considered large corporations, and later, the Soviet Union, to be important parts of Satan's realm, though, curiously, he did not believe that big government fit the same mold. In spite of his religiosity, Truman liked to play poker, drink bourbon, and bestow medals on people, like a gracious monarch. [2]

Harry Truman took office when FDR died on April 12, 1945, and served from 1945 to 1953. He was an extremely unpopular president during his terms of office for mostly the right reasons—such things as his mishandling of Korean and Chinese affairs, failing to put the consumer economy back on a peacetime basis, trying to expand Roosevelt's newly created and already bloated centralized welfare state, and authorizing the atomic bombing of Hiroshima and Nagasaki.

Truman's reputation has grown with court historians for mostly the wrong reasons. For example, he increased presidential power at the expense of Congress and the people, and increased rather than decreased Roosevelt's executive office staff, after purging many of them; he committed the U.S. to permanent entanglement in the political and military affairs of Europe; he created a new secret police establishment, the CIA, which gave both he and future presidents the capacity to interfere in, and even overthrow foreign governments without informing Congress. In fact, in June, 1948, Truman set up a covert operations branch in the CIA to conduct propaganda, economic warfare, sabotage, subversion, and secret aid to favored political movements. No sooner was this branch created, but it intervened covertly in Italy's elections in 1948.[3]

Truman's first official action was to confirm arrangements for the United Nations organization conference, set for April 25, 1945. Truman shared Roosevelt's idealism about the UN, which European powers knew would not work, and Congress had rejected in Wilson's day. The idea was that the new organization would produce an "effortless perpetual peace." It turned out to be a "shadow force . . . (or) an embarrassment." In fact,

2. Whitney, *Biographies*, 303; McCoy, *Truman*, 2, 6, 65, 145.

3. Miller Center, *Franklin Roosevelt—Domestic Affairs; Whitney, Biographies*, 299; Crenson and Ginsberg, *Presidential Power*, 256; Herring, *Colony to Superpower*, 621.

the Russians used the veto Roosevelt gave them twenty-one times by March, 1948, turning the UN "largely into a debating society."[4]

After the assassination of Hitler and Germany's surrender, the new president wrote, "Things have gone so well that I can't understand it, except to attribute it to God. He guides me, I think." Again, "Luck always seems to be with me in games of chance and in politics." He indicated early on that he wanted the extension of Roosevelt's public power program and also trade reciprocity. He appointed high school and Missouri National Guard cronies to high positions in the government. The great majority of his appointees were party men rather than doctrinaire New Dealers. Harry did not want women in his cabinet.[5]

Truman created two new presidential agencies early in his first term, which were tacked on to Franklin Roosevelt's Executive Office of the President (EOP): the Council of Economic Advisers (CEA) in 1946, and the National Security Council (NSC) in 1947. Some in Congress perhaps naively believed that these new agencies should or would serve as independent bodies and therefore serve as checks on presidential authority in fiscal and military matters. But the legislation creating the NSC did not grant the body statutory authority as a decision-making body. Both the new agencies were left wide open to presidential manipulation.[6]

By creating a single defense budget and a more unified military chain of command, the National Security Act creating the NSC also both decreased Congress' ability to influence military affairs and increased the president's control over those affairs.[7] In addition, the NSC, in tandem with the CIA, together became a sort of an unelected shadow government, or Praetorian Guard, used to hide presidential operations and some military operations from view, and thus from accountability. It gave the national government the ability to use thugs and secrecy to accomplish its often illicit objectives.

Truman wanted to keep wartime controls on prices and wages during "reconversion." In other words, he continued the use of emergency power after the war emergency was over. He issued Executive Order 9599 to this effect in August, 1945. In fact, Truman hit the ground running with presidential decrees. He issued 137 executive orders between FDR's death

4. McCoy, *Truman*, 15, 33–34, 134.

5. Ibid., 17–18, 21.

6. Crenson and Ginsberg, *Presidential Power*, 184.

7. Ibid., 248.

and the end of 1945, only a few months later. When coal miners called a national strike, Truman actualized the bluff Teddy Roosevelt had made, and took over the mines, operating them under the Department of the Interior. Truman used peacetime executive orders simply because Congress refused to adopt the policies he personally wished to see adopted.[8]

Roosevelt had been responsible for huge profits for big business while labor's wage rates were basically frozen and strikes prohibited. When Japan surrendered, labor was once again justified in going on strike. In October, 1945, Truman seized twenty-six oil companies on national security grounds when they threatened to go on strike. This was extending the wartime emergency power well beyond wartime. One historian commented glibly, this action was "legally questionable."[9]

Where Teddy Roosevelt stuck his nose into labor-management relations fifty years before, Truman was now body and soul in the business. He happily entered negotiations for wage increases in the auto and steel industries. He asked, "Who is going to run the country?" His answer was, neither labor nor capital, but Truman himself. Unions like bituminous coal began to think that federal intervention, and even takeovers of industries would get them a better deal, so they deliberately provoked trouble. All of this irritated Harry. He was sorely tempted to use the tools in Lincoln's bag of tyrannical tricks. He wrote in a journal, "Declare an emergency, call out troops. Start industry and put anyone to work who wants to work. If any leader interferes, court martial him. Lewis [United mine worker president John L. Lewis] ought to have been shot in 1942, but Franklin didn't have the guts to do it. Adjourn Congress and run the country. Get plenty of atomic bombs on hand, drop one on Stalin." Harry was not kidding about using radical tyrannical methods. When railway engineers and train men struck, he asked for legislation to conscript the strikers into the armed forces as a punishment and strip workers of seniority rights. He cooed, "Lets . . . hang a few traitors." He also wanted the army to run the railroads. Eventually, the strike was settled without his legislation being enacted. One historian noted, "He sometimes responded more like Captain Harry of Battery D than like the chief of state."[10]

Truman used the veto for policy purposes, not because a measure was deemed to be unconstitutional. Oblivious of constitutional legal

8. Whitney, *Biographies*, 305; Cooper, *Order*, 41, 115.
9. McCoy, *Truman*, 49–51.
10. Ibid., 57–61.

tradition, he opined that the veto was "one of the greatest strengths that the president has . . . if he doesn't like something that they're cooking up." He thus used the veto to make himself a one-man wrecking crew. He used the veto twenty-one times in 1945 and thirty-three times in 1946. One historian notes, "He was among the presidents who used this weapon most." Congress passed legislation to return the U.S. Employment Service to the states, but Truman vetoed it. Congress overrode his veto and paid respect to states rights rather than allow the permanent nationalization of a traditional state-based prerogative. Truman vetoed legislation to weaken the ICC, to exclude some people from Social Security, and to subsidize metals like copper, lead, and zinc. Truman also vetoed the 1947 Taft-Hartley Act, whose purpose was to make unions more accountable and assure prospective employees that they don't have to join unions before being hired. Congress overrode his veto. He also vetoed the 1950 McCarran Internal Security Act. The Constitution gives the power of raising revenues to Congress, stating in Article 1, Section 8, that "The Congress shall have the power to lay and collect taxes." In spite of this, Truman twice vetoed tax cut legislation. He was considered "highly combative." Twelve of his regular vetoes were overridden.[11]

Due to decreased war spending, federal spending declined from $98 billion in fiscal year 1945 to $60 billion in fiscal year 1946, while federal revenues declined to $43.5 billion. Thus the debt continued to rise. In 1945–46 the country sent a third of its wheat production to curb the horrendous starvation occurring in Europe as a result of Franklin Roosevelt's unconditional surrender policy. Meanwhile, at home black markets like that during prohibition were sprouting up to pay higher prices for scarce goods, and in November, 1946, Truman was forced to decontrol prices except for rents. He also obtained passage of the Employment Act of 1946, insistent as he was on keeping the national government in charge of employment in the country. The act gave the federal government responsibility "to promote maximum employment, (and) production . . ." He also signed legislation to expand the school lunch program, give foreign aid to the newly independent Philippines, lend money to England, expand the state department, give veterans priority in purchasing surplus property, and create an Indian Claims Commission. He greased the skids

11. Flagel, *Guide*, 132, 136–37; McCoy, *Truman*, 52–53, 62, 98–99; Crenson and Ginsberg, *Presidential Power*, 229; Morley, *Freedom and Federalism*, 20; Whitney, *Biographies*, 305.

for all this legislative love-making by agreeing to increase congressional salaries.[12]

Truman planned to keep the draft going due to America's substantial new colonial demands, which included occupying Germany and Japan and operating post-war military bases worldwide. As a supplement to a continuing draft, he wanted mandatory military training for young men as well. He "worked long and hard" to get Congress to pass a universal training requirement, but Congress did not agree. In fact, the standing army was reduced from three million in 1946 to one and a half million in 1947, and it stayed there until the start of the Korean War in 1950, when it rose precipitously again. This new peace time level in 1947 compares to 335,000 in peacetime 1939. The nation was now five times more militant than it was only ten years before.[13]

Part of Harry's reconversion program was to convert war-time support of nation-building in western and eastern Europe to peacetime nation-building. In support of this, Harry signed the Bretton Woods agreements establishing the International Monetary Fund and the International Bank for Reconstruction and Development. In August, 1946, he stopped Lend-Lease and started to use UN banking and aid agencies to funnel U.S. taxpayer dollars away from local communities and overseas instead. He also indicated he wanted independence for the Philippines Islands.[14]

Not surprisingly, due to Truman's massive continuing government interventionism, Democrats lost control of Congress in 1946, a stirring vote of no confidence in Truman. Truman got the hint and proclaimed the end of World War II on December 31, 1946, thus finally ending war-time emergency powers some 18 months after the war actually ended. But he still could not refrain from encouraging the voluntary centralization of American life. In his 1947 state of the union message, he not only called for a balanced budget, but also the contradictory program of medical care for all Americans and reduction of taxes in the near future. Congress responded with a bill to decrease income taxes now, which Truman vetoed. Congress also gave Truman less for defense, education, housing, agriculture, and transportation than he had asked for. Congress also passed the Twenty Second Amendment to the Constitution, which

12. McCoy, *Truman*, 53–56, 61.
13. Ibid., 83, 116–18.
14. Ibid., 71.

made it illegal for an American president like FDR to serve for life again, whether war or no war. Perhaps this was a hint that Truman, as Roosevelt's partner in crime, should limit his political ambitions as well. But the law grandfathered in Truman, if he wanted to run for a third term. Regarding that prospect, he said "I am sure God almighty will guide me." Apparently God asked him to retire, but only after telling Truman to advise the people not to "go off after false gods," that is, Republicans, in the 1952 election.[15]

In Truman's message to the country in 1948 he made a dishonest call for the country to focus not on party but on the country, and specifically, his program for the country. That program continued to be a call for massive increase in federal government rental housing, federal aid to education, and national health care. Forgetting his speech apparently, later that hear he asked Americans to "vote for the straight Democratic ticket, and everything will be safe for the world." He also usurped the Congressional power of the purse and vetoed a tax cut, but Congress reclaimed its right and overrode the veto. Rather than federal housing rental, Congress instead opted for increasing credit for home-buyers, especially for veterans, and Truman signed the bill. In 1948 Truman vetoed a total of forty-three bills. He portrayed himself as "the people's president," pandering to every conceivable post-war need based on his own agenda, and not that proposed by the people's representatives in Congress. He wanted high price supports for farmers, federal grain storage bins, and civil rights legislation. He issued Executive Orders 9980 and 9981 to combat discrimination in hiring and in promotion of federal employees, including the military.[16]

In the 1948 presidential election, Truman called upon the vast resources of the federal government to win reelection. He used its patronage power, its budgetary support for key segments of the electorate, especially entitlements, and the "unparalleled publicity" power of the government. In the summer of 1948, just before the election, he made promises to tingle in the ears of vast segments of the American electorate. He called for federal aid to education to garner the youth vote (and the vote of suburban parents). He called for an increase in the minimum wage to woo workers and an increase in Social Security benefits to excite retirees (he eventually got Congress to double retirement benefits in 1950). He called

15. Ibid., 91–98, 302.
16. Ibid., 102, 104–9.

for pay raises for federal employees, civil rights for minorities, more in-expensive housing for the poor, agricultural supports for the farmer vote, flood control for homeowners, conservation for liberals, authorization to accept more displaced persons from world War II (immigrants who could be expected to vote for the man or the party who let them in the country), public power for river dwellers and rural homeowners, and a loan for construction of the UN building (to add an infusion of money into New York City). One historian wrote, "He was asking for something for most Americans." Truman barked back at his detractors. He said, "The special interests are trying to frighten the people with the old, warn-out, bugaboo that socialism is taking over Washington." The old, warn-out bugaboo, of course, was the U.S. Constitution, with its rule of law, and its rule of financial sanity, depending as it did upon the pocketbooks of ordinary Americans.[17]

Truman presented America with a totally unrealistic national do-mestic agenda once he won election in his own right in 1948. After the tremendous financial debilitation of World War II, the nation wanted to return to normalcy. This included, for many, mustering out the military, decreasing taxes, deregulating social life, getting the government out of minute regulation of economic affairs, enhancing the power of organized labor, privatizing government programs and deflating the size of the cen-tral government welfare state created by FDR. This is what the nation did after World War I. But Truman proposed to take the nation in the oppo-site direction. He let it be known he wanted to keep the military on a war-time footing, and to enact higher taxes and new public works programs such as airports and river valley development. He wanted to continue the Fair Employment Practices Commission on a permanent basis, provide subsidized housing for the poor, security for farmers, unemployment compensation, regulation of atomic energy, scientific research support, legislation to guarantee "full employment," federal assistance for educa-tion, reorganization of the executive branch, expansion of Social Security, an increase in the minimum wage, liberalized immigration, national price controls, curbs on strikes, assistance for world reconstruction, universal military training, and national health insurance. These kinds of proposals for home and abroad, he said, would bring "lasting peace throughout the world." Of his September message, the House minority leader said, "Not even President Roosevelt ever asked for as much at one sitting." His was

17. Ibid., 152, 158, 165, 172, 175.

a utopian and essentially socialist program whose intent was to vastly extend the New Deal, and Congress and the people rejected it. Of all of these proposals he won passage of only a few: a slum clearance bill and an increase in the minimum wage in 1949, and an expansion of Social Security in 1950. Congress gave him six months for his continuation of economic controls rather than the year he asked for. Truman's plan to de-commission only five million of the twelve million military was bumped up to nine million because of public pressure.[18]

Truman made the presidency a vast institution by his increased use of the Bureau of the Budget to usurp the power of the purse from Congress and screen legislative and budget proposals, and by the use of his new executive office of the president, which included the CEA and NSC, his expanded White House staff, and ad hoc commissions. The presidency was now political big business and was creating a bigger and bigger monopoly on political power in the country. In his 1949 state of the union he asserted the right of America to a "Fair Deal" for everyone in the country. This included a right to housing, education, and nationalized health care. He wanted repeal of the Taft-Hartley law, another increase in the minimum wage, increased contributions to Social Security, new farm supports, and civil rights legislation. All this would require a $4 billion tax increase, which Truman said would also help to reduce the now outrageous $252 billion national debt. He wanted per pupil educational grants to the states, which could even use the grants to pay for textbooks, buses, and parochial schools. He later added expansion of medical, dental and nursing schools, new hospitals, and medical research facilities to his federal health care wish list. He also wanted federal promotion of production, continued regulation of bank and consumer credit, rent and export controls, price and wage control authority, increased taxes on corporate profits and estates, reciprocal tariffs with nations the U.S. was now controlling after the war, and anti-merger legislation. He also wanted to remove from office those who were obstructing his spending plan in Congress.[19]

Truman vetoed Social Security for Indians in Arizona and New Mexico because it would have transferred control over Indian water rights and inheritances from federal courts to state courts. He vetoed

---

18. Miller Center, *Truman—Domestic Affairs*; Boyer, *Oxford Companion*, 785; Whitney, *Biographies*, 308; McCoy, *Truman*, 48, 52.

19. McCoy, *Truman*, 146, 164, 166, 173, 182, 186, 190.

thirty pieces of legislation in 1949, and forty in 1950. In 1951 he vetoed only thirteen laws. In 1952 he vetoed nine laws. One was a veto of a bill to give title to offshore lands/waters, including offshore oil deposits, and other natural resources to the states. Along the way, he vetoed an increase in veterans benefits, but Congress overrode the veto. He vetoed provisions to allow citizenship to Asian immigrants and legislation to allow Congress better access to executive branch records. In 1949 Truman filled two vacancies on the Supreme Court, ensuring a "Truman Court . . . that would usually uphold as constitutional whatever the executive branch and Congress did." He wanted to add 810,000 public apartments to the 170,000 units built under Roosevelt's 1937 legislation. Democrats in Congress compromised with Republicans and in July, 1949, passed the Housing Act, specifying that 356,000 units be built by 1964. In 1949 Truman also seized all of the nation's railways ostensibly in order to prevent strikes, hardly the way to stop talk about socialism. He did not return them to private hands until 1952. In one final fit of presidential power grabbing, he issued an executive order in January, 1953, which added 47,753 acres to the Olympic National Park, taking those acres away from the citizens of the state of Washington.[20]

Truman was enough of a neophyte in international relations that he believed that he could continue Franklin Roosevelt's war-time alliance with what he felt was a democratic-oriented Soviet Union. For example, at Yalta, Stalin had agreed with Franklin Roosevelt to hold free elections in Eastern Europe. When Truman met with Stalin at Potsdam in July, 1945, he accepted at face value Stalin's assertion that he would allow free elections in the nations of eastern Europe where Soviet troops were positioned at the end of the war. He also said of the world's greatest cutthroat dictator, "I like Stalin."[21] When the Soviets did not move to allow those elections, Truman felt that economic assistance to the Soviets after the end of the war might bribe them into honoring their promises at Yalta and Potsdam.

Truman's negotiations with Stalin, together with those Roosevelt had with Stalin, provide the most sordid and embarrassing moments in American history, having immense negative consequences for hundreds of millions of ordinary human beings in eastern Europe. Truman even

20. Ibid., 169, 172, 174, 181, 188, 258, 298, 307.
21. Nelson, *Presidency*, 147–48.

caved in to Stalin's foot stomping to force the continuation of Lend-Lease giveaways to Russia after the war.[22]

Truman considered that he was the sole decider in American foreign affairs. He said of the presidency's stranglehold, "No one else can do the deciding for him. That's his job." But Henry Wallace questioned "whether he has enough information behind his decisiveness." In truth, Truman seemed to understand little about the Soviet Union and did not seem to seek out more knowledge. There is no indication he knew about or cared about the mass deaths in the Soviet Union in the 1920s, 1930s, and 1940s, or about the mass political arrests, exiling, and brutalizing of two million Soviet citizens the U.S. repatriated into Stalin's care after the German occupation of parts of Russia. Truman had a rarified, simplified view of things. He wrote, "I'm not in the slightest alarmed at the world situation. It will work out." This he offered only months before the Cold War broke out.[23]

Truman is credited with a number of major foreign policy initiatives. He authorized the use of the atomic bomb in 1945 and authorized a program to develop the hydrogen bomb after that. He also spelled out the Truman Doctrine in 1947, implemented the Marshall Plan in 1947, the Berlin Blockade Airlift in 1948–49, the formation of NATO in 1949, and finally intervention in the Korean Civil War. These initiatives committed the American people, largely without their consent, to developing and defending new cultures far beyond the homeland, which ultimately impoverished the citizens of the homeland and earned an immense amount of enmity for them from the citizens of the developing nations of the third world.

In fact, Truman authorized the bombing of Hiroshima and Nagasaki even after Japan asked for a cease-fire and agreed to voluntary disarmament if only the U.S. would agree not to occupy the country. Since long-term occupation and possession of a sophisticated Asian colony and economy, and complete political domination of a former enemy is what Truman wanted, he turned down Japan and pulled the trigger on the worst atrocity of all time. One commentator reminds, Truman "never waivered" in his decision to use the bomb. Truman dropped the atomic bomb on Hiroshima on August 6, 1945. He said, "This is the greatest thing in history." But he did worry a bit about killing "all those kids." He

22. McCoy, *Truman*, 34–35.
23. Ibid., 70, 73, 309.

announced a two-day holiday to celebrate the U.S. toasting of Japan. Truman assigned a supervisor to the Japanese congress to assure legislation was passed there to his liking. He was governing Japan like a U.S. colony, somewhat like Puerto Rico and the Philippines.[24]

Once he understood that Roosevelt had been manipulated by the Soviet Union, Truman re-mobilized the American military in 1948 right in the midst of its de-mobilization, after it was learned that Czechoslovakia went communist. He engineered a fear-mongering campaign, telling Americans that Greece and Turkey were about to go communist. He re-instituted the draft, eventually building up the standing army to four million. He declined to withdraw from Europe and declined to insist that the Soviet Union withdraw either. He budgeted many tens of billions to stock up the massive Cold War American bases being built around the world. Truman decided to retain Roosevelt's World War II military bases, "from Alaska to Iceland, and from Japan to Eritrea." Truman then declared a national emergency in 1950 and indicated his intention to intervene in the midst of a civil war in Korea.[25]

Truman made Stalin into a demon capable of taking over not only Europe, but the Western Hemisphere as well. One Truman official opined, "If you imagine two or three hundred Pearl Harbors occurring all over the United States, you will have a rough picture of what the next war might look like." Truman himself predicted the Russians wanted world conquest "in five or ten years."[26]

In an environment created by such statements, in March, 1947, Truman enunciated the Truman Doctrine. After observing Stalin's blithe refusal to honor his agreements with Roosevelt in Eastern Europe, Truman essentially said there would be no further losses on his watch.[27]

Congress appropriated $17 billion for the Marshall Plan for the period 1948 through 1952, quite a jump from the already huge $400 million allocated for Greece and Turkey in 1947. Truman signed the legislation in April, 1948. In Britain, the foreign minister said, "My God! . . . This is manna from heaven." The speaker of the American house of representatives said, "We had to carry the burden of leadership, costly as it was." Truman added, "God Almighty . . . had appointed us to do a job." This

---

24. Flagel, *Guide*, 226; McCoy, *Truman*, 40, 202, 204.

25. Ibid., *Truman*, 134, 140.

26. Herring, *Colony to Superpower*, 597, 609.

27. Flagel, *Guide*, 194.

was essentially an internal improvements program for half of Europe, based on the American taxpayers' dime. The Pax Britannica had been the largest empire of all time during the nineteenth century. One historian wrote, this was the "end of Pax Britannia and the establishment instead of the Pax Americana."[28]

Truman was expecting free elections in Korea, after which U.S. and Soviet troops would withdraw, leaving that nation in a happy state of democratic bliss. But Stalin neglected to uphold his promise for elections, and supported a communist regime in the north part of the country. The Dutch could be trusted to try to handle things in the East Indies, the French in Indo China, and the British in Burma, India, and Malaya, but communists made propaganda inroads in those places too while nationalistic movements came to the fore.[29]

The Senate ratified Truman's NATO treaty in July, 1949. By means of this simple action, "The U.S. had reversed its policy of not entering into entangling peacetime alliances." By 1954, the U.S. was paying seventy-six percent of NATO costs.[30]

Truman's budget message to Congress in 1949 asked for military assistance to North Atlantic nations, the continuation of the Marshall Plan, and aid to Greece, Turkey, Korea, and China. In China the American aid was quickly lapped up by the communists and helped them make their final push to take over the country. Truman had to withstand the embarrassment of watching China fall to communism in December, 1949, the same way Wilson watched the fall of all of Russia to communism in 1921.[31]

In the meantime, Truman gleefully found that he had unleashed immense new lobbying forces for hot and cold American militarism in the form of military contractors, the National Guard, the Selective Service System, the military itself, the National Security Council, the CIA, the state department, the allies and their militaries, not to mention fear-mongering politicians in Congress. The people of the United States were nowhere in sight when it came to trying to put a damper on new

---

28. McCoy, *Truman*, 128–29.
29. Ibid., 131–32, 204.
30. Ibid., 198–202, 260, 286–87.
31. Ibid., 191, 193, 195–96.

American war campaigns. That would become clear enough in the matter of Korea.[32]

Truman gave military aid to South Korean autocrat Syngman Rhee. When the communist north attacked Rhee's south, Truman saw an opportunity to get involved in a limited Asian war that would serve as a practice war for other American involvements against communism in the future. Unfortunately, when Truman entered the Korean War he also sewed the seeds for the U.S.'s long-term and disastrous involvement in Vietnam. Truman committed U.S. forces to Korea without consulting Congress, using UN Military Council approval for his go-ahead. He initially said he would only use U.S. troops for purposes of evacuating U.S. citizens. General MacArthur encouraged Truman to expand the mission to provide naval and air support for the south Koreans, and authorized bombing north of the 38th parallel. Once Truman committed those resources, he still declined to seek a war declaration from Congress. In January, 1951, Senator Robert Taft called for Congressional authorization before Truman sent any more troops, even in connection with NATO.[33]

The debacle in Korea occasioned a huge increase in the military budget. In 1950, Truman had asked for $16.8 billion in military budget authority for the current fiscal year, exceeding his promise of a $14 billion lid, made earlier. The Defense Production Act of late 1950 doubled war expenditures from $15 billion to $30 billion, yet Truman insisted, "We are not at war." For fiscal year 1952 he requested total budget appropriations of $71.6 billion compared to $42.4 a year before. This showed the dramatic effect the war had on the total budget. The Korean War pushed the national debt from $220 billion to $275 billion. Truman pushed through a tax increase to help fund the non-war, the Revenue Act of 1951. He issued Proclamation 2914 giving the executive expanded emergency powers. He obtained the Emergency Powers Continuation Act because after finally securing a peace treaty with Japan, seven years after the war was over, he wanted to extend world War II emergency powers into the Korean War era without a lapse in dictatorial power. Truman went on radio and screamed, "Our homes, our Nation, all the things we believe in are in great danger." "We have no right to feel safe . . . on the home front." However, there were no reported sightings of North Korean or Chinese military in Oregon or Washington. He also got a twenty-five percent

32. Ibid., 212.
33. Ibid., 216–17, 224–25, 227, 229, 250; Flagel, *Guide*, 195.

increase in foreign military aid. In June, 1950 the size of the military was at 1.5 million. By December it stood at 2.5 million, and soon was raised to 3.5 million.[34]

Truman pumped a couple billion dollars into the Japanese economy, to purchase military hardware from them for use in the Korean War, and negotiated agreements for U.S. bases in Japan, which included the use of Okinawa as virtually a colonial possession of the U.S.[35]

With his extension of emergency powers, Truman got brassy. He issued Executive Order 10340 allowing him to take over operation of U.S. steel mills. Resolutions for impeachment were introduced in the House. The Supreme Court ultimately ruled his action unconstitutional. Only lawmakers, not courts, like the Court of Appeals which upheld his action, could sustain such a course. Truman did not think America was ready for junta government, so he backed down from the court and gave the mills back to their owners.[36]

Truman could be an eloquent and heart-rending speechmaker. He once said, "As Americans, we believe that every man should be free to live his life as he wishes." This is an admirably libertarian sentiment that would warm the hearts of the founders and the great states' rights defenders. Truman did not want to stir up the electorate with repressive activities until after he got reelected in 1948. On the quiet, he used the IRS to harass political opponents, including senators. Supreme Court Justice Jackson wrote that Truman used the Korean War as an opportunity "to enlarge his mastery over the internal affairs of the country." In other words, he used fear and insecurity to usurp power in the fashion of all true tyrants. A big part of this included suppressing dissent. FBI updated its list of potentially dangerous anti-war activists and made plans to incarcerate them if another emergency cropped up. He used the CIA for repressive activity abroad. One commentator wrote, "The CIA and the NSC were also beginnings for the use of power in ways that were far from traditional in the United States." Truman continued wartime wiretap activities into peacetime, and set up a permanent loyalty program for government employees. During his terms of office, the CIA illegally opened mail of U.S. citizens who were innocently corresponding with citizens in the USSR. Citizens were encouraged to spy on neighbors and

34. McCoy, *Truman*, 228–29, 242, 247, 253, 283, 288–90.
35. Herring, *Colony to Superpower*, 646.
36. McCoy, *Truman*, 292–93.

inform on one another.[37] This makes Truman a hypocrite writ large on the American scene, and gives credence to the statement by Justice Jackson that Truman had motives other than the best interests of the people.

Truman's War cost 33,600 battlefield lives and well over 100,000 American casualties total. General Omar Bradley said Korea was 'the wrong war, at the wrong place, at the wrong time, and with the wrong enemy."[38] An armistice was not signed until the Eisenhower administration, July, 1953. There was no peace treaty signed until the 1980s. The Korean war thus never started and never ended, but 53,000 Americans died, apparently suffering from military budget dust.

Truman not only ignored Congress in military matters, but ignored the people's policy representatives in treaty matters as well. Using his newly created National Security Council, he began to make treaties on his own by means of "executive agreements." He committed the U.S. to participation in the International Trade Organization without Congress, and signed the GATT treaty without Congressional approval. During his term he signed 1,300 executive agreements, often ignoring Congress. Many of these treaties involved the establishing of American military bases around the world. By the end of Truman's term, the U.S. had more that a million U.S. military personnel manning more than 800 bases in a hundred countries. Congress tried to curb presidential power in foreign relations by means of its Foreign Service Reform Act. Unfortunately, that legislation backfired by giving Truman more institutional capacity to do what he wanted. The State Department expanded from 5,000 in 1940 to 20,000 by the end of Truman's term of office. The foreign aid budget stood at an average of $5 billion a year, and the U.S. was committed to defend 42 nations.[39]

Truman remained ignorant about Stalin to the end. He believed Stalin turned against the west because he had been outfoxed by Truman. He said Stalin "thought he had been cheated by a young man from Missouri," but it was Stalin who had outfoxed Truman. Truman's blunders, whether deliberate or ignorant, had given the Russians control of 90 million non-Russian people. Truman said that communism "requires the

37. Crenson and Ginsberg, *Presidential Power*, 231; Miller Center, *Truman—A Life in Brief,'* Herring, *Colony to Superpower*, 653, 655; McCoy, *Truman*, 84, 141–42, 217, 219, 274–76, 279.

38. McCoy, *Truman*, 294; Herring, *Colony to Superpower*, 644.

39 Crenson and Ginsberg, *Presidential Power*, 246, 254–55; Herring, *Colony to Superpower*, 653.

rule of strong masters," apparently not thinking that his Fair Deal, loyalty program, foreign nation-building, military assistance, and alliances derived from just such a strong and illegitimate master. Truman said of his revved-up executive office of the presidency, "the Office of the President is the greatest and most powerful in the history of the world." Harry knew, because he made it so. One historian wrote, "He played Augustus to Roosevelt's Caesar."[40]

Dwight D. Eisenhower

Dwight David Eisenhower spent an entire career as a soldier keeping order in America's turn of the century colonial possessions. He spent two years after World War I doing duty in the Panama Canal Zone, America's southernmost colony in the Americas. He earned additional tame-the-heathen stripes in the Philippines, where in 1935 he served as military adviser to the Philippine puppet government, helping them to build an army capable of defending U.S. interests there.[41]

After Japan attacked Pearl Harbor, Ike used his experience in the Orient to help plan early strategy in the Pacific aimed at making Japan the newest American colony. Ike was ultimately put in charge of developing a strategy for an invasion of France, then occupied by Germany. He excelled at coordinating efforts of the commanders of other nations. While associated with a series of battles that turned back Hitler's grip, Ike also made the stupendous mistake of allowing Stalin to "liberate" and occupy Berlin before U.S. troops would get there, which was tantamount to putting the fox in charge of the chicken coop. Stalin and Marshall Zhukov promised Ike cooperation, but that cooperation came at the price of money, material, and land, like the land surrounding Berlin. That mistake was more than enough to have disqualified him from political leadership in the United States, but the lust for new territories among the bi-partisan leadership back home was enough to suffocate legitimate political analysis and electoral sanity. Ike was heavily promoted as "America's No. 1 hero," and that sort of imperial patriotism was quite enough to appeal to the senseless masses among the American civic population. Like Wilson

40. McCoy, *Truman*, 134, 191, 304, 308, 312.

41. Whitney, *Biographies*, 312, 315; Boyer, *Oxford Companion*, 218; Pach, *Eisenhower*, 5.

before him, he made a hero's tour of European capitals and a hero's tour of cities in the U.S.[42]

Two years later, Eisenhower became the candidate of the moderate-liberal coalition in the Republican party wanting to prevent the nomination of conservative Robert Taft of Ohio. He became an irresistible candidate when he portrayed himself as a peacenik, promising to go to Korea and end the war if only the American people would elect him to the highest office. In his inaugural he portrayed himself as a great pacifist, calling for the removal of "the causes of mutual fear and distrust among nations." In another appearance Ike's speechwriter had him proclaim, "Every gun that is made, every warship launched, every rocket fired . . . [is] a theft from those who hunger and are not fed, those who are cold and not clothed."[43]

But, exposing a different hand—perhaps his administration's real agenda—he also said in the inaugural, "We must be ready to dare all for our country. For history does not long entrust the care of freedom to the weak or timid . . ." Ike thus positioned himself as the covert dare devil president, who convinced his people he was working peace abroad and at home, while doing exactly the opposite. In fact, while he gave the appearance of restraint in the use of presidential power, with his "genial manner and broad smile," in private he was moody, profane, had a "ferocious temper" and was actually using power "vigorously behind the scenes." In order to avoid disclosing earth-shattering events he was manipulating, he talked in circles or played dumb, often telling reporters "I'll have to look that up." He was dumb like a fox, letting associates take responsibility for decisions, avoiding blame. He even seduced cabinet members, telling them "this idea that all wisdom is in the President, in me, that's baloney."[44]

Proof of the fact Ike required a major makeover in order to make him into what he was not is the fact he was the first president to have an advertising agency produce a television campaign commercial to promote his war hero image. This left substance to the imagination. Ike was not a fan of the press, so he left soft image making to the presidential advertisers. He didn't read newspapers or magazines much. In fact, since the press did not know what he was doing, especially in foreign affairs,

42. Boyer, *Oxford Companion*, 218; Pach and Richardson, *Eisenhower*, 8, 9, 12, 15.

43. Whitney, *Biographies*, 317; Miller Center, *Eisenhower—Foreign Affairs*

44. Whitney, *Biographies*, 318; Pach and Richardson, *Eisenhower*, xii, 27, 29, 33, 41, 44.

there was little need for him to determine what they were saying about the issues of the day. Many worried about a career military man taking control of the reigns of government. That experiment did not go well in the day of Andrew Jackson. They fretted about "Caesarism," or "Mac-Arthurism." In fact, Eisenhower appointed a lot of military associates to his personal staff and high positions in government. He also appointed CEOs from industry. He served in the presidency from 1953 to 1961.[45]

In his first year in office, Ike neglected to submit a legislative program and got criticized for it by those who expected him to fill the shoes of the great legislators Franklin Roosevelt and Harry Truman. He then quickly mended his ways, filing an annual legislative program just like Truman, demonstrating that for him political expediency and reelection were more important than constitutional principle. In his 1954 State of the Union message, he presented an active legislative program and created the first office of legislative affairs to lobby Congress for it. The head of this new office wrote that his job was to "uncheck the checks, and unbalance the balances" of constitutional separation of power.[46]

Eisenhower was notable for his lack of stomach for ending New Deal and Fair Deal "reforms," although his first budget cut Truman's proposed budget by about seven percent. He worked to stop a tax cut measure, but supported a bill to lower taxes on corporate dividends and expand the deduction for business depreciation costs. In further support of corporate America, anti-trust activity tapered off under Ike. Ike opposed a tax break to give $20 exemptions to each taxpayer and for dependents, saying he was trying to cut the federal deficit. In reality, Ike added to central government programming by expanding Social Security (adding ten and a half million more beneficiaries), minimum wage regulation (raising the minimum wage to one dollar), and government construction of housing. He asked for $7 billion in aid to build new schools, but Congress could not agree. He positioned himself for popularity with a seductive promise to "take the nation down the middle of the road between the unfettered power of concentrated wealth . . . and the unbridled power of statism or partisan interests." In the context of the already huge power of the central government, taking this position amounted to merely a slight cool-down

45 Miller Center, *Eisenhower—Domestic Affairs*; McDonald, Presidency, 471; Pach and Richardson, Eisenhower, 19, 34, 38.

46. Healy, *Cult of the Presidency*, 83; McDonald, *Presidency*, 368; Flagel, *Guide*, 307; Pach and Richardson, *Eisenhower*, 23, 49–50; Crenson and Ginsberg, *Presidential Power*, 189, 192.

of the engines of Roosevelt/Truman-style socialism and a happy tolera-
tion of corporate interests, however unethical those interests might be.
The middle of the road is the tyrant's playground, because he can appeal to people on both sides of the middle, by vote buying, flip-flopping
and duplicity, in the manner of presidents like Franklin Roosevelt, and,
later on, William Clinton. Ike had promised, for example, not to do any
public campaigning in the mid-term Congressional elections, distanc-
ing himself from Truman's unseemly barnstorming in 1948. However, he
changed his mind and travelled 10,000 miles and made 40 speeches, thus
massively interfering in local elections. Ike used federal money for projects designed to win votes for "middle" Republicans. He denied White
House access to Republicans who voted against his measures. Ike used
his popularity to force support for his legislative measures, in true tyrannical fashion. He boasted, "It is generally believed that I am in a position
to go to the people over the heads [of Congress]."[47]

Ike was somewhat of a fiscal conservative in that he opposed direct
support for farmers by means of agricultural price supports, opposed
some federal public works projects, and opposed national medical insurance for the aged. He then flip-flopped to fiscal liberalism and proposed
a national health insurance program, but Congress declined to support
it. He also opposed organized labor. Ike made flowery speeches about the
importance of states rights. In a speech to a conference of governors, he
said, "The preservation of our States as vigorous, powerful government
units is essential to permanent individual freedom." To back up his assertion, he turned over offshore oil rights to seaboard states, reversing
Truman's policy.[48]

In fact, Ike's middle road ran right over states' rights and cities' rights
with respect to the program he is most remembered for, the Federal Highway Act of 1956. Eisenhower wanted an automobile economy rather than
a mass transportation one "for greater conveniency . . . greater happiness,
and greater standards of living." But an automobile economy reduced the
traditional American educational economy by diverting personal discretionary income away from college educations for children. It was a statist
dream that inspired him to propose and win a program of 41,000 miles
of national government-constructed and government-controlled roads

47. Drewry and O'Connor, *America Is*, 633; Miller Center, *Eisenhower—Domestic
Affairs;* Pach and Richardson, *Eisenhower*, 53–54, 72–73, 76, 106–7, 135.

48. Cooper, *Order*, 268–69; McDonald, *Presidency*, 291; Whitney, *Biographies*,
318; Pach and Richardson, *Eisenhower*, 56, 106.

in 1956. This was a nationalist internal improvement program of humongous proportions that made Truman's Missouri road building program look like peanuts. Ike saw a need for spacious highways to enable America's now gigantic peacetime standing army to move its manpower, vehicles, and materiel around much more quickly to respond to local, national and international needs and opportunities. His plan emphasized expressways between cities and neglected farm-to-market roads. Others proposed that construction and operation decisions be made by state and local officials, but Ike wanted federal money, and federal control of construction and operation of the highways, since their main utility for him was movement of troops. His bill created the National System of Defense and Interstate Highways, and was 90 percent federal financed. Many objected that it would retard urban mass transit, but military considerations trumped civilian considerations.[49]

In addition to his propensity to support government centralization, Ike had a bit of Truman's pugnaciousness as well. He is number four in the list of top ten veto presidents. He vetoed seventy-three regular bills, and made 108 pocket vetoes. Only two of his bills were overridden. Congress overrode his veto of a continuation of the Tennessee Valley Authority power project. He wanted to privatize TVA, but many wanted to continue government ownership. Ike also expanded the use of presidential "memoranda." These were internal government declarations of encouragement for executive agencies to act in a certain way. Generally, these memos encouraged the huge federal bureaucracy to close ranks around a particular foreign policy. Ike issued forty-three of these.[50]

Ike continued the trend set by the Democrat centralizers by expanding the institutional capacity and thus power of the Executive Office of the President. That office went from a staff of 500 in FDR's second term to 2,500 in Eisenhower's second term.[51] The pre-war State department had 5,000 employees; in Ike's State department there were 20,000 employees to bolster international intrigue and help him hatch monarchist-style, protection racket treaties with nations around the globe.

Ike continued and expanded Truman's overly secretive policy of classification of government documents, using executive orders to do so.

49. Miller Center, *Eisenhower—Domestic Affairs*; Pach and Richardson, Eisenhower, 123–24.

50. Cooper, *Order*, 90.

51. Healy, *Cult of the Presidency*, 83.

As we will see, his dishonesty in foreign affairs reveals that his purpose in such a classification system was to advance activities and policies the public would not necessarily approve of. In 1954, he refused to turn over documents requested by Congress related to government contracting, giving further precedent to the now very current idea of "executive privilege," the idea that elected rulers are above the law. Ike was covering up a scandal involving the Dixon-Yates corporation. One of the embarrassing tidbits he hid from the public was the abusive conditions of government-sponsored radiation tests on human subjects. He also used the CIA to illegally open mail of U.S. citizens corresponding with people in the Soviet Union. He thus used his personal secret police force exactly the way McKinley, both Roosevelts, Taft and Truman ordained it to be used, to squelch dissent. His secret police harassed and abused "suspected" communists and encouraged citizens to spy on one another. He also continued and expanded Truman's federal employee loyalty program.[52]

Ike invoked executive privilege to prevent Congressional interrogation of members of the executive branch regarding communist sympathies, saying such privilege was necessary to allow candid policy discussions in the executive. But Ike really was trying to protect revelation of his private, chessboard-like manipulation of nations around the world. His argument has been called the "boldest assertion of executive privilege in the history of the republic," and was later judged by one constitutional scholar as "altogether without historical foundation."[53]

Ike used religion to develop the cult of his own personality by using religious themes in his speeches. In his inaugural speech he referred in an opening prayer to gods and wars, light and darkness, and said, "Forces of good and evil are massed and armed and opposed." He also made clear that he spoke for his cabinet in his contacts with heaven. He prayed, "Almighty God, as we stand here at this moment my future associates in the Executive branch of government join me in beseeching that Thou will make full and complete our dedication to the service of the people . . ." These apocalyptic references to the Bible reflected his upbringing in a Jehovah's Witness home and gave him justification for his massive program of covert wars, opposing what he figured were evil forces the world over. Ike started cabinet meetings with prayer and created the interfaith White

52 Cooper, *Order*, 25; Healy, *Cult of the Presidency*, 101; Pach and Richardson, *Eisenhower*, 64, 107–8; Crenson and Ginsberg, *Presidential Power*, 262–63, 347; Herring, *Colony to Superpower*, 653.

53. Pach and Richardson, *Eisenhower*, 64, 70–71.

House prayer breakfast as a newly baptized Presbyterian. He used Billy Graham as his unofficial spiritual advisor.[54]

On Flag Day in 1954, Ike signed a bill adding "Under God" to the pledge of allegiance. He also earned the distinction of making "In God We Trust" the motto of the U.S. In 1957, he saw to the motto's inclusion on U.S. coinage. Large portions of the electorate appreciated this, since two-thirds of public schools in the northeast and deep south engaged in daily Bible readings. These actions gave the appearance of elevating God and religion to their deserved place in American society and made him an extremely popular president across the country as well. His re-election slogan was "I like Ike," and much of the country actually did. Unfortunately, Ike personally did much to accelerate the decline of traditional Bible political ethics, since he moved the government further in the direction of Pharaoh-like central power and further away from local, democratic consent in government.[55]

Like most other candidates for national office, Ike promised to balance the national budget. He also wanted to please business interests by promising to keep the federal government off the backs of the private sector. However, a recessionary dip in 1953–54 made him forget both those campaign promises so that he agreed to expand spending, increase the national debt, and use interventionist methods to regulate the economy, all in order to get reelected. Luckily, Ike benefitted from the increases in the income tax during the Truman/Korean war era, which boosted that tax from $45 billion in 1945 to $65 billion in 1955. This enabled him to balance the budget in three of his eight years. He was even able to promote a military buildup, mostly in air and nuclear power, while still holding the federal budget constant. Ike was a lucky tyrant. He was able to please both liberals and conservatives in a something for everybody kind of administration. In 1958 Ike proposed a record peacetime budget. Conservatives screamed about his increases in unemployment insurance, Social Security, and federal health programs. They also complained about excessive amounts for defense. Congress made major cuts in his military budget that year. In 1959 the nation saw the largest peacetime deficit in history, so Ike was forced to veto many spending bills, and saw a budget surplus in 1960.[56]

---

54. Whitney, *Biographies*, 318; Flagel, *Guide*, 42–43.

55. Herring, *Colony to Superpower*, 655; Flagel, *Guide*, 43.

56. Bailyn, *America Is*, 1118–19; Crenson and Ginsberg, *Presidential Power*, 258;

Ike believed in gradualism in civil rights, since he prized the south-ern racist vote. He ordered federal troops to the south to calm racial ac-tivity and pushed voting rights legislation, but did little to ensure actual access to the ballot box, like dealing with poll taxes or literacy tests. He declined to endorse the Supreme Court ruling to desegregate schools. He believed states and localities had responsibility for fairness in employ-ment. He said, "Race relations is one of those things that will be healthy and sound only if it starts locally." However, in 1954 he abolished the last segregated unit in the armed forces, but didn't do much for equality in duty assignments or promotions.[57]

Ike flip-flopped when it came to domestic use of the armed forces. He proudly announced, "I can't imagine any set of circumstances that would ever induce me to send federal troops . . . to enforce the orders of a federal court . . ." But, then along came Orval Faubus, Governor of Arkansas. The governor at first promised to support phased desegrega-tion starting at Little Rock Central High, but then backed away, thinking of his reelection prospects. He ordered the National Guard to prevent the order that had been agreed upon between the school board and the federal district court. When Faubus withdrew the National Guard, a mob of whites tried to stop integration of nine black students. Ike sent 1,000 paratroopers and federalized the National Guard, not to support deseg-regation, but to restore public order.[58]

Eisenhower ran for a second term in order to be able to protect his policies, although no man had reached the age of seventy in the White House, and he was living with a badly diseased heart. He had covered up his first heart attack, then later disclosed it. Ike was the first American president barred from running for a third term of office by the Twenty-second Amendment. He would probably have run if it had not been for that important law. In fact, some fifty-eight percent of Americans polled said they would elect Ike to a third term. For example, "the warmth of Ike's personality" helped carry the south for him in both elections.[59]

Ike's actions in foreign affairs belied the kindly speeches about world peace used to get him elected. In 1952, during his first presidential

Miller Center, *Eisenhower—Domestic Affairs*; Pach and Richardson, *Eisenhower*, 168–69, 212.

57. Pach and Richardson, *Eisenhower*, 137–42.

58. Ibid., 150, 153.

59. Pach and Richardson, *Eisenhower*, 113–17; Nelson, *Presidency*, 156; McDon-ald, *Presidency*, 470; Cooper, *Order*, 219.

campaign, he said that if elected, he would visit Korea and bring the war to an end. As a part of his gambit to end the Korean War, Ike used the strategy of horrific threats that Nixon later used in the Vietnam war. He directed U.S. officials to hint to China that he might expand the war in a way Truman had not wanted to, that is, use nuclear weapons on China, Korea, and Indochina. In fact, he sent nuclear artillery to Okinawa for potential use on North Korea, and tested nuclear artillery pieces in Nevada. Ultimately he passed out candy to the South Koreans by promising South Korea a military alliance with the U.S. if they ended the war when the U.S. wanted.[60] These measures, together with the fact the Russians needed peace to shore up the regime after Stalin passed away, brought North Korea to the table and the parties signed an armistice.

In fact, the Korean War was a seminal event in U.S. political history. After World War II, the initial Truman de-mobilization brought the "defense" budget down to $14 billion by 1948, but soon enough it skyrocket again due to "containment." Ike criticized Truman's "permanent state of mobilization," and so after the Korean War was over, Ike made deep cuts in the military budget in 1954. Robert Taft, in the Senate, wanted even deeper cuts. However, large-scale demobilization never again occurred in the United State of America. For example, Ike funded the "defense" budget at $45 billion after the end of the war, and it took two years to reduce the standing army to a still-muscular one million soldiers. Ike also supported Truman's program for universal military training. Ike's slogan for election was "I like Ike," but his opponent's slogan was "Draft Ike, and he will draft you!"[61]

Ike did not want to have his hands tied in dealing with the world that the U.S. had recently subjugated, so he fought against the Bricker constitutional amendment that would have reigned in the power of the executive to commit the nation to foreign military alliances. Had Ike allowed the popular measure to pass, the Vietnam war might never have come to pass. Thus Ike must be remembered as one of the most consequential constitutional obstructionists in U.S. history.[62]

60 Miller Center, *Eisenhower—Domestic Affairs*; Herring, *Colony to Superpower*, 660–61; M. Nelson, *Presidency*, 154; Pach and Richardson, *Eisenhower*, 26, 87; Flagel, *Guide*, 233.

61. Flagel, *Guide*, 234; Pach and Richardson, *Eisenhower*, 11–12, 21, 77.

62. Herring, *Colony to Superpower*, 657; McDonald, *Presidency*, 408; Pach and Richardson, *Eisenhower*, 59–62.

Ike signed 1,800 executive agreements in foreign policy, often without Congressional involvement, while Truman had signed 1,300. In fact, only 200 treaty agreements were sent to Congress under Truman and Eisenhower put together. Ike maintained a public posture of love for the founding traditions of the nation, while privately despising them. For example, when Ike's secretary of state attacked the traditional American doctrine of neutrality as "immoral," Ike distanced himself from that unpopular statement, as if he believed in keeping hands off other nations. His thoroughgoing usurpation of Congressional foreign policy power by means of his use of executive agreements shows he was a monstrous hypocrite.[63]

It was important for the citizenry to believe that their nation was finally at peace. Therefore, Ike's strategy called for using the president's own private army, the CIA, to fight numerous wars abroad against nations and factions who might conceivably know how to spell the word "communism." The CIA used bribes, subversion, and assassination, all tactics the American people would not have approved had they known. In the event a larger commitment of military was necessary, Eisenhower demanded a blank check from Congress to intervene militarily in any nation he deemed to be threatened by communism. In particular, he wanted freedom to protect Taiwan in its tug of war with mainland China involving the Taiwan Straits.[64] He did not win this broad power, but eventually succeeded in getting it in order to deal with the Middle East.

Eisenhower reorganized the National Security Council via executive order and chaired more than ninety percent of its 366 meetings. He liked the "backroom feel" of the NSC, where politics and military cohabitated secretly. He made sure that its staff grew considerably, since he became a leading proponent of covert action. He established a committee within the NSC to oversee such actions in 1954, despite the fact that Truman's original NSC legislation could not find a source in the U.S. Constitution authorizing covert action in other nations.[65] The Constitution did not authorize such actions for precisely those reasons Ike's illegal activities exposed. Ike's covert ops brought down two governments, Iran

63. Crenson and Ginsberg, *Presidential Power*, 255; Morley, *Freedom and Federalism*, 128.

64. Miller Center, *Eisenhower—Foreign Affairs*; Crenson and Ginsberg, *Presidential Power*, 263.

65. Flagel, *Guide*, 302; Cooper, *Order*, 149, 176.

and Guatemala, and brought serious long-term consequences that plague the homeland down to this day.

Ike covertly overthrew democracies and established dictatorships not only in Iran and Guatemala, but also in Egypt, Laos and Vietnam. In his January 1960 message he repeated earlier promises: "The U.S. has no intention of interfering in the internal affairs of any nation . . . by force or subversion." This from the mouth of one who was intervening covertly in a significant number of the countries of the world the moment those words came out of his mouth. At the same time he was trying to depose Castro, Eisenhower tried to depose Rafael Trujillo in the Dominican Republic. Ike said he wanted to see Trujillo "sawed off." In August 1960 he also gave the go-ahead to the CIA to try to overthrow Patrick Lumumba in Congo, without ruling out "any particular kind of activity."[66]

Ike believed the Indochina nations of Vietnam, Cambodia, and Laos, followed by Burma and Thailand, would fall to communism without U.S. paternal involvement. In fact, the opposite occurred. The nations of Indochina fell to communism because of American involvement. Initially, Ike didn't need to send troops, because there was already a colonial power there exploiting the people—France. Ike used both overt and covert means to assist in the transition from French to American empire there, and thus sewed the seeds for future direct military involvement. He didn't want to commit U.S. troops because he said "The jungles of Indochina would have swallowed up division after division of U.S. troops." The U.S. could supply air, naval, and logistical support instead. At the start of his term, he had a foreign aid budget of $5 billion/year to draw from to accomplish this. Ike used sports and religious celebrities to lobby Congress for foreign aid. By 1954 Ike was paying more than three-fourths of the French costs of the war, essentially using French troops as U.S. mercenaries to advance U.S. interests there.[67]

Settlement of the French war in Indochina made Cambodia and Laos independent, and split Vietnam in half, pending elections. At the end of his term, Ike contemplated invading Laos to install a U.S. puppet government there. To his credit, Ike avoided overt U.S. involvement in a

---

66. Crenson and Ginsberg, *Presidential Power*, 256; Pach and Richardson, *Eisenhower*, 222–23.

67. Cooper, *Order*, 182; Pach and Richardson, *Eisenhower*, 166–67, 179; Bailyn, *Great Republic*, 1207; Miller Center, *Eisenhower—Domestic Affairs*.

hot war in Laos and Vietnam, which his successors JFK and LBJ found to their liking and went ahead with.[68]

Ike's goal was to continue and even expand the Truman policy of permanent mobilization against and "containment" of those nations he wanted the American people to believe could threaten the American heartland. Therefore war spending never fell below fifty percent of the national budget total in his entire eight-year term. While at first he slowed the rate of increase in conventional weaponry spending, he boosted Truman's budget levels for nuclear weapons and Air Force spending. He later flip-flopped on his pledge to decrease conventional military spending and increased it.[69]

Ike's policy was to use tax money for economic and military aid to countries that agreed with his policies, or could be bribed into supporting them. For example, he negotiated with Gamal Nasser to provide $400 million to build the Aswan High Dam on the Nile in Egypt if the leader there agreed to kowtow to him. He used bribery aid to prop up King Hussein in Jordan by helping that monarch survive a rebellion. He dispatched the U.S. Sixth Fleet to let the Jordanian rebels know who was really boss in the region and gave Hussein a cash grant of $20 million to deal with that "domestic affair." The King then disavowed national elections and declared martial law. Ike also sent aid to support King Saud in Saudi Arabia.[70]

Eisenhower moved to expand U.S. interests in the Middle East oil fields that the nation had first corralled militarily during World War II. In Egypt, Gamel A. Nasser charted a neutralist course between the U.S. and the Soviet Union. Nasser then nationalized the Suez Canal. Some two-thirds of the oil for western Europe passed through here. Ike wanted an international authority to run Suez or else to reroute oil shipments and build pipelines. Britain and France opted for war instead in 1956. This war also involved Israel and miffed Ike to such an extent that he intervened covertly and successfully in British national elections.[71]

68. Flagel, *Guide*, 198; Nelson, *Presidency*, 156.

69. Miller Center, *Eisenhower—Foreign Affairs*; Herring, *Colony to Superpower*, 692.

70. Miller Center, *Eisenhower—Foreign Affairs*; Boyer, *Oxford Companion*, 219; Herring, *Colony to Superpower*, 677.

71. Herring, *Colony to Superpower*, 675; Pach and Richardson, *Eisenhower*, 126–28.

Ike's understanding of what nations and which factions were truly threatened by or infected with communism was seriously impaired. Eisenhower mistook nationalism for communism. For example, in 1958 he placed U.S. Marines in Lebanon when a faction there that had communicated with Nasser in Egypt (two removes away from actual communist involvement) actually seized power. He did so without serious consideration of other options. Ike also bungled a CIA operation against Syria in Jordan by attempting to overthrow the government there. The U.S. sent arms to neighbors of Syria and encouraged Turkey to concentrate troops on the border with Syria. The Eisenhower Doctrine of resistance to Arab nationalism ultimately failed to shore up U.S. interests there.[72]

Ike blatantly interfered in Japan's internal political relations by means of covert operations to influence elections there. That intervention assured the long-term continuation of a one-party 'democracy' there. He then forced a military alliance treaty on Japan. Ike re-armed America's new colony Germany in order to obtain a balance of power against the Soviet Union, thus trading our former enemy for a new one, like one might trade baseball cards.[73]

Lying to the American people and to the world at large was an important tool of foreign policy for Eisenhower. He lied about U.S. covert operations in Indonesia to overthrow the government there. Sukarno remained resolutely neutral and was thus suspect to Ike. Ike wanted military allies, not merely peace-minded nations and was willing to reward polarism only. India's Nehru asked about Eisenhower's doctrine, "Why a man with such strong muscles should publically demonstrate his muscles all the time."[74]

Ike lied to the world about the U-2 spy flights over Russia, which actually constituted an act of war. He said the U.S. did not do that kind of thing. When one of the planes was shot down, Ike lied again and said it was merely a weather flight. Imagine the uproar when the Soviets announced they had captured the pilot alive and found that it was indeed

---

72. Miller Center, *Eisenhower—Foreign Affairs*; Herring, *Colony to Superpower*, 677, 679; Pach and Richardson, *Eisenhower*, 191, 193–94; Boyer, *Oxford Companion*, 219.

73. Miller Center, *Eisenhower—Foreign Affairs*; Herring, *Colony to Superpower*, 694.

74. Ibid., 680, 693.

a spy plane. Ike had to admit the spy flights had been going on for four years.[75]

From 1958 to 1960 alone, Ike increased the number of nuclear weapons from 6,000 to 18,000. Ike built submarines capable of launching nuclear warheads, and by 1961 had more than two thousand bombers.[76]

Ike and Dulles encouraged "liberation of captive peoples." This sort of talk by the world's greatest power encouraged revolts against oppression in places like Hungary, Tibet, and East Berlin. But the U.S. lacked a realistic capacity to help all people everywhere, and selectively intervened in nationalist revolts, usually on the side of the oppressor, leading to profound disillusionment and blowback the world over. Ike's most notorious big-nation botches were the East Berlin crisis of 1953 and the Hungarian Revolution of 1956. Harsh economic conditions in East Germany provoked protests in East Berlin, followed by a general strike and rioting. Ike was busy swelling his resume in Korea and looked the other way.

Being in an alliance is like being jumped into a street gang. When a party tries to get out, it gets in all kinds of trouble. When Hungary announced it was leaving the Warsaw Pact in 1956, Russia sent 200,000 troops and 4,000 tanks into Budapest. Hungary expected help from the champion of cold war self-determination, the United States, but Ike turned a cold shoulder. The U.S. had been broadcasting over Radio Free Europe it wanted to liberate people from communism. Ike had even helped organize demonstrations in Hungary. But when things got real, he opted to not hurt his reelection chances in this presidential election year instead of supporting an oppressed people. When Hungarians proposed a multi-party democracy, and Ike had little to say or do, Khrushchev responded with tanks and crushed the revolt, killing 4,000.[77]

Ike made a final World War II/Eisenhower Administration victory lap at the end of 1959 to Europe, the Near East and South Asia. He said, "I decided to make an effort that no President ever was called upon to make. I do feel a compulsion to visit a number of countries . . . to prove that we are not aggressive, that we seek nobody else's territories or possessions." He wanted to show his smile to the world and hide his fangs. No previous president was ever called upon to do this, because no president before Ike had both an overt and covert empire to bask in like Ike did.

75. Herring, *Colony to Superpower*, 698; Whitney, *Biographies*, 321.

76. Herring, *Colony to Superpower*, 700.

77. Ibid., 644, 666.

He didn't seek territories or possessions, because he already had a boatful locked up and subservient to his personal rule. About his trip it was said, "Throngs greeted him in India, Pakistan, Italy and elsewhere."[78]

Ike cemented what he hoped would be the popular view of his presidency with a stirring farewell address. His speechwriter, Malcolm Moos, had him hypocritically warn against the rise of the military-industrial complex, which he described as the union of "an immense military establishment and a large arms industry" that was "felt in every city, every State house, every office of the Federal government . . ."[79] He returned to his earlier political theme of pacifism, saying "Together we must learn how to compose differences not with arms, but with intellect and decent purpose." He spoke as someone who had "witnessed the horror and the lingering sadness of war."

Ike neglected to mention that the military-industrial complex was the demon he helped nurture and turn loose on the world. He could only speak against it once it was too late to do anything about it. Now, he could use agonized and emotional terms to describe the predicament. He spoke of the "three and a half million men and women . . . directly engaged in the defense establishment [in peace time]." He spoke of "the prospect of domination of the nation's scholars" by the military establishment. While historians of his presidency use the term "military industrial complex," the speech really targeted what should be called the "military-industrial-academic complex."

Ike also decried what he spent his two terms of office trying to produce, a new global regime dominated by the United States. He said that the nations of the earth must be "a confederation . . . of equals," certainly an absurd proposition and one he most certainly did not believe himself. He even offered a prayer that "all who are insensitive to the needs of others will learn charity; that the scourges of poverty, disease, and ignorance will be made to disappear from the earth . . . (and) all peoples will come to live together in a peace guaranteed by the binding force of mutual respect and love . . ." This was a Biblical millennial gospel featuring the lion laying down with the lamb. He spoke like a prophet and said "We . . . must avoid the impulse to live only for today, plundering, for our own

78. Pach and Richardson, *Eisenhower*, 209.

79. Miller Center, *Eisenhower—Foreign Affairs*; Pach and Richardson, *Eisenhower*, 230.

ease and convenience . . .." He was perhaps experiencing a tinge of guilt for all he had done to subvert the interests of the American people.[80]

Finally, Eisenhower lamented that he had not been able to reduce "the bitterness of the East-West struggle," totally misunderstanding that that particular struggle was not the basic struggle. In fact, the basic struggle was the struggle of each nation for independence from subjugation by their neighbors, which struggle often pitted them against giant nations like the U.S. Leaders in the U.S. did not really care about legitimate national aspirations when those aspirations were expressed by people of different skin color, and especially if they were not expressed in Christian terms, using the English language.

Years later in Lyndon Johnson's term, Ike endorsed LBJ's sustained bombing of North Vietnam and commitment of American troops on the ground, apparently forgetting his own warning about divisions getting mired in the jungles of Asia. He called war protestors "kooks" and "hippies."[81]

John F. Kennedy

As a U.S. representative from Massachusetts, Jack Kennedy supported Truman's fantastical legislative agenda, which sought to go well beyond FDR's immense expansions of the national government. As a senator he positioned himself for the presidency by becoming ever more liberal, thus following time-honored method in the Democratic party of running hard to the left to win the votes of the less-educated voters with unrealistic promises of government salvation. When Kennedy ran against Richard Nixon for president in 1960, the Democrat party platform and Kennedy's debate speeches promised minorities a quick expansion of civil rights once the Democrats were elected, a promise that was largely ignored once Jack was in office.

John F. Kennedy made extensive use of television to promote his personality and the things he wanted people to think about him. He was extremely ambitious for power, and he started running a half year earlier than presidents had before him. He served in the office from 1961 to 1963. He made considerable use of the tools of political idolatry. During the campaign he handed out label pins depicting his torpedo boat PT

80. Pach and Richardson, *Eisenhower*, 230.
81. Ibid., 235.

109. Later, he allowed TV cameras to come into the White House to film the president, and his photogenic wife and children. He opened press conference to live telecasts. His ratings soared on the basis of his personality, which was witty, cool, crisp, and authoritative. In fact, he worked with the television networks to build a "large, permanent infrastructure of technicians, camera crews, correspondents, and producers solely for the purpose of covering the president's day-to-day activities." It has been said, "Being president had become full-time show-business." Thus, Kennedy inaugurated reality TV long before the masses thought it was a cool idea.[82]

In his inaugural address JFK promised a New Frontier program so far-reaching it might not be realized in his own administration, "nor even perhaps in our lifetime on this planet." His twitterpated admirers called the new America under Kennedy "Camelot." Very little of his Camelot program came to pass in his three years in office, and very little could. He ran into political reality soon after taking office. Ultimately, his was an administration of magical talk of domestic progress and fantastic, and often failed, foreign policy initiatives.[83]

The reason that JFK was not able to successfully push through his sweeping domestic proposals was that JFK manhandled Congress. Even after Democrats won the midterm elections of 1962, Kennedy continued to alienate Congress and fail to get his major domestic legislation passed. Congressional relations was important for Kennedy. He empowered his legislative staff to be visible and pushy and placed legislative specialists in the executive departments. He viewed himself as the greatest benefactor of the people, rather than the Congress. He directed his staff to intimidate the Congress by threatening sanctions if the people's representatives did not conform to the president's agenda, and by offering rewards if they did. He did not use a chief of staff, and relied on a kitchen cabinet rather than a single person. JFK met personally with legislative leaders to try to get them to bypass the usual legislative debate on the issues. Kennedy had given a hint during the campaign of his inclination to usurp traditional legal powers from other agencies when he said, "The American people . . . have a right to know . . . whether (the Presidency) . . . is aware of and willing to use the powerful resources of that office." For him, it was clear

82. Bailyn, *Great Republic*, 1217; Healy, *Cult of the Presidency*, 242; Nelson, *Presidency*, 158; McDonald, *Presidency*, 448–49.

83. Whitney, *Biographies*, 325; Boyer, *Oxford Companion*, 418–19.

some presidents simply were not aware that they could successfully get away with things, preferring to maintain traditional legal distinctions. In order to provide justifications for his legal journeys, he hired a private attorney, Clark Clifford.[84]

Kennedy took office in the middle of a recession and therefore floated up a large raft of legislation to stimulate the economy and win the hearts of voters. He proposed lower taxes, an increase in the minimum wage, federal aid to education, greatly enhanced Social Security coverage, federal health insurance for the elderly, urban mass transit, regional development projects in Appalachia, and a Department of Urban Affairs. Of all these initiatives, the only ones to get passed during his lifetime were the Appalachia development loans and grants, and a small increase in the minimum wage. Congress passed and he signed a $5 billion federal assistance to housing act and a small increase in social security benefits. Congress also gave him new powers to reduce tariffs. Because he wanted more rather than less from Congress, he vetoed few public bills. He did, however, issue signing statements criticizing Congress for requirements placed on his executive measures that he felt were inappropriate or unconstitutional. He also directed the federal government to set guidelines on wages and prices. His Civil Rights Act was passed after his death, largely because it was a political prop that Lyndon Johnson found useful. He asked for tax cuts in 1963 while increasing domestic spending, thus ignoring the budget deficit issue.[85]

Not being able to get Congress to do what he wanted, Kennedy set about to do what he could by presidential decree. In fact, he institutionalized the entire executive order process by enacting Executive Order 11630 in 1962, which established a process for developing this form of illegal legislation, which often included executive orders developed deep within the federal bureaucracy. He issued orders attacking housing discrimination and an order on national security data classification. He issued a series of executive orders in his first month in office relating to labor-management disputes between Pan American Airlines and the Flight Engineers International Union, and days later between the union and five other airlines. He referenced no statute as his authority for doing

84. McDonald, Presidency, 368; Whitney, Biographies, 334; Flagel, Guide, 300–301; Healy, Cult of the Presidency, 80.

85. McDonald, Presidency, 354, 369; Miller Center, Kennedy—Domestic Affairs; Nelson, Presidency, 159; Whitney, Biographies, 334; Cooper, Order, 209; Boyer, Oxford Companion, 419; Drewry and O'Connor, America Is, 646.

this, mentioning only "authority vested in me as President of the United States." He issued similar orders in a merchant marine dispute and regarding a railway worker dispute with seventy-nine railroad companies. After that he issued 26 more executive orders in labor disputes. He also initiated a couple dozen presidential memoranda dealing with issues outside of foreign policy matters.[86]

Kennedy was willing to use Trumanesque and Ike-like illegal black ops to get what he wanted done. JFK and his attorney general, his brother Robert Kennedy, illegally wire-tapped steel industry executives and used the IRS to bully the steel industry, all because of a dispute over steel prices. In a private conversation, Kennedy said that the steel industry "fucked us, and now we've got to fuck them." In ancient great king style, JFK had the sex icon of the era, Marilyn Monroe, sing to him at a private party, thanking him for the bravado he used to deal with big steel. He also set up a strike force at IRS to hurt groups critical of his administration and encouraged the IRS to menace politicians on the other side of the aisle, like Richard Nixon. J. Edgar Hoover and the FBI disliked the intrusive and controlling Kennedy brothers, who used the FBI like personal butlers and private detectives. Even though Nixon had his rights trampled by Kennedy, he was happy to build upon Kennedy's precedent once he himself assumed the throne of power. Kennedy wanted to know everything going on in government and would fire people if anything was kept from him.[87]

It has been said that Kennedy wanted a "more active use of American power" than Eisenhower did. Accordingly, he enlarged the nation's nuclear arsenal beyond even the unconscionable expansion of that arsenal made by Ike. He was known as a "hawk of the highest order." JFK pushed the military to study counter-insurgency methods, to keep pace with his announced policy to commit the nation to operations abroad. In his inaugural address, he used soaring language to commit the United States to a program to "pay any price, bear any burden, meet any hardship, support any friend, oppose any foe, in order to assure the survival and success of liberty." This was surely the complete opposite of John Quincy Adams' saying, the United States "does not go abroad in search of monsters to destroy." It also implied a commitment of the United States

86. Cooper, *Order*, 25, 45, 48, 76, 118.

87. Healy, *Cult of the Presidency*, 102–3, 108; Flagel, *Guide*, 182; McDonald, *Presidency*, 473.

to world-wide political and military entanglement of a breadth and depth that would have caused George Washington to raise a sword and an army. It has been said, "No doctrine had ever been so ambitious."[88]

The first use of his military adventurism was the Bay of Pigs disaster, where he picked up on Ike's plan to invade and overthrow Cuba. When the invaders were overwhelmed by Castro's forces, JFK lied to the American people and to the world and said his administration had nothing to do with the operation. JFK, it seems, cared more about military bravado than he worried about bringing the world to the brink of war. He also authorized covert assassination schemes to kill Castro.[89]

What JFK had in mind with his "go anywhere in the world" statement were the twenty-four new nations joining the Third World during the period 1960–63. He would use economic aid (he built a dam for the people of Ghana because they needed one), military advisers, the Peace Corp, the CIA, and U.S. armed forces to make things right whenever they got wrong. Kennedy wanted to "accelerate programs for underdeveloped countries . . . (through) field visits . . . to a number of selected countries, with particular attention to Latin America."[90] This was pro-active nation building. Kennedy used the national treasury as a personal checkbook in his campaign of worldwide benevolence.

In Vietnam, Kennedy tested his nation-building philosophy by first sending in Army Special Forces to train South Vietnam in counter-insurgency. He did this, however, without consulting Congress. He started out in 1961 with hundreds of military supervisors and millions of dollars of expenditure. He later increased the number of military advisers to 11,000 by one report, and to 16,000 by another, and was then expending billions of dollars. Kennedy must have been delighted to escalate U.S. involvement ever closer to actual commitment of U.S. warriors to hot combat operations. In fact, he mentioned to one of his aides that war "made it easier for a president to achieve greatness."[91]

88. Boyer, *Oxford Companion*, 418; Flagel, *Guide*, 197; Herring, *Colony to Superpower*, xvi, 703, 705.

89. Flagel, *Guide*, 254; Miller Center, *Kennedy—Foreign Affairs*; Boyer, *Oxford Companion*, 419.

90. Herring, *Colony to Superpower*, 714–15; Cooper, *Order*, 154.

91. Miller Center, *Kennedy—Foreign Affairs*; Crenson and Ginsberg, *Presidential Power*, 263; Herring, *Colony to Superpower*, 727; Miller Center, *Kennedy—Foreign Affairs*; Flagel, *Guide*, 255; Healy, *Cult of the Presidency*, 280.

Under Kennedy, the National Security Council grew into a shadow government of 200 employees, so large that it now competed with the publically scrutinized Department of State for foreign policy influence.

Kennedy sounded a heavily cultic tone in a speech he was about to deliver in Dallas on the day he was assassinated. He wrote, "We in this country, in this generation, are, by destiny rather than choice, the watchmen on the walls of world freedom." He thus took a biblical metaphor related to municipal vigilance and expanded it, perverting it terribly, to imply American responsibility for all the nations of the earth. He then alleged that the U.S. had not only the calling but the chops to "achieve in our time and for all time the ancient vision of 'peace on earth, good will toward men.'" This perpetual world peace that was to come at his hand would be accomplished by "the righteousness of our cause."[92]

Lyndon B. Johnson

Lyndon Johnson once reminisced that while he was a high school debate coach he felt it proper to "humiliate [debate students] and embarrass them and make fun of 'em." Lyndon Johnson won a seat in Congress by defending Roosevelt's controversial programs. While there he promoted electrical services for farmers, public housing, naval affairs, and won a pork bill for a dam in his home district. He also placated his white southern constituents with several votes against civil rights. He even supported Roosevelt's court-packing plan in 1937 when he was a Senator. During his time in Congress, he supported both Truman and Ike in their Cold War fear-mongering, and in the meanwhile, Texas benefitted greatly from military spending.[93]

As president, LBJ served five years in office, from late 1963 to early 1969. Johnson was known as a dominating personality. For one thing, he stood six feet five and three-quarters inches tall. For one to receive the "Johnson treatment" was to be bullied into submission. He said once that White House occupants consisted of one "elephant" and the rest "pissants." LBJ was a heavy drinker and was known for frequent outbursts of temper. His own press secretary George Reedy referred to the administration of his dictatorial boss of thirteen years as an "American monarchy." Reedy said, "His manners were atrocious . . . frequently calculated

92. Whitney, *Biographies*, 326.
93. Flagel, *Guide*, 21; Bornet, *Johnson*, 3, 38; Boyer, *Oxford Companion*, 407.

to give offense." Johnson tended to man-handle reporters who asked what he thought were silly or embarrassing questions. In an Oval Office meeting in 1963, he was asked by a reporter why the United States was in Vietnam. He unzipped his royal fly, wagged his presidential private part, and yelled, "This is why." LBJ was being candid, if a bit crude. For him, politics was the use of raw socio-sexual power to intimidate, take, and glorify. One commentator reminds that LBJ "dominated the federal government more thoroughly than had any predecessor . . ." Walter Lipmann said LBJ was exercising "unlimited power." One historian writes, "The president concentrated on what was convenient for him." He had such great success manipulating the legislature that he had little need to veto bills.[94]

Johnson purged all but one of the White House staffers that Kennedy had appointed in his first year. Staff and sympathetic media knew it was their job to pour the glory on his head. The Pulitzer Prize-winning journalist who wrote LBJ's election-year autobiography spoke of Johnson's "gift of empathy," his "sensitive awareness of inner feelings," his "patient fortitude," and his "intellectual processes . . . unique in my experience." He also mentioned that Johnson functioned best in "disaster." One fawning professor wrote, "Not only this generation but their children and beyond . . . get chances . . . they owe to you . . . it will be your harvest." During the course of the administration, many of his new staffers, like Bill Moyers, felt betrayed, however, since LBJ's methods were not particularly admirable. For example, he gave expanded visibility to Califano and Valenti for purposes of courting the Italian-American vote. For his part, Califano returned the favor. He said, "starting with George Washington . . . Lyndon Johnson is in a class by himself." Johnson actively exploited the female vote by making appointments of women to the government, but his own top staff remained all male. He backed off female appointments after he won the 1964 election in his own right. Like John Adams long before him, LBJ made a partisan appointment onslaught beginning in 1967 when he knew he would be leaving the presidency.[95]

Johnson achieved what Truman tried to do but couldn't—expand centralized domestic social welfare programs far beyond what even Franklin Roosevelt had done. In order to do so, he had to cast a spell on the electorate beyond even the "Camelot" vision that Kennedy tried

94. Healy, *Cult of the Presidency*, 264; McDonald, *Presidency*, 302, 354; Bornet, 5, 38, 151, 154–55, 160.

95. Bornet, *Johnson*, 25, 31–36, 39, 104, 238, 241, 343–444.

to convince people was possible. In his first state of the union address to Congress in January 1964, he outlined a national socializing program that expropriated the constitutional role of states and counties in the human services field. He said, "Let this session of Congress be known as the session which did more for civil rights than the last hundred sessions combined; as the session which enacted the most far-reaching tax cut of our time; as the session which declared all-out war on human poverty and unemployment in these United States; as the session which finally recognized the health needs of all of our older citizens; as the session which reformed our tangled transportation and transit policies; as the session which achieved the most effective, efficient foreign aid program ever; and as the session which helped to build more homes and more schools and more libraries and more hospitals than any single session of Congress in the history of our Republic." Johnson said, "We know what must be done, and this nation of abundance can surely afford to do it." One author commented, "Neither statement was even remotely true." In fact, however, Congress responded positively to Johnson's "Great Society" program, in part in order to honor the memory of John Kennedy, but in part, too, to get themselves reelected. The initial session passed many of the laws he asked for except medical care for the retired.[96]

LBJ set up task forces to kick off the war on poverty. The prominent socialist Michael Harrington took an active part in planning the "war." The task forces drew largely from liberal university faculty, but their deliberations were kept secret, since LBJ was planning to go far beyond Roosevelt's New Deal. For example, one of the first task force plans was for the federal government to provide universal American literacy within the next 18 months. This sort of delusional hocus-pocus infected the Democratic Party platform in 1960 as well. That platform had announced, "Now within reach (is) the final eradication . . . of poverty," which it said could be accomplished in ten years. Johnson added his own ten-year plan for medical care. During that time, he wanted "modern medical care for every person, of any age, of every race, of every religion, whatever his means." One author wrote, "Johnson and his speechwriters went far beyond rationality."One author wrote about the secret planning of legislative initiatives, "Here was secret government." Also, "The task forces represented the worse form of intellectual and educational elitism," since both the poor and the media were "frozen out completely."

96. Whitney, *Biographies*, 346.

Masking his own autocratic manipulation of the legislative planning process, Johnson entertained the masses with the opposite feeling. He told
Americans, "Government is not an enemy of the people. It is the people,"
as if the people and all their representatives were involved in the process.[97]

In the election year of 1964, LBJ could claim a list of passed legislation and budget measures that included "the Inter-American Development Bank, the Kennedy Cultural Center, tax reduction, . . . federal aid
to airports, the farm program, . . . control of pesticides, the International
Development Association, the Civil Rights Act of 1964, Campobello International Park, urban mass-transit systems, research on water resources,
. . . civil-service pay raises, the 'War on Poverty,' . . . truth-in-securities,
the Medicine Bow National Forest, the Ozark Scenic Riverway, . . . the
Fort Bowie Historic site, foot stamps, housing, . . . nurse training, . . .
the Fire Island National Seashore, library services, and health benefits for
federal employees." Johnson flip-flopped on his position on civil rights
in 1957, when he had refused to support fair employment practices, by
loudly trumpeting his support for civil rights before the 1964 election.[98]

Johnson's tax cut, the Revenue Act of 1964, was designed not only to
stimulate the economy but to stimulate his election. It contained a provision for a one-time selling of homes without much tax on the gain, and
income averaging cuts for individual and corporations. He promised that
the tax cut would stimulate the economy, increase production and federal
revenues, and allow him to balance the budget. This was classic tyrant
trickery. He would cut taxes and increase spending, and all would be
well! In the meanwhile the money supply increased from $31.6 billion to
$44.8 billion. This, together with spending, causing an inflationary time
bomb and the seeds of 1970s inflation. A Council of Economic Advisers
member said that Johnson's failure to enact a tax increase was "a colossal
error," a classic case of fiscal mismanagement which led to an era of inflation. While the deficit in 1965 was $1.6 billion, a year later it tripled, and
in 1968 it stood at $25.2 billion. To grease up the voting booths he also
provided $600 billion in aid to wheat and cotton farmers. In his Great So-
ciety speech, delivered May 28, 1964 as election day approached, Johnson
made messianic promises: "No child will go unfed and no youngster will
go unschooled." Further, "Every teacher (will have) good pay." In addition, there would be "a job for everyone who is willing to work . . . ," "every

97. Bornet, *Johnson*, 56–58, 119, 128, 237.
98. Ibid., 52, 94–95.

slum . . . gone from every city in America." To punctuate his assurances, he exclaimed, "The place is here and the time is now."[99]

Johnson used indirect or "third party" program administrators, including non-profit corporations, endowments, contractors, government enterprises, and private business to implement his poverty programs. These surrogate program administrators often functioned with little accountability and little standardization. LBJ also expanded federal regional and area field offices, and used state and local governments as well.[100]

One of the methods LBJ undertook to drive states in the direction he wanted them to go was to set "floors" defining minimum commitments for states to meet in policy areas he intended to usurp. The idea was to provide funding to encourage the states to meet the standards. But LBJ also forced the states to provide the funding themselves through so-called "unfunded mandates." Other times, he elbowed states out of the policy area altogether, a political situation called federal "preemption."

Johnson was adept at speaking out of both sides of his mouth when it came to political promises and issues. Regarding criminal justice, he remarked, "The Constitution provides that responsibility for law and order should be vested in the states and in the local communities." But once in office, LBJ systematically expanded the federal criminal code by such means as the Drug Abuse and Control Act, the Law Enforcement Assistance Act, and the Omnibus Crime Control and Safe Streets Act. In one study the LEAA contributed only 12 cents of every dollar spent to actual services. LBJ had promised to "drive crime from our midst in these United States," but in the first decade of LEAA crime rates continued upward: from 1960 through 1978 robbery, murder, aggravated assault, and rape tripled in the U.S. Johnson was especially ambitious to commit central bureaucracy to education reform, long the private preserve of families and local government and school districts. He poured money into preschool, elementary and secondary education, and to colleges to care for poorer students and districts by means of special programs and projects. He signed bills like the Elementary and Secondary School Act and the Higher Education Act.[101]

99. Ibid., 52, 59, 61, 94–95, 99–100, 103, 115, 233, 239, 242–43.

100. McDonald, *Presidency*, 337.

101. Healy, *Cult of the Presidency*, 85; Miller Center, *Lyndon Johnson—Domestic Affairs*; Bornet, *Johnson*, 248–49.

Johnson did not tire of using specious language to promote his own special brand of tyranny. In his inaugural address in 1965 after winning the presidency in his own right, he bound himself together with the American people and with God, saying "On this occasion, the oath I have taken before you, and before God, is not mine alone, but ours together." With these words he recalled Teddy Roosevelt's push for a merging of the nation's personality with his own personality and which allowed him to do whatever he wanted to do for his admiring public. He called this binding-together just like the Bible did, a "covenant," based on "the unchanged character of our people, and on their faith." That marvelous unity of God, ruler and people was now producing "a destiny." But strangely, that destiny, like Johnson's method of governing, was ad hoc, it emanated from the ruler's own mind. And it was hardly "unchanged," for Johnson invited his hearers to be hostile toward history, custom and law: "For some, history decides. For this generation, the choice must be our own." The people, together with the ruler, can do whatever they want to do. In terms of personal spiritual matters, Johnson also used the popular minister Billy Graham to advise him as to God's will, in case at any point he did not understand it fully.[102]

Johnson's reference to "war" against poverty suggested that he would try to use peacetime emergency measures and executive usurpation to achieve his goals. In fact, Johnson's name became associated with abuse of emergency power in both domestic and international affairs. He often failed to rescind his emergency and national security directives, thus creating confusion for incoming presidents. Johnson pushed an Open Housing law for federal regulation of the sale and rental of housing, thus moving emergency war-time housing regulation to peacetime. A New York Times columnist groused, "the Great Society programs are all compulsory."[103]

Johnson had been a Congressional leader himself and he knew how to grease the skids to get things done there. With Lyndon Johnson, there was no longer any pretense that the executive branch should merely be administering the law. He intended to write it himself with or without the legally established policy-making branch and used a variety of methods to do so. For example, he offered White House staff to Congressional leaders to help them write speeches and press releases that would help

102. Flagel, *Guide*, 43.
103. Cooper, *Order*, 13, 71, 193; Bornet, *Johnson*, 221.

advance his agenda. His cabinet made their own policy staff available to the Congress to bolster the executive branch agenda as well. He maintained a congressional liaison staff of nine people. He threatened to withhold jobs appointments if legislators did not vote for his programs.[104]

Johnson kept a file of favors asked and favors given, in order to keep a score sheet he could use during crunch time to call in votes. He then kept a loyalty score sheet on each member of Congress updated with each new vote taken. And the loyalty he sought was not to the Constitution, or to the rule of law, but rather to him personally, to his personal agenda. He neglected the constitutional separation of powers and acted as though he was still a legislative leader in Congress. One author says, "He undermined the institutional integrity of Congress."[105]

Johnson had a stellar legislative year in 1965. He dealt with issues and signed laws relating to: Medicare; aid to education; higher education; the four-year farm program; the Department of Housing and Urban Development; increases in social security; voting rights; immigration; heart disease, cancer, and stroke; the National Crime Commission; drug control; mental health facilities; health professions; medical libraries; community health services; vocational rehabilitation; the Arts and Humanities Foundation; aid to Appalachia; highway beauty; clean air; water-pollution; high-speed transit; presidential disability; child health; regional development; aid to small businesses; weather-predicting services; increases in military pay; the Water Resources Council; water desalinization; arms control; strengthening of the UN Charter; an international coffee agreement; retirement for federal employees; the Delaware Water Gap Recreation Area; the Whiskeytown National Recreation Area; the Assateague National Seashore, and life insurance for veterans. Lady Bird Johnson's legislative program was successful as well, dealing with regulations for highway billboards, parks, open spaces (down to specifying even benches and outdoor lighting), post office issuance of stamps on beautification and conservation, a variety of clean water acts, and measures pushed by the Committee for a More Beautiful Capital.[106]

In the first ten months of 1966, ninety of Johnson's proposed 115 bills were signed into law. His total list of legislation enacted in 1966 included food for India; child nutrition; the Department of Transportation;

---

104. Crenson and Ginsberg, *Presidential Power*, 191; Bornet, *Johnson*, 130.

105. Crenson and Ginsberg, *Presidential Power*, 191–92.

106. Bornet, *Johnson*, 135–46, 122, 126, 220–21, 224, 226.

truth in packaging; model cities; rent supplements; the Teachers Corps; the Asian Development Bank; clean rivers; food for freedom; child safety; narcotics rehabilitation; traffic safety; highway safety; mine safety; international education; bail reform; tire safety, a new GI Bill; increase in the minimum wage; urban mass transit; reform of civil procedures; federal aid to highways; military Medicare; public health reorganization; Cape Lookout Seashore; water research; Guadalupe National Park; Revolutionary War Bicentennial; fish and wildlife preservation, water for peace; anti-inflation measures; exchange of scientific knowledge; exchange of cultural materials; foreign investors tax; parcel-post reform; civil-service pay raise; stockpile sales; protection for savings; flexible interest rates; and freedom of information.[107]

Johnson's list of legislation enacted in 1967 included educational professions; the Education Act; control of air pollution; partnership for health; increase in Social Security; age discrimination; wholesome meat; flammable fabrics; urban research; public broadcasting; the Outer Space Treaty; modern government for the District of Columbia; benefits for Vietnam veterans; the Federal Judicial Center; pay for civilian postal workers; the Deaf-Blind Center; college work-study; summer youth programs; food stamps; settlement of the rail strike; Selective Service; urban Fellowships; the Consular Treaty; the Safety at Sea Treaty; the Narcotics Treaty; anti-racketeering; the Product Safety Commission; aid to small businesses; and the Inter-American Bank.[108]

His list of legislative achievements in his lame duck year of 1968 was not paltry. He signed bills dealing with fair housing; an Indian bill of rights; safe streets; wholesome poultry; Food for Peace; community-exchange rules; U.S. grain standards; school breakfasts; bank protection; corporate takeovers; the export program; truth-in-lending; abatement of aircraft noise; gas-pipeline safety; international monetary reform; the International Grains Treaty; Virgin Island elections; the San Rafael Wilderness; the San Gabriel Wilderness; fair federal juries; guaranteed student loans; an FHA-VA interest-rate program; Eisenhower College; gun controls; Aid-to-Handicapped Children; Redwood National Park; Flaming Gorge Recreation Area; Biscayne Park; hazardous-radiation protection; Colorado River reclamation; scenic rivers and trails; the National Water Commission; vocational education; increase in veterans' pensions; North

107. Ibid., 220.
108. Ibid., 221.

Cascades Park; and the Military Justice Code, among others. In 1968, he also signed another Civil Rights Act, sometimes referred to as "the open housing law."[109]

Regarding LBJ's legislative performance, House Majority Leader Albert said, it was "far greater than Roosevelt's." Ultimately, Johnson's staff worried that LBJ had gotten far ahead of even education lobbying groups in pushing nationalization of education. The secretary of HEW said, "The president is dumping a dozen major education bills on the Congress every year." He introduced sixty education bills overall. Through such means as the Elementary and Secondary Education Act of 1965 and the Higher Education Act of 1965, the federal share of education spending nearly doubled. "Education fell . . . increasingly under the direct or indirect control of the federal government." By 1980, Daniel Moynihan could say, "The federal government has acquired the power to shut down any university it chooses." Harper's Magazine reported, "In exchange for federal aid, the universities and colleges have surrendered their independence to the government." Moynihan glumly remarked, "The conquest of the private sector by the public sector . . . continues apace." By 1968 Johnson not only increased the minimum wage but added ten million more people to coverage under the wage. Also, federal payments to Medicare physicians increased 2.5 times from 1966 to 1969, and payments to hospitals by a factor of 1.5. In a 1968 speech, Johnson said that the Great society "is taking root, it is thrusting up, it is reaching out to banish need . . ." America would soon become "a shining land where rural poverty and urban slums have gone the way of the kerosene lamp." Johnson was a unifier (on his terms), and asked that America "not allow the dividers to succeed."[110]

Lyndon Johnson was interested in quantity more so than quality. The meat of his model cities legislation was written the night before it was introduced to Congress. Some fifteen years later there was no evidence that conditions in those model cities had improved. The important thing was that $1 billion was thrown at the cities in an effort to make some of it stick. And the most important thing of all was that city leaders and congresspersons who supported their president could expect to be rewarded with money to make them look good in front of their city dwellers. Fully forty-eight of the first forty-nine cities awarded money went to districts whose congressmen voted for the bill. Johnson's Office of Economic

109. Ibid., 322–23.
110. Ibid., 126, 164, 226–27, 231, 233–34, 245, 250.

Opportunity (OEO) goals were badly overstated, direct services to the poor were under-provided for, and jobs for liberal administrative personnel at good pay were vastly over-represented in the program. Johnson later admitted of OEO programs, "Some failed completely . . . some were badly managed." OEO tried to spread community action money for 100 programs to 1100, and as secretary Cohen said, "That just could not be done." Further, he said, "We tried to do too much in too many places in too short a time." But the political goal of the OEO for Johnson was achieved: OEO staff and welfare recipients voted seventy-four percent for LBJ. In fact, overall federal civilian employment increased by 200,000, nearly twenty percent during Johnson's administration. Overall, the War on Poverty, including crime and education deprivation programming, was "unusually weak, sometimes hopelessly muddled, and hardly ever efficient." Overall public assistance costs doubled even during booming times, not hard times. Violent crime doubled. The Head Start program was notoriously ineffective. Initially the Job Corp cost more per individual served per year than a Harvard education. After retirement, Johnson said he wished he had known "a little more than I did know when I made the decisions." One historian wrote that Johnson legislated "comprehensively—really without limit—for the people's own good, whether they . . . (came) to recognize the need or not."[111]

One press leader called LBJ "strange, proud, cruel, sentimental, insecure, naïve, and bitterly driven . . ." While Ike had nine staff in his press office, and Kennedy ten, LBJ needed sixteen to trumpet himself. Johnson treated the press poorly, giving little advance notice of press conferences, excluded specialists who could ask penetrating questions, and refused to meet for long periods of time. He was noted for "his tendency to propagandize." Navy photographers published a monthly LBJ propaganda film extolling his exploits.[112]

Johnson took full advantage of the tyrant's method of using executive degrees to enact policy. He contributed to the science of usurpation by modifying Kennedy's guidelines for the issuance of executive orders. He mandated affirmative action in government contracting by means of a decree, and used orders to establish commissions like the National Advisory Commission on Civil disorders, known as the Kerner Commission, in 1967. He added to the corruption of the executive order system

111. Ibid., 131, 191, 235, 239, 331–32.
112. Ibid., 149, 156–58, 222, 227, 232, 327.

by using it to enact private bills, such as the one used to exempt J. Edgar Hoover from mandatory retirement, since he was doing such a good job in discrediting Johnson's political opponents. Johnson also issued ninety-three presidential "memoranda," which were essentially vehicles to "get the word out" on his wishes for the direction that the bureaucracy should be headed. Near the end of his term in 1968, liberal land preservationists wanted to set aside 7,617,000 acres of land from development by having Lyndon use the Antiquities Act of 1906 and make an executive decree. This would have increased the national park system by twenty-five percent. Lyndon, in a fit of royal pique and prerogative, and paying back his well-heeled campaign contributors, preserved only 300,000 acres. One Supreme Court justice interested in such matters wrote that LBJ "gave the heritage of America away to the fat cats and the official vandals who have despoiled us." Near the time of his retirement from the presidency, Johnson took an opportunity to reward those of his celebrity friends who did not require so much of him with the Medal of Freedom.[113]

The president did not have much respect for the American people and their various political points of view. He was very demanding of the people who worked for him. He ordered the FBI to hide themselves in dark corners and do political surveillance of his opponents. He dug up dirt on Barry Goldwater's campaign staff, and ordered his minions to obtain advance copies of Goldwater's speeches. He also bugged Goldwater's campaign plane, and audited Nixon's tax records, as Kennedy had done before him. When a stand-up FBI agent hesitated to get the phone records of 1968 Republican vice presidential candidate Spiro Agnew, LBJ personally ordered him to do so in no uncertain terms. Johnson also spied on Congress and magazine editors. When someone asked FBI director J. Edgar Hoover why he did these things, he answered, "You do what the president of the United States orders you to do." Revealed in this statement is the ethic-less world of political depravity inhabited by political appointees in high places in the Johnson administration. Nixon's world of Watergate was merely a continuation of Lyndon Johnson's service as Spy in Chief of the United States. In 1973, Johnson closed his Oval Office and cabinet meeting tapes to historians for the next fifty years. It was said, "Personal power . . . (was) placed above the Constitution and the law in those years." [114]

113. Cooper, *Order*, 8, 17, 54, 78, 90; Bornet, *Johnson*, 146, 326–27.

114. Healy, *Cult of the Presidency*, 103, 108, 176; Bornet, *Johnson*, 207–08.

The fifty-four agencies of Johnson's FBI, CIA, and military intelligence had 1.5 billion records on individuals, bulging particularly after the 1967 Detroit riots and as the anti-war movement blossomed. When Martin Luther King began to express disagreement with the Vietnam War, Johnson had him wiretapped. Johnson's CIA owned or subsidized more than fifty newspapers, news services, radio stations, and periodicals. The CIA also wrote and published some 250 books of propaganda. "Much of this took place during Johnson's presidency."[115]

Johnson also pressured the army into doing domestic spying on individuals, as well as groups. He made illegal use of the military to monitor local civilian matters under the jurisdiction of the various states. He used federal troops in Watts, Los Angeles, in Detroit, and in Washington, DC to quell race riots. Once it was clear that he had more than a few Vietnam war dissenters on his hands, he asked military intelligence to monitor entire protest groups. He had more intelligence boots on the ground doing this in the homeland than he had monitoring the enemy in Vietnam. It was said, "The army had assembled the essential apparatus of a police state."[116]

Going full-steam ahead with both vote-buying tyranny at home and colonial imperialism abroad is perilous business for a politician. Many of LBJ's Democratic supporters dropped their support of the Vietnam War because it was clear the war was taking money and time away from his domestic welfare agenda.[117]

Johnson felt it important to get his 1964 campaign for the presidency off to a good start by denying he would ever commit U.S. troops to action in the Asian cesspool where so many American boys had died in the Korean debacle. Therefore, he warned the American people like a stern and peace-minded elder of the community, "Some . . . are eager to enlarge the conflict . . . They call upon the U.S. to supply American boys to do the job that Asian boys should do." To that, he answered, "We are not about to send American boys nine or ten thousand miles away from home to do what Asian boys ought to be doing for themselves." Alluding to Korea, he added, "We don't want to get . . . tied down to a land war in Asia." Therefore, Johnson portrayed himself as the peace candidate versus Goldwater the war hawk during the 1964 election.[118]

115. Bornet, *Johnson*, 207, 229.
116. Healy, *Cult of the Presidency*, 106; Miller Center, *Johnson—Domestic Affairs*.
117. Crenson and Ginsberg, *Presidential Power*, 241.
118. Miller Center, *Johnson – Foreign Affairs* ; Nelson, *Presidency*, 164.

But Johnson began to worry about his political opponents more than his political constituency. He thought those opponents would make him look like a sissy if South Vietnam fell to the north before he could be elected in his own right. He did not want to be remembered as the commander in chief that lost Southeast Asia to communism. Or the first American president to ever lose a war. He mused to one of his staff, "If I don't go in now . . . they'll shove it up my ass every time." But Johnson did not "go in" in a clear and flashy way. In the words of one historian, he was "consciously emulating . . . Franklin Roosevelt . . . Johnson took the nation into war by indirection and dissimulation [lying by omission]."[119]

During the 1964 election, Johnson used unconscionable scare tactics to affect the uneducated among the citizenry. One of his advertisements showed an American child's world erased by nuclear war. In fact, as one author exclaims, Vietnam was of "no geographic, economic, or material significance to U.S. national security." But he nevertheless entered the useless war by degrees and persisted in sacrificing tens of thousands of American and Vietnamese lives to his own personal and political insecurities when, numerous times along the way, he could have read the hand-writing on the wall and exited. By the time Johnson left office, 40,000 American troops were dead.[120]

Truman and Eisenhower had sent military "advisers" (i.e., supervisors) to Vietnam, and Kennedy had upped the ante by sending as many as 20,000 Special Forces to direct the show there. Johnson looked for a way to get regular forces directly involved. He started by transferring the task of infiltration of the north from the CIA, his private army, to the military, the public armed forces. He also began planning air strikes. Using the public military required a little more public accountability (it needed an actual visible excuse to get involved), and Johnson found it, or rather created it, in an incident in the Gulf of Tonkin, a body of water off the shore of North Vietnam.[121]

In August, 1964, the president claimed U.S. destroyers had been attacked in the Gulf by North Vietnamese torpedo boats. The question may be asked, what were U.S. destroyers doing there in the first place? Their mere presence was an act of war, but Johnson did not even suggest such a

---

119. Nelson, *Presidency*, 161; Herring, *Colony to Superpower*, 738; Flagel, *Guide*, 255; Bornet, *Johnson*, 82.

120. Flagel, *Guide*, 99, 241.

121. Miller Center, *Johnson – Foreign Affairs*.

thing. In the end, LBJ's story that the U.S. warships had been attacked in the Gulf of Tonkin turned out to be doubtful, but it served as a convenient way to get Congress to pass a resolution allowing Johnson to escalate U.S. involvement. In fact, the facts seemed to show that a U.S. destroyer "took a single bullet to the topside," less than what was fired at many American urban homes during gangster drive-by season in the 1990s.[122]

Johnson began bombing the north, but U.S. air power was ineffective in stopping guerilla attacks. Thus Johnson then sent in Marine ground troops on "search and destroy" missions in the south, believing they would quickly end the war. By November 1965 he had 175,000 troops in Vietnam. Later in 1966 he added another 100,000. He finally had 535,000 there by the end of his one and a quarter terms of office. Ultimately, it could then be said that, despite his eloquent speeches about keeping American boys from traveling 10,000 miles to die in an Asian morass, he ultimately sent fifty boys to Asia for every one of the 10,000 miles the American armed forces had to travel to get to Vietnam. In addition, one out of ten stationed there, or 55,000 American boys, died doing what Johnson said he would never do. Total American casualties amounted to 222,351 during the Johnson years.[123]

The Vietnam war added $3.6 billion a year to the U.S. budget. The budget grew from $117.2 billion to $184.7 billion during his administration, adding to the deficit at the rate of $5.5 billion/year. In 1968 LBJ avoided a huge budget deficit by winning a tax surcharge to help pay for Vietnam. As a result, in 1969 the nation actually saw a budget surplus of $3 billion. However, the national debt rose over Johnson's five year term from $317 billion to $353 billion, an increase of 11.4 percent. Johnson had pushed both "guns and butter" in an unprecedented fashion without raising taxes, and set the precedent for others after him to do so, and balloon the national debt beyond anyone's wildest imagination. Ultimately, Johnson's War cost $842 to $855 billion, including veterans benefits like medical care, loss of wages of dead soldiers, and loss in production of civilian goods of those who volunteered or were drafted.[124]

Lyndon Baines Johnson was clearly not overly concerned about morality in foreign affairs outside of Vietnam either, as he had no problem

122. Flagel, *Guide*, 61.

123. Whitney, *Biographies*, 349; Bornet, *Johnson*, 338.

124. Herring, *Colony to Superpower*, 753; Nelson, *Presidency*, 165; McDonald, *Presidency*, 374; Bornet, *Johnson*, 281, 341.

supporting entrenched oligarchs and military governments around the world. He gave aid to military dictators in Argentina, Brazil, Bolivia and Peru. LBJ's staff informed U.S. military officers they could not oppose a coup in Brazil. The coup leader then went on to suspend human rights for the next ten years. LBJ revived the gunboat diplomacy of Teddy Roosevelt and Wilson in the Caribbean and sent 23,000 troops to the Dominican Republic in 1965. He had earlier backed a coup there by Reid Cabral, who usurped power from democratically elected president Juan Bosch in 1962. But now a rebellion broke out which tried to re-instate Bosch. This was squashed by LBJ's troops. Johnson claimed that Bosch was a communist and a supporter of Castro, but, in fact, he was neither. Nor could the marines find more than a few communists on the scene altogether.[125]

Johnson exercised personal control over foreign aid spending in the Agency for International Development, a major new nation-building program of grants and loans begun under his predecessor in 1961. Johnson took fourteen countries off the $3.4 billion program budget because they were not cooperating with him. Johnson was not a critical reader of history and he lacked a grasp of foreign cultures. He was xenophobic, seeing life on the planet through American eyes only. He did not understand, for example, that Wilson's war "did not end horror in Europe," or that "Roosevelt's war opened the door to Communist expansion worldwide." He did, however, understand the language of the kowtowing that world leaders expressed toward him. The French embassy wrote to him about "your monumental achievements . . . [you are] some superhuman mythical figure . . ." And he enjoyed telling people about his firsts in international diplomacy. For example, he said, "I made the first address by an American president devoted wholly to Africa."[126]

Senator William Fulbright accurately summed up the term of this deeply-flawed tyrant. He said that the Johnson administration fell to that "arrogance of power . . . that over-extension of power and mission, which brought ruin to ancient Athens, to Napoleonic France, and to Nazi Germany." Wartime presidents are virtually always reelected, but president Johnson had been wagging his presidential member for too long in front of the American public and they were tired of his war and his treachery. Early in the process of the 1968 presidential primaries, Johnson was doing

---

125. Herring, *Colony to Superpower*, 733, 735, 738; Miller Center, *Lyndon Johnson—Domestic Affairs*; Bornet, *Johnson*, 165, 176.

126. Bornet, *Johnson*, 164–66, 168, 182.

poorly. He announced he would not seek reelection. He also announced a halt in the bombing to try and go out as a peacemaker president. One propaganda letter from the White House said his decision to retire reflected the fact he wanted to "place the presidency above partisanship." It also reflected "his heartfelt desire for unity in America and peace in Vietnam." However, aside from the distinct possibility of losing the election, his real reason for quitting was poor health, which he had hidden from the American people for some time. He had his White House physician cover up his condition.[127]

Richard Nixon

Richard Nixon is perhaps the darkest character to ever assume the office of the American presidency. He was made up of equal parts deeply flawed character and political savvy. In one television address, as allegations swirled about his dishonesty, Nixon claimed, "I am not a crook." He could believe it, because his presidential philosophy was that the president can do no wrong. But history might well provide him with the title Nixon the Crook. In fact, while becoming a millionaire as president, he had paid only $1,670 in income taxes for 1970 and 1971. He eventually agreed to pay $432,787 in back income taxes for the period 1969–72. He also had used campaign funds to buy his wife Pat diamond earrings and to make improvements in his Florida real estate property.[128]

Nixon was extremely ambitious and opportunistic. After serving as vice president for eight years under Eisenhower, he worked diligently for six years throughout Kennedy's and Johnson's terms to get to the White House. He even changed his home to New York City to better court eastern political interests. During his fourteen year experience as a Republican congressman, senator, and vice president he became known by those close to him as a "ruthless political polarizer who would do anything to win." He was fanatically devoted to secrecy. He strictly limited press access to the White House.[129]

127. Herring, *Colony to Superpower*, 741; Miller Center, *Lyndon Johnson—Foreign Affairs*; Bornet, *Johnson*, 302.

128. Whitney, *Biographies*, 385–86.

129. Nelson, *Presidency*, 167; Whitney, *Biographies*, 362; Boyer, *Oxford Companion*, 555; McDonald, *Presidency*, 473.

Nixon was a determined propagandist and self-aggrandizer. After his term as vice president he wrote a book, titled *Six Crises*, to glorify his career to this point. While he wanted to make others look bad, and took great pains to do so, he wanted himself to look good. Once in the White House he employed an aggressive set of public relations tactics by doing interviews on morning talk shows, prime time broadcasts, and by arranging for satellite coverage for his China trip. He got on television thirty-two times in five and a half years, reaching audiences of as many as 70 million at one time. Nixon used his Director of Communications like a war-time disinformation arm. That office disseminated favorable information, conducted polls, and sidestepped a critical press and communicated directly with the often ignorant American people. This was done to do damage-control.[130]

After his first year in office, Nixon marginalized his own cabinet, after seeing that the career bureaucrats who advised them would not give him the latitude and loyalty he wanted. His inner circle aide John Ehrlichman said of the cabinet: "We see them at the annual White House Christmas party." Having dispensed with the cabinet and its independent-thinking bureaucracy, Nixon set up a "counter-bureaucracy" in the White House by doubling the president's executive office staff to 4,000. This allowed him to not have to deal with the constitutionally authorized federal department leadership.[131]

Nixon's management style has been called "ultra-Byzantine," which, translated, means as bad as the worst of ancient kings. He has been called a liberal, a moderate, and a conservative, since his politics changed with the political weather and appealed at times to all three of those constituencies at the same time. It was said of him, "He was never one to let principle stand in the way of politics." Although Nixon gained a reputation as a conservative in California politics, he actually was a Roosevelt New Dealer, having worked as an attorney in the Office of Price Administration in Washington, DC. He is possibly the only American president who flip-flopped joyfully and triumphantly, almost taunting the American people and the press for their ignorance of tyrannical political method.[132]

---

130. Whitney, *Biographies*, 361; Boyer, *Oxford Companion*, 556; McDonald, *Presidency*, 452; Flagel, *Guide*, 306.

131. McDonald, *Presidency*, 338.

132 Herring, *Colony to Superpower*, 833; Miller Center, *Nixon—Domestic Affairs*; Boyer, *Oxford Companion*, 555; Whitney, *Biographies*, 353.

Nixon was careful to position himself superficially as a defender of the Constitution and the interests of the people. For example, he said, "We have made the federal government so strong it grows muscle-bound and the states and localities so weak they have no power." The states' rights issue was an important one in the decade leading up to Nixon's time in office. For example, a third-party candidate, George Wallace, ran on a states' rights platform, and won 10 million votes in 1968. Nixon therefore proposed and won some revenue sharing with the states in the form of block grants authorized by the State and Local Fiscal Assistance Act. Overall, Nixon took a few halting steps in the direction of addressing this imbalance with his left hand, while at the same time working overtime with his right hand to enhance the institutional capacity of the national executive branch at the expense of the people's local representatives in the Congress. He put a heavy hand on the economy and in his legislative program also tried to be all things to all people. "Probably more new regulation was imposed on the economy than in any other presidency since the New Deal."[133]

The ethics-starved Nixon thought it well to maintain a veneer of religiosity. He, like other presidents before him, used Billy Graham as his national spiritual advisor. In his inaugural address he said that the American citizenry were "ragged in spirit," implying that he had the ability to smooth out that spirit. He started a non-denominational service in the White House, as a public display of personal piety. This Sunday gathering was held in the East Room. He told an associate during the Watergate affair that he had prayed for guidance in leading the nation every night of his presidency. He insisted that no bombing raids take place in Vietnam on Sunday. During the unfolding of the Watergate scandal, the president asked his television audience "for your prayers to help me in everything that I do."[134] At his first inauguration he said, "I have taken an oath today in the presence of God . . . I now add this sacred commitment: I shall consecrate my office, my energies and all the wisdom I can summon, to the cause of peace among nations." The outcome of his efforts, he said, would be "a generation of peace."[135]Nixon's prophecy was ill-timed,

133. Drewry and O'Connor, *America Is*, 660, 668–69; Light, *Agenda*, 293; Miller Center, *Nixon—Domestic Affairs.*

134. Whitney, *Biographies*, 380.

135. Ibid., 372.

coming as it did at the beginning of a generation of hot war-making the world over, much of which originated in the White House.

Nixon acted the part of a usurper of power, as one above the law, in a number of ways. He showed his disrespect for constitutional separation of national power between the legislative and executive branches by using executive decrees to make laws. In some cases, if he felt Congress was going to enact a law, he rushed to enact it on his own so he could get credit for it. For example, he ordered federal contractors to establish affirmative goals for hiring minority workers on federal projects. He also created the EPA when he understood Congress would enact a more liberal version. That way he could make it in the way he wanted it. In fact, he announced he would piece it together out of existing agencies.[136]

Nixon felt he could best get away with taking over Congress' job if he did it by surprise and with great drama so that the people bought into it and muffled Congress' objection. Giving out presidential views to Congress on a given subject became a disloyal act.[137] Nixon wanted to present the nation with a fait accompli before they even knew what hit them. He was the opposite of Hoover in this respect. Hoover wanted science and transparency and long-range public planning.

The executive order is so insidious because it requires no advance notice by law, and no public hearing about its content. It is a perfect vehicle for Nixon's shock and awe method of tyranny. Nixon used the executive order to please business constituents as well as to co-opt Congress. He established in the National Industrial Pollution Council in the commerce department and stocked it entirely with industry executives. He reorganized the executive office of the president (EOP) by restructuring the bureau of budget as a new Office of Management and Budget (OMB) and gave it illegal power to monitor non-executive branch (independent) agency programs and budgets. He announced that the OMB would have the power to "clear" or approve their regulations for the first time. Congress complained because it had intended citizen experts to make these kinds of regulations, not the president. Nixon finally backed off. He established the Cabinet Committee on Environmental Quality and later a Council on Environmental Quality, both by executive order. He re-invigorated the Subversive Activities Control Board by executive

---

136. Crenson and Ginsberg, *Presidential Power*, 195; Miller Center, *Nixon—Domestic Affairs*; Nelson, *Presidency*, 150.

137. Crenson and Ginsberg, *Presidential Power*, 193.

order and conducted illegal activities through it. He also issued sixty presidential memoranda directing government without Congress.[138]

Nixon used declarations of emergency to do things he normally couldn't do. In 1970, he delayed pay raises to federal employees by six months in order to keep spending down. When the nation's postal workers went on strike, he declared a state of emergency and used the U.S. army to force workers back on the job. He then flip-flopped on their wage demands, thus unbalancing the budget he promised to balance. He used a state of emergency declaration to justify Proclamation 4047, which raised the tariff surcharge on some imported goods.[139]

Nixon announced a ninety day wage and price freeze, and controls for another eighteen months after that. Furthermore, he did it by executive decree, E.O. 11615, and by declaring a peacetime emergency. This was deemed "one of the most dramatic uses of executive orders for regulatory purposes." The order was initially set for 90 days, and was then extended by another order for another nine months. Nixon claimed the wage/price freeze was authorized by the Trade Expansion Act of 1962 and the Economic Stability Act of 1970. Later on, Congress retroactively blessed this action by granting authority "to issue such orders and regulations . . . to stabilize prices, wages, and salaries." The court, however, announced that this emergency power delegated by Congress was "incredibly broad, possibly unwise, and even potentially dangerous." Eventually, Nixon lost twenty-five high court rulings, the most of any president. He might have fared better if the Congress had not turned down two of his southern conservative patronage appointees to the court.[140]

Nixon vetoed Congressional legislation for policy or personal reasons rather than constitutional reasons. He used the veto as a weapon against education and social programs, but also experienced a high rate of override, about twenty-five percent. In 1974, Nixon also vetoed an energy bill calling for a rollback of oil prices. Nixon didn't worry about Congress. It was said, "He sought to govern without Congress," essentially by the use of veto, executive order, and impoundment. One author

138. Crenson and Ginsberg, *Presidential Power*, 197; Nelson, *Presidency*, 150; Cooper, *Order*, 31, 90, 121, 132.

139. Miller Center, *Nixon—Domestic Affairs*; Crenson and Ginsberg, *Presidential Power*, 340.

140. Drewry and O'Connor, *America Is*, 667; Nelson, *Presidency*, 149; McDonald, *Presidency*, 293–94, 297, 466 note; Cooper, *Order*, 28, 66, 121; Whitney, *Biographies*, 366.

reminds, "[Nixon could] ignore any and all congressional authorizations if he deemed them . . . contrary to the needs of the nation."[141]

Nixon asked Congress for power to hold federal spending at $250 billion, but Congress declined. Nixon then instituted his unilateral impoundment program. Nixon made the boldest claims to impoundment power of any American president. In one move he impounded billions of dollars Congress authorized to implement the Clean Air Act. While Nixon had previously done a few dozen impoundments per year, in December 1972 and January 1973 he began an intensified campaign of impoundments "designed to end Congressional programs in their entirety." These impoundments were directed at public housing, farmers, and water and sewer money for local governments. Nixon had taken a hard turn to the right to assure reelection. He also set up a campaign group to raise funds for his reelection, which it was later learned raised money illegally and used money for illegal purposes, including the Watergate burglary. He refused to enforce a law if he did not believe in it, essentially using the national executive version of southern state nullification, with considerably less constitutional justification.[142]

Congress, for its part, finally woke up to the unstaunched bleeding of the Constitution and passed the Congressional Budget and Impoundment Act of 1974, dealing with both types of presidential impoundments, rescissions and deferrals. Congress also passed the National Emergencies Act, to try to end national emergencies that continued in effect long after the emergency was passed. It also passed the War Powers Act, limiting presidential authority to commit the nation to war without Congressional involvement. Nixon vetoed this law, which required him to report military actions within 30 days, and withdraw the forces after 60 days if Congress did not approve it. Congress overrode him. Congress also strengthened the Freedom of Information Act, and enacted a new Right to Privacy Act, responding to the Nixon domestic surveillance program.[143]

Nixon cited executive privilege in disallowing a prominent member of his staff to testify in defense of an FBI member who leaked some information to Congress. Concerning the idea that executive privilege disallowed members of his administration from testifying under oath,

141. McDonald, *Presidency*, 355, 370; Whitney, *Biographies*, 383–84.

142. Whitney, *Biographies*, 374–75, 377; Healy, *Cult of the Presidency*, 106.

143. McDonald, *Presidency*, 312–13; Cooper, *Order*, 13, 26; Nelson, *Presidency*, 170.

senator Sam Ervin replied, "That is not executive privilege. That is executive poppycock." In addition to executive privilege, he claimed both national security and the right to privacy in order to withhold certain information from Congress, such as his office tapes. He expanded criteria for classification of information related to national security. His own appointees in the court ruled against him regarding the tapes. He also tried to restrict freedom of the press. For the first time in the nation's history, the national government obtained injunctions to prevent newspapers from publishing documents about the Vietnam War, leaked by Daniel Ellsberg, which showed the government concealed vital information from the citizenry. This included information about acts of terror and sabotage in the early days in Vietnam, and the fact that the government made exaggerated threat assertions.[144]

Nixon ordered wire-taps at will. His Army intelligence people kept files on 100,000 people. In May of 1971 Nixon had 13,400 political demonstrators arrested and jailed in Washington, DC. Four years later a federal court awarded the demonstrators damages for violation of their civil rights. He kept a political enemies list and used the IRS to harass them by auditing them. Kennedy was on that list and he wanted to discredit Kennedy's administration even after his death. He used his Special Investigations Unit to forge documents showing newsmen that president Kennedy had ordered the assassination of, rather than just the coup against, Diem in Vietnam. He directed secret police forces to gather information on psychiatric histories and sex lives in order to discredit people. He also had the FBI kidnap anti-war leaders.[145]

On the vote-buying side, Nixon also signed numerous laws designed to buy affection from a welter of constituencies that might be pleased enough to vote for him. He targeted the labor vote with a bill to create the Occupational Safety and Health Administration and the broad consumer vote with his National Highway Traffic Safety Administration. He proposed not only an Environmental Protection Agency, but a National Oceanic and Atmospheric Administration. He signed amendments to the Clean Air Act to reduce auto emissions and to conduct national testing of air quality. He signed the Noise Control Act, the Marine Mammal

144. McDonald, *Presidency*, 312–13; Cooper, *Order*, 13, 26; Nelson, *Presidency*, 170; Drewry and O'Connor, *America Is*, 671–72; Whitney, *Biographies*, 371, 379; Flagel, *Guide*, 154–55.

145. Drewry and O'Connor, *America Is*, 671–72; Whitney, *Biographies*, 370, 381; Nelson, *Presidency*, 170; Healy, *Cult of the Presidency*, 107.

Protection Act, the Endangered Species Act, and the Safe Drinking Water Act, all to please liberals and environmentalists. He lobbied for a Department of Natural Resources.[146]

In social welfare, he courted the poor and minorities by proposing an expansion of the Food Stamp program, an expansion of Job Corps, and job quotas for minorities in the construction industry. He strengthened the EEOC to court minorities, and, to court women, supported the Equal Rights Amendment. Many suspect he pardoned Jimmy Hoffa in exchange for the political support of the Teamsters Union, the only large union that ended up supporting his reelection in 1972. He courted the elderly and disabled by winning a new program for them called Supplemental Security Income (SSI). He also expanded Social Security, Medicare, and Medicaid benefits. He even undertook dishonest proposals to implement Truman's big hope chest item, national health insurance.[147]

Finally, Nixon proposed a radical welfare reform plan for a "negative income tax," a massive transfer payment program by which the federal government would give $1,600 to each poor family of four. The national health insurance program and the "Family Assistance Plan" did not earn enough supporters in Congress to pass. Nixon, like Truman before him, wanted to get credit for trying real hard to give the people amazing benefits that he knew Congress would not buy, since it was such a transparent tool of populist-wooing tyranny. An aide to the president wrote about his Family Assistance Plan, "[The President] wants to be sure its killed by Democrats and that we make a big play for it, but don't let it pass, can't afford it."[148]

Nixon's most talked about abuse of power was hardly any less or more than what we have listed above under the administrations of earlier twentieth-century presidents. The Watergate scandal is just a summary moniker for what one staffer called "all kinds of other involvements" and one historian called "a host of administration misdeeds." Watergate involved Nixon's use of a crew of criminals to uncover dirt on political opponents by burglarizing the Democratic National Committee offices. Five men were arrested doing the deed. Nixon had also commissioned an illegal secret police group called the Special Investigations Unit to

---

146. Healy, *Cult of the Presidency*, 107; Small, *Nixon*, 199; Nelson, *Presidency*, 167.

147. Boyer, *Oxford Companion*, 556; Nelson, *Presidency*, 167; McDonald, *Presidency*, 309; Flagel, *Guide*, 163.

148. Miller Center, *Nixon—Domestic Affairs*; Light, *Agenda*, 291.

uncover what he thought might be a conspiratorial plan to leak information about his secret domestic and foreign policy initiatives. One author calls this group "his own palace guard." The Special Investigations Unit did wiretapping, examined tax returns of political opponents, stole CIA records, kept the president's enemies list, and schemed to photograph classified information in the National Archives. The Unit had a wide range of technical competencies, and included an Eagle Scout. Nixon's various warrantless break-ins, conduced by a police force not authorized by Congress, constituted one of the articles of impeachment brought by Congress against him.[149]

Nixon eventually made clear the justification for his witch hunt activities: "When the President does it, that means it is not illegal." Anyone who upsets the president's plans or strategies is, by definition, on the outside of the law. Nixon wanted to smoke out all these bad people and crucify them for their unpatriotic and illegal plans. One presidential historian summarized, "Nixon equated dissent with treason."[150] In fact, Nixon was simply projecting his own illicit ideas and illegal activities on other political animals who were not quite as sordid as he. In reality, others were not smearing him; he was smearing them.

In order to facilitate these illegal activities, Nixon tried to chase the FBI out of the investigative loop and rely on the more easily controlled CIA. He also purged members of his staff when they began to protest his stone-walling of Congress. He fired an executive branch special prosecutor who subpoenaed his White House tapes. As in the days of Jackson's tyranny, some of Nixon's staff resigned rather than carry out his orders to fire disloyal staff.[151]

Nixon used hush-money payoffs to quiet the arrested members of his Special Investigations Unit burglar squad. It was learned he promised to pardon one of his employees if he refused to talk to the investigating committee. But, on the other hand, he hung out his close political associates to dry when he declined a proposed plan to pardon the twenty or so caught in illegal activities in his behalf. This gave the lie to his own statement that "The President's decision . . . is one that enables those that

149. Miller Center, *Nixon—Domestic Affairs*; Flagel, *Guide*, 63–64.

150. Healy, *Cult of the Presidency*, 175; Herring, *Colony to Superpower*, 764.

151. Nelson, *Presidency*, 168; Whitney, *Biographies*, 385.

carry it out to carry it out without violating the law."[152] It was fine for him to be pardoned, but he punished those who did his failed dirty work.

The Supreme Court forced him to hand over his office tapes and it was quickly learned that in private conversations he was "conspiratorial, vulgar, anti-Semitic." Another commentator reported that the tapes revealed Nixon as "profane, somewhat paranoid, and thoroughly manipulative individual who was willing to do virtually anything to stay in power." This was the president that the American people reelected in 1972 in one of the biggest landslides in U.S. history. When the Supreme Court and the American people turned against Nixon, Congress finally seemed to get the message. A friendly Senator informed Nixon that he could not stop a conviction vote on impeachment, and Nixon resigned on August 8, 1974, the only president ever to do so. He served five years total beginning in 1969.[153]

Nixon's term was characterized by unprecedented secrecy and manipulation in foreign affairs as well. His clandestine operations and negotiations were apart of a conscious political strategy of surprise and intimidation, whose goal was to prolong his personal political career much more so than to advance sacred community political goals like civil liberty and national independence. He curried favor with prospective big business campaign donors, for example, by intimidating Japan into voluntarily restraining their textile exports to the U.S.[154]

Nixon's program of foreign affairs shut out the lawfully designated agency of international policy activity, the department of state, from actual policy planning and participation. For this reason, secretary of state Rodgers resigned in protest. Nixon kept Congress in the dark as well. For example, Nixon's trusted companion in foreign relations, Henry Kissinger, who was director of the National Security Council, visited China on the first state visit in decades, without the State Department or Congress knowing about it. Nixon enhanced the size and capacity of his private and clandestine NSC foreign policy apparat as well. During his time in office, he doubled its size and tripled its budget. He put this agency hard at work in signing agreements with other nations. In response, Congress passed the Case-Zablocki Act in 1972 requiring the secretary of state to

152. Boyer, *Oxford Companion*, 556; Whitney, *Biographies*, 381–82; McDonald, *Presidency*, 310, 384.

153. Nelson, *Presidency*, 168; Flagel, *Guide*, 323.

154. Herring, *Colony to Superpower*, 785.

send Congress the text of all international agreements other than treaties within 60 days, but Nixon ignored or circumvented this law. The secretary of state did not know much of what Nixon was doing in foreign affairs anyway.[155]

Other agencies of legally authorized power were side-swiped by the president as well. Nixon's own secretary of the air force and air force chief of staff, for example, did not even know about Nixon's bombing of Cambodia. The U.S. military had to use espionage techniques on the president to learn what was going on.[156]

Nixon used total secrecy to cut extraordinarily important deals designed to preserve his own power. For example, in order to make a diplomatic opening with China right before the 1972 elections, Nixon let Zhou En-lai know that he would throw Taiwan under the bus. This constituted an enormous shift in U.S. foreign policy and by all historical, legal and practical measures of political conduct, required broad consultation and agreement rather than unilateral decision-making. He assured Zhou secretly he would take the additional unprecedented step of normalizing relations with the People's Republic of China once he won reelection.[157] Nixon imagined he would take an incredible place under the sun once these policies were revealed to the world, and, to an extent, he was right.

Nixon also wanted to use the Soviet Union and China as leverage to end the Vietnam War, because he knew the U.S. electorate would not reelect him unless he ended U.S. involvement there. He had learned too late what really was needed to be done to continue the war. He saw that three-fourths of the opposition to the war came from resisters to the national policy of mandatory soldiering. In fact, some 200,000 young men had ducked the draft, and 500,000 had deserted after being drafted. Nixon thus took immediate measures to enhance the ability of the executive branch to conduct wars in the future without such opposition. He ended the draft and began the process of converting the mammoth American armed forces to a voluntary participation basis. The American war machine would henceforth essentially be a mercenary army, consisting of enlistees who needed a paycheck and had little idea what they were

---

155. Crenson and Ginsberg, *Presidential Power,* 254; Herring, *Colony to Superpower,* 768–69, 777; McDonald, *Presidency,* 409.

156. Healy, *Cult of the Presidency,* 109; Herring, *Colony to Superpower,* 764.

157. Herring, *Colony to Superpower,* 792; Small, *Nixon,* 63, 121–22.

fighting for. Had he done this earlier, he might have been able to continue the war. Nixon also worked with the Congress to pass a law lowering the voting age to eighteen and later to pass the Twenty-sixth Amendment to the Constitution to make the policy irreversible, which was accomplished in July, 1971.[158] These actions to lower the voting age were aimed at satisfying those youngsters still being processed into America's imperial war in Vietnam and those who would be processed into future American wars. How could modern, high school-educated youth be coaxed into dying in presidential petulance wars if they didn't even have the power to vote?

Getting out of Vietnam was politically tricky business. Nixon cancelled plans for U.S. withdrawal from Vietnam in the spring of 1971 when he figured out that if things subsequently went bad for South Vietnam it would hurt his reelection chances. In June, 1971, the Viet Cong had proposed a U.S. withdrawal that would trigger release of American prisoners. All they needed was a withdrawal date. Nixon's opponents accused him of prolonging the withdrawal date so he could do it just before elections. Many more boys had to die, as they did for LBJ, because the timing was not quite right for him personally to be getting out of war. [159]

Sure enough, in October, 1972, just two weeks before the election, Nixon's staff announced that "peace is at hand" in the Vietnam War. Nixon and North Vietnam knew a deal was in place to benefit both parties, having secretly achieved substantial agreement at the Paris peace conference. Nixon had greased the skids by promising North Vietnam communist leaders a bribe of $4.75 billion to rebuild their country if they would end America's part of the war in time to fulfill his election hopes. He also allowed the North to keep the positions they had overrun in the South as a condition for U.S. withdrawal. He thus capitulated to the communists and betrayed South Vietnam in order to win a cease-fire making him look good at election time.[160] It only remained for Nixon to assure the American people, and all the families of those dead American boys, that he had put in place an effective program of "Vietnamization"—U.S. training of freedom forces capable of holding on to their own democratic

158. Crenson and Ginsberg, *Presidential Power*, 238, 265; Whitney, *Biographies*, 370, 376.

159. Miller Center, *Nixon—Foreign Affairs*; Whitney, *Biographies*, 371.

160. Whitney, *Biographies*, 376; Nelson, *Presidency*, 168.

government. In fact, he knew that there was exactly zero chance of that actually taking place.

Nixon supported puppet leaders not only in Vietnam but in Iran and Saudi Arabia, sending money and weapons. The weapons to Iran amount to half of U.S. arm sales during the mid-1970s. In Iran he refrained from criticizing the Shah's repressions there. Both Iran and Saudi Arabia bought great amounts of weaponry from the U.S. Nixon also supported Pakistani dictator Yahya Khan, whose particular claim to fame was that he suppressed the Bangaladesh independence movement. Nixon also gave Khan military aid in its 1971 war with India, and kept the aid program secret from the American people, who might not have favored it as much as he.[161]

In Chile, Nixon intervened in the election process and gave his blessing to a plot to overthrow the newly elected Chilean leader Salvador Allende by signing National Security Directives.[162] The CIA bribed legislators in Chile and Nixon encouraged the plotters to kidnap General Renee Schneider, who supported the Chilean constitution and opposed the coup plotters.

Gerald Ford

Gerald Ford was a naval officer in the Pacific during World War II. But before the war he had been a member of the anti-European entanglement civic group known as America First. Like so many, his mind was changed when the Japanese attacked Pearl Harbor. He apparently did not understand how presidents had historically provoked American wars far away from the homeland. In time, he learned to look the other way once he figured out how things worked in Big Town. His experience as Nixon's vice president certainly taught him that.[163]

Ford was a popular Republican representative in Congress from Michigan. He was elected twelve times by landslides. Early on, he attacked Truman's Marshall Plan for nation-building in Europe. Later, he opposed an increase in the minimum wage, fought against Medicare, and wanted the U.S. to be all-in for war in Vietnam. As a specialist on defense

---

161. Flagel, *Guide*, 200; Herring, *Colony to Superpower*, 788–90; Boyer, *Oxford Companion*, 556.

162. Cooper, *Order*, 182.

163. Boyer, *Oxford Companion*, 274.

budgets, he supported increased armed forces spending. He sponsored no major legislation during his long time in the House. He was conservative in fiscal matters, moderate on social issues, and flip-flopped to become an internationalist (an alliance-man) in foreign affairs. He followed these propensities once in the seat of national power as well. For example, he initially proposed cuts in government programs, but a Democratic Congress wanted more spending to reduce unemployment and countered his wishes.[164]

In the hearings relating to his appointment by Nixon to take Spiro Agnew's place as vice president, Ford was asked if he would have the power to pardon Nixon if he resigned. He said, "I do not think the public would stand for it." One month after he took over the presidency from his disgraced boss, Gerald Ford shocked the nation by granting Nixon a "full, free and absolute pardon . . . for all offenses," including any offenses he "may have committed."

Ford did not discuss the pardon with Congress, party leaders, the Watergate prosecutor, or the public. It was purely an autocratic decision. While many wanted to end the "national nightmare," most didn't want it to end this way. The Republican party nightmare wasn't exorcised by the pardon, nor was the constitutional nightmare either, as Ford essentially gave a "get off free" pass to a major American absolutist, and thus gave great encouragement to the string of usurpers who came after the Nixon/Ford team. Ford also declined to insist that Nixon apologize or that he give up his presidential papers. Ford's own nightmare as president lasted from 1974 to 1977.[165]

While Ford had said, "Our great Republic is a government of laws and not of men," he had in effect trashed the law and elevated the "men" by his action in pardoning Nixon. In fact, Ford's own press secretary Jerald terHorst resigned in protest, and indeed Ford's popularity rating dropped twenty-one points in a week. Yet, the American people still did little except pout.

The Congress considered, but did not act on, a constitutional amendment to require congressional approval for future pardons. What they did act upon was a resolution discouraging the president from pardoning any others of Nixon's group of clandestine operatives prior

164. Whitney, *Biographies*, 395–97; Flagel, *Guide*, 21; Boyer, *Oxford Companion*, 274.

165. Whitney, *Biographies*, 400; Nelson, *Presidency*, 172.

to conviction, so that they might experience at least some consequence for their misdeeds. As we mentioned in the Nixon chapter, the Congress passed a few measures to curb presidential power, which the American presidents then studiously sidestepped. Ford himself usurped the new 1974 anti-impoundment law by using it not to decrease impoundments, but to increase them. He made 100 or more impoundments a year, where Nixon had only done a dozen or so per year.[166]

Ford showed some basic decency in handling the economic difficulties he inherited, including inflation and unemployment, which had risen to as high as twelve percent. He proposed to do what was right, not what was politically opportunistic. He proposed a tax hike and a decrease in federal spending.[167] But Congress, faced with mid-term elections, refused to do what was right for the country, so Ford modified his proposal and embraced a tax cut and flat spending. Congress finally passed legislation enacting an even larger tax cut and an increase in spending, and Ford signed it. This change of heart fit in well with an election on the horizon. He thus flip-flopped on his promise regarding a balanced budget and instead ran a huge deficit in his first year.

On the other hand, Ford took an activist role after Nixon's departure, not a caretaker role. He was a spender. He signed a $25 billion aid bill for education, a law for public financing of presidential races, consumer protection legislation, an unemployment benefits extension, and a $4.8 billion bill for mass transit. By the end of his term, the Nixon/Ford national deficit had risen by double to $706.4 billion, with Ford's years rising faster than Nixon's. Medicare and Social Security increases during Ford's term helped to make that happen. Ford apparently had been somewhat sincere about want to do what was right, since he began to veto spending bills and finally persuaded Congress to decrease the rate of increase in spending in 1975, after the mid-term election.[168]

Ford sustained or increased executive power in the ever-ongoing battle for horizontal imbalance in national power, while tilting in the direction of democracy in the vertical battle for power between the central government and the states. He believed that Congress was encroaching on executive power in placing the post-Johnson/Nixon curbs. In 1974,

166. Drewry and O'Connor, *America Is*, 675; Herring, *Colony to Superpower*, 815; McDonald, *Presidency*, 313; Whitney, *Biographies*, 401.

167. Flagel, *Guide*, 125; Whitney, *Biographies*, 402.

168. Nelson, *Presidency*, 172; Drewry and O'Connor, *America Is*, 675; Bailyn, *Great Republic*, 1256; Miller Center, *Ford—Domestic Affairs*.

he vetoed a bill to provide a review of the executive branch information classification system. He also institutionalized Nixon's use of rule-making procedure commonly used to overturn Congressional legislation. He enacted a requirement for a rule to pass an "inflationary impact analysis" before it could be enacted.[169]

Ford used executive decrees to enact policy. Ford's surcharge on oil imports constituted an unconstitutional delegation of legislative power to the executive. He also issued fifty-four presidential memoranda during his short term.[170]

Ford wielded the veto as a policy weapon, saying "The veto's not a negative thing . . . and a president ought to use it more freely if he doesn't like what Congress is doing." Ford made forty-eight regular vetoes and eighteen pocket vetoes. He was overridden twelve times, indicating Congressional disgust with his usurpations. Only Andrew Johnson and Harry Truman had as high a percentage of overrides. One of Ford's own aides said, "No president can afford to veto twenty-five bills a year . . . It's too damn much, and Congress won't stand for it." Ford also fought a requirement by Congress for their approval on how he spent funds. He essentially used signing statements to provide himself with a line-item veto.[171]

Ford hired the right man to sustain his ideas about unrestrained executive power. When he ran for the office of president after serving out the rest of Nixon's elected term, he chose Dick Cheney as his campaign manager.[172]

Ford utilized the customary indirect supports of executive branch tyranny well enough. One researcher found that in 1976 Ford made a "newsworthy" appearance before the public and media twice every working day. He considered his appearances before the people an entitlement. When the networks once refused to air one of his speeches, he pressured one network television station into carrying the speech. On the other hand, Ford's propaganda apparatus was not as slick as that of his predecessor. For example, the media portrayed him as a clumsy oaf, when in fact he was arguably the most athletic and agile president ever.[173]

169. McDonald, *Presidency*, 341; Healy, *Cult of the Presidency*, 113; Crenson and Ginsberg, *Presidential Power*, 206.

170. Cooper, *Order*, 90; McDonald, *Presidency*, 294.

171. Flagel, *Guide*, 142; McDonald, *Presidency*, 354; Cooper, *Order*, 209.

172. Flagel, *Guide*, 81.

173. McDonald, *Presidency*, 426, 450, 453.

Ford is generally considered to be one of the most genuinely nice of all presidents, along with Taft and Arthur. Aside from his record of flip-flopping, he was "a determinedly honest and deeply religious Episcopalian." During his swearing-in ceremony, he said "I ask you to confirm me as your president with your prayers. And I hope that such prayers will also be the first of many . . ."[174]

Gerald Ford signed the Helsinki Accords, which finally recognized existing boundaries of European countries which resulted from the military jockeying, political spying, and autocratic deal-making after the second war. The Soviet government got the U.S. to recognize their territorial gains made during and after the war, thus establishing a sort of Eastern European Monroe Doctrine. Many lambasted Ford for approving of the Soviet Union's conquests of territory during World War II, but Franklin Roosevelt and Dwight Eisenhower had made those grand concessions initially, not Ford.

On the other hand, Ford put the brakes on the Case-Zablocki Act of 1972, which required enhanced disclosure of executive agreements with other countries. For example, Ford fired a whistle-blower, William Colby, who revealed the CIA's secret involvement in Angola. Ford was angry when Congress cut off the administration's aid to Angola, some $32 million in covert aid given without the consent of Congress.[175]

Ford exercised illicit executive power just before leaving office by issuing NSDM 344 calling for the building of 157 new naval vessels, thus building the navy on the fly.[176] Ford's 1976 Committee on the Present Danger lobbied for a massive military build up despite détente. It issued a report along the lines of Truman's NSC-68 and pushed for absolute military superiority (soon to become Reagan's mantra as well). Ford sold arms to Turkey to aid their side in a dispute with Greece over Cyprus. Those arms were then used to invade Cyprus after the Greeks seized power there. Ford's policy on Turkey thus substantiated Nixon's stated intent for the U.S. to use of surrogates/mercenaries to fight overseas battles, although in this case both European nations were U.S./NATO allies.

174. Flagel, *Guide*, 56; Whitney, *Biographies*, 390, 399.
175. McDonald, *Presidency*, 409; Herring, *Colony to Superpower*, 825, 828.
176. Cooper, *Order*, 169.

Jimmy Carter

Carter was ambitious for the presidency, and while serving as governor of Georgia began participating in national election campaigns. In December of 1974, Carter became the first of many candidates to announce for the democratic nomination. This was virtually two full years before the November, 1976 election. He campaigned almost full-time until the election. While doing so, he played the tyrant by trying to "curry favor with groups and individuals . . . (he) disliked, and pander to all and sundry." Earlier as governor he had done the same by appealing to segregationist elements while at the same time pushing for civil rights. Carter carefully cultivated a cult of personality by pushing his unique background as a farmer, businessman, born-again Christian, and nuclear engineer. Carter, like Obama after him, published a propagandistic autobiography as one tool to increase his name recognition and popularity once he hit the presidential campaign trail. Carter wrote, "Can our government be honest, decent, open, fair, and compassionate?" He implied that it could if he were running it. He also asked, "Can our government be competent?" He implied that it could if he were running it. But Carter's shortcomings ensured that he would serve only one term as president, from 1977 to 1981. Jimmy Carter lacked two elements for competent national executive leadership: experience in international power politics (including communication and compromise), and historical understanding of the nation's constitutional law system. If he had an inkling of the strengths of the provisions of the Constitution as a result of his state-level political experience, he quickly abandoned them once he was seduced by the power of his new office.[177]

Carter disliked pork barrel projects and back room deal-making outside the public view. He campaigned for the presidency saying he would fight pork, which he then attempted to do once in office by opposing a traditional rivers and harbors bill early in his term. The bill unfortunately had wide support. During the campaign he also promised to balance the budget and cut military spending, so as to diminish the size of the imperial presidency.[178]

177. Whitney, *Biographies*, 416; McDonald, *Presidency*, 460; Boyer, *Oxford Companion*, 107; Flagel, *Guide*, 19.

178. Boyer, *Oxford Companion*, 107; Miller Center, *Carter—Domestic Affairs;* Nelson, *Presidency*, 174; Drewry and O'Connor, *America Is*, 678–79.

Carter gave unmistakable signs that he was to be a Wilson-type, called-by-God president. In his inaugural address, which the New York Times labeled as "a sermon," he announced, "Ours was the first society openly to define itself in terms of both spirituality and human liberty. It is that unique self-definition which has given us an exceptional appeal . . ." He ignored the evidence in his own Christian bible of the myriad of ancient nations whose rulers claimed spiritual qualities and bestowed liberties on the people. In doing so, he set the stage not only for the assertion of a new phase of American moral superiority, but a thinly veiled brand of Christian military imperialism that tended during his administration, and for a long time afterward, to de-stabilize the world rather than stabilize it. His self-proclaimed prophetic sensibility set the tone for the infallibility in executive matters he believed he could demonstrate by micro-management of not only domestic affairs but of American international activity. Like Wilson, he believed in his own intellectual and ethical superiority over others. Carter actually reduced the staff of the executive office of the president because he could not trust others to manage the details effectively. Like Wilson, as well, his self-importance and un-Christian-like lack of humility ultimately sent him into a political, and spiritual, nose-dive at the end of his term. In September, 1979 his approval rating stood at nineteen percent.[179]

Carter felt that as the Christian ruler of the nation, he was entitled to have immediate access to his citizen-parishioners. When the television networks refused to give him presidential air time on one occasion, he turned his request into a demand, and the networks caved in. Carter also pioneered another tool of tyranny, positioning himself to earn popularity points by communing directly with his people. He established a presidential call-in radio program. In March of 1977 he answered some forty-two questions out of 9.5 million calls nationwide seeking to question him about matters of state.[180]

God wanted Carter to de-regulate industry, announce by decree a program of uplift for the economy, limit social welfare, fight for the down-trodden the world over, and improve energy policy. Accordingly, Carter created the energy department to fund research and regulate supplies. God also wanted him to spend money doing some of these things.

179. Whitney, *Biographies*, 418; Flagel, *Guide*, 45; McDonald, *Presidency*, 371, 376; Flagel, *Guide*, 306, 323.

180. McDonald, *Presidency*, 453.

Since his party held control of both houses of Congress, he figured he could get away with sending it an ambitious legislative agenda: welfare reform, comprehensive energy reform, hospital cost containment reform, tax reform, and Social Security reform. Unfortunately, his party wanted to expand social welfare rather than limit it. One author recalls, "He dumped a massive number of bills and waited for Congress to pass them." His was an "amateurish, rationalist approach." He reduced his legislative liaison staff and as a result struggled to get legislation passed. Congress, however, eventually funded many of his programs. Despite campaign promises to balance the federal budget, Carter ran an $80 billion government deficit. Yearly expenditures rose from $403 billion in 1977 to a record $579 billion in 1980. He ultimately increased the national debt from $706.4 billion to $994.8 billion, an increase of forty-one percent during his term.[181]

Carter understood that the previous presidents had bequeathed him a number of precedents which he could use to move his agenda along even in the face of a recalcitrant Congress. He was determined to use executive orders, presidential memoranda and proclamations, and control of rule-making. His first executive order was full clemency for violators of the Selective Service Act between 1964 and 1973. He also doled out 534 pardons during his term of office. Carter used an executive order to place a tariff on oil. Not only did Congress ultimately forbid him from doing this, but a federal judge struck down his fee on imported oil as not being part of "the inherent powers of the President." British citizens had fought the same battle against the king, when in 1606 they sued him for regulating customs without Parliament's consent.[182]

Carter issued Executive Orders 11790 and 12038 to establish price and allocation controls on crude and refined oil products. He also used Executive Order 12092 to set non-binding wage and price controls. Some of his executive orders were supported by statutes, others were not. E.O. 12092 of November 1978 prohibited inflationary procurement practices by the federal government, such as engaged in by the military establishment. Businesses not in compliance with the order were barred from contracts over $5 million. This policy was overturned when the court rejected this debarment of contractors as violating constitutional

181. Nelson, *Presidency*, 174; Boyer, *Oxford Companion*, 107; McDonald, *Presidency*, 371; Flagel, *Guide*, 30; Whitney, *Biographies*, 423.

182. Flagel, *Guide*, 166, 168; McDonald, *Presidency*, 296; Schochet, Oz-Salzburger, and Jones, *Political Hebraism*, 196.

separation of powers. His order 12264 prescribed export restrictions. His Executive Order 13130 created the Presidential Commission on the Accident at Three Mile Island in 1979. This kind of order was used as a method of deflecting public pressure on his office for accountability for the accident. The order and its commission thwarted political harm, preserved his reputation as a man who wanted to get to the bottom of things, and held off any report of mis-management until public concern died down. The report could be left to gather dust on the shelf.[183]

Carter issued twenty-two executive orders not related to the Iran Hostage situation between the 1980 election and the arrival of Ronald Reagan. He thus set a precedent for Bill Clinton's use of massive lame duck legislation during the midnight hour of his 1990s presidency.[184]

In an effort to make government more just, Carter issued executive orders with respect to administrative law procedure. His efforts increased the time consuming aspect of these processes. Carter also began the process of expanding uses of signing statements, which statements were intended to indicate executive reluctance to go along with certain measures passed by Congress.[185]

While executive orders deal with people within government, presidential proclamations deal with people outside of government. Carter's Proclamation 4771 instituted peacetime draft registration as a measure to prepare the country for national emergency events of the sort he felt that the Soviet invasion of Afghanistan provided. He did this despite the fact that twentieth century America viewed it as a blatant corruption of the idea of a volunteer military and a tool of presidential adventurism. In fact, Wilson and Franklin Roosevelt had institute drafts only in accordance with prior congressional legislation, but Carter was now doing it on his own by decree, which made it two removes from constitutional appropriateness. Congress gave its approval to this retroactively, but rejected his proposed policy that women also be registered for the draft. Proclamation 4813 extended energy conservation measures in the wake of the Arab oil embargo. Carter also greatly expanded the use of presidential memoranda. Kennedy had issued only twenty two, while Carter issued ninety-three. One of these was the proclamation regarding the

---

183. Cooper, *Order*, 24, 53–54, 66–68.
184. Ibid., 77–78.
185. Ibid., 201, 209.

Petroleum Import Adjustment Program, the oil surcharge order deemed to be unconstitutional.[186]

Carter sidestepped Congressional legislation he did not like by subjecting rule-making to cost-analysis, alternative programming analysis, and approval of the "least cumbersome" form of regulation. He did this by executive order. He also asked agencies to provide broader notice of rule-making in order to give state and local voices more say.[187]

Carter had promised to reorganize the "horrible bureaucratic mess" in the federal government by bringing the bureaucracy more under presidential control. His Paperwork Reduction Act limited sweeping requests for information, and created the Office of Information and Regulatory Affairs (OIRA) within the Office of Management and Budget. Carter also tried to democratize the federal government to a degree by responding to public pressure after the Johnson, Nixon, and Ford administrations for de-classification of information. He used Executive Order 12065, arrived at via an open and participative process, to come up with the policy of "when in doubt, don't classify." Perhaps as one consequence of this, he was unable to stop cabinet leaks of information.[188]

Carter was particularly active in energy affairs and his policies helped to reduce foreign oil dependency by a significant amount. Early in his term he engaged in fear-mongering, saying the nation faced "national catastrophe" unless they gave up their wasteful use of energy. He called for a $.50 tax on gasoline, a windfall profits tax on oil companies, and the development of synthetic fuels. We mentioned above that Carter used unconstitutional executive power to impose a fee on imported oil, which would have passed along a ten cent increase to the consumer at the pump. Congress repealed the oil import fee, so Carter vetoed the bill. Congress, in the control of Carter's own political party, passed legislation forbidding him to implement the oil fee, then overrode his veto.[189]

Carter diminished states' control over local lands when at the end of his term he signed a bill doubling the size of the nation's national park and wildlife refuge system by taking 104 million acres of Alaska's wilderness from the people of that state. He also usurped private and state responsibility to clean up the environment by creating a $1.6 billion

186. Whitney, *Biographies*, 423; Cooper, *Order*, 90, 119, 133, 142.

187. Crenson and Ginsberg, *Presidential Power*, 206; Cooper, *Order*, 11, 62.

188. Cooper, *Order*, 26, 31, 233; McDonald, *Presidency*, 341, 474.

189. Miller Center, *Carter—Domestic Affairs;* Whitney, *Biographies*, 422.

national "superfund" to pay for cleanup of chemicals spilled or dumped into the environment.[190]

Carter's personal beliefs about foreign affairs were admirable, but he junked many of them once he got sucked into the vortex of policy complexity surrounding superpower relations. He believed the U.S. should promote human rights among its allies as well as its enemies, a laudable goal. He decreased aid to Chile, El Salvador, Nicaragua, Argentina, Uruguay and Ethiopia, because they were ruled by dictators. South Korea came under criticism for repressing dissidents. He said, "My determination is very deep." He asserted an almost messianic calling to intervene in other nations' internal affairs when he told the United Nations General Assembly, "No member of the United Nations can claim that mistreatment of its citizens is solely its own business." In 1977 Carter announced he would allow Cuban refugees to immigrate to the United States. After some 125,000 arrived, including many thousands of criminals released from Castro's prisons, both Carter and Castro stopped the flow. Carter's ambassador to the UN, Andrew Young, helped draft a plan to convert Rhodesia from white rule to black majority rule. The administration also helped pass a UN embargo on arms sales to South Africa, a member nation.[191] Carter urged white minority governments in South Africa and Rhodesia (Zimbabwe) to end apartheid.

In his electoral campaign he had promised not to appoint Washington insiders in foreign affairs positions, but he flip-flopped and appointed the insider Zibignew Brzezinski as National Security adviser, and former Johnson administration and Defense Department insider Cyrus Vance as Secretary of State.

Soon after he took office, Carter approved the sale of seven high-tech AWAC intelligence aircraft and 160 F-16 fighters to Iran, totally misunderstanding the political situation there. For example, he lavished praise on the U.S. puppet dictator there, stating that the Shah provided a bastion of stability for the country. In fact, the Shah had purchased billions in American arms since the American CIA helped him regain his throne in 1953, but that was not particularly laudable, since those arms were used to repress the Iranian people. Only months later an anti-American

190. Whitney, *Biographies*, 423.

191. Drewry and O'Connor, *America Is*, 677; Miller Center, *Carter—Foreign Affairs*; Whitney, *Biographies*, 424–25.

revolution broke out in Iran and the Shah killed thousands while trying to maintain power.[192]

Carter could see things in Iran only through his biased and heavily distorted Christian lens, rather than studying the situation from the point of view of Islamic religion, culture and politics. He thought the best thing by far was to support a western-style oligarchy like that favored by presidents before him. One historian wrote that the "Islamic component of the revolution was beyond American comprehension." On the other hand, Carter laudably declined to get directly involved militarily in the civil war there. Another consequence of the Iranian situation was an oil shortage and rising fuel prices. Carter declared a state of emergency related to the shortage in the U.S. which was still in effect in the first decade of the new century.[193]

In November, 1979, less than a year after the Shah was overthrown, Iranian students took 50 hostages from the American embassy in Tehran. The Iranian revolutionary leader seemed determined to deny the hostages to Carter in an effort to hamstring his reelection chances, and did not release them until Reagan took office. In September, 1980, Carter covertly supported Saddam Hussein in Iraq's invasion of Iran, setting off a nine-year war between the two countries.[194]

In 1980, the president introduced the Carter Doctrine during his state of the union address. He said he would commit the nation to war to protect the oil supply routes of the Persian Gulf: "An attempt by any outside force to gain control of the Persian Gulf region will be regarded as an assault on the vital interests of the United States of America. And such an assault will be repelled by any means necessary, including military force." Carter's assumption of the role of champion of the Persian Gulf showed how American imperialism supplanted British imperialism in the region. In 1903, for example, Lord Lansdowne had said to Parliament, "We should regard the establishment of a naval base or a fortified port in the Persian Gulf by any other Power as a very grave menace to British interests, and we should certainly resist it by all the means at our disposal."[195]

192. Whitney, *Biographies*, 429; Herring, *Colony to Superpower*, 848.

193. Herring, *Colony to Superpower*, 848–49; Boyer, *Oxford Companion*, 107; Crenson and Ginsberg, *Presidential Power*, 342.

194. Boyer, *Oxford Companion*, 107; Nelson, *Presidency*, 176; Herring, *Colony to Superpower*, 878.

195. Whitney, *Biographies*, 429; Flagel, *Guide*, 200.

Carter promised during the campaign to cut military spending and initially kept his promise. Prior to the Afghanistan debacle, Congress approved a measure to spend nearly $2 billion to add a fifth nuclear aircraft carrier to the fleet. Carter vetoed the entire $37 billion defense appropriation measure. A new measure excluding the carrier was then passed and approved by the president. Carter tried to limit arms sales abroad. He also decided to defer production of the neutron bomb, a tactical nuclear weapon. But, when the Soviets invaded Afghanistan in December 1979, Carter pushed for a major military buildup. He asked for a five percent increase in military spending, a massive five-year military buildup, and initiated a military draft to prepare for war. He got the largest build-up of conventional military forces since Truman. He initiated an Eisenhower-like policy to win a nuclear war and to hit civilian as well as military targets, outlined in his Presidential Directive-59.[196]

Despite his record of opposing human rights abuses, Carter set out to make an ally with a nation that had a particularly bad human rights record. While Carter growled at Soviet human rights violations, he winked at China's similar violations. He succumbed to Nixon's fascination with sharing world power with China. He gave China Most Favored Nation status and freed up Export/Import Bank credits for them. He gave full and formal diplomatic recognition to China in January 1979 and tried to make a military alliance with the Chinese communists as well, something Nixon wouldn't have thought of trying.[197] He sold high-tech military technology to them and opened negotiations to sell lethal military equipment and share intelligence with them.

At the same time, Carter unilaterally, that is, without Senate consent, revoked a mutual defense treaty with Taiwan. He did, however, continue to supply arms to Taiwan. In doing so, he carried on the time-honored U.S. tradition of providing both tinder and spark to both sides of pairs of nations engaged in egregious international disputes, thereby greatly enhancing the possibility of continuous world-wide conflagration.[198]

Carter, not content to support dictators in Iran and China, backed the oppressive dictator Mobutu in Zaire. He turned a blind eye to the communist dictator Pol Pot in Cambodia and even gave covert support

196. Cooper, *Order*, 166; Whitney, *Biographies*, 423, 426; Miller Center, *Carter—Foreign Affairs*; Herring, *Colony to Superpower*, 855–56.

197. Herring, *Colony to Superpower*, 840, 846; Whitney, *Biographies*, 424.

198. Herring, *Colony to Superpower*, 855; Miller Center, *Carter—Foreign Affairs*.

to Pol, certainly one of the worst political murderers in history. Carter gave U.S. support to the dictator Somoza in Nicaragua. However, he declined to get involved militarily in the Nicaraguan civil war.[199]

After losing his reelection bid, Carter made a televised farewell address, in which he used apocalyptic verbiage to convince the American people they had needed him at this crucial time in history. He said, "For this generation, life is nuclear survival, liberty is human rights, the pursuit of happiness is a planet whose resources are devoted to the physical and spiritual nourishment of its inhabitants." He thus deftly transformed the neutralist doctrine of the founding fathers to one of commitment of American tax dollars and political support to perpetual international intervention in other countries so that the American leader could nourish the planet with his own peculiar political priorities. His pro-entanglement farewell speech was thus the antithesis of Washington's anti-entanglement farewell.

Ronald Reagan

Ronald Reagan had a rebirth of sorts when he became a public relations representative for the General Electric Company and host of its television shows. Prior to that time he had been a Franklin Roosevelt devotee. After having lived through the Great Depression in poverty and dependent upon national giveaways, he now became an independently wealthy, conservative-sounding elitist. Reagan had an evangelical spiritual bent to go along with his political re-birth. His father was a Catholic and his mother a Protestant. He attended College at a small Disciples of Christ school near Peoria, Illinois. Like a number of presidents before and after him, he paid more attention to extracurricular activities in college than he did to scholarship while there.[200]

As governor of California, Reagan sounded conservative, but acted in a moderate to liberal fashion, a perfect template for the classical populist autocrat. For example, he talked about limited government but he oversaw the doubling of the state budget. While governor, after promising to reduce state employees, he presided over growth in their numbers by more than 40,000.[201] But Reagan did enough on the state level to earn

---

199. Herring, *Colony to Superpower*, 844, 846, 857; Boyer, *Oxford Companion*, 107.
200. Nelson, *Presidency*, 176; Whitney, *Biographies*, 437.
201. Boyer, *Oxford Companion*, 653; Whitney, *Biographies*, 441.

some conservative credentials, leading voters to believe he would act the same way in national office. He cut state aid to medical services, education, and welfare. This led people to believe he would keep his presidential campaign promise to dismantle the federal Department of Health, Education, and Welfare. Once Reagan obtained national power, he did little dismantling at all.

Reagan held the presidency from 1981 to 1989. He was extremely ambitious for the presidency, twice trying unsuccessfully to get the Republican presidential nomination, in 1968 and 1976. He was also living evidence that the country was drifting far away from traditional values. He was the first to win the presidency after having a divorce, and, in fact, helped implement California's no-fault divorce law. He was also the first former leader of a labor union to become president.[202]

Reagan talked like a fundamentalist and won eighty-one percent of evangelicals in his reelection campaign in 1984. He had hard-line evangelicals in his cabinet, such as his education secretary. He was nominally a Presbyterian while president, and called the U.S. "God's Country." He questioned evolution, advocated school prayer, and opposed abortion. He repeatedly used the word "God" in his annual addresses to Congress. In a speech to the National Association of Evangelicals in March, 1983, he described the Soviet Union as an "evil empire" and, deflecting attention from his own usurpations, called it "the focus of evil in the world." The "prophetizing Reagan" also justified opposing atheist communism by military force wherever it raised its head, by using his own interpretation of Biblical authority, saying it "is a sin and evil in the world, and we are enjoined by Scripture and the Lord Jesus to oppose it with all our might." As president, he used Billy Graham as his unofficial spiritual advisor.[203]

Reagan, like his ideological opposite John Kennedy, cared little for high culture, whether in music or literature. In fact, he rarely found time to read. One Soviet lesser official revealed that Soviet leader Gorbachev "had some misgivings about Reagan's intellectual capacities." It has been said that "constitutional law and American history were beyond him." For example, he claimed that the Puritans championed religious freedom, when they had openly persecuted Jews, Catholics, and Quakers. He

---

202. Whitney, *Biographies*, 435–36.
203. Whitney, *Biographies*, 447; Flagel, *Guide*, 43, 48, 52.

was strong on faith, and weak on facts and analysis. When asked about details, he often said a subject was "under study."[204]

In his first campaign for president, Reagan put together a coalition of republicans and "Reagan democrats" disenchanted with "stagflation" during Carter's term of office. He promised to cut taxes, curb central government spending, balance the budget by 1984, reduce the federal deficit, and get tough on terrorism. After Carter had divided up the Department of Health, Education, and Welfare, Reagan promised to do away with the Department of Education and diminish the Department of Health and Human Services. But most of this was election year wind. In his first year of office, he cut out only one tiny federal agency, the Comprehensive Employment Training Act (CETA) program of 1974, which offered job training and public employment through a block grant. He never touched Education or Health. Reagan proposed some reductions in entitlements, like a three-month delay in the cost of living increase for Social Security beneficiaries, and also proposed taxing sick pay, enacting penalties for early retirement, and reducing disability benefits. But he backed off these proposals after only a single week because his poll numbers were falling. Principle was much less important than personal power for Ronald Reagan.[205]

Reagan rescued not only Roosevelt's New Deal, But Johnson's Great Society as well. Congress agreed to modest "cuts," that is, decreases in the rate of increase, in education, veterans' affairs, health, welfare and environment. Specifically, he cut back the rate of increase in food stamps, school lunches, money grants to welfare recipients, Medicaid, Medicare, and college loans. Despite his pledge to dismantle federal education programs and abolish the Department of Education, education under Reagan, "look[ed] very similar to what it did under Presidents Johnson, Nixon, Ford, and Carter," the four chief executives before him. Under Reagan, department of education spending rose by fourteen percent. Reagan eliminated training programs for the unemployed. He also held funding at $600 million for the Job Corp program, but flip-flopped on his promise to eliminate the Small Business Administration. In the area of finance and industry, he implemented de-regulation in banking, natural gas, and environmental protection. Eventually formal charges were filed

204. Flagel, *Guide*, 31, 38, 49, 156, 219; McDonald, *Presidency*, 177, 455.

205. Miller Center, *Reagan—Domestic Affairs;* Whitney, *Biographies*, 443; Flagel, *Guide*, 323; Samples, *Struggle*, 89, 91.

against Reagan for contempt of Congress regarding his handling of environmental protection issues. He also decreased funding for Rosalynn Carter's pet legislative project, the 1980 Mental Health Systems Act.[206]

Reagan gave a hint of his imperial and tyrannical agenda in one seemingly innocuous statement in his first inaugural address. He chastened the American people and said they needed to "believe in our capacity to perform great deeds." The word "great" in historical context is a codeword for expansion of the ruler's programs and power. In fact, there was one particular campaign pledge that Reagan kept, the only one that could really enhance power for him as much as he wanted it enhanced. He had run for president on a platform of militarism. After twenty-five years of peaceful co-existence, and even after inheriting the largest military budget in the world at $192 billion, Reagan rushed back into the Cold War and sponsored the largest military build-up in U.S. history, next to Lincoln's perhaps. Reagan's military buildup was more expensive in adjusted dollars than LBJ's tab for Vietnam. Congress authorized at his request a $28 billion increase, amounting to a seven percent annual increase over three years. Overall, Reagan increased the military budget by forty-four percent in his first three years.[207]

Reagan's promise to deal with the national debt was fundamentally dishonest. Reagan had chastised Carter for his $80 billion annual deficit, and had said "We've got to get control of the federal budget. It's out of control." He also said, "It is time . . . to get government back within its means . . ." But Reagan himself quickly doubled Carter's annual deficit number. His annual deficit grew from $79 billion to $173 billion in six years. It grew from $128 billion in 1982 to $200 billion in 1983.[208]His annual deficit was higher than the entire national budget just a decade before in 1970. Some two-thirds of Americans disapproved of his deficit spending.

Reagan never truly had in mind to cut the national budget. He wanted only to cut the rate of increase in the annual domestic "discretionary" budget (programs that were not entitlements), while proposing massive increases in war spending. Experts of all political colors cried out that his initial budget proposal was a recipe for an unbalanced budget

206. Nelson, *Presidency*, 178; Whitney, *Biographies*, 445; Flagel, *Guide*, 125, 141, 266; Cooper, *Order*, 241; Samples, *Struggle*, 90.

207. Miller Center, *Reagan—Domestic Affairs*; Boyer, *Oxford Companion*, 653; Whitney, *Biographies*, 445; Flagel, *Guide*, 123–24, 201.

208. Whitney, *Biographies*, 444–45; McDonald, *Presidency*, 379.

and a larger national debt. In fact, it contemplated a deficit for the year of $110 billion. He used the sophomoric reasoning that his deficit strategy was to scare Congress into reelection worries, and they would start cutting spending like crazy.[209] What he in fact was proposing was what he felt would be popular with voters, not what was right for the country.

In his first budget message, Reagan declared that national welfare programs for "all those with true need," could not be cut. This included the social safety net for the poor, disabled, and elderly. He said that entitlements and other programs could also not be cut, including Social Security, Medicare, and veterans pensions, free school lunches, Social Security Income (SSI) payments to the aged, blind and disabled, Head Start, and summer youth jobs. This added up to a Reagan protection racket for $216 billion worth of poverty programs.[210]

What Reagan also did was push hard for tax cuts. Unfortunately, his initial tax cuts were three to four times larger than his spending cuts in 1981. He asked Congress to cut the marginal tax rates by thirty percent over three years, and eventually won twenty-five. At the same time he asked for an overall 6.2 percent increase in the domestic side of the budget, which equated to an overall 8.3 percent increase after factoring in $26 billion more for the military. Reagan did not represent the interests of the people who elected him. Some fifty-three percent of them thought the cutting defense spending was the best way to reduce the deficit. The tax plan also included very large cuts for the most wealthy. The average tax rate on the top one percent of earners fell from thirty-seven percent to 27.7 percent. Interestingly, Reagan got legislative backing for his income tax cut by giving them tax breaks for their corporate campaign donors, and for real estate developers and oil companies in their districts. Reagan drove the percentage of national revenue that business contributed down from twenty-five percent to eight percent. In January, 1982, he also dropped the government's suit against IBM, the largest anti-trust suit ever, in process since 1968. He also abandoned other pending cases. One author, writing in 1994, reminds, "No monopolization cases have been filed since that day."[211]

209. Miller Center, *Reagan—Domestic Affairs;* Samples, *Struggle,* 82.

210. Samples, *Struggle,* 84, 102.

211. Samples, *Struggle,* 118, 142, 281, note 55; Whitney, *Biographies,* 445; Flagel, *Guide,* 124, 308; McDonald, *Presidency,* 292, 377.

Reagan never sent Congress a balanced budget during his eight years in the presidency. After a little sweetener tax cut for the middle class in his first year, he proved to be a tax-a-little and spend-a-lot liberal tyrant. In 1982, and 1984 Reagan supported tax increases. His 1982 tax program, the Tax Equity and Fiscal Responsibility Act of 1982, tried to help control deficits which resulted from declining tax revenues. It increased taxes on interest, dividends, cigarettes, telephone services, and air travel. An economic downturn had started in 1981 and lasted through the end of 1982. The Federal Reserve had sharply curbed the money supply and thus restricted growth in an effort to curb inflation, resulting in pressure for the tax increase. Later, in 1986, Reagan returned to tax cuts which simplified the tax code by closing some loopholes but gave the highest tax cuts to the wealthiest Americans. He lowered the top individual rate from fifty percent to twenty-eight percent and taxed about eighty-five percent of individuals at the bottom rate of fifteen percent. This led to slightly lower taxes for two-thirds of all individual taxpayers. It also reduced tax brackets from fourteen to two, and overall introduced the lowest rates since the 1920s. Reagan announced that he was satisfied with the 1986 tax bill because it reduced the higher, or "progressive" tax burden on the wealthy. In today's political terms, it protected the one percenters. During his time of office, middle class family annual income grew by only one percent, while the top twenty percent of earners saw an average income increase of nine percent. The bottom twenty percent of earners saw a decline of annual income of eight percent. The tax bill reduced the top corporate rate from forty-six percent to thirty-four percent. In fact, tax reform in 1986 was the only real achievement in limiting government in his entire second term.[212]

After one year of budget "cuts" (that is, only semi-huge increases), the remainder of his eight-year term was followed by "rapid budget growth." Welfare programs grew forty-four percent; the IRS budget grew by 585 percent; the federal prison budget grew 206 percent; the FAA budget grew thirty-six percent; the WIC feeding program grew fifty-four percent; Medicare increased thirty-one percent; the EPA budget increased twenty-two percent; highway spending increased in real terms; education for the handicapped increased fifty percent in real terms; biomedical research at the National Institutes of Health increased forty-seven percent;

212. Drewry and O'Connor, *America Is*, 700; Whitney, *Biographies*, 454; Nelson, *Presidency*, 179; Samples, *Struggle*, 96–97, 112, 131–32, 149, 152.

and alcohol, drug and mental health spending increased thirty-nine percent.[213]

Eight years of irresponsible deficit spending meant that Reagan tripled the cost of interest on the debt during his presidency. The national debt was $994.8 billion in 1981, but by 1989 it was $2.87 trillion. He increased federal spending from $657 billion to $1,064 billion during his term. Federal revenues increased from $599 billion to $909 billion during the same time. His worst annual deficit was $221 billion in 1986. All of this gave the lie to his protestations of being a Cal Coolidge budget conservative. He had hung a portrait of Coolidge in the White House cabinet room, because Cal had reduced the debt, but Cal's government philosophy had not rubbed off on him.[214]

Reagan's tax and spend program ultimately placed the proud America central government into the hands of foreign creditors. Some twenty percent of his deficit spending was financed by foreign capital, which had a devastating effect on the U.S. economy. The United States of American under Reagan became the world's largest debtor nation. In addition, Reagan presided over increasing levels of foreign imports, which produced a massive trade deficit. Reagan supported protectionist legislation in the auto and steel industries but did not want to veto import quotas that would cut the number of Japanese imports. The yearly trade deficit skyrocketed to a record $159.2 billion for fiscal 1987.[215]

Reagan was a non-confrontational person when it came to personal relationships. He did not want to confront legislators personally and twist their arms as Lyndon Johnson would have done. He chose to deal with Congress through public appeals to congressional voting districts and through his own budget proposals. Still, he vetoed thirty-nine bills in his eight years, and pocket vetoed another thirty-nine. Reagan opposed sanctions against the racist apartheid government in South Africa, but Congress overrode his veto. Reagan narrowly stopped an override of his veto of a joint resolution to stop his sale of arms to the monarchy in Saudi Arabia. He wanted to sell a hundred anti-ship missiles, hundreds of anti-aircraft weapons, and a thousand Sidewinder missiles.[216]

213. Samples, *Struggle*, 74, 78, 80–81, 117, 119, 123, 143–44.

214. McDonald, *Presidency*, 378; Flagel, *Guide*, 123.

215. Herring, *Colony to Superpower*, 916; Miller Center, *Reagan—Impact and Legacy*; Whitney, *Biographies*, 456–57.

216. McDonald, *Presidency*, 354; Flagel, *Guide*, 141.

One historian said that Reagan took on the task of "reversing the decline in presidential authority of the 1970s." The same historian opined, "He enjoyed considerable success in achieving that goal." Reagan made spectacular use of tyrannical methods invented by his predecessors to make sure he used his popularity to put the focus of government on the presidency rather than on the Congress. In fact, one historian mentions that Reagan's election was the turning point after which Republicans gave up their traditional abhorrence for executive usurpation of Congressional functions. In terms of diminishing Congress' influence on the federal bureaucracy, he used the Civil Service Reform Act of 1978 to appoint political cronies to positions deeper down in the federal bureaucracy, and then monitored them like Lyndon Johnson had done to see that they followed his wishes. He used "cabinet councils" like the Economic Policy Council, and the Domestic Policy Council to keep cabinet members more wedded to him than to their professional bureaucracies.[217]

Reagan used the executive order extensively to enhance his power. In the first place he used it to undo the policies of his predecessor. In fact, he was busy figuring out which ones he wanted to erase even during the first campaign. For example, he unilaterally eliminated Carter's controls on oil products, wages and prices, and export restrictions. He also revoked some foreign service intelligence operations and changed the management of classified information. Reagan's Executive Order 12356 expanded his autocratic control over national security information and incited a mini-rebellion among his own cabinet officials. These changes also drew a sharp reaction from Congress, in part because he froze key members of Congress out of discussions on national security classification. Reagan's National Security Directive 84 "dramatically intensified controls on access to information."[218]

But Reagan did not always reverse his predecessor's orders. Sometimes he built upon them. He used Carter's 1980 Proclamation 4771 requiring draft registration as a platform to justify filing criminal prosecutions against those failing to register. Reagan especially targeted "known opponents of the program," and thus used it in a discriminatory fashion.[219] Reagan used executive orders to head off outside investigating bodies.

217. Nelson, *Presidency*, 180; Crenson and Ginsberg, *Presidential Power*, 208; McDonald, *Presidency*, vii, 342.

218. Cooper, *Order*, 61–62, 69, 76, 81, 154, 233.

219. Ibid., 119–20.

For example, one such order, Executive Order 12575, empowered the Presidential Special Review Board to investigate the Iran-Contra affair.

Reagan began to depend heavily upon illegal impoundment deferrals to get some control over the budget. He also expanded the use of signing statements by changing both the substance and importance of them, and making them a major vehicle for hijacking or overriding the intent of Congress's newly passed laws.[220] Rather than take time to research Congressional intent, he used signing statements to give his own interpretation of what he felt should be Congress's intent.

A 1979 survey found that productivity was slowed by the increase in national regulation of occupational safety and environmental protection. Reagan did not think it necessary for the government to try to produce a risk-free society. He therefore reinterpreted the Safe Drinking Water legislation of 1986 so that certain mandatory sections of the law would allow discretionary enforcement. This essentially amounted to presidential nullification of Congressional law. One court found that Reagan was "sever(ing) provisions of a bill with which he disagrees." Overall, Reagan attacked seventy-one legislative provisions during his term of office by means of signing statements.[221]

Political scientist Theodore Lowi noted that in the 1960s and 1970s, Congress had increasingly abdicated its responsibility to provide real structure for the laws it was passing. It delegated broad authority to federal agencies to provide that structure. This was "policy without law," and essentially amounted to national programming without Congressional accountability or legitimacy. Reagan was determined to take advantage of this new latitude. In rule making, Reagan implemented what Nixon, Ford, and Carter fell short of. In order to bend government regulations toward his own policy goals, he created a process for "full-blown presidential control of the rule-making process." Reagan issued Executive Order 12291, which established centralized and essentially personal presidential oversight of executive department rule making. Cabinet agencies were required to use cost-benefit analysis to slow down or derail Congressional wishes. Regulations could not be adopted if "costs" outweighed "benefits," or, in other words, if Reagan's right arm (the White House) was unhappy with what his left arm (the agency) was doing. For

220. McDonald, *Presidency*, 313; Cooper, *Order*, 14.

221. McDonald, *Presidency*, 216; Samples, *Struggle*, 61–62; Crenson and Ginsberg, *Presidential Power*, 198–200.

example, Reagan used regulatory review to block environmental legislation and safety and health legislation. During his eight years, some eighty-five regulations a year were returned to agencies for re-tooling or trashing. OMB usually delayed rule implementation an average of three months.[222]

Ronald Reagan memorized lines in his early career in movies. When it came to foreign policy as president, his favorite line was, "Defense is not a budget issue. You spend what you need."[223] In truth, the "defense" budget since Ronald Reagan has generally not even been included in budget discussions. In order to re-enforce imperial notions about the great danger the homeland faces from day to day, the military is turned into an off-line issue, divorced from domestic thinking, in a category by itself, the domain of the executive branch only. Unfortunately, the real level of danger to the American citizenry from the crumbling communist economies of Reagan's day was a much different story. It would have been closer to the truth if he had said, "You spend what the military-industrial complex wants you to spend, and what you need to spend to scare the people into re-electing you."

Khrushchev tapped out of the Cold War in the Nixon days. He was asking for arms control before even the many hundreds of billions of dollars of U.S. military spending that Ford and Carter poured into the U.S. military machine and thus long before Reagan's monumental buildup even started. The Red Army was large, but behind every conscripted soldier was an enlisted officer pointing a gun at his back, encouraging him to stride forward for the glory of the communist dictator, while his family starved and went without basic human rights. A happy kindergartner in Duluth could have whistled a nursery rhyme and the Berlin Wall would have come tumbling down after so long a dictatorship. Still, Reagan asked for $220 billion for his military, the largest peacetime budget in history.

In order to counter what he claimed was Soviet nuclear sophistication and numbers, Reagan decided to build up U.S. nuclear warhead stockpiles. At a time when the Soviet Union was actually rotting to utter dust from internal political contradictions and economic insufficiency, Reagan engineered a U.S./Soviet stockpile of some 80,000 nuclear weapons.[224]

222. Samples, *Struggle*, 62; Cooper, *Order*, 61, 206–7.
223. Miller Center, *Reagan—Foreign Policy*.
224. Flagel, *Guide*, 168, 220.

In international relations, Reagan supported whichever foreign leader talked a tough anti-Soviet game, regardless of whether the people of the nation supported the leader or not. He declared in highly simplistic and inaccurate terms, "The Soviet Union underlies all the unrest that is going on." He built up the Taliban in Afghanistan with taxpayer money, while taxpayers unfortunately later on were required to tear them down.[225]

Reagan shared one assumption that had guided U.S. foreign affairs since the time of Truman. The globe belonged to the United States and the U.S. had to police things in every part of the world to make them turn out the way the U.S. wanted them to turn out. The U.S. did not really need to consult with other nations, allies or enemies, in taking action in pursuit of this objective to control the world. The Reagan Doctrine, breaking with détente, asserted that the U.S. must support covert insurgencies the world over, whether Middle East, Caribbean, Central America, Africa, or Asia as part of its plan to roll back and "transcend" communism. Reagan became King Covert, and ushered in the "Golden Age" of CIA covert operations. Reagan plunged into covert action immediately upon taking office. By March, 1981, he was in Nicaragua, and soon after in Cuba, Honduras and El Salvador.[226]

Reagan continued the Carter administration's support of El Salvador's efforts to squash liberal/leftist rebels in the civil war there. He sent fifty-four military advisers and aid to El Salvador without Congressional approval. In 1981 several members of Congress claimed that Reagan violated the 1973 War Powers law by supplying military supervisory assistance to El Salvador.[227]

Reagan also gave covert aid to Nicaragua in increasing amounts from 1981 to 1984. That aid went to support a faction that abused the human rights of peasants there. The "Contras" there grew with U.S. help from a force of a few hundred to an army of 9,000. The Contra army was trying to overthrow the leftist government of the Sandinistas, which had support from both Cuba and the Soviet Union. Reagan was convinced the Sandinistas were a communist government and would never allow

---

225. Flagel, *Guide*, 202; Herring, *Colony to Superpower*, 881, 883.

226. Flagel, *Guide*, 201.

227. Herring, *Colony to Superpower*, 887; Crenson and Ginsberg, *Presidential Power*, 335.

free elections. The Sandinistas proved Reagan wrong, eventually holding elections, losing, and giving up power.[228]

In order to continue his support of the Contras, Reagan sold weapons to Iran (he was now supporting the *other* side in the Iraq-Iran War) in exchange for the release of U.S. hostages held in Lebanon by Hezbollah. He then diverted the money to the Contras. Ronald Reagan's adventures in tyranny and imperialism in Latin America have been described variously as "blatant disregard for law," "disdain for Congress," "corrosive secrecy," and "open contempt for democracy."[229] In other words, he operated just like Nixon did, but had a more likeable personality.

Ultimately, Reagan provided covert aid/taxpayer money to Poland, Cambodia, Chad, Ethiopia, Iran, Liberia, Nicaragua, Pakistan, Sudan, Mozambique, Angola, and Afghanistan. He opined in simplistic terms that "Support for freedom fighters is self-defense [for the U.S.]" The money he doled out was not peanuts. He gave the Mujahideen in Afghanistan the same amount in 1986 as Truman gave Germany to rebuild in 1951 under the Marshall Plan.[230]

In summary terms, Ronald Reagan was a terribly incompetent historian, but not a bad practical political scientist. He laid his hands on the national treasury of the world's most productive nation and spent the nation happily into perpetual fiscal crisis and servitude, while protecting his own political interests quite admirably. Like a wild west gunslinger, he announced to the world after bombing Tripoli in Libya, "Every nickel-and-dime dictator the world over knows that if he tangles with the United States of America [read: Sheriff Ronald Reagan], he will pay a price." Reagan was an upbeat tyrant, a feel-good despot. In the midst of spending the nation into oblivion, he insisted at the start of his second term that the nation was "in the midst of a spring time of hope . . ."[231]

George H.W. Bush

George Bush was an experienced government administrator before becoming forty-first president of the U.S. from 1989 to 1993. For eight years prior to assuming the presidency he was Reagan's vice president. He also

228. Herring, *Colony to Superpower*, 889; Miller Center, *Reagan—Foreign Affairs*.

229. Flagel, *Guide*, 324; Herring, *Colony to Superpower*, 915.

230. Flagel, *Guide*, 202.

231. Flagel, *Guide*, 239; Whitney, *Biographies*, 450.

was director of the CIA, liaison to China, and chairman of the Republican National Committee. He did not spent more than a couple years in each job, so ambitious was he for higher office. He had been a supporter of the Vietnam War.[232]

George Bush, like so many presidents before him, came from the wealthy class. His father was an executive of U.S. Rubber and a U.S. senator. Bush was sent to exclusive boarding schools for his education. He demonstrated his political ambition by running twice for U.S. senator and losing both times. He ran for president in 1980 against Reagan before accepting the vice presidential slot on the Reagan ticket that year.[233]

As Reagan's vice president, he logged nearly a million miles in foreign travel and headed some presidential task forces, such as the drug interdiction task force, which many people believed overlooked the Panamanian dictator Noriega's illegal activities. He also attended Reagan's cabinet meetings and had his own offices in the White House.[234]

Although Bush claimed to be "out of the loop" in the Iran-Contra affair, most historians believe he was deeply involved. As a former CIA director, he would have had the kind of experience that would be useful to the operatives implementing the plan. In fact, using Proclamation 6518, he ultimately pardoned high level Reagan/Bush officials involved in the Contra affair. Observers understood the proclamation as an effort to erase a stain on the Reagan and Bush administrations. It also saved his political confidants from facing prosecution and saved himself embarrassment, as it became apparent he would be forced to testify at their criminal trials and reveal his knowledge of the goings-on. Bush's pardons "went well beyond the use of pardon power used by previous presidents," and thus rates him as a precedent-setting tyrant in a long-line of usurpers. In fact, he pardoned Caspar Weinberger, convicted of or awaiting trial on charges of perjury, fraud, and conspiracy, on December 24, 1992, hoping to take advantage of the national Christmas "spirit" to dilute the effect of his action.[235] He pardoned Robert McFarlane and Scooter Libby, about to serve thirty months in prison for federal crimes, and three others.

232. Whitney, *Biographies*, 450, 466; Nelson, *Presidency*, 182; Flagel, *Guide*, 21.

233. Whitney, *Biographies*, 461–62; Nelson, *Presidency*, 181; Boyer, *Oxford Companion*, 92.

234. Whitney, *Biographies*, 468.

235. Nelson, *Presidency*, 182; Cooper, *Order*, 135, 141; Flagel, *Guide*, 167–68.

As an Episcopalian, Bush used religion extensively in his presidential campaign. To get conservative and evangelical voters on his side, he championed prayer and the pledge of allegiance in public schools, opposed abortion, supported the death penalty and the right to own firearms, and mentioned God in almost every campaign speech. His efforts paid off as he won eighty-eight percent of the evangelical vote. In his inaugural address, he said "My first act as President is a prayer. I ask you to bow your heads." Once in power, he dropped his push for prayer in schools, and only played the God card once again, when it was reelection time. Although he retained Billy Graham as his spiritual adviser, evangelicals noticed his obvious posturing, and left his reelection camp in droves.[236]

Bush inherited Reagan's enormous budget deficit and because he promised no new taxes, he could not hope to implement new programs. He talked about charity work through volunteerism (waxing poetically about "a thousand points of light in a broad and peaceful sky"), federal anti-drug enforcement, and federal education reform. During the budget negotiations for 1991 he flip-flopped on the forceful position he had taken on taxes. Many American's remember his famous and deeply seductive line, "Read my lips—no new taxes." But the five-year budget deal he made with Congress, styled OBRA-90 and often mentioned as his best domestic achievement, raised taxes. He tried to cushion his betrayal by calling taxes on luxury items like some boats and autos, gasoline and cigarettes, "revenue increases."[237]

Bush could not put the blame on the previous administration for huge increases in the national debt, because he was vice president in that administration. The overall national debt during his administration grew 51.5 percent from $2.87 trillion to $4.35 trillion. His annual spending deficits, after a slow start, surpassed Reagan's worst of $221 billion, and rose to as high as $350 billion. That huge debt and the fact he made the political miscalculation to leave Saddam Hussein in power, hastened his reelection loss to Clinton in 1992. He also failed to be the promised "education president" and a leader for the environment. Banking on a second

236. Whitney, *Biographies*, 471; Flagel, *Guide*, 43, 52–53.

237. Whitney, *Biographies*, 471; Miller Center, *G.H.W. Bush—Domestic Affairs*; Boyer, *Oxford Companion*, 92; Nelson, *Presidency*, 183.

term, he left many court appointments unfilled, and thus gave Clinton the glory of filling those federal district and circuit court judgeships instead.[238]

Bush busted the budget with a spending bailout of the failing savings and loan industry, which he projected to cost the taxpayers $166 billion over ten years. This was not only the largest federal bailout in U.S. history, but set the precedent for the unseemly and monstrous bailouts to come in the George W. Bush and Barack Obama administrations. Within a matter of months, the expected cost of the bailout ballooned to $300 billion. The subsidized closing of failed banks and sales of assets is now estimated to cost $500 billion by the year 2030. The industry had indulged in risky real estate investments and poor lending practices. Bankruptcies in other industries also increased.[239]

Bush asked for more money for Medicaid, NASA, the National Science Foundation, federal adoptions, and Head Start, all the while calling for budget reductions. He also proposed to elevate the Environmental Protection Agency (EPA) to cabinet status, as he wanted to get credit for supporting environmental causes.[240]

Bush signed the Americans with Disabilities Act of 1990, which fulfilled a campaign promise to give the disabled access to buildings, transportation, and telecommunications. This program was a significant federal invasion into the state and local police power bailiwick.[241]

Bush inserted a signing statement into the 1991 Civil Rights Act. The statement sought to control interpretation of the act, and set boundaries on its impact on business. The Energy and Water Development Appropriations Act of 1992 prohibited the president from spending certain money relating to pricing of hydroelectric power, so Bush inserted a signing statement saying he would not be bound by that provision. The Whistle Blower Protection Act required the Office of Legislative Council to submit information to both president and Congress at the same time, but Bush inserted a signing statement saying he believed the law did not preclude him from reviewing information before Congress got it.[242]

---

238. Nelson, *Presidency*, 184; Whitney, *Biographies*, 486; McDonald, *Presidency*, 305.

239. Whitney, *Biographies*, 485; Nelson, *Presidency*, 183.

240. Boyer, *Oxford Companion*, 92–93; Miller Center, *G.H.W. Bush—Domestic Affairs*.

241. Miller Center, *G.H.W. Bush—Domestic Affairs*; Boyer, *Oxford Companion*, 92.

242. Crenson and Ginsberg, *Presidential Power*, 199; Cooper, *Order*, 203, 207, 212.

Bush also held on to Reagan's hard-line control of rulemaking. He discouraged and delayed new rules, and even tightened up the level of control by removing it from a statutory agency, the Office of Information and Regulatory Affairs, to the more easily manipulated hands of his vice president, Dan Quayle. On the other hand, since he didn't have the kind of positive domestic policy agenda many other presidents had, he did not regularly remind agency heads of their conservative mission as Reagan had done. As a result, "the proliferation of regulations began," resulting in the code of Federal Regulations reachings 200 volumes and 100,000 pages. He also continued OIRA even after Congress refused to re-authorize the Paperwork Reduction Act.[243]

Bush used presidential memoranda in creative ways. He used memorandums of disapproval sixteen times. There was no statutory authority for Bush's Council on Competitiveness, known as the Quayle Commission. Bush did not even take trouble to issue an executive order or proclamation, or memorandum to create it, but initiated it in a press release in April, 1989.[244]

Bush was vocally less belligerent toward Congress than Reagan, but more aggressive in terms of vetoes. During the campaign he promised to work with Congress, but ended up vetoing forty-four bills, only one of which was overridden. Bush used the veto frequently because his party could prevent an override in Congress. He used the veto fifteen times in 1990 alone. He vetoed bills thirty-five times during his term without an override, until near the end of his term on October, 1992, when the Congress overrode a veto of a bill regulating cable TV rates and standards. He also made fifteen pocket vetoes. He also asked for a line-item veto to give himself more power over Congressional appropriations.[245]

Bush vetoed the Family and Medical Leave Act, though seventy percent of working people supported it. He vetoed a bill to raise the federal minimum wage, and also a voter-registration initiative which would have added additional voters to the Democratic party column. In the words of one commentator, his was a "rule by veto." Bush wanted to run things in favor of big business. For example, he protected the arms manufacturing industry by taking a narrow definition of the kinds of weapons that

243. Crenson and Ginsberg, *Presidential Power*, 206; Cooper, *Order*, 93; McDonald, *Presidency*, 32, 344–45.

244. Cooper, *Order*, 31–32, 90.

245. Miller Center, *G.H.W. Bush—Domestic Affairs*; Whitney, *Biographies*, 485; McDonald, *Presidency*, 355; Flagel, *Guide*, 144; Light, *Agenda*, 286.

were banned as assault weapons. For the same reason he approved arms sales that bolstered the economic success of the U.S. military-industrial sector.[246]

Early in his term, in June, 1989, Bush was confronted with a foreign affairs ethics nightmare when the Chinese military squashed a pro-democracy group demonstrating as much as 100,000 strong in Tiananmen Square. They constructed a model of the Statue of Liberty and participated in hunger strikes. Tens of thousands of soldiers cleared the square and killed as many as three thousand protestors, and wounded possibly 10,000 more. Some eight or more student leaders were sentenced to death, and three were publically executed. These actions exposed the U.S.'s favorite trading partner as a brutal dictatorship. Bush clapped on moderate economic restrictions, then soon eased them, and finally removed sanctions altogether. Throughout the economic sanction process, he refused to break political relations with China. Bush thus demonstrated that the corporate economic interests of his election campaign donors far outweighed the human rights needs of the world's most numerous people. The Congress voted to implement new sanctions, but Bush vetoed this move. Bush refused to end China's Most Favored Nation status with the U.S. Later it was revealed he had conducted diplomacy secretively kept from the Congress, which subverted its interests.[247]

Bush was an activist in foreign affairs, and would have nothing of the people's concerns influencing his unilateral decision-making. He ultimately ordered American forces into action three times during his presidency: in Panama, in the Middle East to liberate Kuwait, and in Somalia.

In August, 1990, Iraq invaded Kuwait, thus threatening U.S. oil interests and the U.S. imposed "stability" of the Middle East. Iraq needed money to pay off its war debts and finance its military. Bush went to work building a political coalition of some twenty-nine countries to add troops to those of the U.S. He deployed the results of Carter's and Reagan's military buildups into U.S. bases in Saudi Arabia and the Persian Gulf for their upcoming use against Saddam. This was the Deseret Shield phase of the war, ostensibly to prevent Saddam from invading Saudi Arabia.[248] The U.N. Security Council imposed a trade and financial embargo on Iraq and for the first time authorized the use of national military forces

---

246. McDonald, *Presidency*, 456; Cooper, *Order*, 102, 166; Flagel, *Guide*, 144.
247. Herring, *Colony to Superpower*, 903–4; Whitney, *Biographies*, 473.
248. Nelson, *Presidency*, 183.

not under U.N. command to enforce national sanctions. This essentially gave the lie to the idea that the U.N acted independently of U.S. wishes.

In November, 1990, the U.N. Security Council issued a declaration enabling the U.S. and its puppet forces "to use all necessary means" to kick Iraq out of Kuwait. The U.S. contributed 500,000 troops to the region, and the coalition nations added another 200,000. Military reserves were called up for overseas action for the first time since the 1968 Tet offensive in the Vietnam War. By February 27, 1991, a cease fire was declared. Bush's war gave him an eighty-nine percent favorable public opinion, even though he had lied about Saddam's intent to invade Saudi Arabia in order to get the war jump-started, and even though he used deficit spending to finance the war budget, placing a heavy burden on America's future generations. Bush had been willing to have Americans pay a much higher price, however. In a letter to his children before the war, Bush wrote that casualties for the United States could be in the tens of thousands and there could be a protracted stalemate in Kuwait. In fact, the war took only 100 hours and cost less than 150 U.S. lives, and Bush was withdrawing forces within four weeks.[249]

Bush summarized American dominance of world affairs during his administration with ringing tones: "Out of these troubled times, a new world order can emerge: a new era, freer from the threat of terror, stronger in the pursuit of justice and more secure in the quest for peace. An era in which the nations of the world, east and west, north and south, can prosper and live in harmony . . . a hundred generations have searched for this elusive path to peace, while a thousand wars raged across the span of human endeavor. Today that new world is struggling to be born . . . A world where the rule of law supplants the rule of the jungle . . . A world where the strong respect the rights of the weak."[250]

Between the lines of this incredible sophistry was the clearly unsupportable notion that the United States, and in particular its already impoverished middle class, could and would be tapped to be the savior of the world. The U.S. nation, itself steeped in political and economic corruption, would be the guide, and source, the gate, the path to world-wide justice and peace. Bush's prophecy was so sodden with ignorance and ineptness that history shows his own son in fact triggered the opposite

249. Herring, *Colony to Superpower*, 909; Miller Center, *G.H.W. Bush—Foreign Affairs*; Whitney, *Biographies*, 475; Flagel, *Guide*, 228.

250. Miller Center, *G.H.W. Bush—Foreign Affairs*.

of what the father promised—new wars and deeper and more pervasive waves of terror and injustice and heedlessness of law.

Desert Storm was a prime example of Bush's New World Order, a way to describe the situation the U.S. found itself in after the demise of the Soviet Union. A document leaked under the pen of Bush's Undersecretary of Defense, Paul Wolfowitz, indicated that the real intent of the NWO was actually quite a bit more sinister than just to make adjustments to a happy new balance of power in which the U.S. found itself to be in a leadership position. The goal of the NWO was to prevent any power from challenging U.S. military supremacy in the world. The document indicated that the U.S. should act preemptively to stop any anti-U.S. activity by any power that might potentially have access to nuclear weapons.[251] This policy position did not fully capture the imagination of the elder Bush, but seized hold of the younger Bush, as we shall see.

The Soviet Union had become, in some ways, a U.S. dependency, which it quickly demonstrated by joining with the U.S. in condemning Hussein's invasion of Kuwait. In fact, Gorbachev and Bush signed a pre-alliance type "mutual non-aggression pact," which meant that the U.S. and Soviet Union now "liked" each other, and were "friends."[252]

William Clinton

Bill Clinton was so ambitious for continuing power that when he lost his reelection bid for governor of Arkansas he went into a period of depression and seclusion.[253] As president, he intended to make sure that didn't happen again. Clinton's presidential election promises made clear to astute observers that he intended to be all things to all people. He served two terms over the years 1993 to 2001.

Clinton followed the political maxim for Democrats that dictated "During the campaign, run hard to the left, and once in office, run hard to the center." He promised to deal with almost every economic issue the federal government could possibly stick its nose into, including unemployment, tariff and trade, taxation, inflation, wages, business regulation, organized labor, and affirmative action. During the campaign he also promised to overhaul health, education and welfare programs. He made

251. Herring, *Colony to Superpower*, 922.
252. Miller Center, *G.H.W. Bush—Foreign Affairs*; Nelson, *Presidency*, 183.
253. Boyer, *Oxford Companion*, 136.

the largely contradictory promises that he would bring the federal budget under control by such measures as "end(ing) welfare as we know it," while at the same time promising to enact a national health insurance program, as big a budget buster as anyone might imagine.[254]

As a "centrist" once in office, he could appeal to all varieties of voters, and hopefully offend few. He could take advantage of every political issue that cropped up by promising or delivering some solution to it, and thus become the ultimate political opportunist, the very definition of a tyrant. In fact, the word "Clintonism" became a euphemism for this tyranny, and was marked by disguised "tax and spend" political opportunism, usurpation of Congressional prerogatives, and private immorality. In spite of personal and political lasciviousness, Clinton gave his presidency a cultic focus by promising a "New Covenant" between government and the people.[255] The biblical new covenant restored ancient Israel's original political and cultural values. But Clinton's program took American further away from her traditional ethical moorings.[256]

Clinton was known in political-speak as a "pragmatist," that is, one who is highly flexible and willing to go where the votes are. He felt that there was a great market for votes in the female population and was a "master" at appeal to them. Bill Clinton told women he understood how hard and unappreciated their lot was and that he would protect their economic and social interests. In order to effectuate his promise to protect women and children, he issued memoranda on missing children, child support, teen parents, family friendly work places, family violence, adoption, family medical leave, child care, children's health insurance, family planning, second chance homes for pregnant teens, guaranteed hospital overnights for new mothers, and use of the internet to increase adoptions. Ultimately, however, his administration could hardly be judged socially positive or even socially neutral or harmless. For example, Clinton declined to regulate derivatives in the banking industry, thus playing a key role in forcing tens of millions of families to suffer catastrophic mortgage losses less than a decade after his exit from the presidency during the great recession of 2008.[257]

254. Crenson and Ginsberg, *Presidential Power*, 200; Boyer, *Oxford Companion*, 136.

255. Healy, *Cult of the Presidency*, 124.

256. Light, *Agenda*, 295; Boyer, *Oxford Companion*, 136.

257. David Brooks, PBS Nightly News, 10-19-12; PBS Nightly News, interview with Sheila Bair, author of *Bull By the Horns*, 10-19-12.

Because of his predecessor's slowness in appointing federal judges, Clinton was able to appoint more than 100 federal district and circuit court judges. Clinton also appointed some 300 unelected officials to populate his executive office of the president and help him usurp power. If one factors in consultants, volunteers, security staff and interns, that staff ballooned up to around 6,000.[258]

Clinton's fundamental political strategy was a familiar one when compared against populist tyrants of the past. He intended to be adorable and trustworthy by working overtime to be popular. One commentator says he made "unrelenting effort to cultivate public sympathy." He "virtually never stopped campaigning." He used political consultants who put a wet finger to the wind to determine what direction the crowd was leaning, and then made great effort to lean in that direction too. He was the ultimate example of the "public presidency," and thus of the political opportunist and careerist. After a Republican sweep of Congress in 1994, he let out a rash of "poll-tested micro-initiatives," essentially highly opportunistic vote-buying schemes designed to enhance the glory of his administration even during hard political times. Also, if opinion ran in a direction he did not want to go, he spent money to influence public opinion, often using questionable fund raising tactics to get a hold of the money. In his reelection campaign he used "soft money" for himself rather than divide it among the wide range of Democratic Party candidates it was intended for. He essentially sold access to White House coffees and White House recreational facilities, provided flights on Air Force One and seats in the Kennedy Center presidential box, all to loosen up campaign donations, and thus used public facilities for unauthorized purposes.[259]

In his first year Clinton pushed seventeen legislative proposals, while his predecessor had pushed only five. He touched upon almost every hot button issue the electorate cared about, including campaign finance reform, and health care lobby reform. By the end of his second year he had won approval of a federal family leave law, which was deeply intrusive into state economic affairs, a federal motor vehicle voter registration act, the Brady gun-control law, the NAFTA foreign trade law, and

258. McDonald, *Presidency*, 305; Flagel, *Guide*, 298.

259. Light, *Agenda*, 281; Healy, *Cult of the Presidency*, 125; Adler and Genovese, *The Clinton Legacy*, 143–44.

an increase in the minimum wage to $5.15 per hour. He averaged eight major legislative proposals per year while in office.[260]

Clinton supported a conservative program to limit access to welfare benefits for legal immigrants, but fought attempts to take away public education for illegal immigrants. By executive decree he enacted a "Don't ask, don't tell," policy for gays in the military. This policy was then challenged by Congress in a defense authorization bill.[261]

Clinton pushed the central government deeply into traditionally local education issues. Clinton's policy crew discussed proposals for mandatory school uniforms and a national tutoring initiative. He also stepped into the slippers of Daddy of the Nation by trying to control local criminal justice affairs. He proposed cell phones for citizen crime watch groups and safety locks for handguns, in addition to the television V-chip and a national registry of sex offenders.

Clinton tried to buy votes by a crass means that many earlier presidents refused to stoop to. He distributed extra disaster relief to states that were politically important to his reelection campaign. He holds the record for seventy-five disaster declarations involving federal handouts prior to his reelection campaign in 1996.[262]

Clinton furthered developed the massive internal security spy capability initiated by prior presidents. Civil liberties groups decried his presidential directive PD5-5, which provided for the installation of technology to decode encrypted messages in communications circuits, preparatory to turning on the capability after court order.[263]

The Republicans won both houses of Congress during the mid-term elections in 1994, the first time in forty years. They called for a balanced budget amendment, budget cuts, and reduced taxes. Clinton then announced his deepening commitment to centrist policies like cutting taxes, cracking down on illegal immigration, and changing welfare programs. He also turned against his own budget and announced he would work with Republicans to balance the budget within seven years, with no tax increases. To help him get control of the budget he also asked for a line-item veto.

260. Light, *Agenda*, 278, 288, 293; Boyer, *Oxford Companion*, 137.

261. Miller Center, *Clinton—Domestic Affairs*.

262. Healy, *Cult of the Presidency*, 208.

263. Cooper, *Order*, 189.

After Democrats lost the mid-term elections of 1994, Clinton decided he would legislate without Congress. This he would do by executive decree and related instruments of constitutional usurpation, such as the aggressive use of veto for policy purposes. He vetoed seventeen bills in the next two years, including spending cuts he did not like. He used the vetoes in three main areas: to reverse earlier abortion restrictions; trade and employment; and environment. Clinton left the nation an explanation of his thinking process. "I had overemphasized in my first two years . . . the importance of legislative battles as opposed to the other things that the president might be doing." By the time he had caught on to the possibilities for doing whatever it was he wanted to do, he was able to gleefully announce, "I love this job."[264]

Clinton set a pattern that later presidents would use to justify unilateral tyrannical action. When the other political party recaptured a good deal of political ground it had lost to a president, the chief executive would now re-double his efforts to govern without the opposition. Clinton assailed the general Congressional unwillingness to enact his program by arguing, "I am taking this action today [on privacy protections] because Congress has failed to act." Clinton also had the authority of his own vice president to encourage him. Al Gore's National Performance Review recommended that Clinton skirt Congress and even his own agency rule-making and make laws and policies on his own. After a period of time watching Clinton govern this way, the Christian Science Monitor wrote, "It's been a mark of the Clinton administration to rule by executive fiat."[265]

Clinton's labor friends complained loudly that he "do something" for them. Thus, in 1995 he issued Executive Order 12954 barring federal contracts over $100,000 with firms that use scabs as permanent replacement of strikers. He did this after failing to get legislation through Congress on this in 1994. This "end run around Capitol Hill" was known as the Striker Replacement Order. Later, a circuit court found that this decree conflicted with the National Labor Relations Act. One author indicates that in the matter of the striker replacement order Clinton interpreted the constitutional "duty to take care" to faithfully implement the laws so broadly that it "swallows the rest of the Constitution ."[266]

---

264. Boyer, *Oxford Companion*, 136–37; Whitney, *Biographies*, 503–4; Flagel, *Guide*, 27; Adler and Genovese, *Clinton Legacy*, 7.

265. Cooper, *Order*, 3, 17, 221.

266. Ibid., 55, 238.

Some of the president's executive orders not only wrecked havoc with the horizontal separation of powers between Congress and the executive branch, but also the vertical separation of powers between the central and the state governments. An executive decree on the American Heritage Rivers Initiative overrode land use powers of states and localities. His executive decrees and presidential memoranda also allowed federal agencies to take away money from states and localities where environment consequences adversely affected minorities. In 1996, he set aside two million acres in southern Utah to create the Grand Staircase-Escalante National Monument. In his last days in office, Clinton closed off millions of acres of land to development in ten states, using an outdated 1906 law, The Antiquities Act, to designate these areas as protected.[267]

His western lands proclamations shocked America. This would be like a state bringing back an unenforced, hundred year old adultery law still on the books and enforcing it in the late twentieth century. Senator Larry Craig of Idaho worried, "King William want(s) to reign . . . These are not the King's lands, these are the people's lands . . ." One author lamented "the absolutist pretensions of Bill Clinton, which harken to the swollen claims of the Stuart kings . . ." Clinton signed thirty executive decrees on environmental and national resources issues alone, including the Children's Environment Protection Act.[268]

Clinton had campaigned to enact legislation related to the environment and civil rights. In furtherance of this, he issued Executive Order 12898, known as the Environmental Justice for Minority Populations order. It provided for improved decision-making for industrial "siting" decisions. He did not mention any authority except "by the authority vested in me." He issued a memorandum to go along with it invoking civil rights laws which overruled the permit-making decisions of local communities. He used these two vehicles to get around his own administration's rule-making procedure. Some thirty-four state EPA offices sent letters of protest, and mayors, counties, and governors associations joined in the protest. They claimed that land use regulation was always a state and local function and that the administration's new direction failed to address the economic development side of the equation. States and localities would

---

267. Crenson and Ginsberg, *Presidential Power*, 200–201; Adler and Genovese, *Clinton Legacy*, 8.

268. Cooper, *Order*, 118; Crenson and Ginsberg, *Presidential Power*, 200; Adler and Genovese, *Clinton Legacy*, 8.

be stymied by federal delays and litigation by individuals filing suits before exhausting other remedies.[269]

Clinton also issued significant policy changes via presidential memoranda. Few members of Congress were even aware of this particular "presidential direction action tool." In fact, there is no written process for developing one, no requirement to publish it in the Federal Register, and no numbering or indexing to keep track of them. Clinton issued memoranda to stop the abortion "gag rule" related to counseling of patients in federally-funded family planning clinics, lift a moratorium on funding for fetal tissue experimentation, reverse a ban on abortions in military hospitals, end the Mexico City policy of Reagan which specified that aid be withheld from non-government organizations promoting abortions, re-examine the ban on importation of the abortion pill and push to produce it locally, end discrimination against gays in the military, withhold education funding from states without a strong policy against guns in schools, and outline a national Patient's Bill of Rights. While Kennedy issued only twenty-two memoranda during his term, Ford fifty-four, and Carter ninety-three, Clinton ultimately issued some 536 of them.[270] They are used for a variety of reasons: to circumvent Congress and the Constitution, handle hot problems quickly, generate favorable publicity at a vulnerable moment, take rapid action, pay personal political debts, and reward supporters.

If Reagan and G.H.W. Bush used signing statements for "conservative" purposes, Clinton used them to enhance "liberal" causes. The 1996 Defense Appropriations bill required the discharge of HIV-positive military members even if still fit to serve. Clinton ordered his Justice Department not to defend the HIV ban if it was challenged in court and also backed efforts to change the law. He would only enforce the provision as far as to get a test case in order to try to have it overthrown. Clinton increased by fifty percent the number of signing statements under Reagan, bringing the number of his own up to 105.[271]

Clinton had campaigned to make executive department rules easier to make. But he then kept virtually all of the suffocating Reagan/Bush rulemaking orders in place and added more of his own in Executive Order 12866. For example, he developed a process for making "regulatory

269. Cooper, *Order*, 106–12.
270. Ibid., 81–82, 84, 86, 91, 101.
271. Cooper, *Order*, 217–18; Crenson and Ginsberg, *Presidential Power*, 199–200.

prompts." These were orders instructing agencies to adopt particular regulations over and above the law. Reagan was into prevention of rule-writing he did not want, and stopping the implementation of rules he didn't like. But Clinton was into affirmatively writing what he wanted, that is, pure proactive lawmaking. Clinton published 107 rules that originated in the White House as independent (and illegal) rulemaking. These rules promulgated new laws for health and human services, commerce, labor, agriculture, interior, and treasury. The rules had content related to things like gun-control, water pollution, patients' rights, parental leave, food and drug, and tobacco. Overall, Clinton published forty-three "presidential directives" (executive orders or memoranda), designed to allow him to take control away from administrative agencies and concentrate that control in his own hand.[272]Clinton also extended Reagan's rule process of hard line political review of policies to independent agencies like the Social Security Administration. He required them to submit annual regulatory agendas to him. These agencies were placed by Congress outside of presidential control, but Clinton undid that.

Bill Clinton expanded the concept of executive privilege in an "indefensible manner," given the fact that constitutional scholar Raoul Berger maintains that executive privilege for secrecy does not exist in the U.S. Constitution. Clinton made an early claim for executive privilege when a Congressional committee investigated firings of Travel Office staff in 1993. He made similar claims during the investigation of wrongdoing by agricultural secretary Mike Espy, during Congress's attempt to obtain an anti-Clinton memo written by FBI director Louis Freeh, during the investigation of the Monica Lewinsky affair, and when trying to shield the first lady's conversations with White House attorneys. Clinton asserted the existence of presidential immunity from civil suits. The Supreme Court denied his claim that he had temporary immunity from a civil damages suit (for sexual harassment) arising from before he took office.[273]

He also abused presidential pardon power when he pardoned sixteen members of a Puerto Rican revolutionary organization that had planted seventy or more bombs in restaurants and shopping malls. He did not follow the prescribed pardon procedure and used the pardons to curry favor with New York City Puerto Ricans for his wife Hillary, who was running for the Senate from New York state. He also pardoned white

272. Cooper, *Order*, 61, 63, 82; Crenson and Ginsberg, *Presidential Power*, 208–09.
273. Adler and Genovese, *Clinton Legacy*, xxvi, 58, 66–68, 73.

collar fugitive Mark Rich, whose wife was a prominent fundraiser for the president and the Democratic party. [274]

In the election year of 1996, Clinton sensed the nation was shifting to the right, so he shifted right along with them. He agreed to limit the rate of increase in Medicare, a policy he had previously labeled as extremist. He accepted the idea of tax cuts, without consulting his party, a sure sign of a tyrant in self-aggrandizing mode. His budget agreement with the Republican Congress did allow him some new spending in education and health care for children. He announced that "the era of big government is over," and thus branded himself as a very poor prophet. He took on some conservative Republican themes by speaking out against violent and pornographic depictions in popular culture. He spoke against minority quota programs, and in favor of a constitutional amendment allowing school prayer. He embraced welfare reform passed by the Congress and signed it into law over the objections of his party and his cabinet. The legislation "cut" $55 billion over the next six years, and was a huge shift from the bill he initially proposed, which would have added $10 billion more in one welfare program area.[275] It also ended the guarantee of cash assistance to support children that had been in effect since Franklin Roosevelt's term, and shifted some program responsibility to the states.

In September, 1998, Clinton reported a budget surplus of $70 billion, the first since 1969. He reached an agreement with Congress to set aside the surplus, while winning concessions on education, farm relief, and IMF funding. Congress adjourned without settling how to use the budget surplus, and by default it was used to pay down the national debt. Later in his second term he pushed for Medicaid and Social Security finance reform and initiated a Presidential Initiative on Race. In 1999 Clinton signed the Financial Reform Bill, which allowed banks, brokerage firms, and insurance companies to enter into combinations, thus undermining the century of progress made in limiting trust conglomerations. In his 2000 State of the Union address, Clinton bragged that "the state of our union is the strongest it has ever been."[276] This was only months before the "dot com" recession hit.

As a young man, Bill Clinton had opposed the undeclared war in Vietnam. By the time he finished his presidency he had become a prime

---

274. Ibid., xxvii, 84–85, 121.

275. Boyer, *Oxford Companion*, 136; Whitney, *Biographies*, 504–5.

276. Whitney, *Biographies*, 513–14, 519, 521.

proponent and author of undeclared U.S. wars. As president, he came to realize that war presidents become heroes and less imperialist chief executives get lost in the shuffle of the great ones. He once said, "I envy Kennedy having an enemy." But Clinton was not one to sit and fret. He took up the challenge. He mused, "The question now is how to persuade people they could do things when they are not immediately threatened." By the time Clinton was finished he really got the hang of "doing things." He employed the military eighty-four times in eight years in office. This included cruise missile attacks on Iraq in 1993 and 1996, an invasion of Somalia in 1993, air strikes in Bosnia in 1994, cruise missile attacks on Afghanistan and Sudan in 1998, and an air war in Kosovo in 1999. His war in Bosnia was "the most intensive and sustained military campaign conducted by the United States since the Vietnam War." He was the first to use force in contravention of Congressional refusal to authorize such force against Serbs in 1999. He hinted he would veto legislation requiring him to get authorization for intervention in Haiti. On the soft side of the ledger, he sent his secretary of state to help negotiate peace terms in the Middle East and Northern Ireland, as a good imperial land-master should.[277]

Clinton used the U.S. military to divert attention from his political and sexual scandals at home. On one particular Monday, he admitted his affair with Monica Lewinsky on national TV and gave sworn testimony before the grand jury. Clinton understood that the week would only be going downhill from there and felt he needed a diversion to draw the American people's attention away from him. In fact, on Thursday of the same week, Lewinsky started her second round of testimony in front of the grand jury and it came out that Clinton had given a DNA sample to an independent investigative group studying his behavior. Not so coincidentally, on the same Thursday Clinton ordered surprise strikes against Sudan and Afghanistan involving seventy-five sorties designed to stir the public interest. One author wrote, "It was one of the few times that summer that another event managed to compete with the Lewinsky affair for public attention." He was grasping at straws, particularly in Sudan, where he relied on a trumped-up charge of Sudan having weapons of mass destruction and a serious connection to Osama bin Laden.[278]

---

277. Healy, *Cult of the Presidency*, 280; Boyer, *Oxford Companion*, 136; Herring, *Colony to Superpower*, 936; Adler and Genovese, *Clinton Legacy*, xxvi, 3, 35, 39 .

278. Whitney, *Biographies*, 511–12; Healy, *Cult of the Presidency*, 127.

Later on, on the eve of the House impeachment debate, Clinton began his Desert Fox air strikes in Iraq. His stated reason was that Iraq was resisting cooperation with UN weapons inspectors. This episode of hiding under the cover of military fireworks had the untoward effect of derailing any possibility of an Iraq inspection system for another four years. But more importantly, some viewers of the nightly news focused on Iraq instead of on Clinton's sexual adventures. One author summarizes quite cogently, Clinton was "risking lives to cling to power."[279]

Military spending continued at a high level throughout the Clinton years. It was $325 billion in 1995. At this level, it was six times more than the next six largest national war budgets combined. The electorate expected Clinton to revoke Reagan's active policy of arms sales abroad, but Clinton's PDD-34 in February, 1995 maintained the policy, which underscored the importance Clinton placed on supporting the financial health of the armament industry. Clinton also proposed a scaled-down version of Reagan's Star Wars missile defense system.[280]

In his last two years in office, Clinton pursued trade agreements with China, Vietnam and other nations, thus helping to prop up their communist regimes and undermine American jobs at home. He also urged support of the World Trade Organization, which aimed at increasing global trade and America's participation and leadership in the new trading patterns.[281]

Clinton pushed through NAFTA and a revision of GATT in 1993 and 1994, respectively. These "free trade" agreements institutionalized U.S. economic hegemony in the New World Order. Clinton could not get passage of these treaties using the two-thirds majority required by the U.S. Constitution, so he won their confirmation by means of the fifty percent requirement of a joint resolution. Clinton abused power when he authorized $20 billion in loan guarantees to Mexico from the Exchange Stabilization Fund. Congress said the fund never was intended to be used this way. [282]

Clinton's "free trade" philosophy included, conspicuously, U.S. freedom to trade openly and happily with the regime oppressing by far the

---

279. Healy, *Cult of the Presidency*, 127–28, 199; Whitney, *Biographies*, 516.

280. Cooper, *Order*, 166; Herring, *From Colony to Superpower*, 921.

281. Whitney, *Biographies*, 501.

282. Crenson and Ginsberg, *Presidential Power*, 255; Adler and Genovese, *Clinton Legacy*, 7.

greatest number of human beings on the planet. Like Nixon, Carter, and Bush before him, Clinton ignored human rights violations in China in order to keep the trade flowing between the plutocrats there and American corporate moguls. He gave China Most Favored Nation trading status without any quid pro quo related to political rights for the Chinese people. This made Clinton a flip-flopping hypocrite, since he had only shortly before accused George H.W. Bush of "coddling tyrants from Baghdad . . . to Beijing."[283]

283. Herring, *Colony to Superpower*, 927.

$$7$$

The Twenty-First-Century Presidents

There are only two presidents in our last group of chief executives, George W. Bush and Barack Obama. They represent virtually the beginning of emperorship in America. During both presidencies, the Congress basically abdicated the great majority of their constitutional responsibilities and allowed these two all powerful governors and their bloated bureaucracies to single-handedly rule the nation and the world. The more that court historians and their followers try to make these two into opposites, the clearer it actually becomes they are but flip sides of the same coin. Both have devoted the entire national treasury, including civilian and military accounts, into making themselves great and heroic presidents. The Republican George Bush believes he is the liberator of foreign lands from tyranny and oppression and the protector of the homeland from foreign assaults. The Democrat Barack Obama believes that he is the hero of the oppressed classes at home. Both believe fervently that their holy goals justify unholy, that is, unconstitutional, means. It is too soon to have a clear historical fix on all their many usurpations of law, but an attempt will be made here to provide a brief outline.

George W. Bush

Dead certain, and often dead wrong. George Bush, like Grover Cleveland before him, was a confirmed moralist and an obstinate leader. Speaking of stem cell research, Bush said "It is important that the president be a moral educator . . ."Like Cleveland, he thought the citizenry needed to be led, and didn't want them to get uppity. Bush didn't ask them to stretch themselves very far, saying, "I ask you to lead your lives, and hug your children." But unlike Cleveland, who was right on many of the important issues of the day, George W. Bush got major things wrong—things like whether Iraq possessed weapons of mass destruction and what it means to be a compassionate conservative. He got things wrong because he read court histories, books written to promote the interests of the wealthy and powerful, rather than critical histories, books that go deeper, books that dig down to uncover legitimate dissent and promote the rule of law.[1]

George W. Bush was a small town Texas boy who trafficked as hard as he could on his rural roots when he got into politics. But politically, economically, and culturally he was a big city aristocrat with deep family roots in Yankee New England. Bush famously leaped ahead of 500 applicants for the National Guard to avoid Vietnam combat. In 1976, he was arrested for DUI and was a problem drinker until 40 years old, when he quit for good. He had a "Roman candle temper" and, in the words of his wife, did "pretty much everything to excess." It has been said that Bush had a deep suspicion of intellectuals in high school and college and that he trusted his emotions (essentially, his beliefs and faith) more than his intellect. In fact, at Yale, he was not a particularly good student, and preferred to concentrate on social activities with friends.[2]

Bush ran for U.S. Congress from West Texas. During the race his opponent correctly criticized him for getting the greatest portion of his campaign money from outside the district, from his elite, corporate connections. He lost the race but continued to build an oil business while his father served two terms as vice president of the U.S. Later, Bush sold his oil business and moved to Washington, DC to help his father run for president. On his father's campaign team, he liked to say "I was a loyalty enforcer . . ." After his father's election, he borrowed money, became a managing partner in the Texas Rangers baseball team, and led the drive to build a "glittering new stadium" to entertain the middle class, while the poor living in Texas cities slipped further into abject poverty. His subsequent popularity in the professional sporting world propelled him to the governorship of Texas, where he served two terms of office while Clinton was president. He used his father's campaign organizers to help him run

1. Draper, *Dead Certain*, 125, 155.

2. Flagel, *Guide*, 64–65; Matuz, *Fact Book*, 735; Draper, *Dead Certain*, 31, 35, 39, 45.

for governor, and promised "hot button," hard-nosed reforms in welfare and criminal justice, while also promising local school district autonomy. As governor he styled himself a "compassionate conservative," one who supported government-sponsored welfare and education rather than traditional limited government and individual responsibility. He also pushed juvenile justice and tort reform. Texans love bigness, and George W. was one of the biggest of the big. He frequently bragged that he was governor of "the second biggest state and the twelfth biggest economy in the world."[3]

Bush's personal religious devotional life as a Methodist was sincere, but his interpretation of biblical politics was not well grounded in scholarship. After the September 11 tragedy, he appeared in front of a joint session of Congress and parroted the words of Jesus, saying "Either you are with us, or you are with the terrorists . . . One cannot serve two masters." He did not seem to understand, or did not care, that the "two masters" reference in the New Testament referred, on the one hand, to a politically disengaged lifestyle of ignorant materialism, and on the other hand to tolerant faith, learning, and social activism. The two masters reference had nothing to do with criminal terrorism, but it certainly served to give his military crusade a mask of legitimacy.[4]

Aside from religious soft-heartedness and wrong-headedness, Bush was ambitious, cold-hearted, and willing to say anything and do almost anything to get and keep power. For example, while on the first campaign trail, Bush used rough tactics in South Carolina to marginalize his competitor, John McCain. McCain chided Bush for his methods: "I want the presidency in the best way, not the worst way." He also didn't mind being a hypocrite. In his autobiography, *A Charge to Keep*, he wrote that he was motivated to run for president because "It seemed to me that elite central planners were determining the course of our nation. I wanted to do something about it." In fact, Bush then became one of the most formidable elitist central planners the nation had ever seen, centralizing decision-making in his own hands so thoroughly and expanding federal spending so far that he upped the level of political centralism to new heights. He raised more money than any other candidate ever had, an "obscene war chest" of $193 million.[5]

3. Matuz, *Fact Book*, 736–37; Draper, *Dead Certain*, 21, 44.

4. Flagel, *Guide*, 43–45.

5. Miller Center, *George W. Bush—Campaigns and Elections*; Matuz, *Fact Book*, 733; Draper, *Dead Certain*, 5.

George W. was a corporation-based populist. He took money from financial and industrial interests who understood there were some issues to deal with in society, and used that money, once he was elected, to divvy benefits out to consumers. Those consumers were suffering a loss of economic standing at the hands of those same corporate interests that he represented. They were now feeling a bit guilty for their transgressions. While allowing George some latitude with their money, at the same time the interests would keep an eye on him to see that he did not go too far. George was essentially a Federalist like Alexander Hamilton, and a National Republican like John Quincy Adams. He wanted to expand presidential power and at the same time expand national power, thus making the nation much like a mildly limited monarchy. To achieve these two objectives, he was willing to spend lots of money on people's problems. While conservatives like John Boehner were still calling for closing down the federal department of education, George was promising not to close down the department of education, and instead, to spend $2.9 billion for teacher training.[6]

During the campaign George trafficked in his lack of Washington experience by positioning himself as an outsider. He declined to mention, for example, his many eastern business and Washington political connections. He didn't like being "defined" by others, those others being the press and other politicians. He would do the defining, not them. He and his handlers decided the best persona to project to the people and delivered it with a "micro-targeted message campaign." Near the end of the campaign, for example, the team brought in Richard Cheney to tell the folks in West Virginia that free trader Bush could work with them. He promised tariff protection for steel and steelworkers.[7]

Bush also argued for tax cuts during the campaign, offering the seductive argument that "the surplus is not the government's money; the surplus is the people's money." Bush also spoke of himself in the third person: "President George W. Bush will keep the promise of Social Security . . . no changes, no reductions, no way." Once elected, however, he proposed a radical change in the program and attempted to get it passed. Bush had to try to find a way to reach the humongous voting public. Some seventy percent of adult Americans could vote in 2004, in contrast with only four percent in 1789. According to his "breakout"

6. Draper, *Dead Certain*, 80, 115.
7. Ibid., 99, 101.

new political philosophy of self-definition and micro-persuasion, both of which in actuality came from the Clinton administration, Bush could win the support of women by pushing educational funding, since education was a big female issue. Moreover, increased federal involvement in education could be seen and justified as a response to poverty. He could reach people on the left by demonstrating his concern for green issues. After early-on reversing a liberal EPA announcement relating to carbon dioxide, Bush went on tour to outdoor venues like the Everglades and Sequoia National Park and inhaled the good, green political air and photo opportunities at those places.[8]

Bush was, among other good things of his own defining, a "reformer with results." He also was "a uniter, not a divider." Bush was also into appearances. He wanted the campaign stages he spoke from to "look presidential," and that led to the construction of "sweeping backdrops," like Hollywood sets. Later, during his administration, his Office of Public Liaison staged 400 presidential appearances per year, all tightly controlled to promote the chief and his compassion. He was on one of those events in Florida, speaking to a second grade reading class with lots of African-American kids, when the World Trade Center was hit.[9]

Bush was in favor of big, but didn't know much about the big, bad world outside of the United States. During the campaign he was asked by a reporter to name any of the four leaders of the four hot spots in the world at the time. In his answer, he stumbled badly and was embarrassed. From now on, he would plant questioners in the audience who would ask him questions he knew the answers to, or else would screen attendees for loyalty and friendliness before they could get tickets to his events. Like Grover Cleveland, Bush also turned his back on the press and froze them out of his life. A press conference was an opportunity to lose control of his message, to lose his propaganda edge and fumble it over to a press sharpie. He was vindictive like that. After winning the governorship he said, "Blacks didn't come out for me like the Hispanics did, so they're not gonna see much help from me." As president, Bush was "edgy, incurious, insulated." Others described him as "immaleable," "disengaged," "in denial" about Iraq. There was little learning left in him. He often said, "You know where I stand." And like most tyrants, where he stood was self-preservation.[10]

8. Samples, *Struggle*, 214; Flagel, *Guide*, 55; Draper, *Dead Certain*, 121.

9. Draper, *Dead Certain*, 7–8, 63, 71–72, 75, 78, 100, 134.

10. Ibid., 11, 46, 108, 234, 291, 360.

Bush certainly had a compulsion to accomplish "big things," a type of megalomania common to ancient as well as modern tyrants. Without knowing much about the subject matter (foreign affairs), he told Vladimir Putin of Russia, "Let's not get stuck in history." "[Let's] make history together." Not worrying about the fact Putin had been a life-long KGB agent in Leninist-Stalinist Russia and that re-Stalinization was moving ahead rapidly in Putin's Russia, he announced, "Russia is not the enemy of the United States."[11] He promised, "We will write not footnotes, but chapters in the American story." And true enough, Bush left out any footnotes documenting evidence of weapons of mass destruction in Iraq, and wrote instead a great big fluffy chapter detailing presidential aggression in the Middle East that he hoped would enshrine his name for all time as a great military leader.[12]

Bush promised to hire Democrats in his cabinet and not to engage in partisan rancor like that seen between Clinton and the Republican Congress. But ultimately, Bush appointed only a single Democrat. On the other hand, he went on to surround himself with advisors who had served in his father's administration, and some of the most conservative members of the Ford and Reagan administrations. He picked Dick Cheney as vice president because he was smart, loyal to the Bushes, and did not have any ambition to unseat his boss in the future. George W. was not into sharing the presidency with anybody. He told his staff, "I'm glad to have you, but I don't need you." His agenda was important, not theirs. A group of these came to be called the neo-conservatives, or neo-cons, since they broke with traditional conservatives who had supported smaller government, balanced budgets, and multinational cooperation. In fact, annual federal spending jumped by $400 billion by the end of the first Bush term, as he signed new federal mandates in education, health care, homeland security, and a variety of other spendy measures. The incongruity between his words and his deeds proved once again that political faction names and slogans like "neo-conservative" and "compassionate conservative" serve mainly to obscure real political orientation rather than enlighten the electorate as to the intentions of the politician. The loss of several hundred thousand lives in wars of foreign adventurism could hardly be labeled as "compassionate," unless one was amused by the fact most of the dead were foreigners. In addition, there was nothing new

11. Ibid., 105, 132–33.
12. Whitney, *Biographies*, 528; Draper, *Dead Certain*, 95.

about domestic repression and foreign war. That pairing was as old as the hills.[13]

George Bush was determined to take political advantage of prevailing healthy economic winds at the time of the 2000 presidential election. He had available to him some $500 billion in budget surpluses that had accumulated over the three year period from 1998–2000. He openly concurred with the Congressional Budget Office that there would be a $5.6 trillion dollar revenue surplus over the next ten years. Thus, something had to be done with all this extra cash floating around before the country quite drowned in it. During the summer of 2000, when the federal budget was in surplus, candidate Bush proposed a trillion dollar tax cut over ten years. He said that the surplus was the people's money. He was so determined to curry votes with this policy proposal that his campaign internet site allowed browsers to calculate how much money they would get back if they voted for Bush. If he entertained the right with his tax proposal, Bush would also curry favor with the rest of the electorate with his education proposal. In Texas he had become an absolute nerd on the subject, and centrally-controlled education in Washington, as it had in Austin, would appeal to the center-left. In fact, George W. soon was working with Ted Kennedy to accomplish the plan, which he called No Child Left Behind. In his first term he also pursued other big ticket items. He set up commissions to work on reform in energy policy and Social Security, expanded federal funding for religious social services, and signed a Medicare prescription plan, in addition to tax cuts and No Child.[14]

In Bush's first year in office in 2001, he and the Congress agreed on a $1.35 trillion retroactive tax cut that increased the standard deduction for marrieds (deflating the "marriage penalty"), doubled the child credit, eliminated the estate tax (for the rich), and reduced marginal tax rates for the top three brackets, with the highest bracket getting the biggest break. It also exempted millions from paying taxes and created a new ten percent bracket for the working poor. Also in 2001 he signed a law providing for large subsidies for big agriculture, some $180 billion over ten years. He extended unemployment benefits and gave tax relief for investment in plants and equipment.[15]

13. Whitney, *Biographies*, 527, 533; Draper, *Dead Certain*, 90, 102–03.

14. Flagel, *Guide*, 127; Miller Center, *George W. Bush—Domestic Affairs*; Draper, *Dead Certain*, 113, 117–20, 127; Whitney, *Biographies*, 528.

15. Miller Center, *George W. Bush—Domestic Affairs*; Wikipedia, *George W. Bush*, 8; Whitney, *Biographies*, 534, 545.

Then, in 2002 Bush signed another tax cut which amounted to some $350 billion. Then, again, a year later, in 2003, he gave in to pressure to accelerate some of the phased-in cuts of the initial tax legislation, so he signed the Economic Stimulus Act giving most taxpayers rebates of $600 and lower-income taxpayers $300, just in time to leaven up their votes for his reelection campaign in 2004. He also heavily reduced taxes on dividends and capital gains. With these various tax benevolences he was essentially celebrating his ascension to power and his great leader generosity like an ancient tyrant king. In addition, he claimed his tax cuts were "principled," though they enhanced financial "principal" for the wealthy more so than for the middle class and the poor. The percentage below the poverty line increased each of Bush's first four years.[16]

Bush's tax cuts failed to increase jobs much, though perhaps shortened the "dot com" recession of 2001 somewhat. In fact, the jobs situation was hampered by the Bush administration's continuation of the nation's large trade deficits, a consequence of outsourcing manufacturing overseas. Overall, Bush turned a budget surplus—$230 billion in Clinton's last year—into the largest national deficit in the nation's history by 2004—some $413 billion.[17] Few voting Americans seemed to understand that reducing revenues and increasing spending was irresponsible public policy and would lead to deficits.

Bush's sponsorship of the No Child Left Behind public education bill in his first term marked the final end of the Republican party tradition of bucking unconstitutional involvement of the federal government in local and state school board activities, bucking the usurping of parental discretion in education, and promising to abolish the federal department of education. Bush did not even attempt to act like a traditional Republican. He jumped ship and stuck the central government nose into every school house in America. His was such a big government intervention bill that he had no trouble getting bi-partisan support. In signing the legislation January 2002, he accomplished something like the equivalent of his Medicare Part D spending program in health care, only for education. While liberals complained that Bush slashed funding for the program by $90 million only a month after signing the law, No Child ultimately increased Department of Education funding by sixty percent. For all this effort, the nation saw some minimal increases in math and reading test

16. Whitney, *Biographies*, 549; Wikipedia, *George W. Bush*, 7–8.

17. Miller Center, *George W. Bush—Domestic Affairs*,

scores. However, the legislation forced huge costs on state budgets to administer the law, which offset the increased federal expenditures in the states. No Child passed in early 2002, along with a large budget increase in non-defense discretionary spending, at a time when the nation's deficit was beginning to soar into the stratosphere.[18]

By the time of mid-term elections in 2002, Bush's message had changed from the economy to national security, the war with Iraq was pending, and all hell was about to break loose with regard to Bush's usurpation of the rule of law. During mid-terms, Bush did what traditional presidents refused to do, interfere in state electoral politics. He "vigorously" campaigned for congressional candidates. In the process, he jettisoned the idea of bi-partisan compromise on issues. During his campaigning for Republicans, he stressed Democrat reluctance to support his version of a Department of Homeland Security bill. In March, 2003, Bush created the Office of Homeland Security on his own by decree. His creation of the cabinet-level Office of Homeland Security by use of Executive Order 13228 relied on "the authority invested in me." The new department of government consolidated twenty-two federal agencies and created a large new group of federal employees taking charge of passenger- and baggage-screening at airports.[19] It was the largest increase in federal employment since Roosevelt's New Deal in the 1930s and the largest reorganization of the federal government since Truman's in 1947.

Aside from his tax-cut cash giveaway programs, Bush had an Easter basket-full of happy policy surprises leading up to his reelection effort. One of the brightly-colored eggs in his basket was the federal disaster relief program. Bush increased the number of federal disaster declarations beyond even the world record pace of Bill Clinton. After the Katrina disaster, Bush promised, "We're going to rebuild this place." Just like that. Three years later, however, only fifty percent of the proposed FEMA grants had been paid out.[20] The Katrina debacle demonstrated that the national government was incompetent to handle humanitarian operations at home, much less to handle them in far-flung places abroad.

---

18. Miller Center, *George W. Bush—Domestic Affairs*; Matus, *Fact Book*, 754; Samples, *Struggle*, 215.

19. Draper, *Dead Certain*, 170–71; Miller Center, *George W. Bush—Campaigns and Elections*; Crenson and Ginsberg, *Presidential Power*, 201; Cooper, *Order*, 32; Whitney, *Biographies*, 544–45.

20. Healy, *Cult of the Presidency*, 208; Matuz, *Fact Book*, 752.

In the 2004 reelection campaign, Bush demonstrated he could pass out candy at election time just as admirably as Bill Clinton had. He proposed $23 million for school drug-testing, doubled federal funding for abstinence programs, $300 million for prisoner re-entry programming, doubling participation in federal funding of job training programs, providing every poor county in American with its own health center, and building seven million new low cost homes in the next decade. He made a spirited defense of the sanctity of traditional marriage. He appealed to soccer moms, teachers, criminal justice and social service workers, states, counties, cities, and even the poor folk who actually might vote. With his public housing proposal, he outdid Franklin Roosevelt's proposal by a moon-shoot.[21]

But Bush did not let on that the budget was so badly busted as it was. He promised that deficits would decrease in his second term and that promise tinkled pleasantly in the ears of the 120 million voters who went to the polls in 2004. Bush counted on the fact voters could be guilted into not changing their commander in chief during wartime, and he was right. Bush's second term would feature a proposal to privatize Social Security, which he announced February, 2005. Now that he had been reelected, he would spent his new political capital as the leader of the people and ask for legislation within five months time changing the national retirement program that no one had touched in twenty-two years. In sixty days he went to sixty cities to preach the Bush privatization gospel just like Wilson had preached the League of Nations. He met protesters in each one of the cities, and like Wilson, lost his attempt to usurp Congress' policy-making power.[22]

Bush's federal spending increased at a rate more than double that of Clinton. He was perhaps the most lavish spender in the history of the world to that point. He was the first president in 176 years to go an entire term without vetoing any legislation, so little did he want to stop the growth of government. In his second term his first veto was against money for stem cell research. He also vetoed the State Children's Health Insurance Program in 2006. The national debt rose from $5.8 trillion to $11.4 trillion under Bush, an increase of some 96.6 percent. This compares to $2.7 trillion when the very large tipper Ronald Reagan left office. Under George W. Bush, the U.S. completed the journey from being the

21. Draper, *Dead Certain*, 224–25, 246, 249, 378, 380, 397–99, 401.
22. Whitney, *Biographies*, 552; Draper, *Dead Certain*, 293–97, 301–2.

greatest creditor nation in the world to being the greatest debtor nation in the world, borrowing some $800 billion a year from China, Japan, and South Korea.[23] In 2009, incoming president Obama inherited a $438 billion debt from Bush. Bush thus beat his own previous record of $413 billion set in 2004.

Bush he didn't regard war spending in Afghanistan and Iraq as part of the national budget. National "defense" was absolutely essential, and so it couldn't be included as something to be subject to influence by outside parties, like the people, or Congress. Bush's national domestic budget looked pretty good in 2005, but his off-line war spending that year was $450 billion, a pretty big bundle for a non-existing item. In fact it was comparable to the biggest of the Daddy War Bucks spenders during the Cold War, who were not hip to the later idea that that kind of spending didn't need to be mentioned or discussed.[24]

One Congressman spoke of Bush's term as one of "unbridled executive power and congressional ineffectiveness." Bush was fond of using the tools that the tyrants before him used to usurp the law. This he did with executive orders, signing statements, and rule-making. He was so fond of executive orders, that he did not undo some of Clinton's presidential orders because he didn't want to raise too much public awareness about these relatively new presidential legislative tricks. He chafed at Clinton's seizure and lockdown of state lands by executive order. However, when western states challenged Clinton's unilateral seizures, Bush sent his Attorney General to support rather than dispute Clinton's actions. The methods tyrants share in common tend to bind them together more than the minor policy differences that aggravate them from time to time.[25]

Bush, unlike Clinton, hit the ground running in his use of executive orders, issuing forty in his first year. One prohibited the use of federal funds for international family planning that provided abortion counseling and another limited the use of embryonic stem cells in federally funded research. Bush freed energy companies from a variety of federal laws via executive orders. He used executive orders to create a new government agency, create military tribunals, order the CIA to overthrow governments, freeze assets of foreigners, and hire mercenaries into the

---

23. Matuz, *Fact Book*, 752; Flagel, *Guide*, 44–45, 127; Wikipedia, *George W. Bush*, 8; Herring, *Colony to Superpower*, 961.

24. Wikipedia, *George W. Bush*, 9.

25. Whitney, *Biographies*, 556.

U.S. armed forces. He reversed only those orders that he had severe philosophical differences with. He reversed several of Clinton's pro-labor executive orders and added some going in the opposite direction. For example, Executive Order 13202 blocked use of labor agreements on federally funded financial construction projects.[26] Executive orders made laws into play toys of the great executives, rather than reasoned policies hammered out for long-term benefit of the people.

The use of signing statements, which document reasons and circumstances where new laws would not be allowed to control executive actions, vastly expanded under Bush in order to frustrate laws passed by Congress. Reagan had used signing statements to usurp 105 provisions of law. Bush, on the other hand, usurped more than 500 legislative provisions in his first five years in office.[27]

Bush used a signing statement to change a law on campaign finance reform. It claimed that all sections of the law were "non-severable," so that if a court invalidated any part of the law, the whole thing would have to go. In 2003, he hamstrung Inspector General legislation designed to oversee the Iraq War. He saw to it that certain areas of his activities were off limits. He signed legislation creating a September 11 investigating commission, but indicated he could withhold information from the commission if he wanted. Congress reorganized the flow of information among and between the many varied intelligence agencies, but Bush said this legislation was only "advisory," and not binding on him. Often the Congress was not even aware of administration non-enforcement of parts of the law the president did not like. When Congress was onto Bush over one issue or another, he had a way to deflect them from his trail. For example, he refused to allow his director of Homeland Security to testify before Congress in 2002, citing "executive prerogative." This legal-sounding terminology amounted to "I don't want to, so I won't." Bush derailed the Energy and Water Development Act by effectively creating an illegal line item veto. He announced that he could decide, after study, if and which provisions of the law were "necessary and expedient" (applying the language of Article 2, section 3 of the Constitution extremely broadly). For example, he would only expend monies if he considered them "necessary."[28]

26. Crenson and Ginsberg, *Presidential Power*, 203; Cooper, *Order*, 51, 238.

27. Crenson and Ginsberg, *Presidential Power*, 200–201; Whitney, *Biographies*, 555.

28. Crenson and Ginsberg, *Presidential Power*, 203–5; Cooper, *Order*, 204.

Bush objected to Clinton's policy adventures in liberal executive branch lawmaking, but he liked Clinton's methods—in particular his rule-making usurpations. Bush published a memo saying he wanted federal agencies to "implement vigorously" Clinton's Executive Order 12866 regarding regulatory oversight of independent agencies of government, and therefore the adoption of rules outside the process Congress specified for regulatory agencies. His first day in office, Bush also issued a memorandum on his own Regulatory Review Plan. This provided a 60-day moratorium on new rules, even those already submitted to the Federal Register for publication. Some other rule-makings were frozen indefinitely. He issued another inauguration day memorandum freezing government hiring, as Clinton had done, and making pending hiring decisions subject to political appointments in the new administration. Two days later he reinstated Reagan's Mexico policy and opened a friendly relationship with Mexican president Vicente Fox. He wanted to define his own policy in the matter of the Russians, however. He later traveled to Slovenia and met with Russia's president Putin, plumbing the "soul" of this ex-KGB agent and finding him trustworthy.[29]

In his first year, Bush returned twenty major rules for revision. One such rule was related to auto safety. He continued the use of "prompt" memos to agencies asking them to implement policies he wanted. He sent out five prompt memos in his first year. One was to require the use of defibrillators on job sites, and one was to require the disclosure of the fatty acid content of foods. Bush even asked citizens and industry lobbyists to make suggestions to him for current rules that should be abolished or modified. They could meet directly with presidential staff and thus circumvent lawful legislative and judicial review processes.[30]

Bush had a need to be the single point of light on defending traditional family issues, no matter that those issues had always been the bailiwick of states and localities. So he pushed family law legislation like sex-education. He promoted the abstinence-only variety of sex education, denying funding for other approaches. He also signed partial birth abortion ban legislation in 2003. This implemented a policy requiring non-governmental organizations (NGOs) operating overseas to agree not to perform abortions or promote them. It also withdrew U.S. funding

---

29. Crenson and Ginsberg, *Presidential Power*, 209–10; Cooper, *Order*, 83; Matuz, *Fact Book*, 745.

30. Crenson and Ginsberg, *Presidential Power*, 210–11.

for the United Nations Population Fund because it was facilitating China's abortion policy.[31] On the other hand, Bush was much less concerned about the abortion of human rights in China.

Bush could not legislate all issues from his own engine room. On some social issues he was going to have to please voters on both sides of the aisle. For example, he did not repeal Clinton's executive order banning discrimination on the basis of sexual orientation in the federal civilian work force. But, on the other hand, he threatened to veto the Matthew Shepard Act, which would have included sex orientation in hate crimes. Also, while he opposed embryonic stem cell research approved under Clinton, he found it necessary to support adult stem cell research instead. For another example, while he endorsed the Federal Marriage Amendments of 2005–6, which prohibited same-sex couples from getting legal recognition of their unions, he then averred that it would be best if states would decide the issue for themselves. Nevertheless, he took a hard stand when he prohibited the use of public money by any group recognizing a woman's right to an abortion.[32]

At one time or another, Bush expressed a concern to save the American people from their various cultural disorders and insecurities. In his various state of the union addresses, he listed an ambitious program to rescue American children from gangs, fight steroids in sports, move America beyond a petroleum-based economy, and "lead freedom's advance" around the world.[33]

Bush supported some environmental initiatives while balking at others. He signed the 2002 Great Lakes Legacy Act to clean up local pollution, a nice pork barrel project for the Lakes states. He also signed "brownfield" legislation to clean up abandoned industrial sites so his friends in corporate America would not have to bear the burden. He also signed legislation related to a Healthy Forests Initiative. However, he did not support the Kyoto Protocol on global warning/greenhouse gases. Instead, he asked the question why the U.S. should have to comply while China need not? He failed to mention that his campaign donor friends at Exxon-Mobil didn't like the idea. White House cronies watered down reports published by the national government's own professional environmentalists, suppressing scientific information that negated some

---

31. Wikipedia, *George W. Bush*, 7, 11.
32. Wikipedia, *George W. Bush*, 2–3; Whitney, *Biographies*, 535.
33. Healy, *Cult of the Presidency*, 8.

of his argument against the protocol. This underscored that one of the chief functions of expanding White House staff over the last many decades was to effectively enhance the disinformation capacity of the Chief Executive.[34]

In 2002 Bush pushed the Clear Skies Act of 2003 to amend the Clean Air Act. This expanded emissions control to pollutants like mercury. The overall effect of the legislation was to make sure that sulfur dioxide, nitrogen dioxide, and mercury emissions would be reduced at a nice slow pace over the next fifteen years at the nation's power plants.

In energy matters, Bush in 2006 pledged like all presidents to diminish reliance on foreign oil, which went right along with his unstated policy of increasing reliance on domestic oil campaign contributions. To demonstrate his earnestness he championed the Methane to Markets legislation in Congress. He also supported oil drilling in Alaska's Arctic National Wildlife Refuge.[35]

Bush did not neglect the steel industry. He reversed his long-standing support of free trade and supported tariffs of up to thirty percent on imported steel in 2002. This was the broadest protectionist action in twenty years, and America's own puppet International Trade Organization ruled them illegal. He also imposed a tariff on Canadian softwood lumber to help leaven up donations from stateside forest interests.[36]

Bush had friends in the health care industry, particularly in the drug industry. Bush had won the nomination from his party for his initial run at the presidency in part because he had raised so much money for the party and its candidates in 1999. As the war in Iraq approached, Bush moved to pay off his indebtedness to the health care industry by signing the Medicare Act of 2003, which added pharmacy coverage for retired folks, and, not incidentally, prohibited the federal government from negotiating discounts with drug companies. A century earlier, his own party had curbed rebates to commercial interests in order to control corporate profits, but now Bush was curbing rebates in order to enhance corporate profits. His proposed 2001 national budget had called for an additional $314 billion for Medicare over ten years, including $300 billion for the pharmacy benefit, and other increases like home health funding.[37]

34. Wikipedia, *George W. Bush*, 4.
35. Ibid., 5–6.
36. Ibid., 9–10.
37. Wikipedia, *George W. Bush*, 10–11; Samples, *Struggle*, 216.

Bush saw that the public supported the new drug program if the costs were not mentioned. But many saw the program as a new entitlement designed to buy votes. It was an expansion of the welfare state in the LBJ Great Society tradition. The pay-as-you-go budgetary rules had expired in 2002, so it was not necessary to propose new taxes on seniors, or general taxes, or to cut other programs to pay for it. The new benefit could be divvied out without having to pay for it in the present, a tyrant's dream situation. Some forty-seven percent of seniors opposed the program, even though the costs were either not mentioned, or underestimated. They saw it as a way to benefit drug companies more than seniors. Bush made major concessions to the drug companies, like forbidding price controls and asserting protectionism against foreign drug company participation, which promised the industry above average profit margins. One study showed that the costs were underestimated by $100 billion or more. In 2003 the cost for the program was revised upward to $400 billion over ten years. In time, some fifty percent of seniors said the program was not working.[38]

After the 2006 mid-term elections, Bush made a large number of recess appointments to powerful posts in his administration, avoiding the need for Senate confirmation of them and setting a powerful precedent for his successor Barack Obama to follow. The Rove corruption affair and the recess appointments, along with executive orders, signing statements, and rule-making fiascos led one author to summarize that "a defining characteristic of the Bush administration [was] a broad based, concerted effort to continually bypass the legislature and the courts and to consolidate power in the executive branch."

Just before election day in 2008, the country experienced the serial failure of several major financial institutions, followed by a nation-wide and world-wide market panic in part stoked by the failure of unregulated investment debt instruments. Bush reversed his long-standing policy of not interfering in private markets and called for $700 billion to be spent to keep additional business institutions from failing. His Treasury Secretary Henry Poulson demanded unchecked power over spending the $700 billion in bailout funds. The Bush proposal read, "Decisions by the Secretary . . . are unreviewable . . . and may not be reviewed by any court of law or any administrative agency." This attempt at dictatorial power over the economy was rebuffed by Congress, but Bush didn't

38. Samples, *Struggle*, 229–31, 235, 242.

really care. He planned to do whatever he wanted anyway, as in the case of his auto industry bailout. His proposed $15 billion bailout failed to clear Congress, but Bush went ahead and authorized $17.4 billion for the auto bailout anyway.[39] It was almost as though there were two separate nations at work in the Bush administration, one belonging to the people, the Congress, and the law, and the other belonging to the tyrant and his moneyed minions.

Bush's record in foreign affairs set a new standard for political hypocrisy. As a candidate, he said he would not have ordered the Kosovo or Haitian military interventions because they were nation-building efforts.[40] As president, he then committed U.S. troops and other aid for nation-building in Afghanistan for seven of his eight years in office, a policy that continued well beyond his term. He committed U.S. troops and foreign aid to nation-building in Iraq for most of his two terms and well beyond as well.

Starting from a military budget of around $300 billion, he began a Reagan-like buildup that would amount to a fifty percent increase in the already over-built national armory. This included, as it turned out, putting community-building at home on the back burner, while the chief executive engaged in a massive reculturation process abroad.[41] In order to rebuild those two nations the way he wanted them, many thousands of their citizens had to die, just as many Philippine citizens had to die a century before in America's first imperial adventure abroad.

Bush was engaging in a political photo op by reading to second graders in Florida when he was interrupted with news of a plane crash into one of the Twin Towers in New York City. One week after September 11, 2001, Bush gave a speech at the National Cathedral in which he asked the nation to accept the delusional idea that America now had a calling to "rid the world of evil."[42] It was quite evidently true that U.S. presidents during the previous century had not been able to rid the streets of evil in even one small city in the U.S., let alone all the cities of all the nations of the earth. Perhaps the assertion was George Bush's way of saying he was going to be needing a lot of cash for what he was about to do and that he

---

39. Healy, *Cult of the Presidency*, 303–4.
40. Miller Center, *George W. Bush—Foreign Affairs*.
41. Whitney, *Biographies*, 535.
42. Healy, *Cult of the Presidency*, 2, 148.

would be asking newspapers to commit a lot of column inches to extolling his glorious crusade.

At ground zero in New York City, Bush reverted to the Reaganesque role of wild west sheriff. He said he wanted the perpetrators "dead or alive." Deeply and unabashedly devoted to the religion of retaliation, he said, "The people who knocked these buildings down will hear from all of us soon."His poll ratings soared as he had hoped.[43] The problem was, hundreds of thousands of civilian people who didn't knock those buildings down ultimately heard from the president in bloody ways as well. In fact, Bush soon promised a perpetual global war: "Our war on terror begins with Al Qaeda but it does not end there. It will not end until every terrorist group of global reach has been found, stopped, and defeated." Since the world was now a tightly knit global economic enterprise, most any local terrorist wannabe of any sort could be jerrymandered into Bush's definition of a group with "global reach."

The Bush team knew they had reaped a political windfall with 9/11. Condi Rice, Bush's national security guru, hardly needed to advise him to "try and make big strategic plays . . ."Bush badly wanted to "spend the [political] capital now," that is, exploit the massive insecurity the nation felt after the event and the high approval rating he got after his combative speeches. He wanted to take absolute power as soon as possible after the door to the throne room had been thrown wide open to him. Congress, for its part, caved in giddily to everything he asked for: greater security for airports, bail-outs for airlines, tax cuts, terrorism surveillance through the Patriot Act, and soon enough, authorization to use force abroad however he wanted.[44]

As we mentioned above, before 9/11 Bush had been against the use of the military as "a nation-building corps from America." He said, "Our military is meant to fight and win war," not to rebuild cities and national infrastructure. He had said of Al Gore, "He believes in nation-building." After 9/11 and the decision to invade Iraq, he told three Iraqi exiles, "I pledge to the people of Iraq that the U.S. Army itself will rebuild every power station or installation that might be damaged during the military operations." Even then, Bush and his team had a pathetic lack of knowledge about Iraq's miserable, malfunctioning electrical grid and had to

---

43. Matuz, *Fact Book*, 747.
44. Draper, *Dead Certain*, 166, 173, 279.

resort to disinformation about progress in restoring it. Eventually, they left the promise unfulfilled.[45]

Saddam Hussein's Iraq had not attacked America. House majority leader Dick Armey said, "I don't believe that America will justifiably make an unprovoked attack on another nation . . . it would not be consistent with what we have been as a nation . . ." Armey thought it would be old-fashioned to say that offensive war was badly illegal. He figured such a war was going to happen anyway and that he would register a weak protest in advance of it. George Bush didn't care that offensive conquest, the easy and fun half of the deal, had another half, the long and hard part of ruling a foreign people and trying to convince them they were being liberated rather than enslaved. Colin Powell reminded him, "You'll be the proud owner of the hopes and aspirations of 25 million Iraqis." Did George Bush know what to do with all those desert dwellers? He apparently did not put much thought into what some called the "Pottery Barn" rule of international conquest: If you break it, you buy it.[46]

Bush and his groupies had not done much study of Iraq and its people. They only knew that its rulers were bad. Bush thought that Iraqis were well educated and that they would quickly accept democracy. Who wouldn't, when it was handed to them on a platter? Some advisers told him the people there would mob U.S. soldiers in the streets like the French had mobbed U.S. soldiers when they liberated Paris in World War II. But this was a junior high analysis of Middle Eastern politics. In fact, Iraqis knew a lot about corrupt, totalitarian government and religious bickering, and very little about democracy. They had very bad political habits. Knowing how to work is fundamental to setting up democracy, and many Iraqis were used to working very little to get a paycheck from Saddam. When Iraqis quickly descended into looting and anarchy rather than democracy, Rumsfeld waved it off, saying, "Freedom's untidy, and free people are free to make mistakes and commit crimes and do bad things."[47]

One week after September 11, Bush's attorney general asked for new centralized law enforcement power that would enable the chief executive to search, wiretap and surveil the internet, to hold non-citizens indefinitely, and to use information gained by foreign intelligence domestically.

45. Ibid., 128, 188, 289.
46. Ibid., 178–80.
47. Ibid., 178, 189, 192, 197, 204.

He also asked for tougher penalties for terrorism, and for consolidated judicial appeals. Weeks later, in his 2002 state of the union, he stated disingenuously, "America will always stand firm for . . . rule of law."[48]

In an atmosphere of most unmanly panic, on October 26, 2001 the Congress passed one of the most repressive laws the nation had ever seen, and gave the president virtually everything he had asked for in the Patriot Act. It gave broad new emergency powers to the chief executive and in doing-so marginalized or jettisoned important parts of the Bill of Rights. It passed with no committee report, little public debate, and with "breathtaking speed." Only one Senator, Russ Feingold of Wisconsin, voted against it. As a result of this hasty action, more than 1,000 immigrants and visitors were detained secretly and held without charge. Secret proceedings were held and thousands were secretly deported. Bush increased the controversial practice of holding people as material witnesses, which did not require legal charges to be filed. Not until nearly a year later did a U.S. Court of Appeals rule secret detentions unconstitutional. It wrote, "The executive branch seeks to uproot people's lives, outside the public eye, and behind a closed door. Democracies die behind closed doors."[49]

In November, Bush signed a highly repressive executive order to set up special military tribunals to serve as a parallel legal system to mete out special judgments against foreigners the president fingered as "enemy combatants." The new military court system could apply to unlimited numbers of people, would use very limited judicial procedures in those cases brought to it, and would allow the commander in chief to alter those rules at any time. Bush intentionally modeled his executive order on the military tribunals for German-American citizens that resulted from Franklin Roosevelt's Executive Order 2561. The nation's citizenry were dead to the constitutional implications of that earlier event, and were mummified to an even greater degree now. A few educated people raised eyebrows, however. In one legal brief, the new court system was characterized as "an unprecedented, unconstitutional, and dangerously unchecked expansion of military authority." Bush also asserted a personal right to hold suspects indefinitely with no trial and no access to any type of legal proceeding at all. When these supposed powers were later applied not to a foreigner, but to an American named Jose Padilla, Americans

48. Samples, *Struggle*, 218, 224.
49. Whitney, *Biographies*, 537–38, 556.

caught a glimpse of the potential reach of hastily-devised, ill-informed, emergency powers.[50]

Bush built a new prison at an offshore Navy base in Cuba and transferred as many as six hundred Afghanistan prisoners there, in contravention of the Geneva Conventions that the U.S. had historically supported. This basically put him beyond the reach of law. By 2004, only four of these hundreds had been charged with any crime. That year, federal courts ruled the Bush system was illegal, as was his sidestepping of the Geneva Conventions, but he vowed to appeal and continued to hold prisoners there, while no trials were held during the remainder of his term in office.[51]

Bush implemented a program of "extraordinary rendition" to transfer U.S. citizens to foreign countries so they could be tortured there, since U.S. law said that torture could not happen in the U.S.[52] Thus, Bush instituted a sort of human rights loophole in the law, somewhat like the economic loophole for offshore tax shelters.

When Bush instituted the War on Terror, he made the American homeland a legitimate new battlefield for the security forces, and subjected entire American populations to the rules of war normally only imposed on enemy battlefields. Tapping American phones was re-cast as "gathering battlefield intelligence." Seizing American citizens on American soil and holding them indefinitely in military brigs without charges and without counsel was re-cast as "capturing enemy combatants." The American Jose Padilla was held for three and a half years in a military brig without charges.[53]

Bush used the NSA to eavesdrop on email and phone conversations by Americans with people outside the U.S. He did this by secret executive decree. He avoided the legally empower Foreign Intelligence Surveillance Act (FISA) court and claimed the right to spy on Americans without the knowledge of that court. Bush also figured Congress's Authorization for Use of Military Force (AUMF) allowed the president to ignore laws banning torture and even ignore the federal Non-Detention Act, which said there was to be no detention of Americans except by an Act of Congress.[54]

50. Healy, *Cult of the Presidency*, 149; Crenson and Ginsberg, *Presidential Power*, 331; Cooper, *Order*, 8; Whitney, *Biographies*, 539.

51. Whitney, *Biographies*, 540.

52. Healy, *Cult of the Presidency*, 180.

53. Ibid., 148, 173.

54. Crenson and Ginsberg, *Presidential Power*, 202; Whitney, *Biographies*, 556; Healy, *Cult of the Presidency*, 170–71.

Torture became an issue with the revelations of bizarre, abusive, and sadistic U.S. soldier treatment of Iraqi prisoners at Abu Ghraib, practices that further discredited the U.S. in the eyes of the world and gave the lie to Bush's speeches about the export of justice to all the world. The torture unveiled there violated U.S. law, international law, and U.S. military law.

In case the people, and the other political party, didn't quite see eye to eye with Bush on some of these matters, it was important to keep those matters on the quiet. Bush profusely invoked the Military and State Secrets privilege, used sparingly since World War II. That law shields the government from civil or criminal discovery. It was only invoked for six cases from 1953 through 1976. Then, From Carter through Clinton it was invoked fifty-nine times. But the Bush administration more than doubled that latter frequency. In the past, the law was used to limit only certain aspects of discovery, but Bush used it to quash entire cases involving "extraordinary rendition."[55]

So anxious was Bush to exploit the 9/11 situation politically that he invaded Afghanistan with less than a month of preparation. American troops quickly overthrew its government, comprised of the same Taliban that America had supplied with everything it wanted during Carter's term of office. Bush started the air war on Afghanistan October 7, 2001. That war was joined by our ally Britain, and, with minimal support, also by other economic and political dependencies of the U.S.: France, Germany, Australia, and Canada. The government there fell in a matter of weeks. Rather than turn over the country to its own people, Bush determined to stay and occupy the country in part to enhance his party's chances in the 2002 elections. In the process of "gettin' er done" in Afghanistan, Bush opened up a new American base in Uzbekistan. Bush's pacification program after the air war did not take root in Afghanistan any better than it did later in Iraq. In order that the entire burden of nation-building there would not fall on the American people, Bush collected pledges of some $25 billion in tribute money from international friends to help with reconstruction in Afghanistan. That kind of cash was needed, since the first of Congress' many infusions of money for restoration of banking, education, health care, water, electricity and sewage in Iraq came to the tidy sum of $18 billion.[56]

55. Healy, *Cult of the Presidency*, 179–80.
56. Samples, *Struggle*, 221; Whitney, *Biographies*, 540, 547.

Bush essentially threatened war on every nation where terrorists had found a niche to hide. He asserted, "They will hand over the terrorists, or they will share in their fate." And again, "Our enemy is a radical network of terrorists and every government that supports them."[57] He did not seem to care that some governments might not know where or if terrorists were hiding within. Ironically, the so-called "9/11 Commission" later told Bush that he had not been sufficiently attentive to plotters hiding within his own nation, and had failed to "hand over" the terrorists that he was hiding within his own country.

In Afghanistan, Bush overthrew one nation that gave significant support to Al Qaeda, but during a State of the Union address on January 29, 2002 "padded his terror list with three others that didn't," Iraq, Iran, and North Korea. He reported, "These regimes pose a grave and growing danger." He seemed not to understand that his precipitous invasion of Afghanistan posed a danger to Middle Eastern culture, and that rushing militarily into another nation after Afghanistan would heighten tension immeasurably. Nevertheless, he said, "I will not wait on events." Bush's successor, Barack Obama, seized on this exact language of impatience to justify his own extra-constitutional activities. In just one of an innumerable volley of highly exaggerated accusations about the destructive power of these three regimes, and particularly Iraq, Bush added, "The United States will not permit the world's most dangerous regimes to threaten us with the world's most destructive weapons."[58] Many American citizens did not particularly care for these fighting words and the U.N. was totally opposed to his flawed plan to invade Iraq.

Throughout 2002 Bush built a case for war on the foundation of what he claimed was evidence that Iraq had weapons of mass destruction, including biological warfare capability. He created "the most significant reformulation of foreign policy in fifty years with a new policy known as the Bush Doctrine." This policy emphasized offensive war, marketed by use of the innocent-sounding term "preemption." It also encompassed unilateral action (acting outside alliances), and world-wide dominance through military strength. His strategy document stated, "Our forces will be strong enough to dissuade potential adversaries from pursing a military build-up in hopes of surpassing, or equaling, the power of the

---

57. Crenson and Ginsberg, *Presidential Power*, 302.
58. Healy, *Cult of the Presidency*, 147; Matuz, *Fact Book*, 748.

United States."[59] Here Bush essentially announced that he wanted to intimidate even "potential" adversaries, and thus that he had no intention of drawing down any of American's 800 military bases in some 100 countries of the world. The fact that America already had a larger military than the next ten largest national military establishments combined (and virtually all of those were allies or "friends") was of little use to Bush unless he could flaunt the muscle of that military colossus in front of the nations of the earth. The president was becoming not only the "decider" of domestic affairs but the main decider of international drama as well. So isolated was he in his own cloud of giddy power that he was creating his own reality. He not only solved problems, he created them first, so he could step in and solve them later.

Bush enlisted support from "experts" in his administration to fan the flames of war. David Addington, who worked for the vice president Dick Cheney, made it known that hundreds of thousands of Americans could be killed by terrorists. Actual terrorist death statistics, on the other hand, showed that more Americans were killed by lightning and from allergic reactions to peanuts than from terror attacks, even when the September 11 deaths were added in.[60]

For Bush, "action" consisted mainly of the shock and awe part of war-making. In fact, Bush believed once he had scattered the citizenry, the war was won. In Afghanistan he thought the U.S. would be out in three months and so had did not made plans past the invasion phase. The same could be said about Iraq. Bush began the Iraq War by hitting Baghdad in March, 2003. Only weeks into the invasion, he landed on the aircraft carrier Abraham Lincoln and announced "Mission Accomplished." Bush had estimated that it would cost $74.7 billion for the democratization of Iraq and that turnover of sovereignty to the Iraqis would happen June 30, 2004. But soon enough, the bill in military terms alone had gone up to ten times that and more, up to $1 trillion, some three times the military and financial support the U.S. gave England in World War II in comparable dollars. Bush cushioned the effect of these wildly increasing expenditures by limiting the politically unpopular use of reservists. He converted specialist functions from reserve resources to active duty resources. His military resources could more quickly be accessible without political restraint.[61]

---

59. Whitney, *Biographies*, 533, 543.

60. Healy, *Cult of the Presidency*, 189–90.

61. Herring, *Colony to Superpower*, 953; Whitney, *Biographies*, 548; Flagel, *Guide*,

Meanwhile, back home the International Monetary Fund estimated that Social Security and Medicare, America's own nation-building programs, were underfunded by $47 trillion over the next seventy years. The American poverty rate was rising, fewer companies were providing health care benefits, and home ownership was being procured on fraudulently easy terms, which would lead to horrendous consequences soon enough. Clearly, the money could have been used at home.[62]

The Congress, for its part, continued to put up weak resistance to Bush's ongoing war plans and maneuvers. Civil order deteriorated in Iraq when a Shiite mosque was destroyed. One of the tools Bush used to pacify areas torn under religious strife was to pay bribes to Sunni tribes to police their own towns. Millions ultimately left the country and death squads walked the cities. Many citizens at home and abroad wanted the U.S. to withdraw from its nation-building experiment. Bush, on the other hand, proposed more soldiers to pacify the situation. In 2007, Congress opposed Bush's proposed troop surge of 30,000, but let it happen anyway. It passed a bill setting a deadline for withdrawal of troops but did not override the president's veto. One Democratic congressman introduced thirty-five articles of impeachment against the president on June 9, 2008, but speaker Pelosi did not allow discussion of them. After the mid-term elections in 2006, some sixty percent of Americans said that Iraq had not improved national security. In mid-2007, fifty-five percent of Americans said the Iraq war was a mistake.[63]

Brown University's Watson Institute for International Studies found that in ten years from September 11, 2001, to September, 2011, the cost of Bush's wars came to some $3.7 trillion. This figure included direct war spending, homeland security, costs for post-war care of veterans, and interest on the deficit financing for the war. Some 225,000 to 259,000 persons died directly from warfare, including 125,000 civilians in Iraq. Many hundreds of thousands more died from loss of food, medical care, and drinking water. Some 365,000 were wounded, and 7.8 million exiled from their homes. For every person killed in the 9/11 tragedy, Bush's war policy saw to it that seventy-three were essentially killed in retaliation.

127; Crenson and Ginsberg, *Presidential Power*, 266.

    62. Whitney, *Biographies*, 549.

    63. Matuz, *Fact Book*, 751, 753; Samples, *Struggle*, 237, 242; Whitney, *Biographies*, 554.

Barack Obama

Barack Obama was ambitious for presidential power. In 2005, he became America's third African-American senator. In order to leaven up the population for his "reform" candidacy, he sponsored health and housing bills, and also campaign funding and government transparency bills. Following in the Clinton tradition of making himself adorable to women, Obama sponsored a reintroduced Equal Rights Amendment, an Equal Pay Act, as well as a new child care credit for working women. He traveled world-wide to promote his foreign policy credentials, and spoke to audiences around the country to test the waters for a presidential run. To bolster his national security credentials, he also served on the European Affairs subcommittee and on the Homeland Security and Governmental Affairs groups. He criticized Bush's unwillingness to meet with rulers from Korea and Cuba.[64]

During the campaign Obama promised a swift end to Bush's war in Iraq and a tax cut "for 95 percent of all working families," both titillating vote-buying measures. He made the promise to "end our dependence on oil from the Middle East . . . in ten years," implying if he were reelected he could almost get it done during his term of office. He voted for the FISA Amendments Act of 2008, which gave freedom to telecommunications companies to conduct Bush-style wiretapping without warrants. He signaled his intent to follow in the discredited nation-building tradition of George W. Bush by sponsoring in the Senate the Congo Relief, Security, and Democracy Promotion Act. One author perceptively wrote of Obama, "Real Change, or Bush Lite?"[65]

During the run-up to, and the early days of his presidency, Barack Obama introduced twenty-first century America to a level of political idolatry the country had rarely seen before. In his book *The Audacity of Hope*, Barack Obama wrote, "I know that my satisfaction is not to be found in the glare of television cameras or the applause of the crowd." But Obama self-consciously then became perhaps the most oversold, over-reported, over-televised, overwrought candidate and national office holder in the history of American politics.

As a U.S. senator Obama had missed 290 votes, nearly as many as the 348 votes he actually cast, thus demonstrating a willingness to place

---

64. Matuz, *Fact Book*, 765.

65. Miller Center, *Obama—Domestic Affairs*; Wikipedia, *Obama*, 5–6.

responsible office-holding in second place next to avoiding controversy, and participating instead in extra-curricular popularity-generating speeches and photo opportunities. Obama straddled many issues, leaving people uncertain where he stood. He did this regarding federal abortion funding, whether the uninsured would be forced to buy insurance, and gay marriage.[66]

In his presidential acceptance speech Obama spoke of the "dream of our founders" and the "power of our democracy," implying both had come together in his personage and his victory. As if to deflect this im-modesty, he said "This election has never been about me. It's been about you." Some perhaps noticed that in direct contradiction to this message, he had taken great pains to expose his face and personality live and di-rectly to some 80,000 people, grandstanding at a football stadium (and to some thirty-eight million more watching on television worldwide) rather than at a traditional convention hall to make his acceptance speech. He did something similar time and time again, making photo opportunities out of every dramatic or emotionsl event. For example, at the funeral of a child killed in Arizona during a speech of an Arizona Congressper-son, he took the limelight for himself and used it as an opportunity to magnify the power of his office and his popularity as a policymaker. One African-American writer characterized the early Obama presidency as one devoted to "rhetoric, style, and symbolism."[67]

During the 2008 campaign, he had shamelessly used Germany's Brandenburg Gate as a backdrop, as if he had had a role in post-World War II Cold War victories. He carefully deflected attention away from his limelight hogging and "self-infatuation" with tawdry propaganda state-ments, like "This is not about me," and "This is not about politics." In fact, after using the more humble, royal "we" in a few speeches, as Teddy Roosevelt had done, he dropped his team out of the picture altogether and began using "the naked I." In his first state of the union speech he used the word "I" ninety-six times and "my" or "me" eighteen times. He used the word "I" thirty-four times in his speech on the federal takeover of General Motors. He basked in the obvious congratulatory rhetoric used by his staff and the media to hail the new chief. The vice presi-dent, Joe Biden, was the chief piler-on of the flattery. Biden announced, for example, "This president never backs down." Others spoke of the

---

66. Matuz, *Fact Book*, 769.

67. Yahoo News, 1-13-11; Deseret News, 12-15-10.

president's "excessive need for admiration." The media also did its share of kowtowing. Obama appeared on half the covers of *Time Magazine* in 2008, and by August 2009 had appeared on seven *Time* covers. MSNBC's Chris Matthews said, "The biblical term for it . . . is deliverance. We're being picked up and moved to where we have to be." Not all the press were idolizers. When Fox News didn't give in to Obama's demands to cover a prime-time speech and when the network gave coverage to his behind-the-scenes work to get the Olympics for Chicago, Obama began to refuse to call on Fox reporters at press conferences. The White House itself became a shrine to Obama. One observer said, "There are pictures all over . . . of President Obama . . . It was just one picture after another." Obama put his face in front of the people at a pace that made many understand he was already running Clinton-like for reelection. In his first year he gave 411 speeches, made forty-six trips inside the U.S., and ten foreign trips to twenty-one countries, more than any other president.[68]

As president, Obama made incessant and insufferable use of the oracles of culture to promote himself by appearing at sporting events, musical events, entertainment events, comedy and talk shows, and other television shows. He outdid even Bill Clinton in his need for attention and congratulation. He appeared on television shows like America's Most Wanted, Leno, Letterman, 60 Minutes, and network political analysis shows like Meet the Press, Face the Nation, State of the Union, and This Week. He gave commentary on Final Four NCAA basketball games. He tapped celebrities to help him get reelected. At the final campaign rally of his presidential reelection run in Iowa in 2012, Bruce Springsteen, Jay-Z, Mariah Carey, Ricky Martin, John Mellencamp, Samuel L. Jackson, Derek Fisher, and Chris Rock took the stage with him. He also got Russia's ruler Putin to campaign for him. Beyonce performed for him at his second inaugural festivities. Michelle Obama emailed millions (including this writer) on November 5, 2012 appealing to veterans, students, and women, indirectly reminding that her husband had expanded their benefits during his first term.[69]

Obama made a number of campaign promises that he famously failed to keep. He promised to attack immigration reform in his first term, but did not. In 2008 he promised to end no-bid contracts, but in his first year he awarded a $25 million no-bid to a company owned by a

68. Limbaugh, *Crimes*, 15–19, 23–24, 38, 119–20.
69. Limbaugh, *Crimes*, 25–27; MSNBC, 10-31-12, 11-6-12, 1-9-13.

major campaign donor. Later, he let a large no-bid contract for electrical services in Afghanistan. He promised to end "extraordinary rendition," but did not. He promised to curb earmarked pork-barrel spending, but his stimulus bill and his omnibus spending bills were full of them. Earmarks increased rather than decreased from 2009 to 2010. He promised to put health care debates on television, but instead kept meetings out of the camera's eye. He said he would make himself easily available to the press, and to be the "most transparent administration in history," but his people were soon known as "tightwads on information." He promised proper oversight of stimulus funds, but didn't deliver. He hid controversial provisions in large bills to avoid discovery. For example, he put a provision to nationalize student loan financing in the ObamaCare health legislation. He promised to publish legislation on line for five days before signing it, but broke this promise with respect to most of his first 100 day legislation, including SCHIP and Fair Pay laws. He signed the $800 billion stimulus bill one day after it passed. Only half of early bills were posted on the website, and most signed before the five days promised. He promised $646 billion in new revenue from auctioning off greenhouse gas emission allowances to help balance the budget, but couldn't get the legislation passed. He promised not to raise "any of your taxes," for those making less than $250,000, but then increased federal excise taxes on a wide array of products and services for this group, including on the uninsured. He promised the stimulus funds would create a couple million jobs, but job loss continued after application of the stimulus.[70]

Obama promised to be a "uniter." But before long he settled into a pattern of brow-beating opponents into accepting his views and soon got highly polarized job approval ratings, even higher than Clinton's. His polarization tactics disappointed many followers, but actually were discernible even before he took office. At a campaign fundraiser he said, "If they bring a knife to the fight, we bring a gun." He met with congressional Republicans only one day before Democrats completed drafting the 1,073 page stimulus bill. He talked about Republican roadblocks even when he had a large majority of Democrats in both houses of Congress. He justified his tactics by saying, "I don't want the folks who created the mess to do a lot of talking." One commentator wrote, "Obama's language is highly conciliatory . . . but the method isn't." He promised the Justice

70. Washington Post, 11-10-12; Limbaugh, *Crimes*, 5–6, 28, 60–62, 66–67, 71, 165, 201.

department would be free of politics, but than had Justice dismiss a highly political case against Black Panthers. He promised no political favoritism but observers were concerned that Chrysler car dealerships that contributed to Republican candidates were closed down. He also clearly favored labor unions in a number of cases. There was evidence in a Office of Personnel Management memo of his intent to purge Republicans from the civil service.[71]

A hint of the tendency toward Washington politics-as-usual, rather than "change," came when Obama chose Clinton's former chief of staff, John Podesta, to help assemble his team of cabinet leaders for him. Obama tried to co-opt various factions in the Democrat party by folding their leaders into his cabinet and shadow cabinet staffs, much like Lincoln had done. For example, he appointed his presidential opponents to key positions on his staff. He popped the balloon of his anti-war campaign promise by appointing Bush's defense secretary, Robert Gates, as his man in Iraq and Afghanistan.[72]

Obama also flip-flopped on the issue of taking super PAC (Political Action Committee) money in the presidential election. He favored public financing of those elections, but in both the 2008 and 2012 elections he accepted large amounts of private donations. Good government groups loudly bemoaned Obama's "reversal." Far from serving as a political "uniter," his Priorities USA Action committee pulled out a political "gun" and spent millions of dollars in efforts to demonize Mitt Romney in 2012. It stooped so low as to try to link a woman's death to Romney's tenure at Bain Capital.[73]

In his first few days in office, Obama jumped on his new found power to rule as a popular tyrant by issuing executive orders and presidential memoranda. For example, he changed the law to allow federal money to go to foreign non-governmental organizations that promote abortions. He issued orders to develop plans for a quick withdrawal from Iraq, but then went very slow on the whole process. He ordered the closing of the Guantanamo Bay concentration camp, but later declined to implement it. Jimmy Carter noted that some 160 prisoners remained held there, half of them cleared for release. Obama chilled the Constitution in a more fundamental sense by arguing that water-boarding, and the use of power

71. Limbaugh, *Crimes*, 5–7, 92–94, 98, 103.
72. Miller Center, *Obama—Domestic Affairs*.
73. MSNBC News, 2-7-12; Politico, 10-15-12.

drills and semi-automatic weapons to grease confessions at Guantanamo could not be used as a defense by the accused, due to national security concerns.[74]

Obama followed George W. Bush's path in ways other than sustaining the instruments of extra-constitutional repression of human rights. Even before taking office, he endorsed Bush's $700 billion Troubled Asset Relief Program (TARP), whose first focus was on buying toxic assets, and later on making "capital injections" and "investments" (bailouts). He supported Bush's legally questionable diversion of $18 billion in "bridge loans" to auto companies, and the restructuring (bailout) of AIG, the world's largest insurance company.[75]

Once taking office, Obama used TARP resources on his own to restructure the auto industry, including issuing loans and taking over companies. He ultimately spent some $421 billion of TARP funds. As of summer 2013, a good portion of the money had been paid back, the program thus coming in under some predictions about the overall cost to the taxpayers. Auto manufacturers ultimately recouped a portion of market share, saw improving sales, exports and profitability, and repaid a majority of the loans. Obama authored a Financial Stability plan to do stress testing on banks, make capital infusions to the larger banks, and support small business and homeowners. His spending included reelection vote-encouraging measures, like giving small business owners greater access to some kinds of federal contracting and a Cash for Clunkers program to increase auto sales, which provided $3,500 or $4,500 rebates to consumers.[76]

Obama's restructuring program for the auto industry included $80 billion in loans and tax credits to GM and Chrysler, the sale of Chrysler to Fiat, and eventual nationalization of GM by giving the U.S. government a sixty percent equity stake in the company. Obama also extracted peacetime tribute from the Canadian government, in the form of another twelve percent equity stake in GM. Canada had been smart enough financially to avoid the deep recession, and were thus rewarded with the responsibility to help the U.S. government "shoulder" the crisis. As of November, 2011, some $35 billion of the $80 billion had been paid back. Obama's ethical reputation slipped when he used his executive power to

74. Wikipedia, *Obama*, 8.
75. *Financial Crisis*, 20–21.
76. Ibid., 13–14, 23, 31.

reward organized labor for their contributions to his campaign. In 2009 he implemented an unjust debt payback scheme for investors in the auto industry. He specified that Chrysler bondholders, who were secured and therefore favored creditors, could receive only twenty-nine cents on the dollar payback, while United Auto Worker retirees, who were unsecured and therefore secondary creditors, would get fifty cents on the dollar pay off. He threatened the lawyers for the bondholders with a smear campaign if they continued to object.[77]

During the transition period, the price tag for Obama's own stimulus spending program, set to follow Bush's spending spree, jumped from $400 billion to $800 billion. He ultimately proposed and pushed to passage some $825 billion's worth of vote buying projects under the title of the American Recovery and Reinvestment Act (ARRA), otherwise known as "the stimulus." Obama cried "emergency," and indicated that any delay in his plan would "turn a crisis into a catastrophe." His chief of staff Rahm Emanuel implied that the underlying constitutional agenda of this legislation was to increase presidential power. He was caught bragging, "You never want to let a serious crisis go to waste." One third of these funds was marked to go to state governments to bail them out and make them ever-more dependent on central government for their salvation. Another third was marked for internal improvement projects. These included river flooding reduction projects, urban canal inspection, and wild-land fire management. Some $2.25 billion went for high speed rail to bail out a vastly overspent California project. This second third went to pay not just for infrastructure, but health care, education, and direct relief to individuals. It included a monster building and renovation program for the federal government, and for renovations to turn older government buildings into green buildings. One author wrote, "To the extent the stimulus was stimulating anything, it was government." The final third was $300 billion in tax breaks and incentives, including the Making Work Pay Credit to help the electorate and business understand they had done the right thing in electing Obama. With this gigantic spending measure in tow, he promised a quick recovery of the economy and unemployment below eight percent, a promise that was to haunt him when unemployment rose to ten percent.[78]

77. Freddoso, *Gangster Government*, ix.

78. Reuters, 1-24-12; Fallows, *Obama Explained*, 24, 26; Limbaugh, *Crimes*, 285, 287, 289–90; Limbaugh, *Destroyer*, 146; Healy, *Cult of the Presidency*, 309.

Unemployment actually reached 10.1 percent in 2009. In 2010, economic growth expanded at first, then slowed. Some economists believed the stimulus package increased growth. Some three-quarters of respondents in a National Association of Business Economics survey believed that the stimulus bill had no impact on employment, however. Median household income was down 2.3 percent between 2009 and 2010, and the poverty rate was up one percent in 2009. On the other hand, Obama promoted corporate welfare for corporations other than automakers and banks, by enhancing the profits of giant grain corporations through overseas food aid.[79]

Obama made large investments in housing through his Home Affordable Modification Program (HAMP), designed to reduce principle payments, and his Home Affordable Refinancing Program (HARP), designed to help underwater homeowners. In the meanwhile, the poverty rate hit and remained at a record level of fifteen percent, the highest since 1965.[80]

Obama held the door open to Bush-style signing statement usurpations by stating he felt he could sign a bill into law (and thus get votes for doing that), and then not implement the law (and thus get the votes of those who didn't like the bill). In a March, 2009, memo he indicated he would use signing statements henceforth and then did so for the first time a few days later. He also asserted a strong-arm executive leadership style in other ways as well. For example he defended presidential liberty to appoint White House "czars" without Senate confirmation. These were un-elected, super policy leaders who would help him bypass the congressional legislative prerogative and govern without oversight. Obama's shadow government included an AIDS czar, an Auto Recovery czar, a Safe Schools czar, an Economic czar, a Border czar, a Climate czar, a Science czar, a Green Jobs czar, a Car czar, a Stimulus Accountability czar, an Executive Pay czar, a Safe Schools czar, and a Deposed Green Jobs czar, among others (some 32 altogether). He also overruled EPA anti-smog rule-making, showing he could massage the efforts of his professional staff in whatever direction he wanted to.[81]

79. Wikipedia, *Obama*, 10; Guardian, 7-18-12; Reuters, 1-24-12.

80. *Financial Crisis*, 25–26; Associated Press, 9-12-12.

81. Genovese, *Prerogative*, 138–39, 160; The New American, 1-4-10; The New York Times, 4-23-12; Limbaugh, *Crimes*,120, 149–50.

Obama's crowning first-term achievement was his Patient Protection and Affordable Care Act. He had promised to pursue national health care legislation only at the end of his first term, but flip-flopped once in office in order to take advantage of Democrat majorities in Congress in his first two years. The fact he had rushed the legislation was seen after its passage in the constitutional difficulties uncovered in the law, ultimately ruled upon by the Supreme Court in June, 2012. The law as first proposed was to spend $900 billion over ten years. Most provisions were set to take effect over four years. During the debate process, Obama cut deals to please the pharmacy and hospital industries, which undercut his stated intention to keep the bill budget neutral. He used an executive order to deny funding for abortion in order to get pro-lifers to vote for the legislation. He promised to send $300 million in Medicaid money to Louisiana and give Nebraska a Medicaid expansion waiver in order to get votes from Congressmen from those states. He also made deals for votes from Vermont and Michigan, and reportedly offered judgeships and ambassadorships for votes. He announced on national TV that health care insurance would be required of all Americans, just like auto insurance. He said his bill would deal constructively with all the current problems in the health care scene. The legislation's Payment Advisory Board, however, quickly came under criticism for being a body of unelected government officials who make health care legislation that becomes law at their say-so.[82]

The health care bill, as passed by a partisan Congress and signed by the president, expands Medicaid eligibility, subsidizes insurance premiums for many people, provides incentives for business to provide health care plans, prohibits pre-existing condition exclusions and annual coverage caps, establishes health insurance exchanges in the states, and requires all citizens to obtain coverage or pay a tax penalty. The legislation was geared to offset some of its costs with new Medicare taxes for those with high incomes, by taxes on indoor tanning, by shifting patients from Medicare Advantage to traditional Medicare, and with fees on medical devices and pharmacy companies.[83]

Obama issued waivers from the requirements of the health care law to major labor unions favorable to his presidency. Waivers can rightly

82. Cato Institute *Policy Analysis, No. 700,* 6-14-12; Limbaugh, *Crimes,* 159, 182–84.

83. Wikipedia, *Obama,* 11–12.

be seen as favors to entities who please the chief executive. Such waivers allow the president not only to reward friends but to punish critics, since power to grant a waiver assumes also the power to not grant waivers. Obama allowed states to opt out of the Medicaid expansion provision of the new health care law under certain conditions. He also gave states more latitude in running the federal government's welfare-to-work programs, which effectively undercut federal work requirements that were set in stone in the 1996 welfare reform law. The health care law, strangely, also included a provision to more heavily regulate and tax gold coin and bullion transactions, ostensibly for the benefit of the health care system.[84]

In January, 2010, Obama said he would "end the outsized influence of lobbyists. . . That's why—for the first time in history—my administration posts our White House visitors on line . . . We've excluded lobbyists from policy-making jobs . . ." But Obama then repeatedly gave special waivers to favorite lobbyists, hiring a long list of them into his administration. In fact, both Common Cause and the Center for Public Integrity reported that Obama fell far short of his anti-lobbyist rhetoric. His executive order grand-fathering in former lobbyists now working in the federal government provided a large loophole, applying as it did to some fifty percent of government employment, those in national defense. The White House met secretly with lobbyists at a coffee shop nearby, avoiding disclosing such meetings on the White House visitor log. Also, Obama accepted 2012 campaign money from "bundlers" working for Washington lobbying firms.

Obama pressured Congress to enact the Dodd-Frank Wall Street Reform and Consumer Protection Act, designed to deal with predatory lending and to shine at least a small light on the shadow banking system dealing in derivatives like credit default swaps. This law nationalized regulation of pay day lenders, consumer reporting agencies, and debt collection agencies, in part by consolidating regulatory functions under one powerful agency, the Consumer Financial Protection Bureau (CFPB).[85] Obama coddled financiers who had produced the Great Recession of 2008. Some 2,565 financial industry lobbyists influenced Obama to dilute new regulations. He allowed financiers to repay industry losses with few conditions on repayment, thus protecting the bonuses of corporate executives. Later on, he attempted to nationalize bank prosecutions of

84. New York Times, 7-12-12; Deseret News, 12-15-10.
85. Financial Crisis, 38–39, 48.

those committing fraud leading to the recession. He put pressure on New York's attorney general to forego any future mortgage foreclosure investigations and thus provide immunity for Bank of America and other culprits for future actions. Of bank behavior during this period, Connecticut's attorney general said, "At the best, banks engaged in careless negligence, at worst, outright fraud." Obama wanted the states to forgive and forget, or else give him the power to decide.[86]

In the Restoring American Financial Stability Act of 2010, the Senate had passed a 1,300 page bill in a twenty-one-minute markup session. The legislation included the CFPB in it, with rule-making authority to create and monitor large firms and to provide a permanent, unlimited, bailout authority. The CFPB did not have to consult with Congress on its budget and there was limited review of its activities. It also included a Financial Stability Oversight Council (FSOC) that could put firms in government receivership, or takeover, without judicial review. Many in both parties believed that these agencies had been given unconstitutional power.[87]

Obama believed he had done in his first term what Franklin Roosevelt had done in his, tackling severe economic problems inherited from a previous presidential administration. In February, 2009, Obama said, "Today I am pledging to cut the deficit we inherited by half by the end of my first term in office." This meant the annual deficit would have to decline from $1.2 trillion to $600 billion. Toward this end, he said in 2010 that he would freeze federal spending for three years. One research institute found that his freeze covered only thirteen percent of the federal budget, and didn't cover the stimulus bill. In fact the 2010 deficit reached $1.4 trillion and continued at about that level for the next several years. In 2006, Obama had voted against Bush's increase in the debt limit, saying it was "a sign of leadership failure." Yet Obama himself signed legislation providing for raising of the debt limit from $10 trillion to $15 trillion during his first term.[88]

In fact, Obama was determined to use the atmosphere of economic crisis to be a bigger central government sugar daddy in areas the federal government was not constitutionally authorized to be in. He promised to use the power of the presidency to "transform our schools and colleges."

86. Reuters, 1-24-12; Fallows, *Obama Explained*, 25; Limbaugh, *Crimes*, 67–68.

87. Limbaugh, *Crimes*, 233–40; Limbaugh, *Destroyer*, 3.

88. Limbaugh, *Crimes*, 28, 76, 94, 292; Limbaugh, *Destroyer*, 149, 151.

His Secretary of Education Arne Duncan then initiated the Race to the Top program to create competition among states for $4.5 billion in extra federal funding for schools.

While the atmosphere of economic crisis was deeply instrumental and beneficial to Obama in his effort to enhance presidential power, an environmental crisis provided additional opportunity. In April 2010, an explosion occurred at an offshore drilling rig in the Gulf of Mexico, causing a major and sustained oil spill. Obama placed a six-month moratorium on deep-water drilling. As British Petroleum (BP) was unable to get the spill under control, American citizens called for more federal government involvement, as they had been trained to do by a century's worth of prior American presidents.[89]

In August, 2011, Congress debated on how much to raise the nation's debt limit, which resulted in the compromise Budget Control Act of 2011. This established a faulty and sham procedure to force Congress to work on increasing the debt limit by creating a Joint Committee on Deficit Reduction and an automatic procedure to reduce the rate of growth in spending if legislation was not passed by a certain date. If Congress could not agree, across the board "cuts" were to kick in, including the military budget. This compromise plan prevented the U.S. government from defaulting on its obligations.[90]

Late in his first term, Obama announced the treasury department's Public-Private Investment Program for Legacy Assets, an immense spending spree committing the federal government and its partners to buying up to $2 trillion in depreciated real estate assets. When these deficit spending programs were added on top on Obama's massive new health care law spending, no one was surprised that the president's budget shortfall soared to $1 trillion per year. Later, in another round of "quantitative easing," Obama's fed announced it would spend $40 billion per month in newly minted money to buy mortgage bonds to try to make homes more affordable.[91]

Obama inserted himself into the details of 2010 Congressional midterm elections, touting his economic recovery credentials. The New York Times reported, "some Democrats expressed anger at what they saw as heavy-handed tactics by the president's political team." In 2010 Obama

89. Wikipedia, *Obama*, 12.

90. Wikipedia, *Obama*, 9–10; Time, 7-4-11, 36 .

91. Healy, *Cult of the Presidency*, 303, 309–10; Miller Center, *Obama—Domestic Affairs;* Wikipedia, *Obama*, 9; NBC News, 9-10-12.

had followed up his first year performance with a massive vote-buying program just one month before the 2010 mid-term elections. He pushed the Tax Relief, Unemployment Insurance Reauthorization, and Job Creation Act. This enacted a two-year extension of the Bush tax cuts of 2001 and 2003, a one-year payroll tax reduction to further leaven up the votes of 160 million working people, the continuation of expiring unemployment benefits, and a new rate and exemption amount for estate taxes. If the payroll tax cut had expired, it would have added $1,000 to each family's tax burden, so this was a $1,000 check from Obama to each family in appreciation for their upcoming vote for reelection of his party operatives in the Congress. The bill, which cost $858 billion, was passed with members of both parties supporting it, since it would help the reelection of incumbents on both sides of the aisle. Obama signed it on December 17, 2010.[92]

Obama sponsored the Don't Ask, Don't Tell Repeal Act of 2010. He signed a bill re-authorizing state children's health insurance programs (SCHIP), and reversed Bush's policy on embryonic stem cell research. He proposed new regulations on power plants, factories and oil refineries to limit greenhouse emissions. He signed the Hate Crimes Prevention Act, which expanded the reach of federal criminal law enforcement to include sexual orientation, gender and disability. He signed an omnibus bill making changes in his Affordable Health Care act, increasing Pell grant levels, and stopping the federal government from subsidizing private banks to give out federally insured loans. He changed NASA's priority from moon to Mars, initiated a new rocket type, and authorized continued missions to the space station until 2020.[93]

Obama did not set a very good personal example in how to curb the national debt. He travelled out of the country in a style of monarchic luxury not even dreamed of by icon-breaking globetrotter presidents like Woodrow Wilson and Franklin Roosevelt. On his trip to London, England, to attend the G-20 summit in 2010, he took along with him 500 staff, including 200 Secret Service, six doctors, and his own White House chef and kitchen staff. He also brought thirty-five vehicles, including the presidential limousine, a fleet of decoy vehicles, and a helicopter. He also brought along four speechwriters and twelve teleprompters. Obama could be spendy for purely personal travel as well. He spent nearly $4 million

92. Fallows, *Obama Explained*, 21.
93. Healy, *Cult of the Presidency*, 310; Wikipedia, *Obama*, 8;

in taxpayer dollars for travel expenses for a family vacation to Hawaii in 2011. It cost $182,000 per hour to run Air Force One on its nine hour one-way trip to Hawaii. He found it necessary to bring along a C-17 cargo plane to stow away the presidential limousine and to provide housing expenses for military personnel accompanying him to Hawaii. On another trip, he took an Air Force jet to New York City for a taxpayer-funded date night with Michelle. He took a $3 million taxpayer-funded flight to Copenhagen to lobby for the Olympics for his hometown Chicago.[94]

In October, 2011, after the American people had deposed many Obama legislative supporters in the 2010 mid-term elections and after budget deficit talks broke down, Obama made a conscious decision to make legislative policy unilaterally, that is, without Congress. William Daley, White House Chief of Staff, said the president was determined to "push the envelope in finding things we can do on our own." He thus flip-flopped from the days of his Senate term when he criticized the executive unilateralism of George W. Bush. Obama made increasingly brassy shows of determination and command by acting like a parent with respect to Congress. For example, he notoriously chided Congress on a jobs package, by repeatedly demanding, "Pass this bill." This apparently was a code word for "I will do it if you don't." The usurper mindset, and the obsequiousness Obama increasingly was expecting from Congress, the media, the people, and his own staff was reflected by Nancy-Ann DeParle, a deputy chief of staff. She remarked, "No one opposed doing more." Senator Grassley, a Republican from Iowa, said Obama was acting "more and more like a king."[95]

Obama even coined a propaganda phrase to justify his planned rush of new usurpations—"We Can't Wait." He used this anthem for usurpation even though the Constitution provides no caveat regarding Congressional inaction to justify presidential lawmaking. The propaganda message promoted the variety of "democracy" we discussed above, a democracy that defines Obama and his partisan people as the only real legitimate power and authority in the country. Obama and his people could no longer wait for the kind of consensus or compromise which constituted true democracy. The result of the new campaign for majoritarian tyranny was "dozens of new policies," related to jobs for vets, drug shortages, fuel economy standards, domestic violence, discrimination

---

94. Scripps Howard, 8-2-10; Yahoo News, 12-19-11; Limbaugh, *Crimes*, 37, 42.
95. New York Times, 4-23-12.

by federal contractors on the basis of sexual orientation, re-payment terms for student loans, deportation of young illegal immigrants, land ownership and management, stem cell research, mail delivery, pollution controls on coal and gas and the Keystone pipeline, deepwater drilling, summer jobs, gun safety, and refinance fees for federally-insured mortgages. In 2011, Obama issued a memorandum to use foreign aid to promote gay rights. He directed the Federal Drug Administration to reduce drug shortages by accelerating review of applications to produce drugs. Obama has boldly asserted that he is bypassing Congress with statements like, "If Congress refuses to act, I've said that I'll continue to do everything in my power to act without them." The word "continue" is the operative word here. Obama had already been making legislation by means of executive orders for some time. Earlier in his term he ordered his staff to stop enforcing the Defense of Marriage Act, which prohibited federal recognition of same-sex marriages, after lawmakers declined to repeal it. He also gave state waivers from federal educational mandates of the No Child Left Behind law, which required that students be proficient at grade level in reading and math by 2012, and increased curbs on greenhouse gases by defining carbon dioxide as a toxic pollutant under the Clean Air Act.[96]

As he got closer to the most active part of his reelection campaign, Obama cranked up the unrealistic promises again. In his 2011 State of the Union, he promised a five-year freeze on domestic spending, since even the electorate had become worried about what all the spending would do to the country. He also promised to curb tax breaks for oil companies and the wealthiest two percent of earners. He made the obligatory, and always dishonest, promise to ban congressional earmarks, to reduce health care costs, and a spate of other cynically unrealistic political seductions.[97]

This was just the beginning of a tremendous onslaught of vote-buying programs leading up to the 2012 elections. Obama made halting efforts in housing policy by promoting poorly thought-out "ad hoc" loan modifications rather than a comprehensive program. In February, 2012, he announced a $25 billion foreclosure settlement with the nation's five largest banks. This money was strategically designed to aid people in an election year. It gave reduced principle/mortgage write-downs and

96. Yahoo, 12-6-11; Limbaugh, *Destroyer*, 5–7, 9; Politico, 7-30-13; Washington Post, 6-25-12, 1-25-13; New York Times, 4-23-12, 8-13-12; Limbaugh, *Crimes*, 178–79.

97. Wikipedia, *Obama*, 9.

additional money to help people refinance. It announced that 750,000 people who lost their homes from 2008-2011 would get $2,000 checks to compensate for poor foreclosure practices and that the money would be paid out in the months of April through October, leading up to the election. This was a nice benefit, but many Americans understood it was miniscule in view of the trillions of dollars in decline in home values they had experienced. In May, 2012, in spite of his long-standing opposition, he announced his support for same-sex marriage, just in time to appeal to the gay vote. In addition, recent polls showed that fifty-one percent of the nation now favored it, so he could expect to get political benefit, and perhaps campaign workers, from the announcement. In 2012, Obama caved in to farmers and Republicans and allowed children under sixteen to use power-driven farm equipment, and those under eighteen to work in grain silos, and stock yards. This dismayed child welfare advocates, but boosted his reelection chances. Obama's health care plan provided that people whose insurance plans pay out less than fifty percent of premiums in benefits were to get rebates in the mail before the election. He also declared 1,000 counties in twenty-six states as national disaster areas due to drought lasting eight weeks or longer. This amounted to one-third of all U.S. counties and was the "largest ever USDA disaster declaration." The declaration opened the way for low-cost loan assistance in those states. Obama also championed and obtained passage of an extension of the two percent payroll tax holiday and an extension of the period of unemployment benefits until after the 2012 election. The first saved workers an average of $1,000 right before the election, and the second was worth more than that to the unemployed. He also expanded the Child Tax Credit to many more families, increased the Earned Income Tax Credit for families with three or more children, and signed into law the American Opportunity Tax Credit, worth $10,000 for nine million families supporting college kids. His first term policies providing health coverage up to age twenty-six and free contraception for women helped loosen up the youth vote, and his deportation deferral policy leavened up the Hispanic vote.[98]

But there were lots of things Obama wanted to do but couldn't do before the election because they would be hypocritical or unpopular. He

---

98. Washington Post, 4-30-12; Bloomberg News Services, 7-12-12; Reuters, 1-24-12; 12-12-11; US News and World Report, 10-2-12; MSN Money, 11-9-12; Financial Crisis, 36.

was caught in a "hot microphone" moment telling a confidant that "After my election, I have more flexibility."[99]

In June, 2012, after Obama used executive privilege to avoid handing over thousands of pages of documents relating to a botched federal gun-running effort into Mexico, a scandal called Fast and Furious, Congress recommended a first ever contempt vote for a sitting Attorney General, Eric Holder. Congress also investigated the administration's policy of monitoring and reading email without a warrant. The legislature expressed concern about Obama's waivers for welfare-to-work programs, since Congress had not authorized waivers of TANF work requirements. The Congress also questioned waivers to allow states to opt out of Medicaid expansion.[100]

Throughout his first term, Obama had touted the benefits of environmental legislation. However, Obama shocked the nation by opening up the Arctic Ocean, previously considered untouchable, for drilling there by Shell Oil. Shell Oil had scratched Obama's back by breaking from the rest of the industry and pushing for climate change legislation. Obama rejected a tough ozone standard, which also pleased business, but delayed the Keystone pipeline from Canada and adopted tough air quality standards for power plants, which pleased environmentalists.[101]

Obama took a variety of actions with respect to states rights, most often subverting them, but supporting them when it suited his political purposes. His justice department filed a lawsuit against an Arizona county sheriff, "a rare step for the agency." The lawsuit attempted to assert national hegemony over county government. Obama also tried to prevent states like Arizona from checking the immigration status of Latinos in the state, but a court upheld the "show me your papers" part of the law there. Obama asserted that states are powerless to enforce federal immigration standards without the express blessing of the federal executive, but this negated the long-standing ideal of dual sovereignty and cooperative relations between federal and state government.[102]

In order to purchase the future electoral loyalty of illegal Mexican immigrants for the Democratic party, Obama announced a huge

---

99. Today Show, 10-4-13.

100. Washington Post, 6-21-12; Politico, 6-24-12; MSNBC, 7-6-12; New York Times, 7-12-12, 7-17-12.

101. New York Times, 5-23-12.

102. Associated Press, 5-1-12; Washington Post, 4-29-12; NBC News, 12-12-11.

program to allow 1.7 million illegals to work legally and live openly in the U.S. He did this by executive order, after Congress had declined to pass his Dream Act. This policy of domestic political manipulation dovetailed with his military policy for international imperialism, since Obama openly encouraged new foreign-born residents to join the U.S. military and thus essentially serve as foreign mercenaries fighting for causes they knew or cared little about.[103]

Obama's administration got into trouble for corruption, as many administrations before his had as well. His General Services Administration oversees government facilities, office space and supplies. The head of the agency resigned after admitting that at a Las Vegas conference in 2010 she had spent about $823,000 for private parties at a training conference there. Sadly, for the industry there, but gladly for the American public, that information did not stay in Las Vegas.[104]

Obama filled vacancies in the federal court system not always with dispassionate constitutional scholars, but with partisan hacks who could be counted on to support not only greater federal deficit spending and intrusion into the realm of state sovereignty, but also to support executive power grabs. In fact, Elena Kagan, a successful Supreme Court appointee, had been a legal aide in the Clinton administration, had written justifications which allowed Clinton to usurp congressional legislative power at his convenience, and could be expected to do the same for Obama.

Obama made heavy use of a tried and true method of presidential usurpation of Congressional prerogative in the matter of recess appointments of persons blocked by the Senate. He bypassed the Senate confirmation process to install important new administration officials to the National Labor Relations Board and the Consumer Financial Protection Bureau. Liberals and conservatives alike warned this was a "dangerous precedent."He also asked Congress for departmental "consolidation authority" to merge trade and commerce agencies, so that he could present his administration as a model of efficiency in an election year.[105]

As we mentioned above, Obama campaigned to close the U.S. offshore prison at Guantanamo Bay and signed an executive order to do so on his first day in office. But as president, he chose not to close the prison, and declined to release likely innocent political prisoners until his

---

103. New York Times, 8-13-12; Associated Press, 7-4-12.

104. MSNBC, 4-16-12.

105. Fallows, *Obama Explained*, 4; Yahoo News, 1-4-12; Associated Press, 1-12-12.

government could find nations where they could be exiled. He had also railed against the use of military tribunals, and at first halted military trials. However, later on he decided some detainees would still face military commissions. He also continued Bush's illegal policy of holding some without trial. In order to test the political winds, he leaked the possibility he would make an executive order indefinitely imprisoning some at Guantanamo without trials, but later backed off on publishing the order.[106]

Obama initially encouraged the armed forces to comply with traditional torture policy by following the interrogation standards outlined in the Army Field Manual. Then he flip-flopped and defended Bush-style torture, including Bush's assertion that the federal government could suppress disclosure of evidence about torture and even entire law suits.[107]

During his first presidential campaign, he had asserted he did not believe Article II of the Constitution gave the president unchecked powers in military affairs, such as the power to unilaterally authorize a military attack without an imminent threat, or power to ignore laws on domestic surveillance and treatment of enemy combatants. These were things than only an evil Republican would think of doing. But as president he objected to a spending bill that would restrict his ability as commander in chief to place troops under foreign command. And although his position on domestic surveillance was an explicit campaign promise, the closer he got to the presidency the more inclined he was to change his mind.

In the summer of 2008, he flip-flopped on national security wiretapping. As president, Obama covered up Bush's record of warrantless wiretapping by opposing a case challenging those illegal acts. The ACLU conducted a study of federal agencies regarding reading of internet emails and revealed many details of Obama's change of heart. In 2010, the Obama administration admitted in the U.S. vs. Warshak case that the government had read 27,000 emails without the use of a search warrant. In April 2011, Obama's justice department argued against requiring warrants for email access. Wired Magazine reported that Utah's NSA data center coming on line in 2013 would be capable of monitoring every email and text message sent around the world. NSA was spending $2 billion at the Utah spy center to construct one million square foot facility that will house a "cloud" that stores trillions of intercepted phone calls,

106. Reuters, 1-24-12; Genovese, *Prerogative*, 159–61; Healy, *Cult of the Presidency*, 307.

107. Healy, *Cult of the Presidency*, 308; Genovese, *Prerogative*, 159.

emails and data trails. It was also reported by business's Insider Magazine, that NSA does not spy on Americans directly, but contracts out the job to Israeli firms, who have installed hardware and software in ten to twenty wiretapping rooms across the United States to tap U.S. telecommunications networks like Verizon's. In 2012 it was reported that Obama's use of the FBI to hunt for government whistleblowers/leakers had put a "chill over press coverage of national security issues."[108]

One author wrote of the "unprecedented assault on government whistleblowers and leakers of every sort," especially coming from a president who promised to operate "the most open and transparent [administration] in history." Great concern arose when Obama's attorney general made a speech at Northwest University Law School, in early March, 2012, during which he justified murder of Americans who are a threat to the government. Legal observers suggested that this view played havoc with the Constitution's Fifth Amendment (due process), Sixth Amendment (trial by jury, confront witnesses, obtain counsel), and Eighth Amendment (no cruel and unusual punishment).[109]

In a White House Press Conference held February 23, 2012, Jake Tapper asked Jay Carney why the government was using the Espionage Act of 1917 so frequently, especially to take government whistleblowers to court. Obama had invoked the law six times, but before his term it had only been invoked three times in U.S. history. For example, Obama was suing a CIA officer for providing information about CIA torture. In another case, Obama filed ten felony counts against an employee for saying the U.S. overspent on a program to collect data from an outside source when it could have used an inside source. Tapper mentioned the hypocrisy of the administration lauding the reporting of government brutality in foreign lands, but not in the U.S. The *New York Times* indicated the six cases have to do with administrative secrecy, not national security, or in other words, the government is "hiding its business." On the other hand, no government personnel who authorized or engaged in water-boarding torture was being prosecuted.[110]

As Obama's second term began in 2013, a number of issues came to the fore to test patience with presidential activism. These issues included

---

108. Healy, *Cult of the Presidency*, 307–8; MSNBC, 7-6-12; Business Insider Magazine, 4-4-12; Washington Post, 4-23-12; New York Times, 8-1-12.

109. The New American, 2-29-12; Personal Liberty Digest, 3-12-12.

110. The New American, 2-29-12.

state voter registration laws, automatic spending cuts, aid to Syrian rebels, immigration reform, eavesdropping by the NSA, Hurricane Sandy storm aid, the military pivot to Asia, farm aid and food stamps, aid to Egypt, hunger strikes at Guantanamo, early childhood education, North Korean sabre rattling, repression of tech companies for non-compliance with wiretap orders, drone activity on U.S. soil, IRS targeting of conservative groups, justice department seizure of phone records of journalists, a military sex scandal involving cover-ups, Edward Snowden's NSA leaks, NSA spying in Europe and South America, second term appointments, delays in implementation of ObamaCare, response to chemical weapon use in Syria, a military coup in Egypt, federal support for college students, the level of the debt ceiling, and responsibility for the brief government shutdown that started October 1, 2013. Obama unleashed hardball tactics in pointing the finger at Republicans over the government shutdown. His email propaganda arm, BarackObama.com, used verbiage like "extreme group of House republicans" and "sabotage our economy" to castigate his opponents. This was reminiscent of Woodrow Wilson's hate campaign against German Americans a century before. Media pals spoke of national security vulnerability because intelligence analysts from the FBI and other agencies were furloughed. It was suggested that cancer treatment for children was threatened by National Institutes of Health furloughs.

While many presidents confine their extreme ambition to either the domestic sphere or the foreign sphere, Obama had a high level of ambition for glory in both. In his first year of office, while kicking off huge domestic measures, he traveled abroad more than any other president. In the first two months he sent his vice president and secretary of state to Europe to laid the groundwork for "a new era" in U.S. relations with western and eastern Europe. He also reached out to Iran, Turkey, and Egypt, calling for "a new beginning" in U.S.-Arab relations. In 2010, Obama signed an extended START arms control treaty with Russia, which the Senate ratified according to constitutional procedure.[111]

Relations with Iran soured after that government cracked down on protests resulting from Iran's 2009 presidential election. Later in his term, relations deteriorated even further as Obama accused Iran of developing a nuclear arsenal. He engaged in saber-rattling against Iran by increasing U.S. navy presence in the Strait of Hormuz, Iran's territorial waters, essentially an act of war against Iran. He sent ships and planes to the

---

111. Miller Center, *Obama—Foreign Affairs*; Wikipedia, *Obama*, 12–13.

Persian Gulf on the basis of an idle boast by Iran that it would shut down the Strait. An Obama warship fired upon an Indian fishing boat, which fled the scene in waters off Dubai after the warship killed one of the boat-hands. Once the Syrian debacle got underway in 2012, Obama used CIA operatives stationed there to steer arms to Syrians opposed to the Assad regime. Overall, it was reported that ties with three traditional allies, Israel, Egypt, and Turkey, declined during his first term.[112]

Obama's stance with respect to Israel was judged by some to be cool at first, since he was making such effort to make friends in the Muslim world. Relations with Israel were judged to be at a low. In 2010 he opposed Netanyahu's plan to continue building housing projects in Arab neighborhoods in East Jerusalem. But, at the same time, he also sought to purchase Israeli favor and loyalty, and to please his corporate friends in the military-industrial complex, by increasing military aid in 2010 to finance Israel's missile-defense shield. Obama also sent a record number of troops to participate in joint military exercises in Israel. In 2011, the U.S. vetoed a U.N. Security Council resolution condemning Israeli settlements in Palestinian areas. Obama proposed that the U.S. condition sales of bunker-buster bombs to Israel on Israel's agreeing not to attack Iran "this year," that is, just before Obama's reelection campaign, since that would send oil prices skyrocketing and turn voters against him. He caved in on that demand after Israel objected.[113]

Since Obama projected himself as a strident anti-war candidate, the U.S. electorate believed Obama's promise that he would bring the troops home quickly from Iraq. In 2008, Obama had promised to have "all of our combat brigades out of Iraq within sixteen months . . ." That did not happen. He promised in February 2009 to draw down troops from 160,000 to 50,000 in Iraq by August, 2010, eighteen months later. He met that goal, but by December 12, 2011 he still had 6,000 combat troops there. He then brought them home by the end of the year. Democrat Gary Hart protested that Obama's wind-down of the war was way too slow. In fact, it appears that Obama deliberately extended the war in Iraq, at great cost of lives and treasure, so that he could bring the troops home just before the 2012 elections.[114]

112. MSNBC, 12-28-11; Al Jazeera, 7-17-12; New York Times, 6-21-12; Associated Press, 9-13-11.

113. Fallows, *Obama Explained*, 21; Reuters, 3-9-12.

114. Fallows, *Obama Explained*, 21; Associated Press, 6-19-12; Limbaugh, *Crimes*, 84–85.

In the first 2008 debate with John McCain, Obama had said he would send two or three additional brigades to Afghanistan, some 15,000 troops. Instead of bolstering troops in Afghanistan by a little as he drew down troops in Iraq, Obama increased the war there by a lot, learning little from Russia's ten-year disaster of a campaign there. He first boosted troops there by 17,000, then added an additional 33,000. This tripled the U.S. presence there to about 74,000, and ultimately he grew the number to 100,000, four times the original commitment.[115]

As a candidate for presidential office, Obama had promised he would not intervene in Libya. In addition, he had an agreement with Russia to limit any activities in Libya to protecting Libyan citizens. In March 2011, however, he launched a third twenty-first century war against Muslim peoples by unilaterally engaging U.S. air forces in a campaign to overthrow Qaddafi in Libya. This extended American hubris far beyond what Reagan had earlier demonstrated in that country. After enforcing a "no fly" zone there for a month by use of Tomahawk missiles, B-2 Spirits, and fighter jets, he placed U.S. armed forces under U.N. leadership and pressed on with the continuing war there. Some in Congress worried about his constitutional authority to commit dollars and lives to a war that had not been declared in conformity with law. In fact, the War Powers Resolution was a feeble enough law, since in a time of laser-directed bombing raids, the president essentially could conquer any nation in the world without Congressional approval, as the quick overthrow of governments in Afghanistan and Iraq demonstrated. But even this feeble law, Obama refused to acknowledge. The Libya intervention placed Obama in a position of intervening militarily in one nation of Africa, while ignoring opportunities for humanitarian interventions in other places in Africa like Sudan, Zimbabwe, and Ivory Coast.[116]

Obama promoted a plan to increase profits for the American armament industry, boosting overseas sales by overhauling export rules through his Export Control Reform Initiative. His own Homeland Security group protested that the new rules would move military-type weapons from the controlled Munitions List to the relatively uncontrolled Commerce List and make it easier for drug cartels and terrorists to get weapons. In fact, Obama made a Nixon-like claim of executive

115. Wikipedia, *Obama*, 13; Reuters, 1-24-12; Limbaugh, *Crimes*, 140.

116. Yahoo News, 3-21-11; Ogden Standard Examiner, 6-16-11; Washington Post, 10-8-12; NBC News, 11-19-12.

privilege in turning down Congress's demand for documents relating to the Fast and Furious program. The administration allowed some 2,000 weapons to go to Mexican cartels via straw purchases. Under Obama, the U.S. cornered three-quarters of the global arms market. In fact, 2011 saw a tripling in overseas sales over 2010, and doubled the level under the George W. Bush administration.[117]

Obama then brought the Asian world to the brink of a major war and major new blowback by enacting a raid inside Pakistan to kill Osama bin Laden. This was conducted by Navy Seals. U.S. relations with Pakistan, already low before the uncoordinated invasion of Pakistani territory, sank even lower yet. Obama extended U.S. military involvement into Yemen, Kenya, Mali, and Niger. U.S. drone strikes killed twenty-seven people in Pakistan over a three day period. Obama's drone use threatened fifty years of international law. The CIA positioned in Turkey provided aid to Syrian rebels fighting Assad. Obama further destabilized world affairs by tripling U.S. weapons sales abroad, particularly to Persian Gulf nations, in 2011.[118]

In 2012, Obama made his "Asian pivot," establishing a U.S. base on the north shore of Australia at Darwin, and moving some of the Atlantic-based navy to the Pacific. This startled China. An Australian official insisted that this was not an actual U.S. base on Australian soil. The 200 Marines who landed there were merely doing six-months of "training," as part of Obama's new Asian defense alliance measures, and they were actually at the moment merely using Australian facilities to house themselves. This admission, seen as a good thing, actually signaled that the U.S. was taking tribute from Australia in the form of goods and services in kind, so that the U.S. could extend its world-wide protection racket to a brand new continent. One former high level national security adviser wrote that the "pivot to Asia" was an election year ploy to deflect criticism that Democrats are weak on foreign policy, to distract the public from the shambles in Afghanistan and Iraq and the resurgence of Al Qaeda in Yemen and Somalia.[119]

---

117. Washington Post, 6-21-12; Politico, 6-26-12; New York Times, 8-26-12.

118. New York Times, 6-4-12, 6-21-12, 7-31-12, 8-26-12; NBC News, 6-4-12; Guardian, 6-21-12; Washington Times, 1-16-13; NBC News, 2-22-12.

119. Fallows, *Obama Explained*, 22–23; Amitai Etzioni, Communitarian Newsletter, 6-14-12.

Obama admitted that the Australian force would grow to some 2,500 troops, and would include artillery, aircraft, and armored vehicles. The force, in time, would also have manned U.S. surveillance craft and unmanned drones. To some degree, the pivot reflected the wind-down of American wars in Iraq, Afghanistan, and Libya, and the need to stir up the waters of war elsewhere, particularly in the South China Sea.

Obama attempted to slap countervailing duties on subsidized exports from China and Vietnam, but a court said his commerce department could not do this constitutionally. Part of that activity was to build-up or purchase new allies in the region. Obama, for example, announced new relations with the repressive Myanmar/Burma regime by suspending U.S. sanctions there.[120]

At home, at the same time, Obama began to attack dissent within his own military by repressing the constitutional rights of Marine Sergeant Gary Stein, who had posted remarks critical of the administration on his Facebook page. On that page he announced he would not follow unlawful orders of the commander in chief since he had taken an oath in entering the military to uphold the Constitution. Obama's regulations specified that a member of the military cannot get involved in politics, speak in support of a political movement, or use contemptuous words against senior officials, including the vice president and president. The military brass told Stein he could not use social media sites while on government computers. On April 5, 2012, a military board recommended dismissal from the service, including loss of benefits. Stein, a nine-year member of the Marines, was only weeks away from retirement. On April 25, the military announced Stein would be discharged.[121]

120. Reuters, 3-5-12, 5-17-12.
121. Associated Press, 3-8-12, 3-21-12; MSNBC, 4-5-12, 4-25-12.

Bibliography

Adams, Henry. *History of the United States of America During the Administrations of Thomas Jefferson.* New York: Library of America, 1986.

Adams, John. *The Political Writings of John Adams.* George A. Peck, Jr., ed. Liberal Arts Press, 1955.

Adler, David Gray and Michael A. Genovese, eds. *The Presidency and the Law: The Clinton Legacy.* Lawrence, Kansas: University Press of Kansas, 2002.

Bailyn, Bernard. *The Great Republic.* Lexington, Massachusetts: D.C. Heath, 1977.

Bergeron, Paul H. *The Presidency of James K. Polk.* Lawrence, Kansas: University Press of Kansas, 1987.

Bornet, Vaughn Davis. *The Presidency of Lyndon B. Johnson.* Lawrence, Kansas: University Press of Kansas, 1983.

Boyer, Paul S., ed. *The Oxford Companion to United States History.* New York: Oxford University Press, 2001.

Bunting, Josiah. *Ulysses S. Grant.* New York: Henry Holt, 2004.

Castel, Albert. *The Presidency of Andrew Johnson.* Lawrence, Kansas: University Press of Kansas, 1979.

Clements, Kendrick A. *The Presidency of Woodrow Wilson.* Lawrence, Kansas: University Press of Kansas, 1992.

Cole, Donald B. *The Presidency of Andrew Jackson.* Lawrence, Kansas: University Press of Kansas, 1993.

Cooper, Phillip J. *By Order of the President: The Use and Abuse of Executive Direct Action.* Lawrence, Kansas: University Press of Kansas, 2002.

Craughwell, Thomas J. *Presidential Payola.* Beverly, Massachusetts: Fair Winds, 2011.

Crenson, Matthew and Benjamin Ginsberg. *Presidential Power: Unchecked and Unbalanced.* New York: W.W. Norton, 2007.

Cunningham, Noble E. *The Presidency of James Monroe.* Lawrence, Kansas: University Press of Kansas, 1996.

DiLorenzo, Thomas J. *Hamilton's Curse.* New York: Three Rivers, 2008.

———. *Lincoln Unmasked.* New York: Three Rivers, 2006.

———. *The Real Lincoln: A New Look at Abraham Lincoln, His Agenda, and an Unnecessary War.* New York: Three Rivers, 2003.

Draper, Robert. *Dead Certain: The Presidency of George W. Bush.* New York: Free Press, 2007.

Drewry, Henry N. and Thomas H. O'Connor, *America Is.* Westwell, Ohio: McMillan/McGraw School, 1995.

Fallows, James. "Obama Explained." *Atlantic,* February 9, 2012.

Fausold, Martin L. *The Presidency of Herbert C. Hoover.* Lawrence, Kansas: University Press of Kansas, 1985.

Ferrell, Robert H. *The Presidency of Calvin Coolidge.* Lawrence, Kansas: University Press of Kansas, 1998.

Flagel, Thomas B. *The History Buff's Guide to the Presidents: Key People, Places, and Events.* Nashville: Cumberland House, 2007.

Financial Crisis: Five Years Later. Executive Office of the President, September, 2013.

Fisher, Louis. *Constitutional Conflicts between Congress and the President.* 5th ed. Lawrence, Kansas: University Press of Kansas, 2007.

Fleming, Thomas. *The Illusion of Victory: America in World War I.* New York: Basic Books, 2003.

———. *The New Dealers' War: F.D.R. and the War Within World War II.* New York: Basic Books, 2001.

Freddoso, David. *Gangster Government: Barack Obama and the New Washington Thugocracy.* Washington, DC: Regnery, 2011.

Genovese, Michael A. *The Power of the American Presidency 1789-2000.* New York: Oxford University Press, 2001.

———. *Presidential Prerogative: Imperial Power in an Age of Terrorism,* Stanford, California: Stanford University Press, 2011.

Gould, Lewis L. *The Modern Presidency.* 2d ed. Lawrence, Kansas: University Press of Kansas, 2009.

———. *The William Howard Taft Presidency.* Lawrence, Kansas: University Press of Kansas, 2009.

Han, Lori Cox, ed. *New Directions in the American Presidency.* New York: Routledge, 2011.

Healy, Gene. *The Cult of the Presidency: America's Dangerous Devotion to Executive Power.* Washington, DC: Cato Institute, 2008.

Herring, Geroge C. *From Colony to Superpower: U.S. Foreign Relations Since 1776.* New York: Oxford University Press, 2008.

Hoogenboom, Ari. *The Presidency of Rutherford B. Hayes.* Lawrence, Kansas: University Press of Kansas, 1988.

Jefferson, Thomas. *The Works of Thomas Jefferson.* H. A. Washington, ed. Funk and Wagnalls, 1900.

Krent, Harold J. *Presidential Powers.* New York: New York University Press, 2005.

Light, Paul C. *The President's Agenda: Domestic Policy Choice from Kennedy to Clinton.* Baltimore: Johns Hopkins University Press, 1999.

Limbaugh, David. *Crimes Against Liberty: An Indictment of President Barack Obama.* New York: Regnery, 2010.

———. *The Great Destroyer: Barack Obama's War on the Republic.* Washington, DC: Regnery, 2012.

Matuz, Roger. *The Presidents Fact Book: The Achievements, Campaigns, Events, Triumphs, Tragedies, and Legacies of Every President from George Washington to Barack Obama.* New York: Black Dog and Leventhal, 2009.

McCoy, Alfred W. *Policing America's Empire: The United States, the Philippines, and the Rise of the Surveillance State.* Madison, Wisconsin: University of Wisconsin Press, 2009.

McCoy, Donald R. *The Presidency of Harry S. Truman.* Lawrence, Kansas: University Press of Kansas, 1984.

McCullough, David. *John Adams*. New York: Touchstone, 2002.

McDonald, Forrest. *The American Presidency: An Intellectual History*. Lawrence, Kansas: University Press of Kansas, 1994.

———. *The Presidency of George Washington*. Lawrence, Kansas: University Press of Kansas, 1974.

———. *The Presidency of Thomas Jefferson*. Lawrence, Kansas: University Press of Kansas, 1976.

———. *States' Rights and the Union: Imperium in Imperio, 1776–1876*. Lawrence, Kansas: University Press of Kansas, 2002.

McJimsey, George. *The Presidency of Franklin Delano Roosevelt*. Lawrence, Kansas: University Press of Kansas, 2000.

Miller Center Presidential Profiles. No pages. Online: http://www.millercenter.org.

Morgan, H. Wayne. *William McKinley and His America*. Kent, Ohio: Kent State University Press, 2003.

Morley, Felix. *Freedom and Federalism*, Indianapolis: Liberty Press, 1981.

Morris, Edmund. *Theodore Rex*. New York: Modern Library, 2002.

Napolitano, Andrew P. *Theodore and Woodrow*. Nashville: Thomas Nelson, 2012.

Nelson, Michael, ed. *The Presidency: A History of the Office of the President of the United States from 1789 to the Present*. New York: Smithmark, 1996.

Newquist, Jerreld L., ed. *Prophets, Principles and National Survival*. Salt Lake City: Publishers Press, 1964.

Pach, Chester J. and Elmo Richardson. *The Presidency of Dwight D. Eisenhower*. Lawrence, Kansas: University Press of Kansas, 1991.

Paludan, Phillip Shaw. *The Presidency of Abraham Lincoln*. Lawrence, Kansas: University Press of Kansas, 1994.

Rutland, Robert Allen. *The Presidency of James Madison*. Lawrence, Kansas: University Press of Kansas, 1990.

Samples, John. *The Struggle to Limit Government*. Washington DC: Cato Institute, 2010.

Schocet, Gordon, Fania Oz-Salzberger, and Meriav Jones, ed. *Political Hebraism: Judaic Sources in Early Modern Political Thought*. Jerusalem: Shalem, 2008.

Small, Melvin. *The Presidency of Richard Nixon*. Lawrence, Kansas: University Press of Kansas, 1999.

Smith, Elbert B. *The Presidency of James Buchanan*. Lawrence, Kansas: University Press of Kansas, 1988.

Welch, Richard E. *The Presidencies of Grover Cleveland*. Lawrence, Kansas: University Press of Kansas, 1988.

Whitney, David C. *The American Presidents: Biographies of the Chief Executives from George Washington through Barack Obama*. 11th ed. New York: Readers Digest Association, 2012.

Wilson, Major L. *The Presidency of Martin Van Buren*. Lawrence Kansas: University Press of Kansas, 1984.

Index

W